COASTAL WORKS

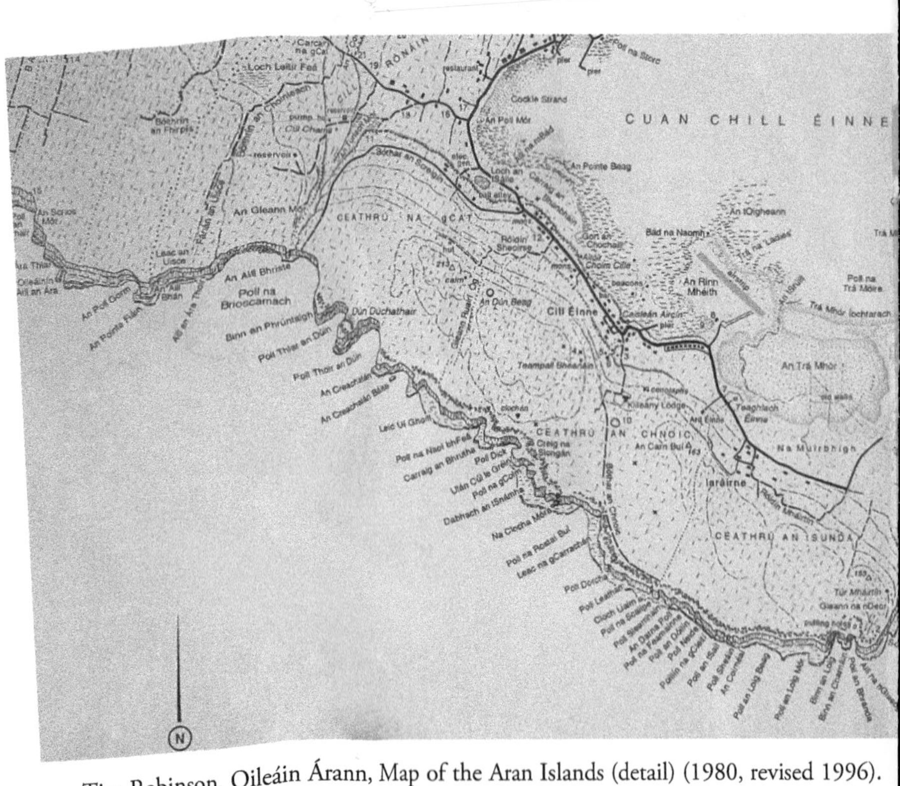

Tim Robinson, Oileáin Árann, Map of the Aran Islands (detail) (1980, revised 1996).

To Máiréad and Tim Robinson

Acknowledgements

The editors gratefully acknowledge the work of Tim Robinson as a source of inspiration for the Atlantic Archipelagos Research Project, now the Atlantic Archipelagos Research Consortium, an international network of scholars working in the humanities. This book has grown out of the many events that this network has organized, for which we are indebted to the generous support of the British Academy; the University of Exeter; Magdalene College, Cambridge; the Moore Institute for Research in the Humanities and Social Studies, the National University of Ireland, Galway; the Druid Theatre Company; University College Dublin; the Willson Center for Humanities and Arts at the University of Georgia; Somerville College, Oxford; and TORCH (the Oxford Research Centre in the Humanities). For providing images, we would also like to thank the staff at the Ashmolean Museum; Tullie House Museum and Art Gallery Carlisle; the Brooklyn Museum; the Scripps Institution of Oceanography; the Natural History Museum of Ireland; the James Hardiman Library, National University of Ireland, Galway; and the Valentia Island Heritage Centre. We are especially indebted to Norman Ackroyd and Tim Robinson for generously allowing us to use their work for the volume's cover and endpapers, and to Elliot Kendall, who created the cartographic frontispieces for each chapter. Our thanks also to Alan Ackroyd, Valentina Bold, Matthew Campbell, Claire Connolly, Eamon Duffy, Hugh Haughton, Kacie Hittel, Robert Macfarlane, Jacqueline Norton, Eve Patten, Nels Pearson, and Alan Riach for their support and encouragement.

Contents

List of Illustrations

List of Cartographic Frontispieces

Artwork by Elliot Kendall

List of Contributors

Nicholas Allen is Franklin Professor of English and Director of the Willson Center for Humanities and Arts at the University of Georgia. He has written and edited several books on Irish literature, including *Broken Landscapes: Selected Letters of Ernie O'Malley* (2011), *Modernism, Ireland and Civil War* (2009), and *George Russell and the New Ireland* (2003).

John Brannigan teaches English at University College Dublin. His most recent book is *Archipelagic Modernism: Literature in the Irish and British Isles, 1890–1970* (2015). He is a former editor of the *Irish University Review*.

Daniel Brayton is an associate professor at Middlebury College and a member of both the Department of English and American Literatures and the Program in Environmental Studies. He is the author of *Shakespeare's Ocean: An Ecocritical Exploration* (2012) and has published numerous articles on early modern English literature, maritime literature, and ecocriticism.

Margaret Cohen is Andrew B. Hammond Professor of French Language, Literature and Civilization at Stanford University, where she is based in the Departments of Comparative Literature and English. Her books include *The Novel and the Sea* (2010), *The Sentimental Education of the Novel* (1999), and *Profane Illumination: Walter Benjamin and the Paris of Surrealist Revolution* (1993).

Nessa Cronin is Lecturer in Irish Studies at the Centre for Irish Studies at the National University of Ireland, Galway. She has written extensively on Irish Literary Geographies and Cultural Cartography, and is co-editor of *Lifeworlds: Space, Place and Irish Culture* (forthcoming 2017), *Landscape Values: Place and Praxis* (2016), and *Anáil an Bhéil Bheo: Orality and Modern Irish Culture* (2009).

Andrew Gibson is former Research Professor of Modern Literature and Theory at Royal Holloway, University of London, and a former Carole and Gordon Professor of Irish Literature at Northwestern University. He has published more than twenty books, including *The Strong Spirit: History, Politics and Aesthetics in Joyce's Writings 1898–1915* (2013), *Intermittency: The Concept of Historical Reason in Contemporary French Philosophy* (2011), *Beckett and Badiou: The Pathos of Intermittency* (2010), and *Joyce's Revenge: History, Politics, and Aesthetics in 'Ulysses'* (2002).

John R. Gillis is Professor Emeritus of History at Rutgers University, now living in Berkeley, California. His work has spanned German, British, and American fields, ranging from cultural to political history. Of late, he has turned to global environmental history, focusing on the margins between between land and water as crucial human habitat. His latest books include *The Shores Around Us* (2015) and *The Human Shore: Seacoasts in History* (2012).

Nick Groom is Professor of English at the University of Exeter and has written widely on literature, music, and contemporary art. He is the author of over a dozen books and editions, including *The Seasons* (2013), *The Gothic* (2012), *The Union Jack* (2006), and *The Forger's Shadow* (2002).

Kyriaki Hadjiafxendi is Senior Lecturer in English at Bath Spa University. Her books include *Crafting the Woman Professional in the Long Nineteenth Century* (2013) and *'What is a Woman to Do?' A Reader on Women, Work and Art c. 1830–1890* (2011), both co-edited with Patricia Zakreski.

Andrew McNeillie is the editor and publisher of the journal *Archipelago*. Among his several publications are a memoir, *An Aran Keening* (2001), and his most recent collection of poems, *Winter Moorings* (2014).

John Plunkett is Associate Professor in the Department of English at the University of Exeter. His publications include *Popular Exhibitions, Science and Showmanship, 1840–1910* (2012), co-edited with Joe Kember and Jill Sullivan, *Victorian Print Media: A Reader* (2005), co-edited with Andrew King, and *Queen Victoria—First Media Monarch* (2003).

Jos Smith is Lecturer in Contemporary Literature at the University of East Anglia. He is the author of *The New Nature Writing: Rethinking the Literature of Place* (2017).

Fiona Stafford is Professor of English Language and Literature at the University of Oxford. Her books include *The Long, Long Life of Trees* (2016), *Reading Romantic Poetry* (2012), and *Local Attachments: The Province of Poetry* (2010).

Damian Walford Davies is Professor of English and Head of the School of English, Communication and Philosophy at Cardiff University. His recent books include *Cartographies of Culture: New Geographies of Welsh Writing in English* (2012) and the poetry collections *Judas* (2015) and *Witch* (2012).

1
Introduction

Nicholas Allen, Nick Groom, and Jos Smith

In 1967, Benoît Mandelbrot suggested a mathematical conundrum that involved answering the seemingly straightforward question, 'How long is the coast of Britain?'[1] The answer is surprisingly elusive and dependent on the scale at which one is looking. Increasing the scale unearths greater detail, time and time again, and so the answer grows the closer one looks. The problem is that any measure, at however small a scale, is forced to simplify complex ambiguities that might otherwise reveal further intricacies of their own. This was an entry-point to Mandlebrot's writings on fractal geometry, but it also chimes with the very ecology and geomorphology of that coast itself, characteristically intricate, ambiguous, and changeable. Large-scale, ocean-facing landforms—such as capes and bays, estuaries, dunefields, and reefs—are well known to have, nestled within them, smaller and often dynamically mobile features such as longshore bars and troughs, berms and beach cusps, not to mention difficult-to-measure caves, inlets, tributaries, and salt marshes. Looking closer still are to be found the ripples, rills, and swash marks of a more minute scale; even within these are to be found the bioturbation structures of intertidal organisms: forms within forms, scales within scales, and worlds within worlds. In the way that it draws the attention down into such minute details as these, while at the same time drawing it up towards an expanse that suggests a space almost planetary in scale, the coast is a highly distinctive geographical environment. And yet it has all too often been overlooked, as if its peripheral relationship to the land has reinforced its peripheral treatment culturally.

For the author, artist, and map-maker Tim Robinson, Mandlebrot's conundrum has been put to a more literal test on the west coast of Ireland. There the question seemed to speak to a way of thinking that had long

[1] Benoît Mandelbrot, 'How Long Is the Coast of Britain? Statistical Self-Similarity and Fractional Dimension', *Science*, 156 (5 May 1967), 636–8.

occupied Robinson about the relationship between culture and the land at its extreme edge. The network of stories and place names he has been documenting over the last forty years there would complicate this conundrum even further: 'there are more places within a forest, among the galaxies or on a Connemara seashore, than the geometry of common sense allows'.[2] For Robinson, this proliferation of places is bound up with the many human experiences of them, indefinitely troubling our ability to calibrate any final measure. Questions of history, community, tradition, disciplinary perspective, and language—or *languages*—open up and multiply a single place into many. This too can be understood as a kind of fractal geography.

A crucial shaping factor in Robinson's recovery of such plurality is the idea of the margin or the periphery. What level of detail has escaped the eye looking out from the centre? What sits precariously on the outer edge of perception or cultural memory? What new encounters become possible the closer we get to the edge of the known landscape? These are questions that numerous authors have explored on the coasts of Britain and Ireland in search of fresh perspectives beyond the usual domestic allegiances. Robinson embraces Mandelbrot's thought experiment here precisely for the rich possibilities it opens up: the coast, the edge, the margins, become the landscape par excellence for this form of investigation, for revealing what he comes to call 'the view from the horizon'.[3] This is a phrase that describes very well the important and timely reorientation enacted by the essays collected here in *Coastal Works: Cultures of the Atlantic Edge*.

Robinson's work offers one of the richest sustained studies of place in the English language and it has come during a time when the uncertainty about our relationship to the places in which we live on this Atlantic archipelago has undergone considerable strain, both politically and environmentally. Such carefully located literary work as this grounds its readership in a dignified attention to detail, the meaningful exploration of which is part of any culture's reflection on its heritage, on its history, and on its future development. The idea for this book is indebted to Robinson's work and its essays are informed by this idea of the coast as a site of open-ended cultural inquiry, and especially as a site from which to reflect on and reappraise certain geographical meanings and spatial relationships over the Irish and British archipelago. These essays explore the coast through authors and artists over a broad historical range, but all are essays that help to locate, to ground, and to investigate the cultural imagination in

[2] Tim Robinson, *Connemara: A Little Gaelic Kingdom* (London: Penguin, 2012), 252.
[3] Tim Robinson, *The View from the Horizon* (London: Coracle Press, 1999).

relation to a distinctive geography on the western extremity of the European coastal shelf and the eastern edge of the Atlantic Ocean.

The Atlantic world has been clearly defined as an historical and cultural field, but the significance of the Atlantic edge, particularly its British and Irish coasts, has yet to be properly investigated.[4] Where exactly is the Atlantic edge, for example? The law concerning the borders and boundaries of seas and oceans may well be clearly understood, but the ways in which this law is applied remain notoriously complex and contentious.[5] Fisheries, the military, customs, the coastguard, scientists of various kinds, and even the public have vying interests and overlapping senses of space when it comes to the Atlantic edge. How many of us could place on the map where the English Channel, the Bristol Channel, the North Sea, or the Irish Sea meet the Atlantic, not to mention all the firths, estuaries, sounds, and bays that further complicate this geography? According to the International Hydrographic Organization, the western border of the English Channel is to be drawn in a line from Land's End south-east to l'Île Vierge off the coast of Brittany, and the western border of the Bristol Channel is to be drawn from Hartland Point to Garland Head, leaving England with a stretch of only about one hundred miles facing the Atlantic in north Cornwall.[6] The greater part of the coastlines of England and Wales open onto waterways that connect them to other regions of Britain, Ireland, and Europe, while the western coasts of Scotland and Ireland (though dotted with archipelagos of their own) are more characteristically Atlantic-facing. This ambiguous tension in which the coastal margins of the Atlantic edge are somehow *both* inward and outward facing, in which they are at once about clustering and connection and about exposure and periphery, is an important one for this book. It collects and connects those margins and waterways with a westerly imaginary akin to the northerly idea of *Ultima Thule*.

The Atlantic, which by the mid-fifteenth century had a recognizable if complex identity, was the vast product of shipping routes, trade, and cartography; it thus has a significant historical, economic, and textual status. The title 'Atlantic Ocean' itself only became widespread in Britain

[4] See David Armitage and Michael J. Braddick (eds), *The British Atlantic World, 1500–1800*, 2nd edn (New York: Palgrave, 2009); Jack P. Greene and Philip D. Morgan (eds), *Atlantic History: A Critical Reappraisal* (New York: Palgrave, 2009); Nicholas Canny and Philip Morgan (eds), *The Oxford Handbook of the Atlantic World, 1450–1850* (Oxford: Oxford University Press, 2011).

[5] Malcolm D. Evans, 'Maritime Boundary Delimitation', in Donald R. Rothwell et al. (eds), *The Oxford Handbook of the Law of the Sea* (Oxford: Oxford University Press, 2015), 278.

[6] International Hydrographic Organization, *Limits of Oceans and Seas* (Monte Carlo: International Hydrographic Organization, 1953), 39.

in the 1740s, before which Britain had treated the 'Western Ocean' more as an extension of fishing opportunities. However, by 1700, the English economy had become reliant on the Atlantic market and it was therefore inevitable that it would have far-reaching effects on the established nations, regions, and cultures along its eastern rim. The Atlantic was not only a reminder of how the mother country was connected to and divided from America, but it also suggested that the international axis was at last shifting away from Anglo- and Euro-centrism. The edge of Europe was coming increasingly to be figured as the edge of the Atlantic, its own mysterious, blue continent on which lives, nations, and economies were being won and lost. No longer was this sea the peripheral Western Ocean, it was the Atlantic: 'that uphill Sea', as Edmund Burke described the immense maritime expanse.[7]

The last two decades have witnessed an upsurge in the idea of the seas and oceans as subjects of literary and cultural study. The 'blue humanities' (or thalassology, as it is sometimes known) is a movement towards an historical understanding of water and its effects on human society. In classical culture the Mediterranean has become a space around which many disciplines meet and the sea generally has been a metaphorical space since at least the time of the Bible. There are any number of examples whereby coastal zones function as contact points between evolving, and sometimes contrasting, experiences of time, space, and motion. These are connected in turn to thinking about tides and currents, each of which connects its own locality to wider questions of circulation. The sea is no longer an absence across which light can be seen on other lands, as it was for Matthew Arnold in 'Dover Beach' (1867). John R. Gillis points to the work of Steven Mentz, Margaret Cohen, and Philip Steinberg as crucial steps in the historicization of water, challenging what Cohen has called 'hydrophasia', the inability to recognize the bearing that sea travel has had on the thought and indeed the aesthetics of literary culture.[8] Steinberg's *The Social Construction of the Ocean* (2001) is also a key work in the building of a contemporary seascape that resonates with our idea in this collection of a coastal culture that is local in context and global in connection.

The coast itself intensifies a particular aspect of the blue humanities: marginal as it may be to some, it is the region of exchange between land

[7] Edmund Burke, 'Speech on Stamp Act Disturbances', in Paul Langford (ed.), *The Writings and Speeches of Edmund Burke: Volume II* (Oxford: Clarendon Press, 1981), 44.
[8] Margaret Cohen, *The Novel and the Sea* (Princeton: Princeton University Press, 2009), 14.

and sea, domestic and international space, where relationships and tensions between geography and culture are felt intensely and are played out dynamically. If the historical development of the Atlantic fundamentally redefined Europe's sense of itself through what Eric Slauter calls 'dizzying shifts that come from viewing familiar phenomena from different angles, different geographies, and different disciplinary perspectives', coasts also present similar opportunities: points or moments of cultural exchange and consequent replottings of identity.[9] Work by the Port Towns and Urban Cultures research group at the University of Portsmouth, for example, has revealed a tradition of such moments in the history of British ports as liminal sites.[10] In this book we aim to show that such dynamic reconfigurations might be tracked across a much wider coastal heritage and culture in Britain and Ireland. As Gillis has argued, the coast has served as 'a kind of frontier, less regulated than the interiors and providing people with a greater degree of freedom to explore new possibilities'.[11]

However, just as the wateriness of the sea has been sidelined in favour of more traditional historical and critical approaches (as Alison Games puts it, 'the Atlantic history that many historians produce is rarely centred around the ocean, and the ocean is rarely relevant to the project'[12]), so something quite distinctive to the coast has been neglected. The very interfacial aspects of coastlines, as lively borders between land and sea, between one country and another, are likewise neglected. Coastal places are diverse and distinctive in their topographies and have a centre of gravity all their own: they offer the littoral perspective. For ecologists, a coastline is an extremely rich and singular space that is understood less as an edge or margin than as precisely this kind of interface. It presents what is known as an 'ecotone', a boundary zone where two ecosystems meet and overlap (where '-tone' suggests the tension between the two).[13] An ecotone often has a biological density far greater than that of the areas on either side of it: both the intensity of its life and death cycle and the diversity of its species are greater, with some particularly hardy 'frontier' species even coming to thrive in its environment. A coastal ecotone (as opposed to that between a desert and grassland, for example) offers an unusually sharp change over a (generally) narrow area and in many ways

[9] Eric Slauter, 'History, Literature, and the Atlantic World', *William and Mary Quarterly*, 55 (2008), 161.

[10] Port Towns and Urban Cultures, http://porttowns.port.ac.uk/about.

[11] John R. Gillis, *The Human Shore: Seacoasts in History* (Chicago: University of Chicago Press, 2012), 76.

[12] Alison Games, 'Atlantic History: Definitions, Challenges, and Opportunities', *American Historical Review*, 111 (2006), 745.

[13] Gillis, *The Human Shore*, 4.

presents the ecotone *in extremis*. Communities, too, have based their lives on this dynamic geographical environment: fishing, harvesting various weeds and shellfish, managing the comings and goings of a harbour or a dock, or providing for the annual migration of holiday-goers. As an ecotone, then, at a range of different levels, the coast represents not the dwindling and petering out of an edge, but the intensification of activity over a border zone.

Managing coastal change for conservationists is now as much a matter of dealing with the effects of human use and pollution as it is with the natural instabilities of the land's edge.[14] Coastal conservation and heritage are a relatively recent post-war development, but one that has gradually become a matter of national interest from the 1960s onward. The National Trust launched Enterprise Neptune in 1965 after a major coastal survey claimed that nearly a third of the coast of Britain had been defaced and spoiled by human leisure and industry. The same survey also claimed that a further 900 miles were both worthy and in urgent need of protection.[15] The following four decades saw one of the largest sustained conservation projects of its kind in Britain successfully define over 730 miles of coastline as 'Heritage Coast', an initiative that is ongoing today as work nears completion on a public right of way allowing a walker to travel the entire coast on foot.

Among the reasons given for coastal heritage and conservation are values concerning the protection of wildlife and biodiversity, beautiful natural scenery, and landscapes of historical, architectural, and archaeological interest. The literary and visual arts have played an important role in shaping these values, articulating them, and understanding the way they have changed over time, and yet there has perhaps been less acknowledgement of this than there might have been. Some of the first powers to be devolved to Scotland and Wales in 1998 were concerned with environment and heritage,[16] and we have since begun to see different attitudes to the coastal landscape emerge between the members of the United Kingdom, with Scotland in particular placing a premium on the legacy of literature in what has come to be called its 'Earth Heritage'.[17] Much could be learned from this Scottish example and brought to bear in government-led projects of coastal heritage elsewhere contributing a rich cultural perspective on the coast from the arts and humanities. More detailed consideration of

[14] Heather Viles and Tom Spencer, *Coastal Problems* (London: Edward Arnold, 1995), 3.

[15] David Evans, *A History of Nature Conservation in Britain* (London: Routledge, 1992), 125.

[16] https://www.gov.uk/guidance-on-devolution#devolved-responsibilities.

[17] John E. Gordon and Vanessa Kirkbride, 'Reading the Landscape: Unveiling Scotland's Earth Stories', Association for Heritage Interpretation, www.ahi.org.uk.

coastal cultures will no doubt reveal more nuanced and more tangible arguments for supporting and researching the cultural activity of coastal regions, arguments to which we hope the essays collected here will contribute.

Coastlines have always been powerful imaginative spaces—from the otherworldly thresholds of the early Irish *immrama* to the 'state of the nation' travelogue that took Jonathan Raban around the coast of Britain in the 1980s—but the meanings that are drawn out of them have been extremely diverse.[18] The coast reminds us of our own domestic and bodily limitations to land, what Douglas Dunn, describing life on St Kilda, has called the 'manacles of place'.[19] Barry Cunliffe has gone so far as to suggest that standing on a coast is a 'timeless human experience'.[20] And yet the coast has seen extraordinary change as well: transport and technology have added to that 'timeless' experience something paradoxically contingent. While limiting, the coast nurtures the possibility of exceeding that limitation. It challenges and stretches the notion of place; exposes it as it describes its circumference; opens the intensely local up to the trans-local, to the archipelagic, to the transatlantic, and the more broadly global, amplifying, at one and the same time, *both* a sense of place and a sense of planet. This is not a recent quality of coastal experience: we might think of archaeologist Cyril Fox's earlier study of ancient, trans-peninsular sea routes or of Gordon Childe's images of the grey coast of north-west Scotland as 'bright with Neolithic Argonauts'.[21] More recently, Godfrey Baldacchino and Eric Clark have described the way the cultural geography of islands has troubled such binaries as 'openness and closure, roots and routes'.[22] In the end, it may be precisely this paradoxical tension between boundedness and exposure, limit and possibility, that makes the human experience of coasts so 'timeless'.

It is perhaps no coincidence that this book focuses so much on the coastal regions of Ireland and Britain in particular. The contemporary awareness of the sea as a significant stage for historical issues is a response in part to the rearrangement of national histories prompted by new departures in the study of empire, postcolonialism, and, latterly, globalization. These critical movements have their political corollary in the

18 Jonathan Raban, *Coasting: A Private Voyage* (London: Simon and Schuster, 1987).

19 Douglas Dunn, 'St Kilda's Parliament', *New Selected Poems: 1964–2000* (London: Faber and Faber, 2003), 70.

20 Barry Cunliffe, *Facing the Ocean: The Atlantic and its Peoples* (Oxford: Oxford University Press, 2001), 1.

21 Ibid., 16–17.

22 Godfrey Baldacchino and Eric Clark, 'Editorial', *Cultural Geographies*, 20 (April 2013), 130.

devolution of the United Kingdom. The roots of that Union were in seaborne expansion. In *The Black Atlantic* (1993), Paul Gilroy was among the first to populate this water world with the stories of those who were exploited to create it. The British Empire's purchase on the far-flung cantonments it controlled was dictated by its sea power. Consequently, the concept of the archipelago, around which this book has been orientated, is important as a way to imagine the influence of world systems on small cultural and geographical territories.

This concept of the archipelago became a critical tool in the study of literature following an extended conversation between historians about the limits of nationalism as a means to describe complex interactions between fragmentary interest groups over extended time.[23] Their debate grew from discussion of the island wars of the seventeenth century before its later extension into the wider Atlantic world. The four kingdoms of Ireland, Scotland, Wales, and England were engaged in the period after the Reformation in a struggle for power and legitimacy.[24] This conflict incorporated several modes. The colonization of land, the marginalization of cultures unwilling or unable to be assimilated into emerging orders, and the expropriation of antagonistic populations were three strategies of conquest. The consequences of these processes, and the varieties of reaction to them, form a tangled history that takes shape on the margins and often at the boundaries of land and sea. 'Archipelagic criticism' has begun to offer a means of, in the words of John Kerrigan, 'stripping away the Anglocentric and Victorian imperial paradigms', and recovering the 'long, braided histories played out across the British-Irish archipelago between three kingdoms, four countries, divided regions, variable ethnicities and religiously determined allegiances'.[25] Here too, the periphery has been turned to in the hope of cultural renewal and the essays presented in this collection will show that the Atlantic coast in particular has offered an ideal landscape to feed such efforts towards that renewal.

If the scholarship of the early modern period offered archipelagic perspectives on the years approaching the formation of the kingdom of Great Britain, a comparable idea has grown from the more recent fragmentation of Britain since the devolutions of 1998. John Brannigan's

[23] Formative works in this concept field include J. G. A. Pocock, *The Discovery of Islands: Essays in British History* (Cambridge: Cambridge University Press, 2005); Philip Schwyzer and Simon Mealor (eds), *Archipelagic Identities: Literature and Identity in the Atlantic Archipelago, 1550–1800* (Aldershot: Ashgate, 2004); and John Kerrigan, *Archipelagic English: Literature, History, and Politics, 1603–1707* (Oxford: Oxford University Press, 2008).

[24] The pioneering account of these relations was Hugh Kearney, *The British Isles: A History of Four Nations*, 2nd edn (Cambridge: Cambridge University Press, 2006).

[25] Kerrigan, *Archipelagic English*, 2.

online lecture series *Scholarcast* in 2011 published a special edition titled 'Reconceiving the British Isles: The Literature of the Archipelago', which offers papers considering geographically relational aspects of twentieth and twenty-first-century literature and culture. Among the key accounts to emerge from this series was Edna Longley's study of the 'criss-crossing' of borders and islands in the travel and thought of W. B. Yeats, Louis MacNeice, W. S. Graham, and Edward Thomas. Brannigan's own *Archipelagic Modernism: Literature in the Irish and British Isles, 1890–1970* likewise explores alternative, devolved literary geographies of the archipelago that are plural, connective, and on the move. In twentieth-century archipelagic criticism such as this there is an emphasis on fluid spatial relations gesturing towards and exploring reconfigurations of cultural identity.[26] Brannigan's contribution to this book explores just such an idea through a reading of the early poetry and later travel writing of Louis MacNeice. He explores an imaginative breadth of space that stretches across the archipelago in MacNeice's life and work and identifies a particular tension between the 'myopic nationalisms of England and Ireland' that the poet so resisted and an alternative world of island utopias off the west coast of Scotland with which he nonetheless found it difficult to connect. Far from idealizing an 'untrammelled' rural way of life on these islands, what Brannigan shows in MacNeice is a more subtle search—plagued with difficulties emerging out of this very tension—for 'new vocabularies of habitation' and 'new geographies of connection'.

Brannigan's work chimes with Andrew Gibson's essay on Norman Nicholson here, which asks the question of where England begins and ends, or even if such an idea of nation corresponds with an imaginative territory representative of the poet's concerns. These concerns are by turn aesthetic, ecological, and messianic, and Gibson follows the logic of Nicholson's writings towards the poet's evocation of the north Atlantic as a boundary to inland constraint. He locates Nicholson's sensibility in the particular geography of Millom, a coastal town in modern-day Cumberland that is invisible to its Lake District neighbours. Millom represents what Gibson calls England's Atlantic edge, a sliver of coastline that is distant from all its immediate neighbours, including those across the Irish Sea. In part, Nicholson's project was to reconfigure the idea of literary space as it applies to national

[26] This tendency towards spatial reconfiguration can also be seen in Glenda Norquay and Gerry Smyth (eds), *Across the Margins: Cultural Identity and Change in the Atlantic Archipelago* (Manchester: Manchester University Press, 2002), and in Stefanie Lehner's *Subaltern Ethics in Contemporary Scottish and Irish Literature: Tracing Counter-Histories* (London: Palgrave, 2011).

identity in his refusal to engage with forms of landscape associated with Wordsworthian Romanticism. Nicholson's is a spare art-in-waiting for the theological transformation of a forgotten place into a land of social redemption. Gibson identifies the foundations of this aesthetic in Nicholson's reading of the Bible, his personal experiences, and, finally, the similarity between historical coastal spaces in Cumbria and Palestine. It is this fluid association that marks Nicholson's poetry as belonging to a liminal zone between land and sea, earth and water, the rising clouds of his English Atlantic a symbol of the towering ocean beyond the nation's borders.

The UK's decision in 2016 to leave the European Union is a matter to which archipelagic criticism seems particularly well positioned to respond. The isolationism that Brexit has intensified culturally, politically, and economically is continuous with the darker aspects of the insular turn towards domestic space and the contraction of interests that Jed Esty has associated with the long withdrawal of Empire.[27] Thinking archipelagically enables us to question such entrenchments of national identity, reminding us that such moments exist within fluid constellations of identity and relation, constellations that are as diversely networked beyond the traditional borders of the nation-state as they are variegated within those borders domestically. At a time when exclusive and nostalgic nationalisms of various kinds are on the rise on both sides of the Atlantic, hardening the borders of their imagined communities, the archipelagic perspective draws attention to the ebb and flow of nations; to nations, regions, and unions of all kinds as contingent and unfolding events with historical as well as geographical edges. J. G. A. Pocock once suggested that 'it is not inconceivable that future historians may find themselves writing of a "Unionist" or even a "British" period in the history of the peoples inhabiting the Atlantic archipelago'.[28] Philip Schwyzer and Simon Mealor have added that, at times, Britain 'seems less like a place on the map than like a tide sweeping back and forth across it'.[29] These are pertinent reminders of precarious historical relationships as the UK faces a radically shifting future. The idea of a relational archipelago with fluid borders might be an unpopular one at the moment, but it might be all the more important for that.

The coast as precarious border to an uncertain national space is also the focus of Daniel Brayton's essay, which sees a maritime novel experiment

[27] Jed Esty, *A Shrinking Island: Modernism and National Culture in England* (Princeton: Princeton University Press, 2004), 41–2.

[28] Pocock, *The Discovery of Islands*, 26.

[29] Schwyzer and Mealor (eds), *Archipelagic Identities*, 2.

with a form of littoral transnationalism. Brayton's reading of Erskine Childers's classic thriller, *The Riddle of the Sands*, confirms the novel as a model of coastal fiction and establishes its position as a major innovation in the representation of maritime space. In real life, Childers was a character caught between the acts; a gifted British intelligence officer, he died an Irish republican. Feted for his foresight in predicting the German threat of world war in *The Riddle of the Sands*, Childers was executed by the Irish Free State in retribution for his opposition to the Anglo-Irish Treaty. Brayton creates a genealogy of coastal fiction in which Childers's work plays a major evolutionary part. The journey of Childers's characters through a north Atlantic archipelago that extends from the German coast draws a line of association between Europe and Britain whose form depends on coastlines, estuaries, and shallows. In following this course, Childers creates a narrative fiction that shifts between charts, borders, and languages. *The Riddle of the Sands* is a model in this respect of later twentieth-century works like those of Tim Robinson that take the coastal zone as a transitional space between specific local micro-cultures and the environments they share. Brayton's final point is the connection between Childers's capacity to imagine the islands of the north Atlantic archipelago and his experience of coastal sailing. Childers remains one of the most accurate writers to describe the practice of sailing, a practice that changed the novelist's perspective not only of narrative, but of nation.

Nicholas Allen extends this exploration of the shifting coast to the urban imaginations of Ciaran Carson, Glenn Patterson, and Kevin Barry. Allen situates their cities by the sea in a longer account of empire and withdrawal that connects literature to memory by attention to a material culture that is shaped by its global, and intimate, history. Carson and Patterson create versions of a maritime Belfast that is a harbour to ideas of cultural association that its violent history oppresses. Carson's liquid narrative of the city's inland lagoons, its rainy streets and squally history, summons a strange assembly of elements to the surface of *The Star Factory*. It is a book that floats Belfast in a sea of flotsam, the substance of which is the debris of its inhabitants' lives. If *The Star Factory* is an assembly of manufactured parts, Patterson's *The Mill for Grinding Old People Young* is resolutely traditional in its literary construction. A story of foiled love and near disaster, its implied subject is the city that grows around its subject, Gilbert Rice. The Belfast of Patterson's novel is an untidy mess of a provincial city and Allen's essay explores how Patterson uses the taming of its waterways as a metaphor for its material development. Barry's *The City of Bohane* operates in a different territory, even if it shares some of Carson's fantastical elements. Bohane is a fictional city of the future, resting uneasily on Ireland's west coast. There is, in fact, no

Ireland here, but gangs, chancers, and wide boys. Barry's writing opens new possibilities for the coastal work, integrating the cultural vernacular of a specific space so long into wider, cinematic traditions of representation. The west coast of Ireland is one of the most deeply inscribed literary spaces in modernity, at least from the time of Synge. Barry shatters this tradition, as Synge did before him, to create a vision of the coastal city that is at once futuristic and historicized, a condition that might be emblematic of these post-imperial maritime spaces.

Scholarship from a range of disciplines has shown a significant interest in what might be called, after Arif Dirlik, 'critical localism' in an effort to rethink the status of place in a global context.[30] There is something of a tightrope to walk here, though. On one side there has been a resistance to any idea of place as essentialized, static, bounded, and insular: Doreen Massey, for example, has gone to great lengths to draw attention to the way that a place's meaning or identity is constituted by its changing social relations to other places.[31] For some this has meant a wholesale rejection of place as a concept[32] (though not, it should be added, for Massey), while for others this has meant simply a considered reappraisal of place, asking whether we can recognize its embeddedness within wider circulations of power and capital, while at the same time finding in 'place-based practices' and 'place-based imaginaries' a critique of that same circulation of power and capital.[33]

Arturo Escobar asks, 'to what extent can we reinvent both thought and the world according to the logic of a multiplicity of place-based cultures?'[34] The concept of archipelago addresses such a question directly: the exploration of places locally grounded but at the same time involved in a network of cultural relationships, the intricate coastlines becoming interfaces of social and cultural exchange, becoming sites of replotting and reconfiguration. Work in the field of Island Studies has helped to develop a theoretical and spatial framework of 'archipelagic thinking' that might be

[30] For example, see Arturo Escobar, 'Culture Sits in Places: Reflections on Globalism and Subaltern Strategies of Localization', *Political Geography*, 20 (2001), 139–74. For examples of literary criticism's 'placial turn', see Neal Alexander and James Moran (eds), *Regional Modernisms* (Edinburgh: Edinburgh University Press, 2013); Michael Gardiner, *The Return of England in English Literature* (Basingstoke: Palgrave, 2012); and Alexandra Harris, *Romantic Moderns* (London: Thames and Hudson, 2012) and 'The Secrets of England's Past Lie Buried in the Land', *New Statesman* (4 April 2011), 40–1.

[31] Doreen Massey, *Space, Place and Gender* (Cambridge: Cambridge University Press, 1994).

[32] Ursula Heise, *Sense of Place and Sense of Planet* (Oxford: Oxford University Press, 2008); Timothy Morton, *The Ecological Thought* (Cambridge, MA: Harvard University Press, 2010).

[33] Escobar, 'Culture Sits in Places', 142.

[34] Ibid.

productively connected with archipelagic criticism's devolved and interconnected account of nations, regions, and locales. Elaine Stratford, Godfrey Baldacchino, Elizabeth MacMahon, Carol Farbotko, and Andrew Harwood have challenged topologies of 'island thinking' that reproduce the binary opposition of 'island-mainland' (inflected as this so often is with assumptions about periphery/centre hierarchies of power). Instead, they have argued for a fresh approach that emphasizes the way *archipelagic* island spaces might in fact emerge as plural networks, 'inter-related, mutually constituted and co-constructed' and from processes of 'connection, assemblage, mobility, and multiplicity'.[35] Informed by just such dynamic processes of spatial reconfiguration in literary criticism, *Coastal Works* sets out to explore an increasingly *place-based* literary geography of the archipelago that has begun to coalesce with a renewed interest in the local. The archipelagic coast is a landform that itself is perched between different understandings of place, in what Edward Casey has called its 'double horizon'; for Casey, the dialogue between inner and outer horizons, in this case the domestic and oceanic horizons, makes any place always an 'essay in experimental living'.[36] Such an awareness of the fluid but grounded nature of place is nowhere truer than on the coast, not only in its lived history, but also in its literature and art.

Fiona Stafford's highly influential work on place and the local has also informed this book's growth over several conversations, and her contribution to this volume offers an innovative literary critical methodology for reading literary works against a background of critical and historical studies of particular regions.[37] In this case, Stafford explores the Solway Firth, initially within a broad context of the language of coastal place names, the traces and memories they carry of exchange and invasion, expansion and inundation, but also in relation to the imaginative, anthropomorphic impulses evident in the language of confluence. She goes on to consider the estuary's peculiar situation as a border between England and Scotland with a complex history from the early conquests through to the coming of the railways, but also as an opening towards the Isle of Man, Ireland, Wales, and the rest of the world. Taking its cue from John Ruskin's claim for the international importance of the Solway, the essay explores Ruskin's own attachment to the area, magnified as it was by

[35] Elaine Stratford, Godfrey Baldacchino, Elizabeth MacMahon, Carol Farbotko, and Andrew Harwood, 'Envisioning the Archipelago', *Island Studies Journal*, 6 (2011), 113–30.

[36] Edward Casey, *Getting Back into Place: Toward a Renewed Understanding of the Place-World* (Bloomington: Indiana University Press, 1993).

[37] Fiona Stafford, *Local Attachments: The Province of Poetry* (Oxford: Oxford University Press, 2010).

Scott, Burns, and Wordsworth. However, it also goes beyond Ruskin to consider a thoughtful response from Ciaran Carson who, provoked by Ruskin's view of the region described in *Praeterita*, imagines him crossing the Irish Sea to encounter modern Belfast. Stafford develops an intricate analysis that reads the literary texts and the language used to represent the Solway in dialogue with the critical and historical study of this particular region, its topography, but also its coastal relations to the other languages and places of the archipelago.

Serving as something of a masthead for contemporary literature with such a focus on archipelagic place has been Andrew McNeillie's literary journal *Archipelago*. In the editorial of the first issue, McNeillie claimed:

> Extraordinary will be its preoccupations with landscape, with documentary and remembrance, with wilderness and wet, with natural and cultural histories, with language and languages, with the littoral and the vestigial, the geological, and topographical, with climates, in terms of both meteorology, ecology and environment; and all these things as metaphor, liminal and subliminal, at the margins, in the unnameable constellation of islands on the Eastern Atlantic coast, known variously in other millennia as Britain, Great Britain, Britain and Ireland etc.[38]

McNeillie tightens the political and historical focus of the agenda of 'archipelagic criticism' to take account of natural histories, the topographical, climatic, and the ecological, in such a way as to make the spatial reconfigurations of the field necessarily grounded in this concrete understanding of place. As Jos Smith demonstrates in his essay here—a study of *Archipelago* and its very distinctive landscape vision—the sense of place the journal promotes is based on fugitive allegiances, on a sense of belonging that is felt all the more strongly for being mobile, for being trans-local in nature, and for being 'between and among islands'. The journal's representation of the archipelago foregrounds the north-western coastal edge and is at a certain 'argumentative tilt' from conventional representations of modern Britain, one that Smith traces back to the editor's experience of living on the Aran Islands for a formative year in his youth. Turning to some recent work published in the journal, Smith shows that the seas between the islands of the archipelago have quite literally served as a stage for collaboration between artists from different regions, as an ambiguous zone for reframing and rethinking the orientation of the isles as a sociable space for creative possibilities.

McNeillie's own contribution to this collection returns to the Aran Islands with Tim Robinson himself. Taking Robinson's review of his

[38] Andrew McNeillie, 'Editorial', *Archipelago*, 1 (2007), vii.

memoir *An Aran Keening* as a starting point, McNeillie spirals through layers of textual allusion and social history before becoming bewitched by the grave of the RAF airman on Aran. This plot, decidedly not a corner of a foreign field that is forever England, becomes a site of meditation for McNeillie, a place where global conflict, family history, personal memory, and the sea meet in a haunting moment of mortality, evanescence, and loss. It is as if the name and stories of the islanders that McNeillie, like Robinson, strives to preserve are all, like Keats's name on his gravestone, 'writ in water'—the shifting water of the sea.

Beyond the work that McNeillie publishes in *Archipelago*, there has been little criticism that explores the archipelagic perspective through such a focus on place in cultural geography or literary studies, though this is changing. One exception to this is Damian Walford Davies's book *Cartographies of Culture: New Geographies of Welsh Writing in English* (2012). It explores a groundbreaking approach to literary cartography that we see extended in his contribution to this collection as he turns his attention to the work of author and naturalist Ronald Lockley. In this essay, Walford Davies analyses how Welsh island space is mediated through an array of written genres in Lockley's published works (what he comes to call the author's 'teasing discursive ecology'): scientific and popular conservationist discourses, narratives of adventure and survival, autobiography, cartography, local history, and not least of all literary and mythological discourses. Like other naturalists that this collection explores, Lockley occupies an ambiguous territory 'between scientific professional and pioneering amateur', and this comes out in both the writing and the life. Walford Davies traces the experimental stylist in a man who made his island world on Skokholm an 'experiment in a way of living'. In doing so, he frames Lockley in relation to a long tradition of island literature and to the contemporary discipline of 'nissology', or 'a science of island thinking', and a highly original way of reading this multitalented man emerges. Links to other Atlantic and North Sea archipelagos allow Walford Davies to explore Lockley's work as a form of 'counter-mapping' that intervenes in traditional British and Welsh identities and helps us to understand his work as a dynamically archipelagic form of writing.

Nessa Cronin also turns to a naturalist in her essay here, but this time to Maude Delap, who lived and worked on the island of Valentia in the southwest of Ireland. Delap is primarily remembered today for her contribution to natural science through her work elaborating the complex life cycle of the jellyfish, and for her contribution to a maritime survey of Valentia Island published by the Royal Irish Academy in 1899, and yet very little academic work has been published about her. As with Davies on Lockley, a careful reconsideration of an under-acknowledged, semi-professional pioneer helps to provoke some searching questions about the relationship between local, national, and institutional cultures. Through a fascinating account of Delap's work on marine and coastal life, based on original archival research, Cronin is able to draw much-needed attention to the peripheral geographies, to the domestic spaces, and to the particular practices of fieldwork that lie behind the construction of modern European science. Located and gendered histories emerge that are all too often overlooked in our understanding of the professionalization and specialization of knowledge. This is explored in the context of the networks and shifting associations between Victorian Britain and Ireland and through the formation of particularized pathways of knowledge via relations between the museums and academies of the city and the outdoor investigations carried out in the field and at the margins on the coast. Locating the emergence of such scientific knowledge in distinctive geographies and field cultures offers as important a contribution to our understanding of coastal heritage as it does to the understanding of the scientific tradition itself.

Kyriaki Hadjiafxendi and John Plunkett consider a slightly earlier example of the fieldwork of mid-nineteenth-century naturalists on the coast of Devon around Ilfracombe and Torquay. Here the rise in popularity of elite forms of environmental tourism in these westerly locations would have a considerable influence on Victorian popular science thanks to such key figures as George Henry Lewes, Marian Evans Lewes (soon to rise to fame as George Eliot), and Charles Kingsley—all of them popular authors in their own right. The essay contrasts an area considered culturally remote—peripheral in various ways to Victorian England—and the wealth of ecological knowledge that it provided for those who would search it out. But Plunkett and Hadjiafxendi also trace the commercialization of this environmental tourism via the subsequent surge in popularity of the household aquarium. This movement in environmental tourism became infused with an almost exultant 'romance of natural history' that encouraged city-dwellers to come away and explore a remote world, 'stranger than ever opium-eater dreamed'. However, aquariums soon enabled the domestication of these exotic ecosystems as the coast itself became 'mobile and reproducible' in the city and drawing room. The essay provokes questions about the sustainability of tourist cultures and the commodification of the periphery by vested interests in the centre.

Margaret Cohen's account of the phenomenology of observation under water overlaps with the aesthetics of the aquarium but shifts the emphasis away from commodified spectacle. In her study of Zarh Pritchard's early twentieth-century submarine paintings, Cohen ranges from the science of perception at depth to the scientific challenges that faced engineers and artists in their attempts to see beneath the surface. These were problems addressed in the nineteenth century by writers like Robert Louis Stevenson, himself the child of a marine engineer, and Jules Verne, whose idea of deep-sea worlds may have come from his visits to a Paris aquarium. Pritchard was among the first artists to realize that colour and line had different qualities at varying depths. Turner shared a similar attention to the effect of water on light above the sea, his mists and fogs the trace of an aesthetic that diverged from what Cohen identifies as the Enlightenment demand for clarity. Pritchard was Anglo-Irish and travelled widely. His two favourite sites to paint underwater were the west coast of Scotland and Tahiti, two environments far removed from each other in temperature, light, and ecology. Cohen reads this diversity as evidence of a general trend towards an 'ocean internationalism' in the work of marine artists of many forms and styles. The ocean was no free space, as the slave trade had shown. Ruskin, indeed, had discussed Turner's 'The Slave Ship (Slavers Throwing Overboard the Dead and Dying)' in his *Modern Painters* as far back as 1840. Still, the offshore offered the opportunity to engage with an imaginative space outside the boundaries of empire and nation, boundaries that were in violent flux as Pritchard painted. As Cohen suggests, his immersive art offered both a new subject for art and a new way of seeing. That Pritchard's painting is now largely forgotten is suggestive of the degree to which such art lost its place in a century in which the nation-state grew to powerful prominence.

Finally, Nick Groom's essay challenges us to entertain the remarkable hypothetical of an Atlantic archipelago without an Irish Sea. This essay brings to light a hitherto overlooked satirical pamphlet, *Thoughts of a Project for Draining the Irish Channel*, published anonymously in 1722. The pamphlet is a satire on both the South Sea Bubble and Anglo-Irish politics of the time. Its combination of land reclamation projects and political arithmetic, and the comprehension of the sea as a process that could be directed or influenced rather than be accepted as an absolute given, has profound implications for thinking about the relationship between land, coasts, and the sea. The conceptual leap made in *Draining the Irish Channel* is that the sea can and should be improved: in other words, done away with. Conceived thus, Groom shows, the sea could become not only the medium, but the very ground of British colonialism. Land could be created from unproductive water and the Irish Sea could literally become a new territory. Groom's highly original essay—part-detective story, part-literary criticism, part-political history, part-thought experiment—demonstrates how fields as diverse as maritime law and local folklore necessarily contribute to historicizing coastal and marine identities.

The essays gathered here offer a variety of case studies that reveal the rich interconnections between archipelagic criticism, the blue humanities, and Island Studies from some of the leading researchers in these fields. Each deploys an innovative critical methodology for rethinking the cultural and political relationships that stretch across this constellation of islands. They do so with a particular sensitivity to the distinctive and interwoven historical geographies of place as they have been imagined and reimagined by authors, by visual artists, and by pioneering natural scientists. They are offered in the hope that they might inspire further replottings of cultural history and literary geography that contribute to the continuous unfolding of these archipelagic identities.

In 2010, the editors of this collection, with Andrew McNeillie, began the British Academy-funded 'Atlantic Archipelagos Research Project'.[39] The project set out to take an interdisciplinary view on how Britain's partially devolved state 'inflects the formation of post-split Welsh, Scottish and English identities in the context of Ireland's own experience of partition and self-rule'.[40] It began by celebrating the work of Tim Robinson in the Druid Theatre in Galway and has since expanded into the Atlantic Archipelagos Research Consortium, including a great many more active participants, most notably John Brannigan, Fiona Stafford, and Frank Shovlin, who have helped to bring archipelagic events to Dublin, Oxford, Liverpool, Sapelo Island, and Cornwall. The project's interest in coastlines has been fed in particular by Brannigan's work bringing together perspectives (from literary criticism, maritime history, and marine biology) on the Irish Sea, which he has described as 'the geographical centre of the archipelago'.[41] Recognizing the sea at the heart of the islands in this way encourages us to think of these nations, regions, localities, and people as less firmly determined by the ground beneath their feet than by the challenge that connecting with one another has represented. More than anything, this book is an exploration of the contours of this challenge.

[39] Now a consortium: see http://aarco.org.

[40] http://humanities.exeter.ac.uk/english/research/projects/aarp.

[41] John Brannigan, *Archipelagic Modernism: Literature in the Irish and British Isles, 1890–1970* (Edinburgh: Edinburgh University Press, 2015), 64.

2

Draining the Irish Sea

The Colonial Politics of Water

Nick Groom

> Do you not hear the sea?
>
> John Keats to J. H. Reynolds, 17–18 April 1817.[1]

In Arthur C. Clarke's 1972 science fiction novel *Rendezvous with Rama*, a character remarks in passing that the Mediterranean has been drained to assist archaeological study; as preposterous as this sounds, perhaps in the twenty-second century heritage tourism will be more important than life or death. Clarke adapted the idea from Philip K. Dick's 1962 counterfactual history, *The Man in the High Castle*, in which the Nazi Chancellor Martin Bormann has drained the Mediterranean for territorial gain. But the idea had already been around since at least the 1920s, when it was seriously proposed by the German architect Hermann Sörgel as a way of creating the new land of Atlantropa. Not to be outdone, in September 1930, the magazine *Modern Mechanics* reported a similar scheme to drain the North Sea to ease problems of European overpopulation:

> If the extensive schemes for the drainage of [the] North Sea are carried out according to the plan . . . conceived by a group of eminent English scientists, 100,000 square miles will be added to the overcrowded continents of Europe. The reclaimed land will be walled in with enormous dykes, similar to the Netherland dykes, to protect it from the sea, and the various rivers flowing into the North Sea will have their courses diverted to different outlets by means of canals.[2]

The Irish Sea covers a more modest 40,000 square miles. Nevertheless, in 1722 an anonymous author styling himself with the degree 'A. M.

[1] Keats misquotes Shakespeare's *King Lear* IV. vi. 4.

[2] 'North Sea Drainage Project to Increase Area of Europe', *Modern Mechanics* (September 1930), 169.

in Hydrostat' published a satirical proposal in Dublin with the title, *Thoughts of a Project for Draining the Irish Channel.* It is a scintillating pamphlet, and it has been entirely overlooked.

Draining the Irish Channel is a satire on both the South Sea Bubble and Anglo-Irish politics. It capitalizes on the craze for projects and speculation, scientific advances in hydraulics and circulation, resource management and political arithmetic, and improvement and reclamation. It was also an almost immediate response to local plans to improve the port of Dublin by dredging.[3] Reclamation, as an expansion of territory beyond the immediate borders of one's own land, was a striking metaphor for both the fatal imbalance of Anglo-Irish policy, and for imperialism more generally: not only did it redefine physical geography in political terms, it also literally redrew the map of the world. Thus, draining the sea—like draining marshes, water meadows, and floodplains—is a radical example of the impact of commercial ecology on identity, which today raises pertinent questions of regional connectivity and environmental sustainability. Indeed, from the mid-nineteenth century there were repeated proposals to excavate a tunnel under the Irish Sea, and these plans were seriously revived in 1956 and again in 2014, and featured in the 2015 UK General Election campaign.[4] This chapter therefore historicizes coastal work by blending textual criticism, political and legal analysis, regional folklore studies, and counterfactual history with striking new evidence. The significance of the Irish Sea as the axis around which 'The Isles' (Britain and Ireland) defined themselves is revealed through the ultimate endgame: removing the very sea itself.

But before the Irish Sea is drained, the political context needs outlining. By the mid-eighteenth century, English (originally Anglo-Norman) control extended across the whole of the Atlantic archipelago.[5] In Ireland, of course, this was the Age of Ascendancy, which had effectively begun with the Treaty of Limerick (1691). Dublin expanded massively in this period—from a small town to the second largest city of the British Empire. It was built in a fashionable Georgian style that rivalled Edinburgh and was a significant cultural centre. David Garrick performed at Thomas Sheridan's theatre, and Handel's *Messiah* was first performed at

[3] See H. A. Gilligan, *A History of the Port of Dublin* (Dublin: Gill and MacMillan, 1988), 18–25.

[4] See *Hansard*, vol. 70, col. 168 (23 February 1915); *Hansard*, vol. 550, cols 1641–88 (23 March 1956); Chartered Institute of Logistics and Transport Report, *Vision 20:35 Cymru Wales* (reported in *Global Construction Review*, 24 November 2014); and *DUP Westminster Manifesto 2015* (Belfast: Democratic Unionist Party, 2015), 11.

[5] J. G. A. Pocock, 'British History: A Plea for a New Subject', in J. G. A. Pocock, *The Discovery of Islands: Essays in British History* (Cambridge: Cambridge University Press, 2005), 39.

Dublin City Hall.[6] Yet Ireland was ruled by a minority Protestant élite who were increasingly subordinate to the British government. In 1720, Westminster passed the 'Declaratory Act' (known as 'Sixth of George I'), which asserted British power over the Irish Parliament 'to bind the kingdom and people of Ireland' and determine foreign policy, and in 1751, control of the Irish economy also moved to Westminster. Imports of Irish woollen goods were banned by Westminster, and imports of food were only allowed after 1748. Ireland was in effect a cash cow for absentee landlords and served as a vast garrison for the British army when it was not on campaign.

Opposition to British rule had been fiercely articulate since William Molyneux's attack *The Case of Ireland being bound by Acts of Parliament in England* (first published in 1698). Molyneux was a friend of Jonathan Swift, and in the 1720s, Swift himself was, reluctantly, one of the foremost critics of the British government in his 'Drapier's Letters' and other satirical pamphlets. These included his attack on Wood's ha'pence (1724, in which a new coinage with a debased intrinsic value was introduced to Ireland) and his *Short View of the State of Ireland* (1728, which attacked the trade restrictions on Ireland), and culminated in his notorious cannibal polemic *A Modest Proposal* (1729). At the same time as he was writing the 'Drapier' and pamphleteering, Swift was also completing *Travels into Several Remote Nations of the World*, which would be published in 1726 under the name 'Lemuel Gulliver'. As Swift wrote in a letter on 19 January 1724, 'I have left the country of the horses, and am in the flying island, where I shall not stay long, and my last two journeys will be soon over'.[7]

This, the third of Gulliver's voyages and the last to be written of the four, describes Gulliver's encounter with the flying island of Laputa and the philosophers and projectors to whom he is subsequently introduced. These episodes were derived from earlier Scriblerian satire developed with John Arbuthnot, John Gay, Robert Harley, Thomas Parnell, and Alexander Pope. But Swift gave a decidedly Irish spin to the island in a passage that ferociously described the Wood's ha'pence debacle as an allegory, arguing that it could have deservedly brought down the British government and monarchy. In this censored scene, the citizens of 'Lindalino'

[6] See Frank Welsh, *The Four Nations: A History of the United Kingdom* (New Haven and London: Yale University Press, 2003), 208–13.

[7] Jonathan Swift, *The Correspondence of Jonathan Swift*, ed. Harold Williams, 5 vols (Oxford: Clarendon Press, 1963–5), iii. 5; see Robert P. Fitzgerald, 'Science and Politics in Swift's Voyage to Laputa', *Journal of English and Germanic Philology*, 87 (1988), 217.

(Dublin) threaten to 'kill the King and all his Servants, and entirely change the Government'.[8]

In addition to its blistering political satire, *Gulliver's Travels* is laced with topical references to the South Sea Bubble, the ruinous stock market crash of 1720.[9] In 1721, Swift had written a poem, 'The Bubble', on the over-speculation, fraudulent dealing, fantastical money-making schemes, and nascent capitalist greed of the times:

The Sea is richer than the Land,
I heard it from my Grannam's Mouth;
Which now I clearly understand,
For by the Sea she meant the *South*.[10]

'Bubbles' were joint-stock companies that dazzled credulous investors with the empty promise of fabulous profits yet had the life expectancy of a soap bubble; they were symptomatic of the 'Age of Projectors'—projectors being the innovators and financial backers of get-rich-quick wheezes. Daniel Defoe was a typical example, investing (and rapidly losing) money in the manufacture of roofing tiles, the farming of civet cats for perfume, and the development of a bathyscaphe (a primitive submarine) to recover lost treasure from the seabed.

Hence, during Gulliver's visit to Balnibari, Swift describes a 'Club of... Projectors' from the Academy of Lagado who propose diverting a river and digging a canal to direct water, by means of 'Pipes and Engines', to a new mill on the side of a mountain, 'Because the Wind and Air upon a Height agitated the Water, and thereby made it fitter for Motion: And because the Water descending down a Declivity would turn the Mill with half the Current of a River whose Course is more upon a Level'.[11] However, after employing a hundred men for two years, the project is abandoned. It is surely no coincidence that the Grand Canal (Ireland), connecting Dublin with the River Shannon, was first proposed in 1715; that project, however, was eventually completed in 1779.

As Pat Rogers has pointed out, these sorts of activities are examples of the 'commercial exploration' of natural resources.[12] Pumping water seems to have been particularly appealing to projectors. In his *Tour*, Defoe noted

[8] Jonathan Swift, *Gulliver's Travels* [*Travels into Several Remote Nations of the World*], in *The Writings of Jonathan Swift*, ed. Robert A. Greenberg and William B. Piper (New York and London: W. W. Norton, 1973), 1–260, 146 [see 145n].

[9] See Pat Rogers, 'Gulliver and the Engineers', *Modern Language Review*, 70 (1975), 260.

[10] Jonathan Swift, *The Bubble: A Poem* (London, 1721), 7.

[11] Swift, *Gulliver's Travels*, 151–2.

[12] Rogers, 'Gulliver', 261; see John Carswell, *The South Sea Bubble* (Stanford: Stanford University Press, 1960), esp. 14–16.

an innovative new mill devised by George Sorocold, an engineer specializing in hydraulics, and many others, including Thomas Savery and Thomas Newcomen, the most celebrated engineers of the period, built contraptions for pumping water out of mines—and were themselves satirized in the broadside *The Bubblers Mirrour; or England's Folley* (1720):

> Come all ye Culls, my Water Engine Buy,
> To pump your flooded Mines and Coal Pits dry:
> Some projects are all Wind, but ours is Water,
> And tho' at present low, may rise hereafter.[13]

Pumping water out of flooded mines was, however, small beer compared with the possibilities of pumping water out of flooded land. Land reclamation had already been underway in agriculture for decades and was an established aspect of land management. The second chapter of John Mortimer's *The Whole Art of Husbandry: or, The Way of Managing and Improving of Land* (4th edn, 1716), for example, is devoted to reclamation: draining and improving bogs, fens, and marshes. Projectors and modern agriculturalists both agreed that water was something to be controlled and restricted. And it was consequently a small step to think not merely of reclaiming land from waterlogged environments, but of reclaiming land from the sea itself: a reversal of the Deluge accomplished by the expertise of science and industry, the salvaging of the primal Biblical catastrophe, and a recovery of the mythical realm of Atlantis.

This potential transformation of the sea into land received intellectual impetus not only from the practice of land reclamation, but also from theories of circulation. The body had been redefined as a circulatory system by William Harvey in 1628, yet Harvey's ideas on the circulation of the blood were, according to the dissident thinker Ivan Illich, slow to spread, as 'To accommodate circulation, the quivering and symbol-laden flesh of tradition must be recast as a functional system of filters, conduits, valves, and pumps'.[14] Illich notes that by the early eighteenth century, the notion of 'circulation' was being applied by botanists to sap, then to the spread of ideas, and around 1750 money is described as 'circulating'.[15] But in fact the term was being used some half-a-century sooner than Illich

[13] Quoted in part by Rogers, 'Gulliver', 264. This broadside exists in variant forms: see Anon., 'The Bublers Mirrour', in Paul Langford (ed.), *Walpole and the Robinocracy: The English Satirical Print* (Cambridge: Chadwyck-Healey, 1986), 38–9.

[14] Ivan Illich, *H_2O and the Waters of Forgetfulness: Reflections on the Historicity of 'Stuff'* (Dallas: Dallas Institute of Humanities and Culture, 1985), 42. Illich has, after Gaston Bachelard, described the relationship between water and space as a relationship between form and matter (3–6).

[15] Illich, *H_2O and the Waters of Forgetfulness*, 43. 'Liquidity' was likewise used throughout the century as a scientific property applied to other areas.

claims. Already by the early eighteenth century, 'circulation' was being used in England to describe the passions, and there are instances of its fashionable use in seventeenth-century popular literature.[16] By at least 1701, credit in the economy was being described as 'circulating', and Samuel Johnson's *Dictionary* (1755–6) quotes Swift himself writing on the '*circulation* of human things'.[17] The sea too was conceptualized as a circulatory system rather than an inert body, most notably in a treatise by Joseph Mead, which had the self-explanatory title,

> *An Essay on Currents at Sea; By which it appears, There is Reason to Apprehend, that the Sea is not a Fluid in a State of Rest, except those Motions which are caused by the Impulse of Winds, and that [are] known by the Name of Tides: And consequently, That this Earth is not of a uniform Density, according to the Supposition of Sir Isaac Newton; but that the Currents of the Gulph of Florida, also on the Coast of Brasil, and the Northern In-Draught on this Western Coast, are Currents of Circulation, kept up by different Densities in this Earth, and its Motion round its Axis* (1757).

But if the sea was a circulatory system, it was also accountable—as suggested by the allusion made here to the innocuous field of tide tables. Britain, as a maritime island nation, had a calendrically sound structure of national tide tables in the period.[18] The ebbs and flows of tidal currents could be predicted with impressive accuracy. This was not meteorological forecasting or weatherlore, still less astrological prognostication, but the application of new astronomical science to maritime and commercial interests. Such principles of calculation could moreover be applied to all sorts of areas: political economy was given a new mathematical basis—which was of course rapidly and scathingly attacked in Swift's *A Modest Proposal*. But political arithmetic was the new orthodoxy and provided, for example, the ideological basis for the control of the Highlands after the Battle of Culloden in 1746, underpinning road-building programmes and Ordnance Survey cartography.[19] The unruliness of the sea was similarly measurable and, if it could not be controlled, it could at least be reliably governed in the interests of trade and empire. In the case of the 'Irish Gulph', which had a well-deserved reputation for turbulence, this was a

[16] See, for example, Edward Ward, *The London-Spy Compleat* (London, 1700), pt iv, 1 (February 1699).

[17] See Charles Davenant, *A Postscript to a Discourse of Credit, and the Means and Methods of Restoring it* (London, 1701); Samuel Johnson, *A Dictionary of the English Language* (London, 1755–6), quoting 'Swift on Modern Education'.

[18] See, for example, Nathaniel Colson, *The Mariners New Kalendar* (London, 1701), 33–8.

[19] See Rachel Hewitt, *Map of a Nation: A Biography of the Ordnance Survey* (London: Granta, 2010).

crucial issue.[20] In one of the letters that comprise his *Journey through England* (1724), John Macky described 'the Wind being generally very boisterous in these narrow Seas', and '*As unquiet as the Irish sea*' was a common proverb in England.[21]

Whatever the crossing conditions, the Irish Sea was the sole trade route between Ireland and Great Britain. In *A Tour Thro' the Whole Island of Great Britain* (1724), Daniel Defoe comments that the English westward trade was split between Liverpool and Bristol: 'One has all the North, and the other all the South of Britain to correspond in', and '*Ireland* is, as it were, all their own, and shared between them as above'.[22] Defoe also notes that Whitehaven on the Cumbrian coast is England's third biggest port for exporting coal, after Newcastle and Sunderland, as it supplies Dublin 'and all the Towns of *Ireland* on that Coast'. He observes of the maritime traffic on the Irish Sea that "tis frequent in time of War, or upon the ordinary Occasion of cross Winds, to have two hundred Sail of Ships at a Time go from this Place [Whitehaven] for *Dublin*, loaden with Coals'.[23] Coal was also supplied to Ireland from Irwin in Scotland, which exported to Belfast and Carrickfergus, as well as to Dublin.[24] Below the waves, the waters were mainly fished for herring and salmon, and there were allegedly no lobsters in the Irish Sea.[25]

The problem with Dublin harbour, however, was that it contained a significant bar, or bank of sand, which presented a serious obstacle to ships and therefore to trade. As Gerard Boate described the situation:

> DUBLIN haven hath a bar in the mouth, upon which at high flood and spring tide there is fifteen and eighteen feet of water, but at the ebbe and nep tide but six. With an ordinary tide you cannot go the key of Dublin with a ship that draws five feet of water, but with a spring tide you may go up with ships

[20] Edward Barlow, *An Exact Survey of the Tide* (London, 1722), 155.

[21] John Macky, *A Journey Through England. In Familiar Letters from a Gentlemam* [*sic*] *Here, to his Friend Abroad*, 2 vols, 2nd edn (London, 1724), ii. 140; Gerard Boate quotes the proverb, but disagrees: see his *A Natural History of Ireland, in Three Parts* (attrib. to 'several hands', Dublin, 1726), 28–9.

[22] Daniel Defoe, *A Tour Thro' the Whole Island of Great Britain, divided into Circuits or Journies*, 3 vols (London, 1724; subsequently enlarged and updated), iii. 203.

[23] Ibid., iii. 230. [24] Ibid., 'Account and Description of Scotland', iii. 77.

[25] James Saunders, *The Compleat Fisherman* (London, 1724), 37, 53. Donal Flood notes the local trade in cockles, and the tradition that following a glut, herring had suddenly abandoned Dublin Bay (see Donal T. Flood, 'Dublin Bay in the 18th Century', *Dublin Historical Record*, 31 (1978), 129–41, 132); there were also significant north Cornwall fishing grounds for pilchards at St Ives, Newquay, Port Isaac, and Padstow, which by the nineteenth century had collapsed due to overfishing (see Alan Southward, Gerald Boalch, and Linda Maddock, 'Climatic Change and the Herring and Pilchard Fisheries of Devon and Cornwall', in David J. Starkey (ed.), *Devon's Coastline and Coastal Waters: Aspects of Man's Relationship with the Sea* (Exeter: Exeter University Press, 1988), 33–57).

> that draw seven and eight feet. Those that go deeper cannot go nearer Dublin than the Rings-end, a place three miles distant from the bar, and one from Dublin. This haven almost all over falleth dry with the ebbe, as well below Rings-end as above it, so as you may go dry foot round about the ships which lye at an anchor there.[26]

Ships therefore risked running aground because of the combined hazards of the shallow channel and the windswept bay. Moreover, as silt and sand was used for ballast, boats jettisoning this into the bay to lighten their load had raised the bed of the bay and eroded sand banks. In 1707, this led to a Ballast Board being established, but the problem required a much more radical solution.[27]

In September 1713, the hydraulic engineer Capt. John Perry arrived in Dublin at the invitation of Sir Alexander Cairnes to assess 'a Proposition of mine for the making of a better Depth of Water going over the Barr'.[28] Perry spent three months studying the problem before returning to London on a commission to repair the Thames Embankment.[29] Perry, who had studied Dutch water management technology and worked for the Russian tsar Peter the Great building canals, dams, and locks, visited Dublin again in 1720–1 and published *An Answer to Objections against the Making of a Bason, with Reasons for the bettering of the Harbour of Dublin* (1721).[30] In this treatise, he proposed building a 'New common Shore . . . parallel to the River'.[31] This channel would be properly drained and sealed to answer objections that the seawater would stagnate or flood districts, affecting property and land rights. From the current size and unloading practices of ships, Perry estimated the probable effect on the size of cargoes and the consequent impact on imports—coal, for example, would become cheaper.[32] He compared the potential expanded capacity of Dublin with the increased harbour size at Liverpool, which from the end of the seventeenth century had begun to compete with Dublin as a route to North America and the West Indies, and also remarked on a sea wall built at Teignmouth to reclaim land. Perry was back again in 1725 to survey and map the bay, but his proposals to make the port more navigable were

[26] Boate, *Natural History of Ireland*, 15.

[27] Geoffrey Corry, 'The Dublin Bar: The Obstacle to the Improvement of the Port of Dublin', *Dublin Historical Record*, 23 (1970), 143.

[28] Quoted by Flood, 'Dublin Bay', 138.

[29] Perry's work on the Thames is described in *An Account of the Stopping of Daggenham Breach* (London, 1721).

[30] See John Perry, *The State of Russia, under the Present Czar* (London, 1716), and the *Oxford Dictionary of National Biography* (*ODNB*).

[31] John Perry, *An Answer to Objections against the Making of a Bason, with Reasons for the bettering of the Harbour of Dublin* (Dublin, 1721), 7.

[32] Ibid., 18.

ultimately rejected.[33] By this time, some 1,834 ships totalling 90,758 tons entered the harbour annually, accounting for more than half the imports into Ireland.[34]

The early eighteenth-century emphasis on the Irish Sea as a prized trade route and a rich fishery was a mercantilist redefinition of the waters that attempted to eclipse (or rather quell) the deeper currents of identity. But the Irish Sea not only irrigates Irish identity, it defines the archipelago: without it, the 'Isles' would simply be the 'Island'.[35] As Émile Durkheim conjectures, space is not an absolute or abstract set of coordinates, but is constituted by relative relationships inflected by emotional and therefore social values.[36] This, then, is best shown by imagining what would happen if the Irish Sea ceased to exist.

The anonymous author of the pamphlet *Draining the Irish Channel* begins by confirming the boisterous weather fomented by the narrow passage of the Irish Sea:

> the Channel is so cramp'd by the Shores on each side, that in Winter time, for want of Elbow-room, you'll find nothing but the Sea foaming, roaring, bouncing, frisking, skipping, jerking, heaving, setting, tossing as if in a Ferment, and full of frothy and fiery Billows.[37]

Consequently, 'Commerce is hindered, Passengers drown'd or starv'd,... Ships and Goods lost, Merchants ruin'd, Trade destroy'd'.[38]

Such calamities will obviously be avoided if the Sea is drained, and Perry is nominated as the man to do so. The author of *Draining the Irish Channel* is suspicious of Perry's reasons for visiting Dublin to date, suggesting that his dredging proposals are a money-making project—something Perry had explicitly denied in his *Answer to Objections*.[39] But the anonymous satirist points out that draining the entire sea instead will provide far richer benefits than simply improving the harbour: 'there will be found (without doubt) immense Treasure, enough to defray all the Expence, and to pay very well for the Trouble of doing the same'. This will

33 Desmond F. Moore, 'The Port of Dublin', *Dublin Historical Record*, 16 (1961), 137–8; *ODNB*.

34 Figures for 1723 are from Arthur Dobbs, *An Essay on the Trade and Improvement of Ireland* (Dublin, 1729–31), 15–16; see also Sir William Petty, *A Geographical Description of the Kingdom of Ireland, Newly Corrected & Improv'd by Actual Observations* (London, 1728).

35 Hence, Pocock objects less to the Anglocentrism of the term 'British Isles' than 'British history': see J. G. A. Pocock, 'The Atlantic Archipelago and the War of the Three Kingdoms', in *Discovery of Islands*, 77–93, 77.

36 Émile Durkheim, *Elementary Forms of the Religious Life* (New York: Free Press, 1965), 15 (quoted by Illich, *H_2O and the Waters of Forgetfulness*, 8).

37 Anon., *Thoughts of a Project for Draining the Irish Channel* (Dublin, 1722), 8–9.

38 Ibid., 9.

39 Perry, *Answer to Objections*, 26–7.

encourage projectors to invest no less than £100,000 in the scheme, at a remuneration of 'a Pound for their Peny'. Our projector-author speculates on the precious submarine minerals that will become free to be excavated—'vast Quantities of Gold, Silver in Bullion and Specie, Pearl, Rubies, and Diamonds'—and from the larger sea-game a variety of sea-ivory can be harvested.[40]

Anticipating the Admiralty's objection to the loss of military bases and routes, as well as duties, the anonymous author balances this against the potential savings: there will be fewer ships required. Locks at either end of the drained sea will allow passage upriver on the longer waterways of the Liffey and the Mersey and will administer custom duties more effectively, and land transport will be a safer way of traversing the distance: 'instead of being at the Expence of Packet-Boats, we will have Post-Horses and Post-Boys'.[41] Despite the British preference for travelling by sea, land transport is promoted as a way of employing 'Millions of poor Families'. Other rivers will be 'carried away in large Trunks' (i.e. conduits). The success of the whole construction project is assured by the construction innovations in canal and sluice building on the continent, and Capt. Perry's Dutch training.[42]

Details are provided as to where the locks would be best positioned. Their design is to be based on those currently on the Liffey, and they can be constructed from the salvage of 'vast Quantities of noble Timbers' already seasoned by the sea.[43] The locks will also double as fishing traps for large marine livestock such as whales and sharks, as well as sea cows (which apparently taste as good as veal), and once the Sea is drained, huge stocks of crabs and lobsters with claws as big as the antlers of elks will become available. Marine phosphorescence will be reaped to provide illumination for everything from streets to lighthouses. Shooting stars generally fall into sea and may be gleaned as sources of light and heat, and every old Moon has also sunk into the depths and so may be fished out for similar commercial advantage.

A variety of sea monsters will be available to furriers—'*Sea-Goats, Kids, Rabits, Hares, Cats,* and *Sea-Kitlings, Apes, Baboons, Monkeys*'—from which can be manufactured tippets (stoles) and riding breeches;

> and would it not be a pretty Sight to see a *Sea-Horse* at the Tower? Such a Present was never known to be made to any Monarch on Earth, who knows what may happen in this Reign.[44]

[40] *Anon., Draining the Irish Channel*, 10–11, 11, 14.

[41] Ibid., 12. Much detail is provided for an Irish readership: Mardyke is part of Cork, Tuskard is an Irish port mentioned in James Deacon Hume's *The Laws of the Customs* (London: Eyre & Strahan, 1826).

[42] *Anon., Draining the Irish Channel*, 13, 23, 5.

[43] Ibid., 14.

[44] Ibid., 19.

descending there again'.[58] *Draining the Irish Channel* does, however, succeed in monetarizing the Irish Sea and predicts the potential profits from its various yields.

The principal beneficiaries of the sea's yield would have been the Crown and the old landowners. The legal rights of ownership of *wreccum maris* ('wreck of the sea') were disputed for centuries in an attempt to square the proprietary claims of the original owners (or survivors) with the ancient law of 'right of wreck' and its relationship to coastal, regional, and national interests. If *wreccum maris* were washed ashore as flotsam or jetsam, it was supposed to be delivered to the local lord of the manor or a local official such as the coroner, and if not claimed after a year and a day, the finder was entitled to the salvage rights paid by the owners—although in practice this was often not forthcoming. However, if the 'wreck' was not claimed and there were no survivors, it became the property of the Crown or of the lord of the manor as the Crown's delegated agent, via the principle of royal prerogative. This ruling also applied to lagan (cargo or wreckage on the seabed), derelict (abandoned goods or vessels), and even 'royal fish' (such as whales). However, shipwrecked goods that did not reach land—meaning the coast, or at least near enough to be salvaged, and specifically those floating beyond the low-water mark—were by the end of the seventeenth century under the authority of the Admiralty Court, which could claim the said property itself via 'droits of Admiralty'. Simultaneously, of course, it was believed by the common populace that they had their own rights to what they might find on a beach or on the rocks. But wreck law was amended throughout the eighteenth century: first, to revoke the old system of feudal rights and make it consistent with Lockean property rights, and second, to bring it under the jurisdiction of Customs law, which was responsible for delivering revenue to the state in the form of trade duties, and which thereby further eroded manorial rights. By the 1760s, there were some 600 Customs acts, and only in 1771 was it finally settled that assets remained the possession of the original owner—even if lost at sea with all hands.[59]

In practical terms (and for the proposals put forward in *Draining the Irish Channel*), the monarch ultimately collected '*Flotson* [*sic*], *Jetson*, and *Lagan*, where the Ship perisheth, but not when the Ship is saved', a principle reiterated in 1717 pertaining to Ireland, whereby the revenue of wreck, flotsam, jetsam, or lagan was due, respectively, to 'the King, or

[58] Waldron, 'Description of the Isle of Man', 165.

[59] In fact, the original Statute of Westminster (1275) had defined a survivor not only as 'a man', but also as 'a Dog, or a Cat': see Cathryn J. Pearce, *Cornish Wrecking, 1700–1860: Reality and Popular Myth* (Woodbridge: Boydell Press, 2010), 42–4, 99, 54, 175–7, 168–9.

any Patentee or Grantee of the Crown, or any Lord of a Mannor [*sic*]', while any salvage rights were liable to pay duty.[60] Clearly, the difficulty of tracing the original owners of long-wrecked vessels and their booty that were exposed by evacuating the Irish Sea would have been of enormous potential financial benefit to the sovereign and members of the House of Lords, although in the event this may well have been challenged in the courts by the Admiralty.

The Irish Sea evidently has a history. It was named by the Romans *Oceanus Hibernicus* (that to the south was the *Oceanus Vergivius*), and by the eighteenth century it was also known as St George's Channel. Its identity was fluid and nationally conditional: in *The Compleat Fisherman* (1724), for example, James Saunders remarks that 'the *Irish* and *Welsh* Seas, that is to say, the *Severn Sea*, [is] vulgarly call'd the *Bristol Channel*, and the Sea between *England* and *Ireland*, call'd *St. George*'s *Channel*'.[61] But it has a history not only in its name, but also in its material being: the entire body of water and its social, political, and cultural significance. This history of the deep sea can thus be excavated in the same way that the history of the deep land can be excavated: as a catachthonic investigation into subterranean—or submarine—identity.[62] And although seafaring and the island mentality is acknowledged to run deep in *English* identity, the sea—specifically the Irish Sea—is also the medium of communication and interaction with Ireland. This is best shown by imagining what would happen if the Irish Sea ceased to exist and is, I think, the nub of this satire: can the Irish Sea be considered the axis around which the Isles define themselves? I would therefore like to conclude with a thought experiment, taking the satire *Draining the Irish Channel* at face value and projecting what could have been the consequences if the Irish Sea really had been drained in the 1720s.

How would this new 'Erstwhile Irish Sea' ('E.I.S.') territory be defined, named, and governed? From the seventeenth century, Britain has had

[60] Alexander Justice, *A General Treatise of the Dominion of the Sea: and A Compleat Body of the Sea-Laws*... (London, 1709), 669; Matthew Dutton, *The Office and Authority of a Justice of Peace for Ireland*... (Dublin, 1718), 30; see also, for example, *Acts and Statutes made in a Parliament begun at Dublin, the Twelfth Day of November, Anno Dom. 1715* (Dublin, 1719), 96.

[61] Saunders, *The Compleat Fisherman*, 37; see also Guy Miège, *The Present State of Great Britain and Ireland, in Three Parts*, 5th edn (London, 1723), 20. John Chamberlayne, among others, comments that Anglesey is completely surrounded by the Irish Sea: *Magnæ Britanniæ Notitia: or, The Present State of Great Britain; with Divers Remarks upon the Antient State Thereof* (London, 1726), 23.

[62] For 'catachthonic history', see Nick Groom, 'Gothic and Celtic Revivals: Antiquity and the Archipelago', in Robert DeMaria, Jr, Heesok Chang, and Samantha Zacher (eds), *A Companion to British Literature*, 4 vols (Oxford: Wiley-Blackwell, 2014), iii. 361–79.

considerable problems in conceptualizing the relationship between the four nations: no part of the British Isles (if that itself is an acceptable term) is actually solely British, but has a primary identity as English, Irish, Manx, Scottish, or Welsh. The E.I.S. would be an area with a very different history to that of the pre-existent land, a reminder of the profound influence of history, particularly political history—or perhaps rather of memory—on British identities. Presumably, the mystical liberties embedded in the matter of Britain would influence the status of the new territory, and thereby all contiguous territories. Lord Mansfield famously declared in 1772 that the air of England was too pure to be breathed by a slave; consequently, it was believed that any slaves who set foot on English ground were instantly free. With the creation of the E.I.S., would English ground and its proclamations of liberty now literally run continuously to the west coast of Ireland, with all British subjects sharing similar status, rights, and opportunities?

Consider the following scenario. Parliamentary union between Britain and Ireland would have occurred much sooner because the four countries would now occupy a single land mass: a continental island. New Britain would not be able to sustain multiple structures of government—the dual constitutional, legal, and ecclesiastical structures of England and Scotland were difficult enough to manage and only really eased by the successes and profits of Empire. A single parliament would therefore govern, and the head of state would be the monarch of England, Scotland, Ireland, and France (which still formed part of the royal style). The E.I.S. would initially be run as a colony on the model of the American territories—indeed, the American colonies should also be included in this model of the archipelago.[63] It would have needed a very stable monarchy to keep all of this together—would George III have been the man? Possibly an emperor would prove a better head of state, ceding more power to constituent territories; less likely would be a confederacy of devolved parliaments, which would place too much power in the hands of career politicians for eighteenth-century tastes.

Pragmatist aspirations would rapidly incorporate the E.I.S. and the American colonies as full nations of New Britain, perhaps with the upshot that the American colonies would never have become independent—or at least not so rapidly. A state-of-the-art infrastructure consisting of turnpike roads would connect the internal territories, funded by the huge profits made from the drainage project. The North Devon and Cornish coasts and the South and West Irish coasts would be developed as transatlantic

[63] Pocock, 'Atlantic Archipelago', 78.

shipping centres to connect with the American lands of New Britain (because the waters flowing towards Cardiff and Bristol would now be less turbulent). Access to copious and untapped new natural mineral resources would speed the industrialization of landlocked cities such as Dublin and Liverpool, which would expand as Birmingham would later do, driven by the intellectual advances of the E.I.S. Enlightenment.

National attention would be focused on internal affairs: the global colonial project would be diverted as thousands of square miles of new territory (an area larger than Maine) would now be available on the British doorstep. The reduced coastline and shipbuilding centres would also slow trade and imperial expansion, and consequently lead to a more isolationist foreign policy. The new nation would, however, be prey to foreign expansionist ambitions. A successful Jacobite invasion in 1745 might place a Catholic Stuart on the throne of Scotland, with the result that Scottish Presbyterians would be driven into the fertile new domains of the E.I.S., but the King of Scotland would only rule by permission of the Hanoverian Emperor of New Britain to circumvent the risk of civil war. Hence, restrictions against Catholics across the land would be lifted, encouraging a neoteric ecumenicalism. The European context for the former archipelago would almost completely disappear, its attention confined to home policy, North America, and Atlantic-world foreign policy; there would be little energy to pursue colonial activities in the southern hemisphere.

What this scenario suggests is that the contradictions of British historiography and governance are brought into a much sharper focus if they are not mentally compartmentalized by the intercession of the sea. Some things happen more quickly (union and emancipation), and some things might not happen at all (the global expansion of empire). The Whig account of British history as being predominantly a narrative of progress would be replaced by a model of expediency and contingency. The E.I.S. could, however, become something quite different. Driven by profit and bubbles, it could be seen as priming for a new age of commercial exploitation: a huge industrial site mercilessly mined to fuel the ever-growing empire, around which Liverpool and Dublin could expand exponentially into sprawling and oppressive megacities at the centre of an ecological disaster area—a Georgian Gothic dystopia over which remote Londonopolis would exert its imperious rule.[64]

[64] Or 'Londinopolis': see James Howell, *Londinopolis; An Historicall Discourse or Perlustration of the City of London, the Imperial Chamber, and Chief Emporium of Great Britain* (London, 1657).

Whatever the outcome of the drainage project, while Ireland would continue to exist as a material territory, without the sea it would no longer exist in the same way as a social or cultural identity. But then the lack of oceanic permanency would be fatal to all the traditional identities of England and in fact Britain as well, not to mention the Atlantic—which would now be being eyed speculatively by the next generation of projectors. The 'unnameable archipelago' (in the words of Andrew McNeillie), 'the unknown subject' (in the words of J. G. A. Pocock), rests on the sea, and the removal of the 'silver sea' would historicize the archipelago out of existence.[65] Although the sea has certainly been thought of as a mere adjunct to the land—as the other side of the coast—it is not simply *terra infirma*. It has its own tales to tell, if we will attend to its voice.

[65] Andrew McNeillie, 'Editorial', *Archipelago*, 1 (2007), vii; Pocock, 'Atlantic Archipelago', 77; for Pocock, archipelagic history is 'pelagic, maritime and oceanic' (78), and Pocock subsequently argues for overlapping autocentric and heterocentric historical approaches ('The Third Kingdom in its History', in *Discovery of Islands*, 95).

3

The Roar of the Solway

Fiona Stafford

In his final, fragmentary work, *Praeterita*, the great artist, critic, and social reformer, John Ruskin, concluded his lifetime's reflections with a remarkable tribute. At the very end, after recollections of his valedictory trip to the Alps, Ruskin turned to acknowledge a profound and deeply personal debt to an area much closer to home:

> to the living reader, I have this to say very earnestly, that the whole glory and blessing of these sacred coasts depended on the rise and fall of their eternal sea, over sands gilded with its withdrawing glow, from the measureless distances of the west, on the ocean horizon, or veiled in silvery mists, or shadowed with fast-flying storm, of which nevertheless every cloud was pure, and the winter snows blanched in the starlight. For myself, the impressions of the Solway sands are a part of the greatest teaching that ever I received during the joy of youth.[1]

These are the words of an old man, addressing his readers as if from another age. Their commanding seriousness halts the flow of memories to reveal a great truth, apparently withheld until now. And, when the revelation comes, it is startling enough. Why would a man whose life's work was so indebted to his Continental travels turn at last to this relatively unknown estuary on the north-west coast of Britain? In earlier chapters of *Praeterita*, Ruskin had already announced that the three 'tutresses' of all he knew were Rouen, Geneva, and Pisa, his 'two bournes of Earth', Venice and Chamounix.[2] None of these were very close to the Solway in either location or character. In his later retrospections, however, which oscillated between past and present, global and individual, sacred

[1] John Ruskin, *Praeterita*, in E. T. Cook and A. Wedderburn (eds), *The Library Edition of the Works of John Ruskin*, 39 vols (London: Allen, 1903–12), xxxv. 549.

[2] Ibid., 156, 296. In the *Library Edition* of *Praeterita*, Venice and Chamounix are 'homes', but Ruskin had originally written 'bournes', as adopted by O'Gorman in his recent edition (Oxford: Oxford University Press, 2012), 188.

and secular, Ruskin identified the seashores of Southern Scotland and Cumbria as a spiritual home. The wider significance of this border region had been made plain a few paragraphs before:

> it seemed to me that this space of low mountain ground, with the eternal sublimity of its rocky seashores, of its stormy seas and dangerous sands; its strange and mighty crags, Ailsa and the Bass, and its pathless moorlands, haunted by the driving cloud, had been of more import in the world's history than all the lovely countries of the South, except only Palestine.[3]

Although the idea of finding inspiration in the wild North was familiar from *The Nature of Gothic*—Ruskin's famous diatribe against the deadening mechanization of modern society—this later, unequivocal statement of the border region's international significance is of a different order. For the elderly Ruskin, it seems, the personal and local had become the public and universal: at the very end, the Alps were bowing before the Solway Firth.

What was it about this area that mattered so much to him? Anyone visiting the Solway today is likely to be struck by the emptiness of the great stretch of water and sand, the sparseness of the building along its shores. Unlike the Mersey, the Thames, the Liffey, or the Clyde, there is no great port for the world's tankers in which to disembark, nor even a terminal for ferries crossing the Irish Sea. Seaside towns, too, are thin on the ground, for the shores of the Solway attract gulls, geese, redshank, and oystercatchers more readily than families with buckets and spades. Reaching the sea often means taking the tiniest roads, before tramping through rough areas of coarse tufty grasses, mossed pools, and mudflats that sink down towards choppy water, whirling with treacherous currents. There are warning signs about quicksands and rapid tides, and everywhere the shimmering layers of sand, sea, and sky seem on the brink of dangerous transformation. But there are signs, too, of people whose ways of life have been oddly impervious to time and tide, whose cattle graze calmly on the bright sea-soaked patches of grass or whose haaf nets have been left stretching out to dry, ready for the next plunge into the waves of passing salmon. It is easy to understand why the elderly Ruskin, horrified by the 'Storm-cloud' belching from dirty, industrial cities to darken his age, should have found solace here.[4]

And yet, the celebration of the Solway in *Praeterita* suggests more than refreshing breezes or pastoral retreat. The area, in Ruskin's eyes, was

[3] Ibid., 545.

[4] Ruskin, 'The Storm-Cloud of the Nineteenth Century', two lectures delivered in February 1884, *Works of Ruskin*, xxxiv.

second only to the Holy Land in its importance to 'the world's history'. Such a singular response to the Solway sands invites investigation of the place itself and its cultural legacies. This chapter, accordingly, explores not only Ruskin's puzzlingly powerful response to the region, but also whether such a personal account can be representative of more general truths. An individual writer may offer special insight into a particular place, but fuller understanding of its cultural significance often depends on multiple responses and contrasting points of view. But perhaps these can be inferred from a single impression, especially if it is informed by those of earlier residents and visitors to the same shores. A single text may sometimes be seen as a small square through which layers of earlier experience can be slowly exposed, or, to use a less archaeological metaphor, as a patch of calm water, beautiful in itself but also offering a space through which to dive and see what lies beneath. In the case of Ruskin's vivid paragraph, we might wonder what is hiding in those fast-flying shadows. Interpretation of coastal works involves knowledge of both the spatial and temporal dimensions of the place being represented and so what meets the eye may well be a rather misleading aspect of what is below the surface. In coastal areas, especially, unexpected things wash up and wash away.

Understanding the Solway and its depiction in literature demands awareness not only of an unusually fluid physical terrain, but also of a history as shifting as the sands. For centuries, what now seems to be peaceful, empty coastland was a crucial strategic stronghold, so fiercely contested by successive forces that it has been described as 'the most militarised stretch of country in the Islands'.[5] The Romans built a huge fortress at Bowness-on-Solway, at the end of Hadrian's Wall, to consolidate their position and defy incursions from the tribes of Brigantes in the North and those to the West in Ireland. In the ninth century, the Danes arrived and in their wholesale attack on Carlisle killed all the inhabitants and razed all the buildings to the ground. The next millennium saw the region being seized and lost by Scottish and English kings, their castles built, ruined, and rebuilt. In 1307, Edward I breathed his last at Burgh-by-Sands, leaving orders for his bones to be boiled and carried North on all future campaigns against the Scots. The early death of James V was thought to have been brought on by grief over the disastrous defeat of his army at the Battle of Solway Moss in 1542. Even after the border between England and Scotland was finally settled, the Solway continued to form a key

[5] David Brett, *A Book Around the Irish Sea: History Without Nations* (Dublin: Wordwell, 2009), 76; see also Philip Nixon and Hugh Dias, *Exploring Solway History* (Derby: Breedon, 2007) and Gordon Irving, *The Solway Smugglers* (Dumfries: Robert Dinwiddie and Co., 1971).

battleground for opposing armies in the Civil War, the wars of Montrose, and the Jacobite Risings. At the same time, the Isle of Man's independent policies on customs and excise meant that the Solway coast was also a major route for smugglers secretly carrying brandy and tobacco into Britain. The border region was famous, too, for ancient bloody feuds between local families, and even after these had largely receded into folk memory, it remained a destination for young, star-crossed lovers from the south because of the difference in Scottish Law governing parental consent to marriage. Such a history of conflict, open and clandestine, left permanent traces on the Solway shores, whatever Ruskin's natural panorama might initially suggest.

With such a shifting history, anyone might be forgiven for seeking out the fixed and the permanent—the features that seem to predate human accounts and, transcending time, offer a promise of the future. William Wordsworth, for example, perplexed by his own cultural moment 'of dereliction and dismay', still found hope by dwelling on the Cumbrian mountains and lakes as 'enduring things'.[6] There is nothing quite as solid about the Solway sands, however, and though enduring in some senses, the seashore is constantly changing. Coastal boundaries are especially fluid—where does Scotland stop or England begin, and where do their waters become Irish? The sea is promiscuous, and whatever human ingenuity might do with maps and charts, it never keeps to its own, allotted space. The borders of the Irish Sea ripple with estuaries: the Severn, the Liffey, the Mersey, or the Dee, but none is as uncertain as the Solway Firth. Its very name is mysterious, deriving either from the Old Scandinavian *súl* or pillar, or *súla*, which meant solan goose. 'Way' appears to be from the Old Norse *vath*, or Old English *waeth*, which survives in the Cumbrian dialect word, 'wath', and refers to the places where the great estuary can be forded at low tide. Whether the Solway was named after migrating birds or ancient marker stones (the 'pillar' was probably the Lochmaben Stone), it has always been associated with dangerous, opportunistic crossings.

The word 'firth', derived from the Old Norse, *fjord* (still widely familiar from the Norwegian coastline), is also oddly ambiguous, defined in the *Oxford English Dictionary (OED)* as 'an arm of the sea; an estuary of a river'. To the invading Vikings, of course, the Solway Firth was an arm of the sea—through which to extend their power inland. From Scotland or England, however, the Solway Firth was just as much the destination of local rivers, a great estuary where the mouths of the Nith, the Kirtle, the

[6] William Wordsworth, *The Prelude*, II, 457, I, 436, in *William Wordsworth: Twenty-First Century Authors*, ed. Stephen Gill (Oxford: Oxford University Press, 2010).

Sark, the Esk, the Eden, and the Wampool all flowed out into the sea. In coastal regions such as this, even great physical features appear quite differently when viewed from different perspectives. Even 'estuary' has two distinct meanings. The first is 'a tidal opening, an inlet or creek through which the tide enters; an arm of the sea indenting the land', and the second, 'the tidal mouth of a great river'. These definitions are oddly anthropomorphic. An 'arm of the sea', though deriving from its obvious human sense, is, according to the dictionary, 'in ancient use and quite transferred'. So the sea has had 'arms' for a very long time. Such definitions of natural phenomena are relics, perhaps, of older ways of perceiving the world, rare legacies of what William Blake called the 'enlarged and numerous senses of the ancients' who 'animated all sensible objects with Gods or Goddesses'.[7] Blake was familiar with the old literary convention of personifying and even deifying natural phenomena, but it is surprising to see the ancient anthropomorphic impulse still at work in the *OED*. (The noun, 'bosom', for example, in one of its definitions (n2), can be 'applied to the surface of the sea, lake river or ground'; but in another meaning (4c) it is 'a concave bend in the coastline, or the part of the sea embraced by it'. This is remarkably figurative as definitions go.) Something about the earth and sea must nourish and preserve the imaginative impulse, even in the face of the most rigorous scholarly objectivity. Though the term 'estuary' comes from the Latin, *aestuarium*, meaning 'heat, boiling, bubbling', it still reflects the older tendency in its two definitions: an estuary is both a mouth and an arm—a site of incongruous encounters and unsettling transformations.

The essential uncertainty of a great estuary, which is at once an end and a beginning, emerges powerfully in an early Irish poem describing the 'cry' of the magnificent river Garbh as it meets the Atlantic swell. The anthropomorphic impulse is only too obvious in the great 'wrestle' of the flood tide and the cold ebb, 'the mighty river torrent of the great Garbh and the seawater thrusting it back'.[8] The speaker, Sweeney, responds to the estuary as a place of disputed power, where uncontrollable forces clash, while at the same time delighting in the natural 'music' of the river, the sea, the sighing wind, the groaning ice, and the melodious current. The river's voice becomes most insistent as it meets the sea, either disappearing or being thrust back towards the land, as the tide swells and overwhelms

[7] William Blake, *The Marriage of Heaven and Hell* (Oxford: Oxford University Press, 1985).

[8] 'Suibhne praises the Garbh', in Kenneth Hurlstone Jackson (ed.), *A Celtic Miscellany*, rev. edn (Harmondsworth: Penguin, 1971), 74. Garbh means 'rough water' and the poem is probably set in the Waterford estuary.

the current. It was perhaps the ancient, elemental sounds of the Solway Firth that Ruskin was still trying to catch before the threatening clouds of his own age extinguished them forever.

Ruskin's declaration of his attachment to the Solway Firth, which conjures up an expanse of coast suffused with shifting light, suggests a stronger sense of the visual than aural, however. In the few lines quoted at the beginning of this chapter, he recreates an almost celestial vista, 'gilded', 'pure', 'silvery', and radiant with 'glory'. The revelation nevertheless seems to defy definition, with its 'measureless' distances, misty veils, shadowy storms, and 'withdrawing glow': everything shines momentarily before slipping away. If the sense of 'fast-flying' visions suggests a vein of melancholy, the unmistakable wonder of this restless coastline prompts a more powerful surge of thanksgiving nevertheless. Physical phenomena become the language through which to suggest visitings of divinity as well as reflecting the human mind's heaven-sent capacity to receive and preserve. Ruskin's writing rises to the challenge of the landscape, meeting it with impressionistic sentences that transform ordinary nouns and adjectives into signs of something extraordinary. The relationship between different details resists precise visualization, but taken altogether, the cumulative effect is dazzling.

There is nothing peaceful in Ruskin's description of the fast-flying storm or the rise and fall of the eternal sea. It is a kind of word-painting, akin to the art of Joseph Mallord William Turner, whose work he had championed and whose spirit lingers in these last, glimmering recollections. Ruskin had been studying natural phenomena and describing skies for many years, keeping notebooks to record what he saw. This deeply personal response to a carefully observed landscape, however, is also conditioned by those who had known it long before. For Ruskin, the borders were inseparable from the art he most admired and his own memories of the glimmering Solway estuary were magnified by Turner's evocative landscapes. In *Praeterita*, first-hand physical descriptions of the Solway flow almost imperceptibly into recollections of Turner:

> the five *Liber Studiorum* subjects—'Solway Moss', 'Peat Bog, Scotland', 'The Falls of Clyde', 'Ben Arthur', and 'Dunblane Abbey' remain more complete expressions of his intellect, and more noble monuments of his art, than all his mightiest after work, until the days of sunset in the west came for *it* also.[9]

Ruskin's image of the sands was gilded with the sea's withdrawing glow and with Turner's sunsets, admired since youth, but now inseparable from

[9] *Praeterita*, 549. For Ruskin's earlier trip to Scotland to see 'favourite sites of Turner', see the Preface to *Modern Painters V, Works of Ruskin*, vii. 3.

'glimmered bright upon the wet surface of the sands', could still be felt in Ruskin's prose, written in response to the same stretch of coast.

Scott's novel appealed strongly to Ruskin's highly visual imagination, but *Redgauntlet* also demonstrated the importance of sound. In his exploration of the region, Scott seemed to have captured something of the ancient elemental forces that now seemed in danger of disappearing. Only a few years before, Ruskin had praised Scott and Wordsworth for painting the people of the Borders 'with absolute fidelity' and in so doing, representing the 'body and soul of England before her days of mechanical decrepitude and commercial dishonour'.[12] In *Praeterita*, Ruskin's great tribute to the Solway arises when he is recalling an attempt to identify the location of Wandering Willie's tale. Scott's memorable character appears early in *Redgauntlet* and though not apparently central to the narrative, the enigmatic presence of the travelling fiddler haunts the entire book, filling it with snatches of intermittent music. He is the figure who most captivates Ruskin, with his unique understanding of the area. Wandering Willie, whose name derives from traditional Scottish song, is blind, but so receptive to local sounds that he perceives far more than the young protagonist of the novel, Darsie Latimer. Scott offers a very clear contrast between the travellers, in terms of age, class, and personality, but it is the difference in their perceptual capacities that is most important and which seems to have resonated with Ruskin.

When the two characters first meet, Darsie, the young Englishman, has been walking near Dumfries:

> The air I breathed felt purer and more bracing. The clouds, riding high upon a summer breeze, drove, in gay succession, over my head, now obscuring the sun, now letting his rays stream in transient flashes upon various parts of the landscape, and especially upon the broad mirror of the distant Frith of Solway.[13]

Darsie is invigorated by the sea air and the dazzling effects of sunlight flashing on the sea. Willie, in contrast, is introduced through the sound of singing and fiddle music. When Darsie asks whether he is 'of this country', Willie's reply is prompt:

> '*This* country! .... I am of every country in broad Scotland, and a wee bit of England to boot. But yet I am, in some sense, of this country, for I was born within hearing of the roar of the Solway.'[14]

[12] Ruskin, 'The Extension of Railways in the Lake District: A Protest', *Works of Ruskin*, xxxiv. 137–43, 141.

[13] Ibid., 78. Darsie uses the Scots form 'Frith', rather than Firth, reflecting his upbringing.

[14] Ibid., 80.

Where Darsie has been viewing the Solway like a picturesque traveller, keeping the Firth at a pleasing distance and making it a 'broad mirror' to reflect his own preconceived ideas, Willie, the blind wanderer and Borderer, characterizes his native coastland by its *roar*. At this stage, Darsie does not quite understand what he hears, any more than he grasps the meaning of Willie's tale about his grandfather's journey to Hell, in which even the dread border between life and death can be crossed and recrossed. It is not long before the resounding truth of Willie's words comes home, however, as the 'roar' of the Solway threatens to drown any words from Darsie Latimer.

Much of the action of *Redgauntlet* takes place around the Solway, but the most dramatic moment occurs *in* the Firth itself, when Darsie is forcibly taken at night from a fishing hut on the Scottish coast. He is injured, bound, and helpless, lying in a cart in the darkness and only able to guess where he might be. Gradually, the slow movement of the cart, 'sinking' and 'sticking', makes him realize he is in 'the formidable estuary which divides the two kingdoms', mired in the mudflats, surrounded by quicksands. This is a place of meeting and division—where rivers meet the sea, where earth meets firth, where Scotland meets England, north meets south—and where the estuary divides all. In the darkness, Darsie's normally sharp sight becomes redundant, and as the surrounding sounds are accentuated, he hears first the sudden, alarmed dispersal of his mysterious captors, and then the terrifying approach of the tide:

> There lay my native land—my own England—the land where I was born, and to which my wishes, since my earliest age, had turned with all the prejudice of national feeling—there it lay, within a furlong of the place where I was; yet was that furlong, which an infant would have raced over in a minute, a barrier effectual to divide me for ever from England and from life. I soon not only heard the roar of this dreadful torrent, but saw, by the fitful moonlight, the foamy crests of the devouring waves, as they advanced with the speed and fury of a pack of hungry wolves.[15]

There is nothing reassuring about the sound of the Solway. The ancient impulse to animate the physical phenomena seems as natural as the fear inspired by the sound of the approaching tide. This is an image of terrifying inundation, as the waves are transformed into a wolf pack, roaring hungrily. The vivid focus on the hapless figure, whose struggle for personal identity against overwhelming external forces drives the entire narrative, enables Scott to convey the formidable power of the estuary, where at one

[15] Ibid., 159.

Figure 3.2. 'Solway Viaduct at Bowness-on-Solway' (1914). Courtesy of Tullie House Museum and Art Gallery Carlisle.

feels like his hero Turner, lashed to the mast, experiencing the sea-storm for the sake of his art. But Ruskin is at sea in the modern city, amid the 'industrial Armada' where there is no distinction between sea and air, where the writhing cloudscape collapses into 'terraces and sinks and troughs'. As he struggles against the overpowering environment, Ruskin is surrounded by fragments of his earlier writings, including a line about an angel painted by a medieval Irish artist, who 'put red dots into the palm of each hand, and rounded the eyes in perfect circles, and I regret to say, left the mouth out altogether, with perfect satisfaction to himself'.[26] It is not surprising that Carson should have been struck by this passage, with its heavy humour at the expense of the Irish character, and in his poem, Ruskin is haunted by 'that blank mouth'. At first, his reluctance to see the mouth open seems to express fear of what an Irish mouth might say, whether in response to his ill-judged lecture, or more pressing ills. On the other hand, absence may be safer, because another poem in *Belfast Confetti*,

[26] The quotation in Carson's poem is from a lecture Ruskin delivered in Dublin on 'The Mystery of Life and Its Arts', which explored the decay of national arts in Ireland after an early flowering; see *Sesame and Lilies*, in *Works of Ruskin*, xviii. 173.

entitled 'The Mouth', demonstrates the terrible consequences of voicing certain opinions or letting certain things be known—of being 'a mouth'. But if the blank mouth is 'closed against the smog and murk of Belfast', Ruskin's prayer may relate instead to the dark, polluting, urban cloud of his day and his own desire to shut it out.

The river that gives Belfast its name could hardly be less like the shimmering Solway Firth celebrated by Ruskin, Turner, and Scott. In *Belfast Confetti*, Carson observes that the 'river, the stream, the sewer trickles from a black mouth and disappears down a black hole'.[27] Since *Béal* 'means a mouth, or the mouth of a river', the passage connects Belfast with both 'The Mouth' and the 'blank mouth' threatening 'John Ruskin in Belfast', reinforcing its darker possibilities. Carson goes on to puzzle over the place name 'Fast' or 'Farset' (*fearsad*), and whether 'Belfast' means simply 'the town at the mouth of the river', or as a nineteenth-century Irish language specialist suggests, it is bewilderingly multifaceted: 'a shaft; a spindle; the ulna of the arm; a club; the spindle of an axle; a bar or bank of sand at low water; a deep narrow channel on a strand at low tide, a pit or pool of water; a verse, a poem'.[28] Etymologies are problematic in a city where Irish, English, Ulster Scots, and Scots Gaelic mix uneasily, but somewhere within the fluid ironies of the place name is that old anthropomorphic impulse, now twisted and blackened in this modern urban space. Carson, alert to the shifting currents of language, seizes on the etymologies to 'let Belfast be the *mouth of the poem*', before concluding that the 'river Farset, the hidden stream, is all of these things'—an axis, a maze of channels, which remembers 'spindles, arms, the songs of mill-girls' but, at the same time, 'remembers nothing'. Perhaps the early Irish painter knew more than Ruskin suspected and omitted the angel's mouth because it was unpaintable, defying any single perspective or straightforward representation? Carson's collection is filled with references to the shifting nature of the modern city and the difficulty of finding ways in which to express it. In the prose piece, 'Revised Version', he recognizes that 'everything is contingent and provisional', that old maps reveal the ghosts of streets that have vanished as if they never existed. Lost buildings live on in old photographs and engravings, a precarious existence dependent on the flimsiest paper and blurred printing. This is, of course, true of any city, with the centuries' layers of buildings and streets laid out and lost again, but in modern Belfast the desirability of remembering or forgetting was especially unclear. In the knitted, knotted streets of the 1980s, where the river ran along the axis of the Falls Road and Shankhill,

[27] Carson, *Belfast Confetti*, 47. [28] Ibid., 48.

disappearing into the dams and sluices, before being lost in its final culvert, it was not easy to hear a single clear voice or to interpret what the mouth might say.

Ruskin's answer to the troubling 'blank mouth', as ventriloquized by Carson, was to adopt it, quite unexpectedly: 'Let that missing mouth be mine', he says,

> as one evening in Siena,
> I walked the hills above, where fireflies moved like finely broken starlight
> Through the purple leaves, rising, falling, as the cobalt clouds—white-edged, mountainous—
> Surged into thunderous night; and fireflies gusted everywhere, mixed with the lightning,
> Till I thought I'd open up my mouth and swallow them, as I might gulp the milky way.[29]

Suddenly free of what had seemed an all-engulfing storm cloud, Ruskin is drinking in the visionary moment in Siena—or the Solway. For this is the closing image of *Praeterita*, where all words cease. Ruskin's response to Belfast, as intuited by Ciaran Carson, was to make the mouth not an organ for speech, but a means for drinking in eternal truths and suckling on natural beauty. Instead of uttering a cry, the river mouth might, after all, draw life from the rise and fall of the eternal sea.

If Carson was taking Ruskin to task for his sympathetic failures in Ireland and the modern industrial city, then, his poem also demonstrates a deep, intuitive understanding of the visionary moment in *Praeterita*. As Carson's Ruskin gazes 'into its opalescent mirror' of Turner's 'The Dawn of Christianity', the image seems poised between hope and despair, as faith in the eternal delivery is set against the massacre of infants. The meaning of the image, in which the Nile and the sky flow into each other, depends largely on the perspective of the viewer. Ruskin may have been out of place in Belfast in the 1980s, but his capacity to open at last, in spite of the surrounding gloom, to stories from the dawn of time, to the sounds of hope and flashes of transcendent light, is caught as surely in Carson's poem as all the fragments of unwanted lectures or doom-laden prophecies. 'John Ruskin in Belfast' is part of a collection in which 'the contingent and provisional' threaten to obliterate, but in the end create more enduring meanings. Belfast, viewed through two centuries of maps and plans, seems every bit as elusive as the Solway Firth, and though its modern incarnation could hardly be more different from the empty coastline on the far side of the sea, its history of building and rebuilding offers new light on Ruskin's

[29] Ibid., 98.

impressions of the sands. As Carson uncovers successive plans for streets and squares, parks and canals, he recognizes that building projects are also visions, and that maps are mirrors for engineers. One man's storm cloud may be another's Eden.

In *Praeterita*, Ruskin blamed that other great prose writer and Solway native, Thomas Carlyle, for listening too much to the pressures of the present. But his own refusal to represent all that he saw on the Dumfries coast in the 1880s laid Ruskin himself open to charges of selective hearing. His tribute to the Solway is deeply idiosyncratic and can hardly be taken as representative of anything other than Ruskin late in life. And yet, the passage still leads in many directions, to other pens and places, to things half-buried in the elusive sands. Absences are often more resonant than the things most evident. Since one of Ruskin's last published pieces was a somewhat hyperbolic letter to *The Times* about the evils of railway building, it is unsurprising that he should have refused the viaduct entry into his celebration of the Solway Firth. For Ruskin, railways were 'the loathsomest form of devilry now extant, animated and deliberate earthquakes, destructive of all wise social habit or possible natural beauty, carriages of damned souls on the ridges of their own graves'.[30] As such, the Solway viaduct would have seemed rather out of place in his late prose hymn to the border coastline, though it may well have inspired the thoughts of Jeremiah. For those who designed and built the railway across the Firth, however, it was just as visionary as the flashes that lightened Ruskin's dark horizon.

In the Solway, Ruskin heard the eternal roar, and though it was probably magnified by the railway viaduct, he chose not to make that explicit in his autobiography. Time has shown that Ruskin's prophetic tone was not entirely misplaced, for now the viaduct has gone again—it was dismantled in 1934 and the area has since become a nature reserve. In the tiny village of Bowness, there are buildings raised with the stones of Hadrian's Wall and houses constructed for the railways—strange, anomalous survivals from eras that have vanished almost as if they never were. 'Station House' is as much a remnant of a lost age as the Victorian buildings of Belfast, and all around the coastline are traces of earlier, half-forgotten lives and other people's visions. Ruskin's omission of contemporary details was not necessarily a refusal to acknowledge what was really there, but may reflect the sudden clarity of old age, when the present became only a small detail in a much larger picture. Even the gloomy portrayal in 'The Storm-Cloud' of 'harmony now broken' and

[30] Ruskin, *Works of Ruskin*, xxxiv. 603–4.

darkness gaining inexorably on the day still concluded by affirming man's capacity 'to live in Hope' and 'in Reverence of something to be worshipped...and cherished for ever'. At the end of his life, Ruskin had learned to seek hope not from the solid forms of mountains, but from the shifting Solway sand-scape, where sudden light could still break through and he could just catch the roar of the eternal voice. His own glimpse of redemption was empowered nevertheless by the very different visions of his contemporaries, which met across an estuary broad enough to mirror and escape them all.

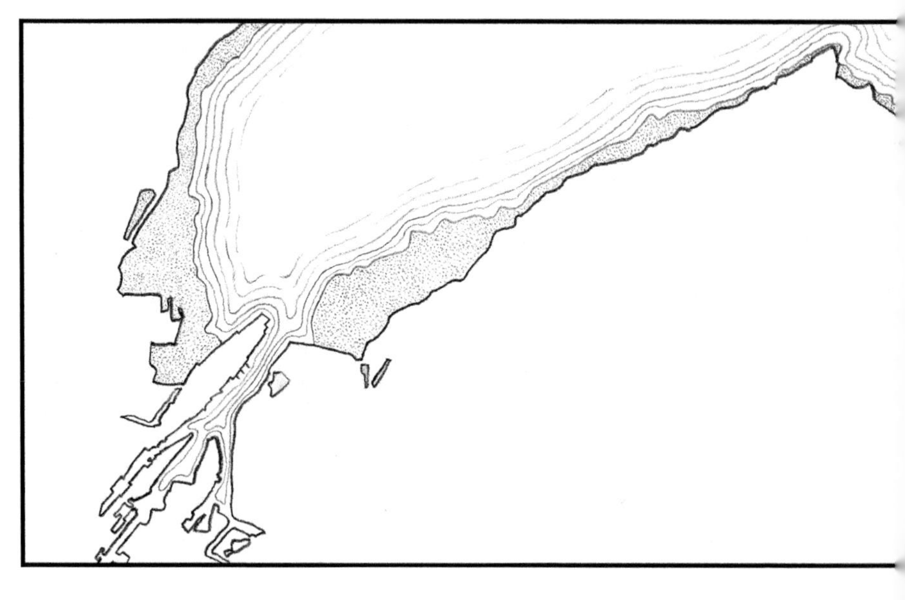

4

Ireland, Literature, and the Coastal Imaginary

Nicholas Allen

The idea of the coast as a significant and definable cultural space has been remarkably understudied in literary criticism as it relates to Ireland. The dynamics of Irish nationalism have marginalized liminal forms of historical affiliation, a tendency that has tended to obscure those geographical zones that sit in the middle distance between land and sea. There is surprisingly little discussion in the critical literature of Ireland's place as an island whose imaginative connections are with the water that surrounds it, rather than with the landmasses about it.[1] There is a significant tradition of island literature in the corpus, but what criticism there is on this subject concentrates on the connections between sovereign territories, with less thought given to the water ways between.

This is curious, not least because water keeps finding its way into Irish literature. There are serial examples of the sea as a medium for invasion and exchange back to earliest times, and in the nineteenth and twentieth centuries the symbolism of water rose in the cultural register as new trends of global migration applied themselves to the island's population. In the nineteenth century, the catastrophe of the famine was backdrop to the many political and cultural movements that shaped Irish society from 1850 to 1922, and it could be argued that campaigns as diverse as Home Rule, the Literary Revival, and the War of Independence all had

[1] Thirty years ago, John de Courcy Ireland lamented that 'maritime history has been a subject rather neglected in most countries, and in this country positively ignored' (*Ireland and the Irish in Maritime History* (Glendale Press: Dun Laoghaire, 1986), xi). This situation is not now so extreme, in part because of the influence of emerging historical forms, from the Atlantic to the postcolonial, that by necessity focus on transnational contexts for their operation. This territory is cultural background to John Brannigan's excellent *Archipelagic Modernism: Literature in the Irish and British Isles, 1890–1970* (Edinburgh: Edinburgh University Press, 2015). See also Michael McCaughan and John Appleby (eds), *The Irish Sea: Aspects of Maritime History* (Belfast: Institute of Irish Studies, 1989).

significant transoceanic contexts. The British colonial system ensured constant contact with ideas and opportunities in other continents, and many prominent nationalists, both constitutional and militant, had experience of living abroad. Certainly all of them were well read in the political literature of other nations, British dominated or not.[2]

The British Empire against which all these agitations were directed was a global dominion of ports and sea trade that facilitated wide circulation of capital goods, information, and people.[3] In Ireland, the port of Dublin was subject to extensive renovation and development from the mid to late nineteenth century.[4] Northerly, Belfast became a world centre of industry, primarily in shipbuilding, but also in the manufacture of rope and linen.[5] Belfast was a late historical arrival to sea trade when compared to Dublin, Cork, Limerick, or Galway, and its rapid growth over the late nineteenth century created an urban culture that was imprinted deeply by its transformation from provincial outpost to a world city, a transformation that still speaks to the city's particular history. If coastal ports were the obvious centres of the imperial maritime economy, other communities felt the effect of British power at sea in more subtle ways, through seasonal migration, service in the Royal and Merchant Navies, and access to the material culture of other places.[6]

[2] The seven signatories to the Proclamation of the Irish Republic in April 1916 were a group of well-educated and well-travelled radicals, many of them educationalists and propagandists. As the proclamation suggests, they were well aware of the multiple political traditions they appealed to in their call for Irish independence. For more, see Liam de Paor, *On the Easter Proclamation and other Declarations* (Dublin: Four Courts, 1997).

[3] For a comparative survey of maritime history, see David Cannadine (ed.), *Empire, the Sea and Global History* (London: Palgrave, 2007). For more on Britain's maritime empire, see John Darwin, *The Empire Project: The Rise and Fall of the British World-System (1830–1970)* (rev. edn, Cambridge: Cambridge University Press, 2011).

[4] 'The port of Dublin, particularly after passage of the Dublin Port and Docks Act at Westminster in 1869, developed into one of the best-run harbours in Europe. Between 1860 and 1914 tens of millions of tonnes of debris were dredged out of the Liffey, new berths, docks and a whole new basin, the Alexandra Basin, were added to the port amenities' (de Courcy Ireland, *Ireland and the Irish*, 245). The impact of Dublin's neglect of infrastructure on its maritime trade registers in Mary Daly, *Dublin, The Deposed Capital: A Social and Economic History (1860–1914)* (Cork: Cork University Press, 1985).

[5] By the First World War, this last industry was so important that after it Lord French said the 'war in the air was won on Belfast wings' (quoted in Alfred Stewart Moore, *Linen* (New York: Macmillan, 1922), 162).

[6] This was a product in part of two conditions. First, it was the merchant marine, and not the Royal Navy, that travelled most regularly in non-European waters for the purpose of trade. Second, 'the British maritime world was always much bigger than the British seaborne empire itself ever was' (Cannadine, 'Introduction', *Empire, the Sea and Global History*, 4). With regard to Ireland, this suggests that ideas of insularity, self-reliance, and the peripheral might be reconsidered in terms of island history.

In short, Ireland was an island shaped by the sea, and its coast is still the permeable barrier through which a series of cultural exchanges, literary, historical, political, and environmental, take place. These exchanges were intense in Ireland in relation to Britain's rise and fall as a maritime empire, and a provocative way to think of this is to consider the backgrounds and interests of the revolutionary generation that entered the public mind with the Easter Rising in 1916. As the main force of insurgents dug into the General Post Office, the rebels' aims were codified in a republican proclamation that was posted on the walls of Dublin city, the ideas for which owed much to the political traditions of France and to the United States of America. Patrick Pearse, Thomas Clarke, and James Connolly were actors in a bipolar British world that was part-formed of intense local attachment and transnational migration. Of these, Patrick Pearse was the figurehead of the rising, a poet, educationalist, and militant whose English father had come to Ireland to build a business in religious statuary. Before the war, Pearse travelled Europe and visited America to fundraise for the Irish republican movement. This migrant perspective informs one of his finer poems, 'On the Strand at Howth', which is a translation from the Irish and set between Dublin and Paris, 'boat and ship / With sails set / Ploughing the waves'.[7] Paris was the haunt of revival writers like George Moore and John Millington Synge, who discovered the modern movements in art and learning from impressionists and anthropologists that revolutionized their representations of Irish life.[8] If separatism is the exclusion of outside influences from an indigenous culture, such exclusion was impossible in Ireland, as the presence of the sea and waves in Pearse's strand poem suggests.

This border between land and water is mutable and evocative, a geography that provokes the senses to hold more than one place in mind, a tradition that holds from Matthew Arnold's 'Dover Beach' to Seamus Heaney's 'North'. From the coastal perspective, the security of land peters out from the shore with a kind of diminishing sovereignty, its last grasp the forelands and islands that splinter into the sea. Patrick Kavanagh drew on this idea when he compared his land-bound life as a farmer to being cast adrift in the far ocean:

[7] Patrick Pearse, 'On the Strand of Howth', *Plays, Stories, Poems* (Dublin: Talbot Press, 1966), 329.

[8] For more on the influence of continental scientific thinking on Synge and company, see Sinead Garrigan-Mattar, *Science, Primitivism, and the Irish Revival* (Oxford: Oxford University Press, 2004).

Oh, Alexander Selkirk knew the plight
Of being king and government and nation.
A road, a mile of kingdom. I am king
Of banks and stones and every blooming thing.[9]

There is intimacy between the literary idea of the island and of self-governance, which takes particular charge in a culture that, like Ireland, has experienced the long receding wave of empire as violence, partition, and persisting disputes over identity. This is the setting for Ciaran Carson's *The Star Factory*, a prose labyrinth of memory and imagination whose foundations are the historic conditions of the city of Belfast. These foundations are stilts set in a muddy estuary that made the early borders of the city uncertain, and this meander of water through the urban space has had a series of sensory effects in literature about Belfast since. One is a fascination with water as a metaphor of expanding distance, which makes the coast, as Tim Robinson has described it in Connemara, a long line of variable associations whose beginning and end are impossible to find.[10] Carson, like Robinson, creates an imaginative geometry in response, a mathematics of memory that has aesthetic consequences for the composition of *The Star Factory*. Another is an uncertainty of place that predates Belfast's troubled late twentieth-century history, even if that history intensifies this condition. Another again is a fascination with misplaced things and orphan objects, which are relics of Belfast's history as a maritime city through which the odds and ends of the imperial world passed, and sometimes stayed.

Carson is an ideal witness to all this as a writer who bridged the destructive period between late empire and its undoing. Aside from his poetry, Carson's prose can be read with W. G. Sebald as an anatomy of the twentieth century's sufferings, and like Sebald, he has an interest in the architecture of space, that frozen poetry of motion in which the human environment is configured as a register, and sometimes a restriction, of desire.[11] *The Star Factory* is built on Carson's memories of childhood and

[9] Patrick Kavanagh, 'Inniskeen Road: July Evening', in David Pierce (ed.), *Irish Writing in the Twentieth Century: A Reader* (Cork: Cork University Press, 2000), 456.

[10] Tim Robinson's two-volume *Stones of Aran: Pilgrimage* (Dublin: Lilliput, 1986) and *Labyrinth* (Dublin: Lilliput, 1995) created a new genre of land and seascape writing that reshaped the literary imagination of the west of Ireland. His style and insights have application to many following forms, most notably Robert Macfarlane's journey through the English countryside, *The Old Ways: A Journey on Foot* (London: Penguin, 2013). Carson and Robinson were correspondents during the 1990s, a connection I hope to develop in a later essay.

[11] Carson refers to Sebald's writing in a letter to his then editor Neil Belton of June 1998. Thinking of a book to follow *The Star Factory*, he 'noted W. G. Sebald's saying in an interview that the more he writes the less he knows how to do it, and that is very true. Every time is a first time' (Ciaran Carson papers, Manuscripts and Rare Book Collection, Emory University, box 3, file 18).

the stories of his father, its imaginative range the bog meadows at the edge of the city's housing, territory he wandered in on days off from school. There he travelled an internal sea with 'the dimensional configuration of the archipelago', Belfast a swamp of bayous and everglades, the curious hybrid of northern industry and southern lassitude a by-product of post-war imagination.[12] In this Belfast exotic, Carson found 'a secret place of mine, where I would sit alone for hours on a minor sand-bank'. Thinking perhaps of the thriller *Odd Man Out*, he imagines if he was ever on the run, 'an IRA man, say', he would become part of the area's 'teeming ecosystem', 'a detail of its verdurous glooms and winding mossy ways, whose divarications, and the routes and tributaries between them, were innumerable'.[13] Towering over all are 'lagooned archipelagos of moving cumulus and jigsaw-puzzle sky'.[14] This is life as a dream in which the child maps possible geographies on the limited space of his experience. It is a dream whose subconscious is the coastal history of the imperial port. This history is afloat in the detritus of British withdrawal from the island of Ireland and visible from Carson's water bank perspective. The key passage is his fantastical separation of the Shankill from the Falls as he untwines the sectarian arteries of the city. A space opens,

> from which emerge, like flotillas salvaged from the bottom of the North Atlantic, the regurgitated superstructures of defunct, Titanic industries: tilted, blackened spinning-mills; the loading-docks of great bakeries at dawn, illuminated by the smell of electricity and yeast; waterworks in convoluted ravines—dams, races, bridges, locks, conduits, sinks, culverts, sluices, ponds, and aqueducts; tentacles and cables of Leviathan, swarming to the surface from a buried ropewalk; catacomb-like brick-kilns.[15]

The industries of the coastal edge are the end points of a transoceanic infrastructure that Carson imagines to exist beneath the surface of sea and memory. This suggests the close connection between the idea of water and of childhood, and of the historical context for both in the maritime city of Belfast. It is a critical given that any reading of Carson's work must proceed from its representation of the Troubles, but *The Star Factory* suggests a different genesis for comprehension, which is the idea of Belfast as a city at sea. There are serial examples of this in the book, one of which is the narrator's construction of an underwater grotto beneath his bedclothes, one the turning of a public toilet into a submarine. In the first,

[12] Ciaran Carson, *The Star Factory* (London: Granta, 1997), 89.
[13] Ibid., 99. [14] Ibid., 101. [15] Ibid., 134.

> Every night, on retiring, I would tent my bedclothes over my head to make an underwater grotto, whose interior of furls and crumples was thrown into chiaroscuro by the beam of the annual torch I got in my Christmas stocking. I was practically unaware of my body, since it formed part of the structure—supporting columns of the knees, flying buttresses of elbows—and my breathing was a rhythm of the coral tide.[16]

In the second,

> cramped in a dank stall, one could think oneself to be in the bowels of a U-boat; the plumbing hissed and whispered as if under marine pressure, for a depth-charge had gone off nearby, an illusion perfectly maintained by the IRA bombing campaign of the 1970s (it is gratifying to note that the toilets' glass brick roof, or pavement, has survived unscathed).[17]

The connecting tissue of these passages is Carson's submerged aesthetic; as diver or submariner, the underwater secures a series of effects that are invisible from land. These pockets of alien space survive in a city that is itself only part of the material world. If Carson transforms Belfast into hybrid mutations of his own imagination, his imagination has its own genealogy, which is part-human, part-built, and wholly at home in this marooned city of the Atlantic edge. As a place, Ireland rarely figures in *The Star Factory*, even if the Irish language runs right through the book. Instead, Belfast is a coastal hub connected to other singular places that all share a past imperial connection, and the history of empire and its wars has its late form in Carson's attention to the technology of military surveillance. Thinking of bugs and wiretaps, Carson goes back again to childhood:

> At this point, the efficacy, or otherwise, of children's tin-can two-way radios occurs to me, their empty Ovaltine receivers connected by a cricket-pitch length of a postman's string. Although your correspondent was within normal earshot, you suspended this belief for the buzz of imaginary distance: your nearby accomplice would suddenly dwindle off into a little-known adjunct of the Empire—Sarawak, or Borneo, perhaps—and reproduce its sound-effects of squawking birds and monkeys whooping through the trees, as he dispatched an urgent order for machetes.[18]

The overlay of one place on another is a standard diagnosis of postcolonial dislocation, and the inability of the local place to assert itself as a coherent geography of social, political, and cultural associations can be read as the triumph of a metropolis over a periphery as the heart of empire pumps thin blood to its extremities. There are elements of this condition in Carson, but they do not dominate. Belfast is joined to Borneo by tenuous

[16] Ibid., 159. [17] Ibid., 239. [18] Ibid., 172–3.

lines of imperial association, which have their material reality in the infrastructure of Britain; Ovaltine and the postman's string are two mid-century objects that were connected intimately to the child's imagination of the sensory exotic.

The capacity to hold these disparate elements together is a product, again, of Belfast's coastal condition as a late imperial port, in decline by the time of *The Star Factory*, but marked all the same by its disparate global histories. At the time of Carson's writing, these histories had receded from public view, partly a consequence of Britain's own imperial dissolution, partly the decline of the late nineteenth- and early twentieth-century economy, and partly the emergence of new ways to understand the local place's relationship with the outside world. The revising genius of *The Star Factory* is to put these elements back together in new forms that incorporate contemporary innovations. This aesthetic alchemy happens in the dank mists of the coastal city as the fog drifts inland to cover Belfast's landmarks. Clarity is available only as a line of association, the connection between past and present a 'worm-hole of the riddled memory' whose dimensions are governed by a 'non-Euclidean geometry'.[19] The Black North of the shipyards and ropeworks has produced, in *The Star Factory*, an alternative literature in which modernity is represented as something more than the oppression of the senses in service of capital. Carson moves towards this wider recognition in the later stages of *The Star Factory* when he rehearses his imaginative practice in other contexts, as in a memory of his mother knitting cardigans that prompts him to think of Lord Cardigan and island life.

> For a moment I indulge a fantasy of the Shetlands (official name until 1974, Zetland), where Fair Isle is situated, as a Welsh-speaking archipelagic colony, and envisage the great Shetland-pony-wool-spinning, wind-powered factories, the extensive, unwalled orchards of windmills perched on the sides of mountains.[20]

The Celtic archipelago is a self-sustaining ecology of linguistic hybridity. Carson's northern gaze includes a wink towards earlier literary excursions into the unfamiliar, notably Auden and MacNeice's *Letters from Iceland.* In *The Star Factory*, he develops the genealogy of the coastal work to include the internal archipelagos of the river-born city, the ribs of which are its bridges. Belfast came into being as a ford, and the idea of crossing is central to many aspects of the modern place. The end of the Troubles invited a new phase of redevelopment with the construction of a new bridge across the Lagan to join the north and west side of the city with the east. The Lagan Bridge swoops over the river and opens up a new view of Belfast Lough. In reality, the motorway and the bridge compress the

[19] Ibid., 208. [20] Ibid., 229.

maritime history of the city beneath the concrete. Symbolically, they are an aerial artery that oxygenates Carson's aesthetic of the contemporary city. He writes:

> I have to admit I love this bridge: driving on its flyover, admiring the stylized white lines printed on the clean black tarmac, I feel I am taking off from an aircraft carrier—I think of HMS Formidable, for instance, launched by Harland and Wolff in 1939 from East Belfast, where I am coming from in 1996. I soar on a gradual aerial curve above the harbour and the docks, seeing them in a new, sunlit perspective, like Wordsworth on Westminster Bridge:
>
> *Earth has not anything to show more fair—*
> *Dull would he be of soul who could pass by*
> *A sight so touching in its majesty:*
> *This City now doth, like a garment, wear*
> *The beauty of the morning; silent, bare,*
> *Ships, towers, domes, theatres and temples lie*
> *Open unto the fields, and to the sky;*
> *All bright and glittering in the smokeless air.* [21]

The view from the bridge offers a perspective between land and sea that was traditionally observed by the poet from a beach or cliff. The citation of Wordsworth connects Belfast to London as cities made of water, the liquidity of global exchange finding material form in bridges, factories, and ships.[22] These arrangements inform an aesthetic that Carson finally brings to light near the end of a book whose general climate is fog and rain. The effect is to ask, after Wordsworth, what the morning promises, and this is the moment where *The Star Factory* reveals itself as a book in which the constraints of the Troubles begin to break. The obverse of this opening out is Carson's fascination with tight spaces throughout the book. His father begins the story by talking from the outside toilet, his lit cigarette dancing in the dark. Bedrooms, libraries, pubs, and cinemas all shape the internal architecture of the book. They are drawn in prose that represents Belfast as a city of miniature partitions, the assembly of which reaches its greater scale in the construction of the *Titanic*, a ship that sank because a section of its hull gave way to the sea. Carson represents this failure as a problem of space and time. Thinking of childhood, the narrator writes:

[21] Ibid., 237–8.

[22] Carson's interest in Wordsworth had been noticed elsewhere, as in John Goodby, 'Space, Narrative and Surveillance', in Elmer Kennedy-Andrews (ed.), *Ciaran Carson: Critical Essays* (Dublin: Four Courts, 2009), 66–85, in which the critic compares both poets' interest in walking as suggestive of their apprehension of the world.

> I remembered *A Night to Remember*, for example, long before I saw it, for my father had told its story, the sinking of the *Titanic*, many times, and the actual film, when I first saw it in the Broadway cinema in the fifties, only served to corroborate his descriptions of the implacable properties of icebergs and supposedly watertight bulkheads, and the temerity of building Babel boats. I felt the chill of his Atlantic language.[23]

The sinking of the Titanic represents for Carson the end of an aesthetic whose foundations were the separation of one form from another. The hard water of the iceberg breaches the titanic ship in an act of creative destruction in a disaster that is emblematic, and perhaps inevitable, because it confirms Belfast's symbolic reality as a coastal hybrid of land and water.

Another rendition of this cultural form is Glenn Patterson's *The Mill for Grinding Old People Young*, his sixth novel and a book, like *The City of Bohane* and *The Star Factory*, that creates narrative from the liquid perspective of the maritime place. *The Mill* is set in Belfast and tells the story of a young man, Gilbert Rice, and his infatuation with a Polish immigrant in the early nineteenth century, a passion that unsettles his mind so much as to lead to his planned, but unsuccessful, assassination of Lord Donegall. Belfast was Donegall's inheritance, and he controlled its political life, much to the aggravation of the merchants and engineers who wished to develop the port so that a town built on estuarial sludge could become a city anchored in heavy industry such as increased shipping could service. *The Mill* begins with Gilbert in old age, now a solid member of the city's upper class, but in youth an impetuous and intelligent clerk of the ballast board. This had the effect of educating him in the possibilities of Belfast's seaward expansion, and one of the early high points of the book is his sally by rowboat around the inner harbour with the visiting engineer, James Walker. The transformation of coastal space into a site for productive capital is the story of engineers, of charts and of exploration, the social effect of which is the backwash of Patterson's novel since Belfast's place in the Atlantic world is connected historically to its eighteenth-century political radicalism. Belfast was the city of Theobald Wolfe Tone and Henry Joy McCracken and offered for a brief time an opportunity for the reconciliation of Planter and Gael in a northern republic.[24]

That dream died in the rebellion of 1798, and Patterson uses the chart of Gilbert Rice's life to map its diminution. Evidently, this is where the novel shows its own debt to the present, with twenty-first-century Belfast

[23] Carson, *The Star Factory*, 238.

[24] For a view of this world, see Marianne Elliot, *Wolfe Tone: Prophet of Irish Independence* (London: Yale University Press, 1989).

a city of reconciliation once again.[25] Patterson extends the idea of solidarity beyond familiar Irish boundaries of religion and class by insisting on the particular aspect of Belfast's maritime location, with a view to testing the city's tolerance for outsiders. The nineteenth-century reality of industrialization in its global phase merged world commerce with local space, creating hybrid alliances and complex challenges for a culture defined by its coastal proximity to other port and river cities. For example, Rice's office contains a wall map of the world that is spiked with little flags, each of which represents an outbreak of cholera. The intention was to match these outbreaks with the quarantine of incoming ships whose point of origin matched the latest reports of infection:

> Forcade, the Superintendent of Quarantine . . . had circulated to all who worked in the Ballast Office a memorandum on an outbreak of cholera, which, it was feared, from its first stirrings in Bengal, was making its way inexorably across the continent of Europe . . . the cholera was in Sebastopol, St. Petersburg, Vienna, Prague; a ship from Cadiz bound for Liverpool had put in at San Sebastian with all on board dead or dying.[26]

As infection, cholera is the equivalent of those many unintended consequences global trade has for the coastal city. Another is the arrival of a Chinese trading ship with a multiracial complement, which poses the question as to what landing rights can be assigned such a motley crew. The answer is a temporary campsite on the foreshore, an outpost that leaves its mark on the city in tea, silk scarves, and the perfume of spiced food.[27]

These incremental intrusions adjust the ways in which the citizens of Belfast imagine themselves and their city. The ballast office in which Rice works represents the standardization of centuries-old knowledge of tides, routes, and trade networks. That knowledge still lingers in the margins of official society, as the reader sees when young Rice and his companions go drinking in the night town of pubs. One character earns his money for drink by swimming submerged from one side of the Lagan to the other; others conduct their own business at the snugs and counters of the alehouses.[28] One of the novel's two pivotal relationships begins in *The Mill for Grinding Old People Young*, the pub from which the book takes its name, when Rice meets the Polish émigré Maria. She has her own story of national struggle, her father a patriot in rebellion against Russia

[25] Caroline Magennis reads the relevance of contemporary contexts to Patterson's work in 'Re-writing Protestant History in the Novels of Glenn Patterson', *Irish Studies Review*, 23 (2015), 348–60.

[26] Glenn Patterson, *The Mill for Grinding Old People Young* (London: Faber, 2012), 88–9.

[27] Ibid., 107.

[28] Ibid., 55.

and her beloved a Polish officer who she struggles to follow through newspaper reports of the fighting. Maria came to Belfast because her father had met Tone in Paris and so convinced her of the city's dedication to liberty. Rice confuses his infatuation for her with the idea that freedom for Belfast can come only with the removal of its overlord, Donegall. There follows an elaborate plot to murder Donegall that fails when Maria discovers Rice's plan and contacts his grandfather, who intervenes. The plot nods here to Thomas Hardy's *Tess of the d'Urbervilles*, with its final scenes set in the Giant's Ring, a Belfast Stonehenge in minor key. The choice is significant as it connects all these events, as does Hardy in England, with a deep time that extends beyond the social disruptions of nineteenth-century industrialization, the effects of which still shape Belfast today.

The early morning mist that shrouds Rice's mad plan is water as a metaphor of uncertainty, as occurs so often in Irish literature, the national territory historically complex and in dispute. The coastal work is a means to represent the cultural heterodoxy that follows, operating as a chart through time of evolving relationships between characters and their environment that are governed by unpredictable incursions. The image continues into the novel's closing moments as Maria departs Belfast on the steamer *Hibernia*. If this is a foreshadowing of partition as Ireland sails from Ulster, it is also a suggestion that the subtlety of human witness will outlast the strictures of race and religion. Gilbert watches *Hibernia* all night as the boat waited in the Lough for a change of tide:

> The moon in surrendering the sky had dragged the clouds with it and the sun rising behind the *Hibernia* was from its first showing above the funnels almost impossible to look into, but I told myself that if she did not quit her post I would not close my eyes, would not, would not, whatever the cost. I lost her finally not to darkness but to dazzle, trying to keep the boat in sight, until I could not distinguish between the Lough, the Lagan, the tears brimming up inside me, filling my head to bursting.[29]

In a general sense, this proximity of sea to land, and the coastal line between, creates a zone of tidal change that extends in Patterson's novel into the human subject.[30] There are serial twentieth-century examples of the coastal work in Irish literature (and Joyce's *Ulysses* might rank first among them), and all share a set of common concerns, namely formal

[29] Ibid., 237.

[30] This is particularly true of the prose epics of Tim Robinson, which map the geological dimensions of the cultural habitat of Ireland's west coast, working out in a radius from Galway Bay; the aesthetic configuration of these written arrangements of life in the largest scale has established its own genre in Irish writing in the last three decades, for which Robinson's early maps might be taken as a starting point.

innovation, an attention to material objects as registers of human interaction, and a labyrinthine combination of source materials.[31] This is immediately true of *Ulysses*, as it is of *The Mill*, *The Star Factory*, and, on the west coast, Kevin Barry's *The City of Bohane*. All these books inhabit a shifting ground between history and fiction and all represent, each in their different way, an engagement with a long twentieth century in Ireland, a major context of which is globalization, either in the retreat of the British Empire or the rise of international capital. This is a provocative claim, given that the British state in Ireland was in disarray with the Easter Rising in 1916 and in withdrawal after independence in 1922, partition notwithstanding. This, perhaps, is a point where the political and cultural histories of the island of Ireland diverge. The history of nationalism in Ireland privileges the construction of the state as a sovereign and self-sustaining entity, while the island's cultural history suggests a different dynamic, which the late history of the British Empire helps us to understand. Water was the global medium of its transactions and consequently, the representation of seas, estuaries, and coastal zones provides a trans-, or even extra-, national context for the narratives created around them. *The Mill*, *The Star Factory*, and *The City of Bohane* all fit this model, and each book is anchored in a tidal space between the city, the coastline, and the immediate interior. Each also shares certain narrative structures, which are common to the coastal work in the period of late empire and after, and each is a miniature epic of space and time, intimately tied to the material and cultural history of the places in which they are set. Despite the novel's futuristic setting, Kevin Barry establishes Bohane early on as a classic city in this mode:

> Our city is built along a run of these bluffs that bank and canyon the Bohane river. The streets tumble down to the river, it is a black and swift-moving rush at the base of almost every street, as black as the bog waters that feed it, and a couple of miles downstream the river rounds the last of the bluffs and there enters the murmurous ocean. The ocean is not directly seen from the city, but at all times there is the ozone rumour of its proximity, a rasp on the air, like a hoarseness.[32]

If Barry nods towards Joyce in his prose, he extends the logic of a global exchange of goods to the immigration of new populations to the island of Ireland. *The City of Bohane* is home to unexpected ethnicities of Asians and Caribbeans, which has the further effect of shifting the social taboos of

[31] This is part of the subject for Nels Pearson, *Irish Cosmopolitanism: Location and Dislocation in James Joyce, Elizabeth Bowen, and Samuel Beckett* (Gainesville: University of Florida Press, 2014).

[32] Kevin Barry, *The City of Bohane* (London: Vintage, 2011).

settled society by the central role travellers play in the narrative.[33] The social architecture of post-independence Ireland still exists, but its power is now symbolic, as if nationalism lost the long war against the continual migration of people within and across state borders. So Barry describes the life of De Valera Street as an ethnic promenade:

> Here came the sullen Polacks and the Back Trace crones. Here came the natty Africans and the big lunks of bog-spawn polis. Here came the pikey blow-ins and the washed-up Madagascars. Here came the women of the Rises down the 98 steps to buy tabs and tights and mackerel . . . De Valera Street was where all converged, was where all trails tangled and knotted[34]

This Ireland is not made of ideals, but signs, and objects signal the global networks of which Bohane is a fictional part. Irish nationalism's obsession with cultural purity can be read as a postcolonial reaction to imperial sovereignty; another perspective might suggest that the relationship between characters and things is the most constant guide to the continual migrations that are the push and pull of coastal life. Ireland exhibits this condition strongly as one island attached by history to another, the archipelago of which extended across the oceans. If that global empire has long receded into political history, its material structures still remain, sedimented now with the history of the nation-states that followed it. The crisis that these modern states face is still global, and Barry's novel emerges as uncertainty grows that nationalism can answer the financial and environmental challenges it faces. This uncertainty registers in Bohane's condition as a place of seepage, the peninsula on which it is built 'a many-hooked lure' for the senses.[35] The sound of fado carries over a variegated landscape of bogs, poppy fields, and turloughs in which memory is a rendition of the city's global past, as registered in the presence of cloths, scents, and furnishing. The Gant approaches an old lover, Macu, and finds her in a 'pair of suede capri pants dyed to a shade approaching the dull radiance of turmeric, a ribbed black top of sheer silk that hugged her lithe frame, a wrap of golden fur cut from an Iberian lynx'.[36] This is a description at once historic and fantastic, the old association of the west of Ireland with Spain dressed now in the fur of a wild animal.

The description is in tune with the novel's sensuous tone; Bohane is a city of distraction and desire, a place of fairs, pubs, and opiates. This, again, is a coastal condition. In a passage reminiscent of scenes from Jack

[33] For more on this subject, see Mary Burke, '*Tinkers*': *Synge and the Cultural History of the Irish Traveller* (Oxford: Oxford University Press, 2009).

[34] Barry, *The City of Bohane*, 31.

[35] Ibid., 60.

[36] Ibid., 140.

Yeats's sketches, Barry describes the arrival of a carnival to the dockside of Bohane:

> And of course many a carnie was sprung from the peninsula originally. We would be the sort, outside in Bohane, who'd run away with the Merries as quick as you'd look at us.[37]

The king of this fair day scene is Logan Hartnett, and he too is dressed in a worldly fashion, with 'a pair of Spanish Harlem arsekickers' and a 'dress-shkelp in his belt, ivory-handled'.[38] Ivory is an established symbol of Ireland's imperial connections, at least since Joyce's *A Portrait of the Artist as a Young Man*.[39] It is an essential part of the material archaeology of the city's social system, a system built with the flexibility of the coastal place in mind. This is the last point to make regarding *The City of Bohane*, which is that the city and the sea are partners in the construction of human habitation. The infrastructure of this mutual possession begins at the coastal fringe and seeps into the city through estuaries, docksides, quays, and wharfs. The motion of water throughout represents a liquid transition between the expanse of the ocean and the interlocked streetscapes of the city. Barry describes this as a 'North Atlantic drift', a transitional space between land and sea that is defined by its colour and conditions:

> Bohane was green and grey and brown:
> The bluish green of wrack and lichen.
> The grey of flint and rockpool.
> The moist brown of dulse and intertidal sand.[40]

As the borders of the coastal city peter out in the intertidal zone between land and sea, the coastal work's origins in the novel form may be traced back to the fictions of Erskine Childers and James Joyce, both of whom observed the coastal margins of island life as symbolic terrains of global modernity.[41] Patterson and Carson renovated this tradition in their books

37 Ibid., 266. 38 Ibid., 245.

39 In one vivid passage, Stephen Dedalus imagines empire and India through the recitation of schoolboy Latin, a gesture itself to the twin powers of Rome and London in his formation: 'The word now shone in his brain, clearer and brighter than any ivory sawn from the mottled tusks of elephants. Ivory, ivoire, avorio, ebur. One of the first examples that he had learnt in Latin had run: *India mittit ebur*' (James Joyce, *A Portrait of the Artist as a Young Man*, ed. John Paul Riquelme (New York: Norton, 2007), 156).

40 Barry, *The City of Bohane*, 249.

41 Erskine Childers published his classic work of maritime espionage, *The Riddle of the Sands*, in 1903. Its combination of literary flair, knowledge of sailing, and warnings of a war with Germany gave the book a reputation for insight that it still enjoys. Childers had a turbulent and fascinating life as a British establishment figure, Irish gunrunner, and eventual victim of the Irish Civil War. See, for example, Andrew Boyle, *The Riddle of Erskine Childers* (London: Hutchinson, 1977).

about Belfast a century later, but all are connected by their attention to the long decline of the British Empire and its legacies in Ireland. Barry returns to the early twentieth century's fascination with the western seaboard in his treatment of a fictional city, but he too integrates Ireland with a world tide of objects and ideas. The flotsam and jetsam of the old empire washed up on an island that had turned its back on the sea. Carson, Patterson, and Barry are three examples of authors who took these fragmentary forms to mould novels whose imaginative territory is the seeping ground that is both land and sea. This, it seems, is the Ireland of contemporary literature, a transition zone whose history, like its future, is visible only in the change of the tides.

5

'At the Dying Atlantic's Edge'

Norman Nicholson and the Cumbrian Coast

Andrew Gibson

This chapter is about Norman Nicholson, born 1914, died 1987. In his time he was widely regarded as, to quote the *Times* obituary, 'the most gifted English Christian provincial poet of the century', and was a noteworthy figure on T. S. Eliot's poetry list at Faber, which set so much of the tune from 1945 onwards.[1] Nicholson's poetry suffered something of an eclipse in the seventies and after: the times were not on its side, and its concerns were apparently not theirs. But there are now at least some signs of a serious Nicholson revival, notably in David Boyd's biography and the scholarly work of David Cooper. Nicholson came from west Cumberland, where he spent almost the whole of his life. He might be defined as in effect the only major west Cumbrian poet, and therefore, since R. S. Thomas was, of course, Welsh, perhaps the only major modern writer of the English Atlantic edge—particularly in that he was singularly committed to his liminal space, what the poem called 'On Duddon Marsh' calls 'the line dividing. . . / Europe from the Atlantic', and spending his whole life in the small, rundown, forgotten industrial town of Millom, at the very south-western coastal tip of his county.[2] Millom had its brief moment of national fame—or notoriety—when, in 1969, its Co-operative Society was forced to close, sparking fears of a domino effect across the country.[3] But it has otherwise long languished in obscurity and comparative remoteness. Not only does the twenty-fifth edition of Ward and Lock's very popular *Guide to the Lake District*, published in the early 1950s, fail even to mention it, but while in the sketch of Cumberland on

[1] Neil Curry, 'Introduction', in Norman Nicholson, *Collected Poems*, ed. Neil Curry (London: Faber and Faber, 2008), xv.

[2] Nicholson, *Collected Poems*, 193.

[3] Bill Myers, *Millom Remembered* (Stroud: Tempus, 2004), 108.

the cover, Keswick, Ambleside, and Windermere are marked with large black dots and large capital letters, Penrith and Cockermouth with medium-size dots and capitals, and Barrow, Broughton, and Ulverston with small ones, Millom is not marked at all. Its name does not appear. This is symptomatic: Millom, as it were, has long been a national blind-spot, a dead zone, off the radar. But from Nicholson's identification with it in its very destitution, I think, its inexistence for the culture, something rather special springs.

National mythology, literature, criticism, and tourism have coincided in presenting Cumbria (until 1974, Cumberland) as in effect an inland space or territory, the 'Lake District'. This imaginary construction serves as both a national heartland, analogous to Kent, the 'Garden of England', and a privileged repository of the national soul, cherished in its beauty by poets and solicitously tended by its wardens. Cumbria functions in effect as what Cooper, quoting cultural geographer David Matless, evokes as a 'social-spiritual space . . . a topography in which the mystical rubs shoulders with the legislative'.[4] As such, however, it excludes another space. This Cumbria is the coastal area that begins with the western fells and ends further west at the Irish Sea, running from the Solway Firth in the north to the Duddon estuary in the south. The 'grey unphotographed waste acres of West Cumberland', as Nicholson describes them, border on the Atlantic.[5] On its eastern side, it includes some of the county's most beautiful, if remote and empty, lakes and valleys, and its highest mountains. But, as Cooper remarks of Nicholson's Millom, though Wordsworth engages on occasions with a westerly Cumbria, the features of the western region that I have just stressed in fact remain marginal to the normative mythology, to the Romantic and post-Romantic Lake District, and to the tourist trail. The western fells cannot be construed as integral to a heartland as the sense of the coast looms large there. On the western peaks, from Scafell to Coniston Old Man to Black Combe, one is vividly aware of how far Cumbria is a culture of the Atlantic edge, that it ends at the sea. This Atlantic edge is invisible or ignorable from within the heartland, at least if we think of the heartland as represented above all by, say, Ambleside, Hawkshead, or Wordsworth's Grasmere. Here, one might think, the myth of the inward and self-enfolded spirit of the island race runs out into the silts and shallows of the Duddon estuary. At the same time, the coast not only has its often bleak and austere beaches, but is

[4] David Matless, *Landscape and Englishness* (London: Reaktion, 1998), 84; David Cooper, 'The Poetics of Place and Space: Wordsworth, Norman Nicholson and the Lake District', *Literature Compass*, 5 (2008), 815.

[5] Nicholson, 'Landing on Staffa', *Collected Poems*, 356.

strewn as, here and there, are the western fells, with the marks of an invasive modernity from which the heartland has been carefully protected (though it has actually assumed its own forms of modernity, too; there is some point to saying, as did W. H. Auden, that the Lake District was 'another bourgeois invention, like the piano'): long-gone mines, mineral railways and blast furnaces, the coastal railway, the nuclear plant at Sellafield (or Windscale), the MOD's so-called 'equipment-proving', big gun-firing range at Eskmeals, the landscapes intermittently, casually contaminated with industrial (and increasingly radioactive) waste and ruination.[6]

Norman Nicholson is the poet par excellence of Cumbria's Atlantic edge, in geographical and geological terms, the Cumbrian coastal plain. Both his books on Lakeland and his scattered poems on the Lake District show him defining his poetic identity in contradistinction to the Lake poets. Cooper sees the coastal area of Cumbria as 'geographically and imaginatively distant from the Wordsworthian centre', like the spoke of a wheel to its nave; distant, that is, but nonetheless connected to it. Nicholson's endeavour is therefore to reconfigure the space of the region, collapsing a 'post-Romantic hierarchization of regional space'.[7] But that is not a vision of it, I think, that Nicholson's *poetry* exactly promotes; and we should remember that Nicholson considered himself to be primarily a poet, that his reputation prior to his death was chiefly as one, and is likely to continue to be so. 'I thought of myself as a Millom boy', writes Nicholson, 'not as a Cumbrian'.[8] True, as Cooper emphasizes, Nicholson explicitly raises the question of Wordsworth's vision of the area in his 'To the River Duddon':

> Wordsworth wrote:
> 'Remote from every taint of sordid industry'.
> But you and I know better, Duddon lass.
> For I, who've lived for nearly thirty years
> Upon your shore, have seen the slagbanks slant
> Like screes sheer into the sand, and seen the tide
> Purple with ore back up the muddy gullies
> And wiped the sinter dust from the farmyard damsons.[9]

But Nicholson does so (as Cooper knows) because of Wordsworth's distinguished Duddon river sonnet sequence: he is squabbling with Wordsworth over border territory, perhaps reproaching Wordsworth for fencing off a domain that would imperil his vision of his own, and putting in a claim

6 Auden quoted in Cooper, 'Poetics', 815.
7 Cooper, 'Poetics', 815, 816.
8 Norman Nicholson, *Wednesday Early Closing* (London: Faber and Faber, 1975), 131.
9 Nicholson, *Collected Poems*, 25.

for a less obviously romantic patch of Cumberland turf. Otherwise, Cooper's argument is above all sustainable in the terms in which he chiefly makes it, on the basis of Nicholson's prose works—it is notably confirmed by *Greater Lakeland*—which were produced with a more commercial end in mind and partly addressed a rather different readership.

Nicholson's poetry, then, I would suggest, is scarcely a poetry of the Lake District as such at all. It is a poetry of the Atlantic edge. This is arguably most obviously the case with the first two volumes, *Five Rivers* and *Rock Face*, and the late volume *Sea to the West*. But I would also claim that it determines the content of all the other volumes, with the possible exception of *A Local Habitation*, that the themes of the poet of the Atlantic edge continue, if sometimes also in rather different versions and guises, in the other volumes. In other words, the space of the Atlantic edge fairly comprehensively determines the character of Nicholson's vision and the substance of what he has to say. I will give a brief account of several crucial features of this vision.

As I have already indicated, Nicholson's is a landscape largely bounded in the east by the western fells. He only very seldom makes reference to the northern fells (those to the north of Keswick, including the Skiddaw range), central fells (those to the east of Borrowdale, from Derwent Water to the Langdale Pikes), or eastern fells (those centred on Helvellyn). Even a poem like 'Skiddaw Slate' turns out to be about, not Skiddaw, a northern peak, but Black Combe, a south-western one, because Black Combe is composed of the slate in question. Yet, at the same time, what is striking is that Nicholson almost never looks out on the Atlantic. The 'maiden' in one of his 'Songs of the Island' feels 'the tug in the blood' at the shingle's edge; but this is very rare.[10] In Nicholson, prospects seldom beckon, vistas almost never spread wide. Nicholson had Irish blood in him and, according to Boyd, there was a substantial Irish immigrant presence amongst the early Millom workers.[11] But save for the occasional reference to winds blowing in from Ulster or, perhaps more interestingly, Sligo, Nicholson the poet has little or no interest in Ireland, or indeed the Isle of Man—which is clearly visible from his Atlantic edge—and seemingly none in the history of their relations with England. Unlike so many comparable Irish writers, he also has little or no interest in the American horizon, a distant America and the freedom of its open spaces. Indeed, he very explicitly turns away from the American will o' the wisp, in what the title of one poem calls 'the affirming blasphemy':

[10] Ibid., 35.
[11] David Boyd, *Norman Nicholson: A Critical Biography* (Seascale: Seascale Press, 2014), 11.

There is grass on the earth though the nettles grow through our ankles;
There is fruit on the trees though the brambles tear at our thighs;
There is manhood in our fingers though the ape howl through our blood.
That to which we cannot return is not to be found before us:
There is no other garden beyond the bright sea.[12]

This has several effects, all relevant to my argument. Geographically speaking, Nicholson's theme is a stretch of land separated from the north and south by estuaries, and from the east by mountains. Imaginatively, he operates within a narrow coastal strip, with its single coastal road:

Between the pine trunks, red as blood,
Like a long wound is gashed the road.
Straight and deep it stretches forth
In front, behind, or south or north,
Backward and forward is the same.[13]

This sense of spatial constraint has major consequences for the poetry. It is further enhanced by the poet's indifference to looking outward. On Nicholson's coast, the Atlantic comes in to 'die', to peter out into estuarial mud, silt, sands, stonescapes, and marshlands, to lose itself in obscure miscellanea and debris, 'wrack and rubble'.[14] Yet Nicholson's imagination is also repeatedly haunted by the notion that the sea may violently rise up, overwhelm, and devour the land. This doubtless had its roots in historical fact: before the construction of the Hodbarrow Outer Barrier in 1905, the biggest civil engineering project seen in Millom, there was a real danger that, as the *Millom Gazette* put matters on Thursday, 20 April of that year, 'Hodbarrow and Millom might be wiped out by the watery element which the [Hodbarrow Mining] Company has had to fight for so long'. (Fascinatingly, the Barrier incorporated a slab of polished red granite from that great British colonial construction, the Aswan dam, which had been opened just three years earlier.)[15] Nicholson's poetry repeatedly comes back to images that, in effect, take the side of the sea against the Company and what it represents. Again and again, he imagines a moment when 'the tall waves / Bound over the mountain tops', as, perhaps above all, in 'The Bow in the Cloud':

The sea bludgeons the shore's long flanks,
Bursts through the dykes like a fleet of tanks,
Smashes like a heel on a matchbox the roofs of the town,

[12] Nicholson, *Collected Poems*, 411, 90–1.
[13] Nicholson, 'The Garden of the Innocent', *Collected Poems*, 85.
[14] Nicholson, 'Whitehaven' and 'Ravenglass Railway Station', *Collected Poems*, 18, 202.
[15] Myers, *Millom Remembered*, 33.

Breaks chimneystack and derrick down,
Tears belfry from steeple, tombstone from grave,
While the broken bell cracks upon the wave.
The water floods the lowlands and the dales,
and fills the ghylls and gullies of the fells.[16]

At all events, again and again, the land-sea vector points inwards, not outwards.

Nicholson is abundantly aware of the history of the coast: incursions of 'the galleys that came to Ravenglass'; the Romans, the Vikings, the Scots, and Picts 'forag[ing] down from Solway Moss'; the English from further south, the Industrial Revolution, and the discovery of haematite ore; the rise, brisk decline, and eclipse of mines, iron, and steel works; the arrival of evacuees during the Second World War (the 'children hurried from a german Herod'); the transfer of art from the Tate Gallery to Cumbria at the same time; and so on.[17] But his grasp and presentation of this history is as an episodic one. He deliberately refuses to grace it with any larger meaning or coherence. His poetry does not reflect or countenance any larger historical narrative of the coast; say, a quasi-colonial one (the word is nonetheless not idle: Nicholson himself writes of 'colonizing voices').[18] Nor does it struggle to produce such a narrative. His project is not in that sense integrative. This is even more strikingly the case in that, though his poetry ranges from Maryport to Whitehaven, St. Bees, Cleator Moor, Egremont, Ravensglass, Silecroft, above all, Millom, and indeed Walney Island, at least in his poetry, Nicholson has no interest in a culture or cultures. If he does claim in *Greater Lakeland* to have 'a sense of belonging', this makes little appearance in the poetry.[19] Indeed, as a poet, he is more likely to treat such a concept ironically, as in the poem 'Nicholson, Suddenly', where he remarks on the death of his Millom namesake:

For I'm left here,
Wearing his name as well as mine,
Finding the new one doesn't fit,
And, though I'll make the best of it,
Sad that such things had to be—
But glad, still, that it wasn't me.[20]

[16] Nicholson, *Collected Poems*, 109.

[17] Nicholson, 'Five Rivers', 'Egremont', and 'Carol for Holy Innocents' Day', *Collected Poems*, 4, 12, 14.

[18] Nicholson, 'Askam Visited', *Collected Poems*, 39.

[19] Norman Nicholson, *Greater Lakeland* (London: Robert Hale, 1977), 22.

[20] Nicholson, *Collected Poems*, 301.

This kind of detachment is notable in that Nicholson was in large part writing in an era that granted a specific prestige to the concept of the 'organic community' as promoted by F. R. Leavis and Denys Thompson in the 1930s, especially in their *Culture and Environment* (1933). But in western Cumbria there is no 'organic community'. The Millom Nicholson knows is in fact 'a decaying Victorian settlement' that began in the mid-nineteenth century as 'a miserable encampment of huts and sheds' struggling up out of 'a waste of dune, salt-marsh and swampy fields', as he tells us in *Greater Lakeland*.[21] It was in reality a 'frontier community' that initially struggled 'to keep public order and maintain basic standards of building and health'.[22] In 1866, what the *Ulverston Mirror and Reflector* of 7 July called 'serious riots' took place in the area. The rioters stole rum, set upon the local constable, and chased at least one naked woman the distance of a mile.[23] Eight years after that, the *Barrow Daily Times* for Friday, 13 March was referring to Millom as 'the antithesis of paradise'. It was thinking in particular of the 'highly unsatisfactory and dangerous state' of the town's sanitary arrangements, its 'common land adorned with dirty pig sties', its 'small and very much overcrowded house[s], built on marshy ground, and surrounded with reeking puddles and loathsome nuisances'.[24] Less an organic community, it would seem, than a combination of sump, mire, and Wild West lawlessness. It was precisely during this period, and only two generations before his own, as Nicholson is acutely aware, that, in 1867, his grandmother arrived from across the Duddon estuary in a cart, still possessed of memories of farmland.

So, too, he is keenly aware of how far the mining communities of the west—Wales, Scotland, Ireland, Cornwall, Cumbria—were not in fact deeply and stably rooted in their worlds and that they had frequently been in large measure made up of incomers who remained itinerant and transient, moving (or being moved) where the work moved:

> Seventy or eighty years ago and more
> Before the days of the railway, travellers crossed the sands
> On horseback or in carts, starting from this shore...
>
> The land was eager then for settlers, opened heart and hand
>
> To men from Wales and Ireland, strange in name
> And cult and dialect.[25]

[21] Nicholson, *Greater Lakeland*, 15, 17, 20.
[22] Myers, *Millom Remembered*, 8.
[23] Ibid., 20.
[24] Ibid., 23.
[25] Nicholson, 'Askam Visited', *Collected Poems*, 39.

He is equally aware of just how fast and how drastically macro-economic change afflicts such a precarious world (see, for instance, 'Hodbarrow Flooded', 'The Riddle', and 'On the Closing of Millom Ironworks'). This is one reason why, in his early poems, he thinks of nearby Askam ('Askam Unvisited', 'Askam Visited'). The discovery of iron ore actually took place earlier in Askam than in Millom, and, for half a century, as in the case of Millom, immigrant labour had flooded in and the village grown rapidly. The Millom and Askam Hematite Iron Company Limited had formed in 1890 and run the two ventures jointly. After the First World War, however, there was a sharp downturn in the iron market, and economic constraints dictated that the company close one site down. By 1938, the Askam works had simply vanished, and Askam, though 'real enough and clear to be seen / Across the estuary, a mile and a half at most', had nonetheless also become

> A place on a map that hands let fall
> Out of the carriage window or into the fire, a letter lost
> In the post.[26]

Brusquely, poignantly, in harsh contradiction to the official narratives of industrial progress, the phases end:

> Down
> On the ebb-tide sands, the five-funnelled
> Battleship of the furnace lies beached and rusting;
> Run aground, not foundered;
> Not a crack in her hull;
> Lacking but a loan to float her off.[27]

In effect, thus, for Nicholson, there is no coastal culture, only the often-brutal effects of historical and economic contingencies. In this respect, he separates himself not only from the Lake poets, but also from the whole tradition of English 'provincial' poetry (Crabbe, Clare, Hardy, early Lawrence) to which his work has more often been linked. Historically, too, this is a land of detritus, the incoherent offscourings of history.

The sense of spatial constraint in Nicholson's poetry pushes him in particular directions. In his poetry, at least, he cannot see and largely refuses to imagine eastward beyond the western fells, and turns away from the oceanic perspective westwards. But equally he cannot look to the south, either. There is scarcely a reference to an England south of Widnes. This is hardly surprising in a poet from a part of the country distant and in some degree alienated from southern values. If Nicholson's imagination

[26] Nicholson, 'Askam Unvisited', *Collected Poems*, 37.
[27] Nicholson, 'On the Closing of Millom Ironworks', *Collected Poems*, 297–8.

does expand, it is rather northwards, in small part to Scotland, but above all to Scandinavia and the Arctic:

> Turn, then, the face to the cold north,
> To the green sky and the white earth,
> Where frost is nutmeg to the tongue,
> Coltsfoot to the coughing lung.
> And let the Eyes stretch out beyond
> Horizons of the yellow hand
> To where beneath the North Star roll
> The Arctic Circles of the soul.[28]

The only foreign country with which any of the poems are concerned is Norway (the only foreign country, apparently, that Nicholson ever visited; according to Boyd, the British Council wanted him to go further afield, but he refused, on health and domestic grounds).[29] In Nicholson's poetry, thus, the relevant Atlantic edge runs from the Irish Sea to the Skaggerak and the Norwegian Sea as far as the Barents Sea. The north is where vast cold and chilling winds come from. It splits Cumbria off from the England to the south. The north claims Cumbria for its own. To think of Cumbria and the north together is also to think of England disintegratively, to think of the Atlantic edge as where Anglo-Saxondom fades and starts to perish and that other great founding British people after the Roman Empire, the Norsemen, assert their cultural sway. Indeed, insofar as Nicholson was interested in the Irish strain in the population of Millom and Cumbria generally, it seems in large measure to have been because he was, in turn, particularly interested in the Viking strain in the Irish and therefore how far, in a sense, the Irish might be claimed for the north. Nicholson is acutely aware of and knowledgeable about the historical Viking presence in Cumbria, as *Greater Lakeland* again makes clear. His poem 'For the Grieg Centenary' even suggests that his feeling of true artistic kinship might be with the great Norwegian composer as much as the provincial English poets, not least because, as is evident in various of his writings, he is so aware of Norse thickening the English he speaks and writes:

> the crackling northern tongues,
> The dialect crisp with the click of the wind
> In the thorns of a wintry dyke,
> So that Solvieg sings
> In the words which bind the homes of Cumberland.[30]

[28] Nicholson, 'Frost Flowers', *Collected Poems*, 127.
[29] In conversation with the author.
[30] Nicholson, *Collected Poems*, 36.

But the narrowness of Nicholson's world as he defines it also has another spatial consequence: if the Atlantic edge for him is only ever a thin strip, whether it runs from the Duddon estuary to the Solway Firth or the Duddon estuary to Tromso, Hammerfest, and beyond, the narrowness also encourages the mind to follow the perpendiculars of the western mountain ranges, the eyes to lift towards what Nicholson calls 'my parochial complement of sky'.[31] The paradox is that, for Nicholson, to think of the Atlantic edge is also to think of the vertical. Nicholson's imagination is constantly drawn upwards. No doubt this reflects a religious drive; yet the vertical dimension in Nicholson's poetry is not principally the dimension of transcendence, as the 'The Bow in the Cloud', admittedly a wartime poem, suggests:

But the iron silts with sand beneath the yellowing moon.
It waits for the time when the bell again will swing,
And the iron crack in the wind and the boulders ring like steel
And the moon and the pebbles and the dead sand on the shore
Fall into file at the eighth word of creation,
And the dumb sea shout with the voice that once was shamed by man.[32]

This hardly seems to betoken any meditative release. The vertical dimension is rather, as Cooper has it, eschatological or, better, I think, messianic. See, for instance, the evocation of dawn over west Cumbria which opens 'The Holy Mountain', or, later in the poem, the invocation of the refining fire:

The earth shall burn to the sky; like the six
Candles before the altar shall burn the six peaks
To the glory of the Lord:
Everest, Sinai, and the seven-fold hill of Rome,
The tripod of creeds,
Helvellyn, megalithic Gable, and Wetherlam,
Burning above the orchards.[33]

Let me put the point this way: in reality, Nicholson's coastal strip is, categorically, an unredeemed land, one that has never tasted even the possibility of historical salvation, one that lies comprehensively beyond the bromides of progressives. Historically, one might suggest, it has never really come into existence at all. There is nothing to be hoped for from west, east, or south. If Cumbria and its history belong anywhere, it is with the north. But, like the Scots and Picts, 'the Norsemen foraged down the dales'; the axis to the north, like the axis to the south with the Romans and

[31] Nicholson, 'The Elvers', *Collected Poems*, 275.
[32] Nicholson, *Collected Poems*, 104. [33] Ibid., 101.

English, is an axis of violence.[34] So 'There is no rest, no refuge, there is no *predicted* hope'.[35] There is God, then, or there is nothing; or rather, there is the event of God. According to Boyd, Nicholson's letters to Sylvia Lubelsky in the Rylands Library show that, after the period of his tuberculosis and his transferral to a sanatorium in Hampshire, he went through a spell of agnosticism, blaming religion for the world's ills.[36] Boyd suggests that it was the encounter with and influence of Eliot's poetry that got him out of this; yet if, to some degree, in passages of his life, he balanced on a knife-edge of faith and faithlessness, this seems to me to be consistent with his poetic vision.[37] Nicholson's God occurs in and as events. He happens, because for Nicholson he must happen if he is to have meaning, as justice. In a whole series of poems in *The Pot Geranium*, taking a more scientific turn than he had in previous volumes, Nicholson addresses the theme of the rare, almost inexistent reversal of self-evidence, as for example in 'The Undiscovered Planet':

> No man has seen it; the lensed eye
> That pin-points week by week the same patch of sky
> Records not even a blur across its pupil; only
> The errantry of Saturn, the wry
> Retarding of Uranus, speak
> Of the pull beyond the pattern:
> The unknown is shown
> Only by a bend in the known.[38]

As Nicholson sees matters, the poet must precisely attend to 'the pull beyond the pattern', the possibility—the imminence—indicated by 'the bend in the known', the sense of constraint from which there is a rare 'errantry' or deviation perhaps mirroring the relationship between poetry and justice and the narrowness of Nicholson's coastal strip.[39] This, too, is surely the gist of 'Song for Pelagius', a poem that can only be read ironically, as a counterblast and rebuke to Pelagianism and, no doubt, specifically, the strain of Pelagianism and wistful if not facile benevolism in the modern Anglican church:

> When the rain rains upward,
> And the rivers siphon the sea,
> When the becks run backward,
> And the sunset swells into day...

[34] Nicholson, 'For the Grieg Centenary', *Collected Poems*, 36.
[35] Nicholson, 'The Holy Mountain', *Collected Poems*, 100 [my italics].
[36] Boyd, *Norman Nicholson*, 50. [37] Ibid., 36.
[38] Nicholson, *Collected Poems*, 211. [39] Ibid.

When oaks and elders
Pump sap into the soil,
when props and pitshafts
Stuff the earth with coal,
When the bright equator
Illuminates the sun,
Man of his will
Shall hoist himself to heaven.[40]

Here the reversal of the land-sea vector comes together with a clutch of images of the reversal of the self-evidence of the natural order to plead the case for the (almost impossible) messianic exception, as opposed to Pelagian optimism and trust in the redemptive powers of human endeavour without grace. Few poems provide a better sense of what is truly at the core of Nicholson's vision.

But, in the end, 'from the angels in the sky / No trees [can] shutter [men] away'.[41] God turns upon the Atlantic edge in judgement of all who have oppressed, failed, and betrayed it over 'Centuries of feudal weight': industrialists, entrepreneurs, governments, and landowners, as Boyd's account of *The Old Man of the Mountains* underlines.[42] The very image of betrayal, in 'Windscale', Nicholson's fine poem about it—according to Boyd, it was written after 'the 1957 reactor fire and catastrophic radiation leak'—is the demonism of the nuclear installation at Sellafield:

The toadstool towers infest the shore:
Stink-horns that propagate and spore
  Wherever the wind blows.
Scafell looks down from the bracken band,
And sees hell in a grain of sand,
  And feels the canker itch between his toes.

This is a land where dirt is clean,
And poison pasture, quick and green,
  And storm sky, bright and bare;
Where sewers flow with milk, and meat
Is carved up for the fire to eat,
  And children suffocate in God's fresh air.[43]

Indeed, in some of the poems, God sends the Atlantic spilling over its edge into the wasteland, not only or even chiefly destructively or in wrath, but

[40] Nicholson, *Collected Poems*, 76.
[41] Nicholson, 'The Holy Mountain', *Collected Poems*, 94.
[42] Nicholson, *Collected Poems*, 15; Boyd, *Norman Nicholson*, 76.
[43] Ibid., 100; Nicholson, *Collected Poems*, 282.

as a messianic image of radical justice. So, too, in the comparatively early novel *The Fire of the Lord* (1944), Benjamin calls upon the fire as an instrument of messianic purification. Nicholson's conception of the Atlantic edge is as an absolute boundary which forces the mind to think the impossible, vertical transaction, of which the idea of justice is a principal manifestation.

Finally, Nicholson's biographical account of his early years, *Wednesday Early Closing*, suggests certain key moments, at least, in his youthful development towards a career as a poet. I will list them in the order which I take to have a certain bearing on his poetry, rather than their chronological order. There is the introduction, via the Anglican church, in which, for pragmatic reasons, he was confirmed—he did it to get to college, he tells us—to a superlative religious language (interestingly, he specifies Thomas Cranmer).[44] Self-evidently, there is his discovery of poetry, poetry and locale together: 'I fell in love; I discovered poetry, I discovered Cumberland'.[45] There is the great moment, inspired by reading George Bernard Shaw, when he turns his habitual view of Millom inside out, converting it into a vision, a vision of devastation: 'the land, almost everywhere, collapsing like a punctured tyre', devastated, abandoned, stagnant, overlooked, a land of rot, decay, rust, weeds, 'a smother of hopelessness'. Suddenly, this explodes into emotions of 'anger, resentment, compassion and a paradoxically exhilarating feeling of disgust'.[46] He became acutely alive to what, in an earlier passage, he describes as 'the scandal, the injustice, the waste, the muddle' of Millom history.[47] He discovered that he had a genuine, coastal wasteland as a subject, to which Eliot's influence would later help him to give a spiritual (but by no means obviously Eliotic) dimension. This made him for a while, he says, a socialist 'in the Trevelyan-Macaulayan tradition' (though he also convicts himself of 'pure adolescent romanticism').[48] But what most crucially matters is the moment of radical estrangement from an unreflective relation to a familiar context.

This estrangement would later be confirmed by the period of Nicholson's tuberculosis and his transferral to a sanatorium in Hampshire, which effects a kind of double displacement. Perhaps most significantly of all, however, reeling back earlier in the life, there is a time when, attending the local Methodist church before the necessary move to Anglicanism, he is transfixed by a thought of the Holy Land. 'The landscape of the Bible', he writes, 'was far more familiar to us than the geography of England'.[49]

44 Nicholson, *Wednesday Early Closing*, 165.
45 Ibid.
46 Nicholson, *Wednesday Early Closing*, 176.
47 Ibid., 151.
48 Ibid., 176.
49 Ibid., 94.

Nicholson reimagines his Atlantic edge in Biblical terms, bearing in mind that the Biblical landscape is also a seaboard landscape. Boyd points to the same conflation, of Palestine and Cumbria, in the play *The Old Man of the Mountains*, the radio broadcast 'Millom Delivered', and the later play *Birth by Drowning*.[50] Nicholson rethinks his territory in and through his vision of devastation, but also as a landscape that requires the impossible redemption. This, together with the boy's love of poetry and his seduction by the beauty of a religious language, establishes the core of his poetry as messianic. Nicholson's poetic thought as a whole and the rest of the poetry are substantially organized around this core.

[50] Boyd, *Norman Nicholson*, 70, 79.

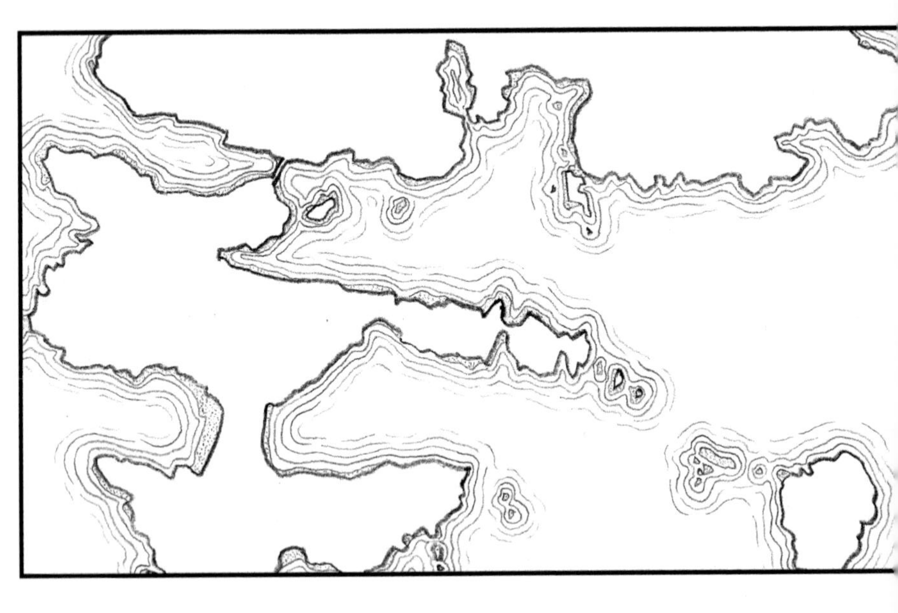

6

'Felt Routes'

Louis MacNeice and the North-East Atlantic Archipelago

John Brannigan

In 'Ode', the final poem in his collection, *Poems* (1935), Louis MacNeice writes of the necessity to 'become the migrating bird following felt routes . . . And without soaring or swerving win by ignoring / The endlessly curving sea and so come to one's home'.[1] Much has been written about MacNeice's search for 'home', his fraught and critical relationship with Ulster, Ireland, and England, and about the difficulty of his 'place' within either Irish or English literary traditions. John Kerrigan has suggested, however, that MacNeice might be seen more productively as a 'self-consciously archipelagic' poet:

> the Anglo-Irish polarity that structured MacNeice's reception during the Troubles is starting to seem restrictive. It can only enhance his standing that so many more of his qualities are visible if he is thought about in the context of what the Good Friday Agreement calls 'the totality of relationships among the peoples of these islands'.[2]

Placing him in such a context, or ascribing to his work the epithet 'archipelagic', is not merely a laudatory gesture, however, but a recognition of the significance of cultural precursors in the work of thinking through the complex negotiation of devolution, and the local ecologies of the British and Irish islands. MacNeice's work, particularly in the 1930s, is constantly struggling with the very restrictions Kerrigan has observed in his later critical reception. It is imbued, of course, with neo-Yeatsian snarls

[1] Louis MacNeice, *The Collected Poems of Louis MacNeice*, ed. E. R. Dodds (New York: Oxford University Press, 1967), 58.

[2] John Kerrigan, 'The Ticking Fear', *London Review of Books*, 30 (7 February 2008), 15–18.

at commercialism, and liberal jibes at the puritanism and atavism of the societies in which he grew up and lived, but these tendencies are equally weighted with the impulse towards, and longings for, the 'felt routes' of alternative northern and Atlantic geographies, new poetries of what Andrew McNeillie calls the 'unnameable archipelago',[3] which is, like MacNeice's conception of the world in 'Snow', 'Incorrigibly plural'.[4] In common with his immediate precursors of the Irish Revival, and indeed contemporaries such as Hugh MacDiarmid, MacNeice was drawn towards the Atlantic edges of the archipelago for much of his experimentation with ideas of place and belonging. In his joint venture to Iceland with W. H. Auden (*Letters from Iceland*, 1937), his ironic travelogue of the Hebrides (*I Crossed the Minch*, 1938), and many of his poems published in the 1930s, there is no untrammelled island utopia, but instead a sensing of the need for new vocabularies of habitation, new geographies of connection and living between the islands.

'Ode' begins with two figures of disillusioned utopia, the town of Bournville in the English midlands which, for all its vaunted aspirations as a social model, pollutes the air with a smell 'coarse with chocolate', and the poet's 'frivolous nostalgia' for 'the Atlantic', which is likened to 'celluloid abstractions', a metaphor perhaps conscious of those abstractions of rugged Atlantic coast life which Robert Flaherty had produced in his film, *Man of Aran* (1934).[5] In 1928, writing on a cruise to Norway, MacNeice had written to his friend, Anthony Blunt, that he 'Might go to Aran Islands like Synge. & eat lobsters and salmon all the time',[6] but although the romantic appeal of the West of Ireland is a recurrent theme in MacNeice's work, it is frequently undermined by a hard-won scepticism of the mythology of the West. So between the industrial dream of a model and mechanical social order, and the agrarian dream of a remote, peasant culture, MacNeice's 'Ode' attempts to ply a new route. Written as an expression of MacNeice's hopes for his son to grow up unencumbered by such useless illusions of utopia, and with some noted resemblances to Yeats's 'A Prayer for my Daughter', the poem is drawn repeatedly back to 'the shore of the regular and rounded sea' as a site in which it is possible to imagine 'one's peace while the yellow waves are roaring'.[7] At its bleakest implications, it is a poem written on the birth of his son that looks forward to a peaceful death for his son, that sees the passing of generations as the

[3] Andrew McNeillie, 'Editorial', *Archipelago*, 1 (2007), vii.

[4] MacNeice, 'Snow', *Collected Poems*, 30.

[5] MacNeice, 'Ode', *Collected Poems*, 54.

[6] Louis MacNeice, *Letters of Louis MacNeice*, ed. Jonathan Allison (London: Faber, 2010), 192.

[7] MacNeice, 'Ode', *Collected Poems*, 58.

only meaningful marker of human existence on earth: 'I remember all the houses where parents / Have reared their children to be parents'.[8] In part, this is all he can hope for, since the store of sensory memory to which he turns for consolation—the sounds which awaken in him a sense of 'summer's athletic ease', for example—are also possibly an 'augury of war'.[9] There are no absolutes he can pass on to his son, no god or science on which his son can depend, so instead the poet and his son 'Must become the migrating bird following felt routes'.[10] It is an interesting metaphor, not least because the motivational factors of bird migration—breeding and feeding—are tied by analogy in the poem to generational anxieties about human migration, but also because in the 1930s, when MacNeice wrote 'Ode', the science for understanding the 'felt routes' of bird migration was underdeveloped. The practice of ring-tagging birds, which had been widely employed only since the beginning of the twentieth century, told ornithologists the range of bird migration, but not how birds navigated precise routes, often across oceans and continents. Whether by instinctual sense of direction, astrological and solar navigation, visual memory, or some kind of genetic memory, bird migration scholars such as Landsborough Thomson and Charles Patten were uncertain, and so MacNeice's poetic emphasis upon the 'felt' navigational routes of birds is rather apt.[11] In being both remarkable and habitual, the migration of birds serves MacNeice as an appropriate metaphor for human existence, neither nomadic nor sedentary, following routes long charted by others, but nonetheless singular, and extraordinary.

The 'felt routes' of MacNeice's own migrations took him from his birthplace in Belfast, with holidays to the much romanticized West of Ireland origins of his parents, along the shore to Carrickfergus, across the Irish Sea to schools in Sherborne in Dorset and Marlborough in Wiltshire, university in Oxford, and lecturing jobs in Birmingham, London, and briefly in New York. Later jobs for the British Council and extensively for the BBC took him to Greece, India, Egypt, Ceylon, Ghana, and South Africa from his home in England, with Ireland an infrequent destination for visits and holidays in his adult life. The pattern is one dictated by work, and only partly by feelings, with the exception, of course, of MacNeice's profound sense of the impossibility of 'living' in Ireland, nor indeed of 'feeling oneself' in England, as he wrote to his friend, E. R. Dodds.[12] His BBC commissions took him on a sometimes riotous, often drunken, tour

[8] Ibid. [9] Ibid., 57. [10] Ibid., 58.

[11] See A. Landsborough Thomson, *Bird Migration* (London: Witherby, 1936), and C. J. Patten, *The Story of the Birds* (Sheffield: Pawson and Brailsford, 1928).

[12] MacNeice, *Letters*, 459.

of the closing days of empire, the lights of one powerful notion of Britishness dimming darker with every tour, and as Alan Gillis argues, the reputation of his late poetry is really as 'a laureate of homelessness and alienation'.[13] But the dead ends of empire, and the suffocating nationalism of the new Irish state, were already evident in his poetry of the 1930s. The 'felt routes', to which 'Ode' directs MacNeice as well as his son, are not the well-worn paths of his later biography, but rather the uncharted waters of an alternative geography of connection and belonging which began to take shape in his early work. Yet it is difficult to discern the shape, since, as Terence Brown has argued, traffic, travel, and tourism become key metaphors and motifs throughout his work, and develop finally into 'a metaphoric uniformity—the journey . . . towards death'.[14]

To discern a new direction for his migrations, a new shape for his belonging, MacNeice first embarks upon a rigorous criticism and abandonment of the various claims upon his identity. 'Valediction' is as clear a declaration of independence from everything which the newly formed states of Ireland and Ulster symbolized as could be written. The poem directs the reader through a series of injunctions to 'see Sackville Street', 'See Belfast', 'Park your car in Killarney, buy a souvenir', and 'swank your fill, / But take the Holyhead boat before you pay the bill'.[15] Ireland, both north and south, is depicted as cold, fake, murderous, and drably sentimental, which romanticizes its own origins and shrouds its petty miseries in 'Sham Celtic crosses' or 'leaps to a fife band'.[16] Yet MacNeice recognizes too the powerful hold of the island on him: 'I cannot be / Anyone else than what this land engendered me', even though he vows also to 'exorcise my blood / . . . I will acquire an attitude not yours / And become as one of your holiday visitors'.[17] Strikingly, MacNeice uses the two most popular and charged metaphors for racial and national belonging here—blood and land—to signal his own difficult entanglements in what he depicts as a mythology of Irishness. And the verbs—engender, exorcise—make it clear that the desired transformation from subject, or son, to the carefree attitude of the holiday visitor who can treat the land as a scenic confection or casual playground will be painful and uncertain. The renunciation is an act of denial, a denial of pleasure as well as pain: 'I must go east and stay, not looking behind'. The poem announces

[13] Alan Gillis, '"Any Dark Saying": Louis MacNeice in the Nineteen Fifties', *Irish University Review*, 42 (2012), 106.

[14] Terence Brown, '"What am I doing here?" Travel and MacNeice', in Fran Brearton and Edna Longley (eds), *Incorrigibly Plural: Louis MacNeice and his Legacy* (Manchester: Carcanet, 2012), 83.

[15] MacNeice, 'Valediction', *Collected Poems*, 52–3.

[16] Ibid. [17] Ibid., 53.

none of the possible promise of going east, nothing of futurity other than the calculated return of the casual visitor, but instead dwells on his extrication from 'your drums and your dolled-up virgins and your ignorant dead', from the litany of violence, ritual, and myth which seem to the poet indefatigable.[18]

In the poem, 'Birmingham', MacNeice continues this process of demythologizing the places of his belonging, for English cities present no antidote to the rural mysticism of Ireland, or the grimy veneers of Ulster. Birmingham is depicted in Eliotic terms as the unreal city, composed of facades and tricks, whatever beauty it has is 'jerry-built', and exploitative of 'sweated labour'.[19] After the 'Saturday thrills', the summer entertainments, or the respite of lunch hour, the factory chimneys still 'call . . . sleep-stupid faces through the daily gate'.[20] The conspicuous modernity of MacNeice's England renders it no less a sham, and ultimately no less dreary in its delusions, than the romanticized scenes of Irish and Ulster atavism. A survey of MacNeice's early poetic renderings of his various residences in Ireland and England might conclude with his own blunt, proto-Larkinesque line from 'An Eclogue for Christmas' that 'One place is as bad as another'.[21] Yet this would miss the point that what MacNeice is doing in his early poetry is not an expression of existential alienation or archetypal modernist rootlessness, but a clearing of the accumulated mythologies and ideologies of place in the British and Irish Isles. This is accomplished through a relentless uprooting and scouring of place: 'Train to Dublin' refuses the destination, and gives the reader instead a series of images as ephemeral as 'the shadow of the smoke of this train upon the grass;'[22] 'Belfast' comprises geological and maritime images of the city's people, formed of 'basalt' and 'mica', 'And the salt carrion water brings him wealth', a city built upon commerce and murder, with no sense in the poem of how it might be called a home;[23] both 'Valediction' and 'Upon this Beach', in very different ways, advocate the life of the 'tripper', consciously opposed to the life of the settler;[24] and perhaps most emphatically, MacNeice's poem about his childhood hometown, 'Carrickfergus', recalls the sounds, smells, and sights of that town, but ends in Dorset, remembering the 'steamer . . . that took me to England— / Sweat and khaki in the Carlisle train'.[25] Migration is a persistent theme and trope in MacNeice's poetry, but it is always a migration from ideas of

[18] Ibid., 54. [19] MacNeice, 'Birmingham', *Collected Poems*, 18.
[20] Ibid. [21] MacNeice, 'An Eclogue for Christmas', *Collected Poems*, 33.
[22] MacNeice, 'Train to Dublin', *Collected Poems*, 27.
[23] MacNeice, 'Belfast', *Collected Poems*, 17.
[24] MacNeice, 'Upon this Beach', *Collected Poems*, 19.
[25] MacNeice, 'Carrickfergus', *Collected Poems*, 69.

place as much as a migration from places themselves. As Peter McDonald argues, one reason why MacNeice has struggled to gain full recognition in either Irish or English literary canons is the constant destabilization of the very categories of 'Ireland' and 'England' implicit in his work.[26]

MacNeice's most famous poem, *Autumn Journal* (1939), similarly works to demythologize national narratives of belonging, juxtaposing them with local and planetary scales of geographic meaning. Place is defined in MacNeice's poem only through movement, through a traversal of place. Indeed, place names of distinctive localities appear most noticeably in lists of the towns along a railway line—'West Meon, Tisted, Farnham, Woking, Weybridge'[27]—or along a road—'Bewdley, Cleobury Mortimer, Ludlow'[28]—where their significance as 'places' is erased by their function merely as names glimpsed at speed by the traveller passing by. If there is a conscious acknowledgement of Edward Thomas's 'Adlestrop' here, the poem also makes clearer than Thomas the accelerated process of transformation which renders places into mere names on a map, the barest signals of routes taken. *Autumn Journal* is, of course, a record of transformation, of the intense period of anticipation prior to the outbreak of the Second World War, and is a poem preoccupied with the differing scales of time—daily, seasonal, and historical—and of place—local, national, and planetary—in which human life is meaningful. It is particularly concerned, however, to dislodge myths of insularity associated with contemporaneous Irish and English nationalist discourses. It famously admonishes Irish isolationism, which would shape the policy of Irish neutrality during the war: 'There is no immunity in this island either'.[29] Against de Valera's protectionist policies of promoting Irish self-sufficiency, MacNeice counters with the acerbic analogy of 'A cart that is drawn by somebody else's horse / And carrying goods to somebody else's market'.[30]

In similar ways to the poem 'Valediction', MacNeice is scathing in his critique of romantic Ireland, but Ireland is not the only target of his attack on insularity. The words 'insulates', 'insulated', and 'insulate', used across the poem, connect three separate references to myths of protection from the encroachments of the world outside the islands. The first instance appears in the opening lines of the poem, in coastal Hampshire, where 'close-clipped yew / Insulates the lives of retired generals and admirals', but presumably, with the impending signs of war, not for long.[31] Section XII of the poem uses the word 'insulated' also in the sense of a

[26] Peter McDonald, *Louis MacNeice: The Poet in his Contexts* (Oxford: Clarendon Press, 1991), 1–9.

[27] MacNeice, 'Autumn Journal', *Collected Poems*, 102.

[28] Ibid., 115.

[29] Ibid.

[30] Ibid.

[31] Ibid., 101.

desperate last illusion of peace before the onset of war, when 'the legions wait at the gates'.[32] The third instance of the word balances the myth of insular Ireland with the equally false sense of a protected England: 'There is straw to lay in the streets; call the hunchback, / The gentleman farmer, the village idiot, the Shropshire Lad, / To insulate us if they can with coma / Before we all go mad.'[33] The poem draws us forward and back, shrewdly across the British and Irish Isles, between the myths of insularity which define nationalist narratives of exceptionalism, be they agrarian idylls of frugal self-sufficiency and world-oblivious localism, or pastoral dreams of a 'merrie' rural retreat from modernity. MacNeice returns forcefully to this point at the end of *Autumn Journal* when he poses the question about what should fill our dreams: 'Of Tir nan Og or South Sea islands, / Of a land where all the milk is cream / And all the girls are willing?'[34] Or instead, MacNeice asks, shall we not dream of 'a possible land / Not of sleep-walkers, not of angry puppets, / But where both heart and brain can understand / The movements of our fellows'?[35] Against the myopic nationalisms of England and Ireland, then, with their dreams of island utopias, or rather island hideaways, MacNeice poses instead an alternative geography, a geography in which the 'hungry faces' of Spain are connected to the 'generals and admirals' on the Hampshire coast, in which we are all 'Following the curve of a planet'.[36] *Autumn Journal* critiques Irish and English nationalisms, then, not just by showing their reliance on the same myths of rural and island insularity, but also by showing their interdependence upon global scales of transformation and belonging. And, just as in the 'felt routes' of 'Ode', it is the *movement* of people, not their rootedness, which demands understanding, as if indeed human scales of belonging can only be understood in terms of motion, migration, and traversal.

It is precisely along these lines that we might consider MacNeice's travel narratives of the period—*Letters from Iceland* and *I Crossed the Minch*—as sharing the same preoccupations as his poetry. The term 'travel narratives', of course, does not adequately describe these books, which are idiosyncratic compendia of prose and poetry, letters and journals, fictional personae, and travel reportage. The very assemblage form of both books suggests a radical indeterminacy of approach, or an underlying irony to their very pretence to be travel records. Auden and MacNeice collaborated on *Letters from Iceland*, which goes, almost comically and certainly briefly, through the motions of pretending to be a travel book, with a section 'For Tourists' advising on customs and expectations, and another 'addressed to John Betjeman' which compiles quotations from diverse sources on every

[32] Ibid., 124. [33] Ibid., 137. [34] Ibid., 152.
[35] Ibid. [36] Ibid., 158, 102.

aspect of Icelandic geography, culture, and history.[37] Similarly, *I Crossed the Minch* contains a 'Potted History', and journal accounts of MacNeice's tour of the Hebrides, but MacNeice begins with the admission that he set out for the islands without knowing that the inhabitants predominantly speak Gaelic, thus limiting his ability to 'become intimate with the lives of the people', and thereby turn authoritative guide for his prospective readers.[38] In the case of both books, there is an important question of tone raised by their glib assemblage of the conventional ingredients of the travel narrative, which certainly in English writing has long and involved associations with cultural imperialism. MacNeice's acknowledgement of his ignorance of the language of the Hebridean islanders might be regarded as cavalier, and perhaps characteristic of the presumptuous disposition of colonial travel narratives, which may claim authority to depict others without having gained intimacy or acceptance. Likewise, Auden and MacNeice in *Letters from Iceland*, although they acknowledge from the outset that a 'travel book owes so little to the writers, and so much to the people they meet', proceed to provide accounts of their travels and of the island which adopt an attitude that might certainly be read as condescension. In both cases, however, the tone is inseparable from the general frivolity evident in the juxtaposition of fictional personae, poetry, letters, and drab journal records of diet and weather. A travel narrative which informs the reader that 'The sitting-rooms of Icelandic farms are all rather alike', or that 'One waterfall is extraordinarily like another', may be regarded, perhaps, as treating its subject matter with some scepticism, even irony.[39] To be fair, also, even the titles of both works make no claim to authority on their respective subject locations, and MacNeice's *I Crossed the Minch*, in particular, begs to be considered a mock-heroic title. There is an argument to be made, then, that *Letters from Iceland* and *I Crossed the Minch*, if they seem to belong to the genre of travel writing, are in some regards deconstructive of that genre, playfully ironic with its conventions, and frankly dismissive of its claims to cultural knowledge. Yet, in the context of MacNeice's already established poetic interest in islands and insularity, the decision to travel to, and write about, Iceland and the Hebrides, to turn to a northern hopscotch tour of islands, raises serious questions about an underlying archipelagic theme in his work.

[37] W. H. Auden and Louis MacNeice, *Letters from Iceland* (1937; London: Faber and Faber, 1967).

[38] Louis MacNeice, *I Crossed the Minch*, introd. Tom Herron (1938; Edinburgh: Polygon, 2007), 7.

[39] Auden and MacNeice, *Letters from Iceland*, 113, 135.

Much of *I Crossed the Minch* is shaped by a scaling of the Hebrides against the measure of MacNeice's experiences and perceptions of other places, so that MacNeice draws comparisons between the Hebrides and Ireland, Ulster, Achill, Connemara, London, Birmingham, Cumberland, Iceland, and Norway. 'The lava-fields of Iceland cured me of the idea that a landscape cannot be too bleak', he writes, comparing the stones of Iceland with the stones of Connemara, which in turn are compared to his hopes of finding 'the right ratio of life and barrenness' in the landscape of the Hebrides.[40] Throughout the book, MacNeice makes clear that the distinctiveness of the islands could only ever be defined in relation to its archipelagic neighbours. Ireland, in particular, is a recurrent figure of comparison: 'the islanders, like the Southern Irish, show a disregard for time and penny-in-the-slot efficiency'.[41] So, too, MacNeice's depiction of the islands must be differentiated from an already established genre of travel writing about them, a genre to which he happily, perhaps opportunistically, contributes, but of which he is deeply sceptical: 'you should never believe what people in England tell you about other countries', he writes, and that warning undergirds the constant measuring of MacNeice's observations of the islands against the sentimental expectations he has acquired from travel writings about the islands.[42] *I Crossed the Minch* is a narrative of deflated hopes and misplaced expectations, conveying even in its formal dedication to MacNeice's 'native informant', Hector MacIver, that it is a book likely to disappoint his island hosts, being the 'book of an outsider who has treated frivolously what he could not assess on its merits'.[43]

Yet, however appropriate it is to see *I Crossed the Minch* as a 'potboiler', written for financial gain, the conscious, even strategic, frivolity of the book's deflationary approach to the distinctiveness and value of the islands requires some explanation. MacNeice explains that his purpose in going to the Hebrides was to find his own sense of Celticism reflected and amplified in the islanders, 'a sentimental and futile hope' as it turns out, and a hope, moreover, about which his earlier poetry had already shown healthy scepticism. The idea of some vague sense of racial affinity which might mysteriously crystallize in MacNeice on sustained and close contact with some actual Gaels is dismissed in the same sentence in which it is raised. If there is an archipelagic sense of affinity and connection to be constructed in the relations between the Hebrides and other parts of the north-east Atlantic, MacNeice swiftly dismisses the racial discourse underpinning such a notion in its Yeatsian version. So, too, the idea of a common coastal

[40] MacNeice, *I Crossed the Minch*, 33. [41] Ibid., 13.
[42] Ibid., 70. [43] Ibid., 3.

consciousness shared along the Atlantic seaboard simply does not accord with MacNeice's disappointed reaction to much of the coastal landscape of the islands. In Mull, for example, he complains that 'The grass seemed to run down to the sea. I do not like this. There should be no philandering between sea and land'.[44] In Claddach, he protests melodramatically at the 'mere vomit of a sea, flats of slime and seaweed, a dead lagoon of limbo', which lies between Claddach and Kirkibost Island.[45] It compares unfavourably with his romanticized vision from his childhood of the Atlantic seen for the first time in the West of Ireland as 'a regular leap of white like the flash of an animal's teeth'.[46] MacNeice is clinical, perhaps even scathingly unsentimental, in casting a cold eye on the romanticization of the landscape and people of the Hebrides, and, if the travel book as a generic type relies upon selling the idea of remote places to a largely metropolitan readership, MacNeice perversely and persistently discourages further travel. His apparently melancholic declaration on the opening page, 'I doubt if I shall visit the Western Islands again', turns out over the course of the book to be a more frank, and measured, summary of MacNeice's assessment of the real interest of the islands to the unconnected traveller.[47]

There is scant reference in *I Crossed the Minch* to other books about the Hebrides, although, as Tom Herron records, it was a popular subject of travel books in the 1930s.[48] MacNeice records meeting Barra's most famous resident, the writer Compton Mackenzie, who would become even more famous as an island writer when he published *Whisky Galore* (1947), but he engages with Mackenzie as a celebrity rather than as a writer.[49] However, in MacNeice's playful demythologizing of Celticist and romanticist tendencies in island writings, it is difficult to accept that he was unaware of the exaggerated extent of such tendencies in books such as Seton Gordon's *Islands of the West* (1933). Gordon combined the keenly scientific approach of the expert naturalist with a deeply romantic sense of the Western Isles as a world still governed by Celtic spiritual beliefs in the power of the tides: 'True it is that when the Atlantic at the imperious bidding of the pale moon pours in a mighty irresistible stream north-east past Malin Head and Tory Island, past Barra, Mingulay and Mull of the Great Hills, the clustered shore clans of the Isles awake'.[50] MacNeice's book eschews both: he sheds little light on the particularities of natural or human habitation of the islands, and he responds to the drunken feeling of being at one with the Celtic lore of the islanders by

44 Ibid., 115. 45 Ibid., 74. 46 Ibid., 26. 47 Ibid., 7.

48 Tom Herron, 'Introduction', in MacNeice, *I Crossed the Minch*, xi.

49 MacNeice, *I Crossed the Minch*, 97–104.

50 Seton Gordon, *Islands of the West* (London: Cassell, 1933), 7.

rushing off to Stornoway 'to try and buy a copy of the *Listener*', which would at least give him the sense of being back in touch with his cherished metropolitan literati.[51] MacNeice prefers to constantly remind his readers, self-reflexively, that he is a thoroughly metropolitan being, and this might be read as an effective means of subverting the assumptions of the travel genre. Yet what both Gordon and MacNeice share, albeit expressed in quite different ways, is a sense of the islands as belonging to an archipelagic geography which defies conventional state or national boundaries. Gordon traces the language, customs, and beliefs of the Hebrides through connections with Connemara, Tory, Inishbofin, and the Scilly Isles, mapping an arc of islands and fractal coastlines fringing the Atlantic, which for the most part share in common the Gaelic language, and the persistence of Celtic myths and lore. The Irish newspapers reflected some sense of this archipelago when reporting on Hebridean affairs, and there is some evidence of interest in the Hebrides among Irish readers.[52] MacNeice bears out something of this geography in the way in which the Hebrides conjure in his mind comparisons with Achill, Connemara, and Iceland, but it is devoid of romanticism. In returning to England, for example, MacNeice sees a 'flashy poster' in a railway station, advertising 'Visit the Western Isles: A Wonderland of Colour', to which his trenchant response is that 'there was more colour in Birmingham'.[53]

Such anti-romantic expressions in *I Crossed the Minch* might be regarded as examples of what Tom Herron describes accurately as the 'tonal promiscuity' of the work, but MacNeice's 'promiscuity' masks a deeper search for a sense of connection, for some idea of place which might be called home, and most pertinently here, his search seems repeatedly to take him to islands, and to ideas of islands, which might, magically, bear within them the seeds of an alternative way of life. The search was not his alone. Valentine Cunningham has written insightfully of the remarkable alignment of left-wing pastoralism of the 1930s with a training in classical scholarship, and perhaps even more strikingly how many of these same intellectuals had immediate familial connections with Northern Irish Protestantism, most notably E. R. Dodds, Cecil Day Lewis, George

51 MacNeice, *I Crossed the Minch*, 8.

52 See, for example, a report on Compton Mackenzie's account of life in Barra, 'Living off the Map', broadcast on BBC radio on 7 October 1936, in 'A Happy Island', *The Irish Times*, 13 October 1936, 6, which laments that the 'virility' of the Outer Hebrides as described by Mackenzie is not to be found on Ireland's Atlantic islands. Boswell's *A Tour to the Hebrides* was among the most widely read books in Dublin in December 1936: see 'What Dublin is Reading', *The Irish Times*, 5 December 1936, 7.

53 MacNeice, *I Crossed the Minch*, 106–7.

Thomson, and MacNeice himself.[54] Thomson is most notable among them for his explicit depiction of the lives of twentieth-century Blasket islanders as the cultural analogues of Homer's Greeks:

> The conversation of those ragged peasants, as soon as I learnt to follow it, electrified me. It was as though Homer had come alive. Its vitality was inexhaustible, yet it was rhythmical, alliterative, formal, artificial, always on the point of bursting into poetry. . . . Returning to Homer, I read him in a new light. He was a people's poet.[55]

For Thomson, visiting the Blaskets enabled him to see, and to argue for, Homer as a prototypical poet of proletarian life, *avant la lettre*, but also, of course, this entailed seeing life on the Blaskets as an idyllic mode of pastoral existence. As a Marxist, Thomson could find some inspiration in the idea that pre-capitalist economic relations persisted in such 'outlying or secluded communities', which he celebrated as 'a simple culture, but free from the rapacity and vulgarity that is destroying our own'.[56] Auden saw something of this vitality of 'folk-poetry', which he believed comparable to pre-industrial Europe, in the frontier and prospecting communities of America.[57] MacNeice was immersed in the classical pastoral, however, like Thomson, and perhaps this is one notable source of his attraction to 'the Celtic or backward fringes' of the British Isles which he hoped remained the home of 'natural (some will call it primitive) culture'.[58] Yet, MacNeice distrusts the terms of this investment of proletarian romance and nobility in the supposed outliers of the British Isles, which has 'made a Mecca of the Blaskets', and distrusts the association of the Hebrides with ideas of primitive dignity and self-sufficiency, not least because his allusions to dependence upon the dole and tinned food suggest 'an island invaded by the vices of the mainland'.[59] Those 'vices of the mainland' are walked in to the islands on the boots of 'trippers' just like MacNeice, of course, who is keenly aware of the responsibilities of the travel genre in which he writes both for the idealization of remote places and the corresponding demise of their remoteness.

MacNeice craves the idealization of the Hebrides, and his happiest moments on the islands come when walking alone with a map, 'not

[54] Valentine Cunningham, 'MacNeice and Thirties (Classical) Pastoralism', in Brearton and Longley (eds), *Incorrigibly Plural*, 85–100.

[55] George Thomson, *Studies in Ancient Greek Society: The Prehistoric Aegean* (London: Lawrence and Wishart, 1949), 540.

[56] George Thomson, *Island Home: The Blasket Heritage* (Dingle: Brandon, 1988), 80, 85.

[57] W. H. Auden, 'Introduction', in W. H. Auden (ed.), *The Oxford Book of Light Verse* (London: Clarendon Press, 1938), xix.

[58] MacNeice, *I Crossed the Minch*, 7.

[59] Ibid., 74–5, 8.

meeting a person on the way', or when, in the company of islanders, he can imagine that somehow this community embodies a 'Celtic timelessness'.[60] It is certainly the case that these moments are rare intrusions in a narrative which is predominantly characterized by scepticism and incredulity, and yet *I Crossed the Minch* cannot wholly abandon the hopes or fantastical notions upon which it was founded. Just as Thomson imagines the Blaskets as not only a remnant of pre-capitalist society, but also as a harbinger of a future model of community, so too MacNeice is drawn towards the idea of the Hebrides as embodying similar potential:

> Their traditional language needs no artificial cultivation, their population is small enough to allow of a genuine community feeling, their social life is still homogeneous (though commercialisation may soon drive rifts through it), lastly the sea still separates them from their neighbours.[61]

At this point in the narrative, MacNeice quotes a line in Greek from Aeschylus's *Agamemnon*, spoken by Agamemnon's wife, Clytemnestra: 'There is the sea and who shall drain it dry?'[62] The line might be interpreted both as a statement of some arrogance, claiming power over the sea, which Clytemnestra acknowledges in her subsequent lines has been the source of great wealth for her household, and as a statement of futility, akin to the Irish mythological tale of Cuchulainn's fight with the waves, or the English legend of King Canute commanding the tides to stop. It has little significance for the point MacNeice is making, other than to suggest resonance between the seafaring communities of ancient Greece and those of the Hebrides. It is precisely the resonance which Compton Mackenzie remarks upon to MacNeice, that the landscape glimpsed through 'a little ship's window' in Mackenzie's Barra house 'was the nearest thing to Greece this end of Europe'.[63] Like Thomson, then, MacNeice glimpses ancient Greece in the familial, 'primitive' communities of the Gaelic-speaking Atlantic seaboard. The continuity proposed by such an analogy is registered in some of MacNeice's poems which figure the sea as timeless, most notably 'The Sea' from *Blind Fireworks* (1929) and 'Thalassa' (1964). Yet the analogy is more interesting than a specious form of universalism: the classical parallel poses a challenge to the notions of blood kinship or racial continuity which underpin Celtic Revivalism, precisely by proposing instead similarities which are cultural and material, and more precisely which relate the

[60] Ibid., 200, 209. [61] Ibid., 14.

[62] Ibid., 14. The translation is from MacNeice's own translation of *Agamemnon*, which he published in 1936: see Louis MacNeice, *The Agamemnon of Aeschylus* (London: Faber, 1936), 45.

[63] MacNeice, *I Crossed the Minch*, 101.

cultural to the material. For MacNeice this is crucial, since his initial assumption of affinity with Gaelic islanders is misplaced: such affinity would be based on a mythology of race, whereas it is clear in *I Crossed the Minch* that the changing cultural patterns of life on the islands are directly connected to changing material circumstances. To affect affinity to a folk or peasant primitivism (for which MacNeice interestingly uses the image of 'Synge's hobnailed boots chasing girls' naked feet'[64]) would, in such conditions, be an empty formalism: it would falsify the terms of his relationship to the islands, which, as he realizes melancholically, can only be that of a 'tripper'.

Cunningham is too quick, however, to lump MacNeice's 'The Hebrides' and 'Leaving Barra' in with a species of 'travelmaniac' writing which he criticizes as a 'literature living greedily off its authors' experiences of foreign places', too ready to accept MacNeice's own sense of complicity in tourist voyeurism and exploitation.[65] MacNeice mocks himself as a 'tripper', but his trips are really searches for connection, quests for affinity which even if they fail nevertheless ask questions about the relations between 'these islands'. For MacNeice, although he cannot belong to them, the homogeneity, longevity, and finitude of the Hebridean communities constitute ripe conditions for the survival of a kind of island nationalism, while he can see little possibility of this in Scotland, and for a socialist dreaming of 'a federation of differentiated communities'; nationalism, even if reactionary, might at least have its provisional uses in defining the terms of such differentiation.[66] However, as MacNeice acknowledges of his more romantic moments on the islands, perhaps the comforts of nationalism are always about the illusion of insularity, a point that becomes particularly significant in MacNeice's caustic address to Ireland in 'Neutrality' (1944), where the sea becomes a source of moral rebuke: 'to the west off your own shores the mackerel / Are fat—on the flesh of your kin'.[67] The Irish government's declared policy of neutrality in the Second World War was, for MacNeice, a coldly logical extension of the insularity nationalism fostered. It confirmed and exaggerated the sense already evident in his poetic depictions of Ireland in the 1930s that the myth of islandness was less a product of romance than of cold indifference to those outside the bounds of the nation. Yet, as Clair Wills suggests in her account of MacNeice's prolonged stay in neutral Ireland at the beginning of the war, there is perhaps some censure of his own temptation

64 Ibid., 212.

65 Valentine Cunningham, *British Writers of the Thirties* (Oxford: Oxford University Press, 1988), 351.

66 MacNeice, *I Crossed the Minch*, 16.

67 MacNeice, *Collected Poems*, 224.

to remain in Ireland masked in his later depiction of neutrality as cold-blooded escapism.[68] The insularity of islands was not wholly without appeal in a world descending into genocide and mutual mass destruction. 'You will find in this book no picture of island Utopias', declares MacNeice in the introductory chapter of *I Crossed the Minch*, but while this is incontestable, it does not capture the book's lingering sense of a man in search of island utopias.[69]

The reviewer for *The Times* distinguished the poetry included in *I Crossed the Minch* from its prose, praising the poetry for not containing any of the 'smartness or sophistication' which comes between the poet and the islanders in the playful fictional interludes and ironic tone of much of the prose.[70] It might be argued that the 'smartness' and 'sophistication' is a register of MacNeice's uneasy relationship to the ready urbanite sentimentalism and misty Celtic romanticism about islands, and especially Atlantic fringe islands, which had become a cliché of Irish and British writings in the early twentieth century, and perhaps even long before.

It might also be argued that the poetry included in *I Crossed the Minch* should be considered in intimate relation to, even in dialogue with, that 'smartness' and 'sophistication' of the prose. Yet, as the final section of *I Crossed the Minch*, the poem 'On Those Islands' (also published in the collection *The Earth Compels* (1938) as 'The Hebrides') does suggest a closer affinity between the poet and the islands, an affection that survives and outlives the smart, breezy dialogue of MacNeice's fictional personae of 'Hetty and Maisie'. Terence Brown alludes to the poem as 'richly celebratory of Hebridean life', and Heather Clark sees in it 'several stock Revivalist motifs', perhaps even 'a dialogue with Yeats's "The Lake Isle of Innisfree", whose speaker also dreams of surrendering to an island other-world free from time and modernity', except that, as both Brown and Clark point out, the poem also recognizes island life as a fantasy only for someone like MacNeice who is not from the islands.[71] The poem dramatizes this distance of the speaker from the intimacies of the island communities in its refrain, repeated twelve times, 'On those islands', with its deictic word indicating a spatial, and an implied emotional, detachment. MacNeice clusters together a series of images of the islands which conform

[68] Clair Wills, *That Neutral Island: A Cultural History of Ireland During the Second World War* (London: Faber, 2007), 71–8.

[69] MacNeice, *I Crossed the Minch*, 18.

[70] 'A Poet in the Hebrides', *The Times*, 5 April 1938, 10.

[71] See Terence Brown, *The Literature of Ireland: Culture and Criticism* (Cambridge: Cambridge University Press, 2010), 137, and Heather Clark, 'Leaving Barra, Leaving Inishmore: Islands in the Irish Protestant Imagination', *Canadian Journal of Irish Studies*, 35 (Fall 2009), 32.

to conventional expectations of remote, rural life: 'No one hurries', 'peasant', 'The houses straggle', 'fragrant peat', 'No one repeats the password for it is known', 'ancestral rights', 'unspoiled by contact', 'their land though mainly stones', 'a lost breed', and many more.[72] These images of quiet and intimate peasant life jostle with the encroaching signs of modernity, some already familiar in Synge's *The Aran Islands*: 'The photos . . . of the successful sons / Who married wealth in Toronto or New York', 'the bus, not stopping, / Drops a parcel for the lonely household', the 'dole' and 'old-age pensions'.[73] Cunningham emphasizes how many of the movements figured in the poem appear to be negative.[74] It is more striking, however, how many of them are ambivalent. 'No one hurries' may be read, for example, as a sign of pastoral ease, or of systemic lethargy. 'No one repeats the password for it is known' may be read as a sign of communal familiarity, or of pathological insularity. Equally, 'the bus, not stopping, / Drops a parcel for the lonely household' could be an action that either compounds or relieves the loneliness of the household. The more one appreciates the ambivalence of such figures in the poem, the more evident it becomes that 'On Those Islands' is an exercise in studied (even affected) detachment, an attempt to depict islands and their peculiarities without romanticizing their 'primitivism'.[75]

MacNeice concludes by alluding to the survival of neighbourliness and the preservation of familial and communal customs. The islands are places 'Where a few surnames cover a host of people / And the art of being a stranger with your neighbour / Has still to be imported', where people 'still can live as their fathers lived'.[76] In themselves, these lines are also ambivalent, and can be read as celebrations of island life only in juxtaposition with the figure of 'the tyrant time', absent from the islands, which signals 'people to doom / With semaphore ultimatums tick by tick'.[77] On the islands, 'There is still peace', to which MacNeice immediately adds the caveat, 'though not for me and not / Perhaps for long'.[78] MacNeice constructs here an elaborate depiction of the dependence of the islands upon the mainland, and vice versa: the 'peace', neighbourliness, and traditionalism of the islands belong to a figurative system in which they are meaningful only in relation to the 'tyranny' of modernity, only, that is, in relation to the very metropolitan norms to which they appear to contrast. It is impossible, in other words, to see them outside of that system of representation in which island life is constantly exoticized as peaceful,

72 MacNeice, 'The Hebrides', *Collected Poems*, 64–6.
73 Ibid.
74 Cunningham, *British Writers of the Thirties*, 358.
75 MacNeice, 'The Hebrides', *Collected Poems*, 65.
76 Ibid., 66.
77 Ibid.
78 Ibid.

harmonious, and frugal. And yet, encoded into those representations of island life are the lingering ideals of knowable, human communities, in which each death is a communal death, and each life a noble bearing of communal values.

MacNeice's poem might be read as a lament for the perhaps inevitable passing of this way of life, but the poem is at the same time a hymn to a possible future, a mapping of the forms of communal life which in Raymond Williams's terms are now residual, but which might become emergent.[79] Thus, MacNeice's imaginative preoccupation with the islands of the north-east Atlantic archipelago, critical and sceptical always, nevertheless finds in them not the dying remnants of a primitive life beyond modernity, but instead models of how such thoroughly modern, globally connected, and penetrated spaces still manage to maintain, even if only for some time, forms of communal living strange to, and estranging of, metropolitan society. This explains the artful oscillation in MacNeice's island writings between intimacy and disavowal, proximity and distance, sincerity and irony, for ultimately it is only by preserving the strangeness of islands, their constant ambivalence as figures of totality and eccentricity, that MacNeice understands their usefulness as models of survival and re-inhabitation, beacons by which one might, like the migrating birds following their 'felt routes', eventually 'come to one's home'.

[79] Raymond Williams, *Marxism and Literature* (Oxford: Oxford University Press, 1977), 122–3.

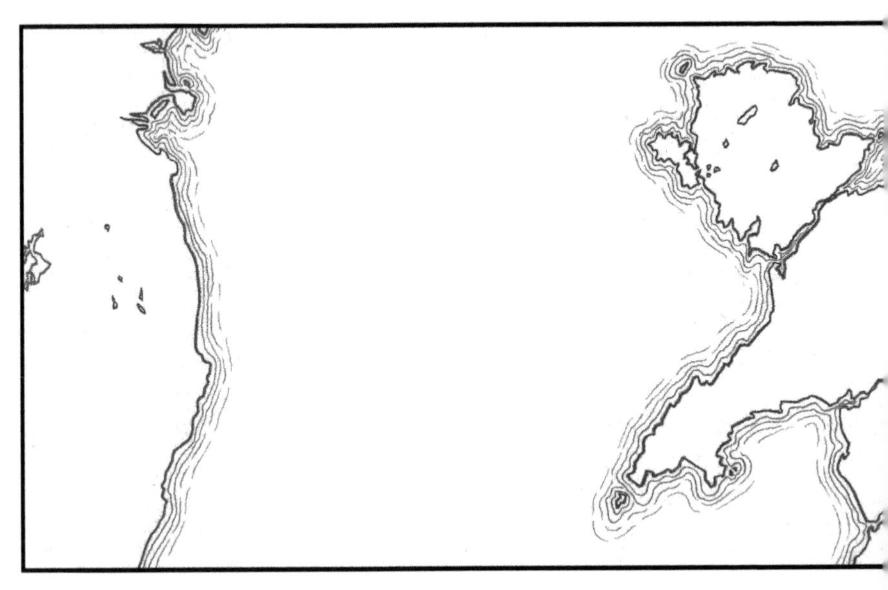

7

The Riddle of the Sands

Erskine Childers Between the Tides

Daniel Brayton

The beauty of the seacoast often clouds the mind. It is a commonplace for tourists—and some scholars—to emote about seacoasts and seascapes as 'timeless' features of the planet and of human experience. To do so is not only to indulge in the most hackneyed of postcard platitudes, it is also to perpetuate a destructive mythology of the ocean's essentially ahistorical nature.[1] Not only are the chemical, biotic, and physical dimensions of seacoasts (and of the global ocean) constantly changing by means of human activity as well as natural processes, but the physical contours of seacoasts themselves are dynamic and their edge effects unstable.[2] We might choose instead to pursue a nuanced understanding by which the historicity and dynamism of the marine environment—its biogeochemical complexity and myriad cultural meanings—constitute intriguing conceptual challenges that resist easy categorizations. The seacoast, as distinct from the open sea, has proven particularly elusive to those wishing to define, chart, or imagine it as a physically or semantically static entity. Christoph Singer's claim that 'the shore is transformation spatialized' seems particularly apt, for the seacoast is both an ever-shifting biophysical reality and a culturally dynamic zone of meaning; the coast is a transformative zone where language, culture, politics, and the imagination meet to become constitutive dimensions of a physical geography that is distinctive and difficult to define.[3]

[1] As I have argued elsewhere, the mythology of the inexhaustible ocean has deep roots in Western culture and enormous consequences. See Dan Brayton, *Shakespeare's Ocean: An Ecocritical Exploration* (Charlottesville: University of Virginia Press, 2012). See also W. Jeffrey Bolster, *The Mortal Sea* (Cambridge: Belknap Press, 2013); and Callum Roberts, *The Unnatural History of the Sea* (Washington, DC: Island Press, 2007).

[2] Barry Cunliffe, *Facing the Ocean: The Atlantic and Its Peoples, 8000 BC–AD 1500* (Oxford: Oxford University Press, 2001), 1.

[3] Christoph Singer, *Sea Change: The Shore from Shakespeare to Banville* (Amsterdam: Brill Academic Publishers, 2014), 11.

In his study of the cultural history of the New England seacoast, the landscape historian John R. Stilgoe argues that 'for all that tourists and tourist-trappers wax eloquent about the timelessness of the sea, the seacoast itself is deeply historic', the product of a cultural history inscribed on 'postcards, travel posters, and advertising', as well as on nautical charts, literary texts, and landscape paintings. 'Once historians abandon it to ecologists, conchologists, and other scientists', Stilgoe continues, 'or dismiss it as a summertime playground, a child's place, a realm to be visited during nonthinking vacations, the seacoast floats in the national imagination as timeless as the sea, but somehow quaint and weather-beaten, too'.[4] Stilgoe's focus is the New England coast, but his point has broader relevance. The task of mapping the cultural significance of the coastal zone is a hermeneutic endeavour that necessitates a cultural excavation just as much as an historical one. It is just such an excavation that Alain Corbin provides in his study *Territoire du vide: L'Occident et le desir du rivage, 1750–1840*; translated literally, 'Territory (land) of the void: The West and the desire for the shore, 1750–1840', a title that contains a conspicuous irony which gestures to his argument.[5] Corbin's topic is not the sea, but the seacoast (*rivage*). The early modern European seashore, according to Corbin, underwent a several-centuries-long cultural transformation from signifying the 'repulsive' edge of oceanic chaos to what I have elsewhere characterized as 'a source of fascination that eventually leads to a vogue of seaside vacationing, bathing, early beach culture, and marine art'.[6] The shore transforms from void to aesthetic plenitude.

Writers and mariners of various stripes have been drawn to the representational challenge of describing seacoasts and their own solitary adventures on them at least since the dawn of the eighteenth century, when William Dampier published his *New Voyage Round the World*, and, soon thereafter, Defoe penned *Robinson Crusoe* and *Captain Singleton*.[7] But it is not until the middle of the nineteenth century that we can locate the emergence of narratives of coastal navigation written in English. As Jonathan Raban argues, the 'notion of taking a boat and grandly coming to terms with one's native land is one that regularly presents itself to a certain dubious breed of Englishman'.[8] The Victorian-Edwardian vogue for solitary small-boat voyaging—and vogue it most certainly was—generated

[4] John R. Stilgoe, *Alongshore* (New Haven and London: Yale University Press, 1994), ix.

[5] The title of Jocelyn Phelps's translation, *The Lure of the Sea: The Discovery of the Seaside in the Western World, 1750–1840*, fails to capture the ironic richness of the original.

[6] Brayton, *Shakespeare's Ocean*, 56.

[7] See Margaret Cohen, *The Novel and the Sea* (Princeton: Princeton University Press, 2009), 1–14, 60–88.

[8] Jonathan Raban, *Coasting: A Private Voyage* (New York: Simon and Schuster, 1987), 26.

a literary tradition to which sailor-authors have contributed ever since. Raban traces a literary genealogy of Victorian coastal adventurers back to John Macgregor's bestselling 1867 narrative *The Voyage Alone in the Yawl 'Rob Roy'*. Next in this lineage came Empson Edward Middleton, whom Raban characterizes as a disgruntled ex-Indian Army officer. Inspired by reading Macgregor in 1868, Middleton had a slightly larger version of the *Rob Roy* built and took her sailing, resulting in his book *The Cruise of the Kate*.[9] Next came R. T. McMullen, whose *Down Channel* is considered a classic of the genre and still widely read. Raban then traces this literary line to Hilaire Belloc (Raban describes him as a fascist sympathizer), who published *The Cruise of the Nona* in 1925, emphasizing the reactionary ideological commitments of the authors in this corpus.[10] 'These lonely saltwater romances', Raban opines,

> are all products of suburbia and the city; they are postindustrial dreams at heart, as urban in their own way as the glass-and-steel romances of St. Pancras Station and the Crystal Palace. In part, at least, they belong to the literature of national pathology. They express the simple claustrophobia of living in a country that has suddenly grown too small, too smoky, too intimate, too man-made and civilized for comfort.[11]

Yet this is hardly all that these narratives do; expressing claustrophobia in tales of their own small-boat exploits is a reductive approach that requires Raban to cull the corpus to a barebones handful of books. By characterizing the literature of small-boat navigation as the written record of a set of failed imperialists, muscular Christians, crypto-fascists, and other dubious Englishmen, Raban fails to mention the many writer-mariners whose views did not conform to Raban's notion of coastal voyaging as a refuge for disgruntled ideological reactionaries. A more complete genealogy would include the writings of E. F. Knight, such as *The Cruise of the Alerte*, and those of Alain Gerbault, such as *The Fight of the Fire-Crest*, and other books that have been published in the various iterations of a literary canon that achieved material fruition in the form of The Mariners Library.[12]

Many of the authors who contributed to the literary corpus of coastwise navigation were not even Englishmen. From the opposite side of the North Atlantic came equally gripping and influential narratives of small-boat voyages, some of them written even earlier than Macgregor's

[9] Ibid., 29. [10] Ibid., 26–43. [11] Ibid., 41.

[12] I refer to the series of nautical books published by Rupert Hart-Davis between 1948 and 1963. The corpus of literary works to which I refer here, which I have characterized as a 'genealogy', 'canon', and 'tradition' of narratives of coastal navigation in small boats, itself constitutes a subset of this series. Not all the books I describe (e.g. *Carter's Coast of New England*) are included in this series.

'*Rob Roy*' narrative, including Robert Carter's delightful coastal travelogue-cum-natural history essay *A Summer Cruise on the New England Coast*, published in 1864 as dispatches in the *New York Tribune* and later in book form by a little-known journalist and editor named Robert Carter. Carter's account of a four-week cruise of coastal New England undertaken in the summer of 1858 is now generally known as *Carter's Coast of New England*.[13] Composed of equal parts travel narrative of antebellum coastal New England, natural history essay, and piscatory eclogue in prose, it predates Macgregor's *Voyage Alone* by several years and differs markedly in its wry, slightly comedic tone. Another American 'classic' of coastal navigation is Henry Plummer's *The Boy, Me, and the Cat*, which recounts the author's voyage from Massachusetts to Florida and back with his son aboard their twenty-four-foot catboat in 1912–13. The list goes on, with literary gems abounding.

All of the above titles belong to the category of non-fiction, but some nautical fiction from the period squarely belongs in the coastal mariner's canon. Foremost among these are Conrad's nautical fictions, such as *Heart of Darkness*, with its frame narrative set in the Thames Estuary, and 'The Secret Sharer', another conspicuously coastal tale, and such novels as *The Shadow Line* and *The Rover*, with their detailed descriptions of coastal navigation and seamanship. We can trace a literary genealogy of sea fiction, following Thomas Philbrick, to James Fenimore Cooper, and Captain Marryat, or we can follow Margaret Cohen further back in history to the writings of Dampier and Defoe.[14] But the burgeoning Victorian-Edwardian corpus of nautical narratives is also the product of a particular historical conjuncture; it is a canon that attests to the enormous significance of the global ocean in the empire-building of the United Kingdom and, to a lesser extent (at the time), the United States. This corpus can be seen as a symptom of a growing tension between the imperial nation-state and the liberal subject whose ability to circulate on the coastal margins engendered new perspectives and affinities. The historian John Darwin has argued that the British Empire was 'unfinished', by which he means it was a loosely woven fabric of ports and cantonments rather than a more traditional empire consisting of a vast coextensive territory (such as that of the Mongols or Alexander the Great):

> After 1860, nearly half the British army was stationed in British cantonments, many miles and days from the nearest seaport. Much of the empire,

[13] An edition of *Carter's Coast of New England*, revised and introduced by Daniel Ford, was published by the now-defunct New Hampshire Publishing Company in 1969.

[14] See Thomas Philbrick, *James Fenimore Cooper and the Development of American Sea Fiction* (Cambridge, MA: Harvard University Press, 1961); and Cohen, *The Novel and the Sea*.

> with the exception of India and Canada, resembled a vast archipelago strewn round the world from Hong Kong to the Falkland Islands. 'The British empire is, for the purpose of a war with any Power except Russia and the United States, equivalent to a number of islands scattered over the oceans', remarked a Late Victorian expert.[15]

Inland cantonments formed the nodal points of a dispersed and heterogeneous aggregation of possessions, dominions, monopolies, and territories that would come to be known as the British Empire, the most important nodes of which were the seaports themselves. From Queenstown (modern Cobh) to Cape Town, deepwater harbours were the basis for the British domination of oceanic space. During the later years of empire, Britons became particularly aware of the nautical nature of their global possessions. Nautical narratives reflect a growing awareness of the potential for individual subjects to circulate within interstices of this world system—along coastlines and shipping lanes, between islands, and across bays, sounds, and straits. Indeed, Conrad's career as a merchant mariner transpired mainly in such spaces; his literary career is one long meditation on his experiences there.

Rivalling Conrad's nautical fiction for sheer narrative vividness and technical accuracy is a fictional one-off, Erskine Childers's 1903 nautical spy thriller *The Riddle of the Sands: A Record of Secret Service*.[16] Childers has been described as 'one of the brightest and most glittering [minds] of his generation'.[17] In some respects, his biography resembles the spy thriller for which he is best known. The son of an English father and an Anglo-Irish mother, Childers attended Haileybury College and then Trinity College, Cambridge, where he joined the debating society and pursued rugby and rowing. He became a fervent sailor only after a lower back injury ended his rugby and rowing careers, mastering his seamanship on small boats in the thin waters of the Thames Estuary, Wicklow Harbor, and the Frisian Islands of Germany. Childers haunts modern British and Irish history as a ghost of several guises—as a popular novelist who penned the novel many consider to be the first modern spy thriller; as a military strategist who employed fiction to sway early twentieth-century British public opinion about a possible German invasion by sea; as a veteran soldier whose experience in the Boer War led him to write a telling and controversial critique of the disastrous cavalry tactics

[15] John Darwin, *Unfinished Empire: The Global Expansion of Britain* (New York: Penguin, 2012), 306.

[16] Born Robert Erskine Childers, he is conventionally referred to by dropping the first name.

[17] John O'Beirne Ranelagh, *A Short History of Ireland*, 2nd edn (Cambridge: Cambridge University Press, 1994), 172.

employed in that ill-conceived war; as an intelligence agent who worked with Churchill to plan a possible invasion of Germany plotted on the reciprocal course to the one he imagined in his spy thriller; for a brief time as a Liberal candidate for Parliament; and, finally, tragically, as a political dissident whose passionate espousal of the cause of Irish Home Rule led to his execution by a Free State firing squad in 1922.

Childers wrote several widely read books on diverse topics, but *The Riddle of the Sands* was his only novel. His other writings are telling: his *German Influence on British Cavalry* was a critique of the ineffective cavalry tactics employed in the Boer War, while his 1911 political road map for dominion status for Ireland, *The Framework of Home Rule*, argued for the economic advantages of a semi-autonomous Ireland, with its own Parliament but as a dominion of Britain.[18] Between 1911 and his death in 1922, Childers was increasingly drawn to the cause of Irish independence, however, and by the outbreak of full-scale military hostilities between 1916 and 1922, he would become a member of Sinn Fein and a prominent public figure. The most telling chapter of Childers's biography, for my purposes, and the focus of this chapter, centres upon a fateful sailing voyage undertaken at the start of the First World War. In the summer of 1914, Childers and his friend Sir Roger Casement purchased Mauser rifles and ammunition in Germany and Belgium, which they then smuggled to the Irish Volunteers, off-loading in Howth, near Dublin, and Kilcoole, County Wicklow.[19] Childers's attraction to the Irish cause was met by suspicion and hostility among his peers. Both Childers and Casement were avid amateur sailors as well as compelling propagandists who realized that running guns to the Irish coast was both a tactical manoeuvre and a symbolic one. Childers sailed with 900 rifles and 29,000 rounds of ammunition stowed aboard his sailing yacht *Asgard*, landing this peculiar freight on 26 July 1914.[20] The remaining weapons and ammunition were similarly transported aboard the *Kelpie*, a sailboat owned by Childers's friend Edward Conor Marshall O'Brien, another serious amateur mariner.[21]

[18] Childers informs the reader directly, 'My purpose in this volume is to advocate a definite scheme of self-government for Ireland' (Erskine Childers, *The Framework of Home Rule* (London: E. Arnold, 1911), 1).

[19] After the failure of the 1916 uprising, Casement was arrested, charged, tried, and hanged for high treason.

[20] Since 2012 ,the National Museum of Ireland has housed an exhibition entitled '*Asgard*: The 1914 Howth gun running vessel conserved at The National Museum of Ireland, Collins Barracks in Dublin', showcasing the Childers' yacht.

[21] O'Brien would later become a nautical author of note with the publication of *Across Three Oceans* (London: E. Arnold, 1926).

The Howth gunrunning was a peculiar historical episode. Wooden sailing yachts generally make poor instruments of war, yet they possess an unusual potential for stealth. The largest sailing vessel Childers ever owned, *Asgard* was a fifty-one-foot gaff yawl of twenty-eight tons burden designed and built by the celebrated Scots-Norwegian naval architect Colin Archer and paid for by Childers's American father-in-law. Childers and his wife Molly (née Osborne) shared a passion for yachting and, in time, a fervour for the cause of Irish independence. Molly was an equal partner in their sailing adventures, having supported Irish independence for years, and played a key role in the gunrunning. An American citizen who grew up on Boston's Beacon Hill, Molly came from a city noteworthy for its longstanding support for the idea of a free Ireland. Hampered from an early age by a debilitating physical condition, she was nevertheless a capable sailor. The Mausers delivered to Howth would be used in the Easter Uprising of 1916, and in the tumultuous years of civil war that followed, Childers would become, as the historian John O'Beirne Ranelagh notes, 'the principal propagandist of the Irish republican cause'.[22] When in 1922 the independence struggle in Ireland intensified into civil war, with ambushes and executions taking place, carrying an unlicensed firearm was made a capital offence. At this moment of peaking violence and suspicion, Childers was captured by the forces of the Irish Free State at his home in Wicklow and charged with carrying a semi-automatic pistol of Spanish manufacture. The circumstances could not have been more opportune for Childers's adversaries, who considered him a dangerous propagandist; they seized their moment. With his appeal pending, Childers was executed by firing squad on 24 November 1922. His last words, spoken to the firing squad about to end his life, were 'Take a step forward, lads. It will be easier that way'.[23] Earlier, he had asked his eldest son, Erskine Hamilton Childers (1905–74), who would later become the fourth president of the Republic of Ireland, to forgive the men responsible for his capture and execution. Today, the newly restored *Asgard* sits 'on the hard' as a permanent exhibit at the National Museum of Ireland at Collins Barracks, a wooden testimonial to the two passions that consumed and would come to define its owner: coastal navigation and the cause of Ireland.

[22] Ranelagh, *A Short History of Ireland*, 206.
[23] Andrew Boyle, *The Riddle of Erskine Childers* (London: Hutchinson, 1977), 72.

Revered in Ireland for his role in supporting Irish independence as well as by generations of readers who consider *The Riddle of the Sands* a masterpiece of nautical literature, Childers left a legacy of riddles pertaining to national affiliation.[24] How could such dyed-in-the-wool Englishmen as Childers and Casement, who dedicated the first part of their adult lives to the cause of national security, and in Childers's case, contributed major works of fiction and non-fiction to the topic, become martyrs to the Fenian cause? I submit that Childers's conflicted affiliations are profoundly linked to his passion for coastal navigation and can be decoded in the text of *The Riddle of the Sands*. Childers's thriller is an inquiry into the indeterminacy of coastlines, those zones of transformation where empire and nation meet. In *The Riddle of the Sands*, Childers reimagined the relationship between the individual and the late imperial nation-state. His fictional exploration of the geophysical interface of the seacoast developed his talent for reimagining national affiliation. Childers understood the seacoast as a geocultural ecotone rich with latent significance and immanent with political potential. Life imitates art, as another Irishman once pointed out, and it does so in ways frequently overlooked by those who imagine landscapes, seascapes, and national identities as fixed and timeless categories.

In his introduction to the Dover edition of *The Riddle of the Sands*, Norman Donaldson argues that, far from being a traitor to his country, Childers was a lifelong patriot:

> patriotism—though he seldom employed the word—was the key to the author's life. Loyalty to England was the mainspring to this, his only work of fiction; devotion to his mother's land led to his death.[25]

If both of these claims are true, then Childers's national-political affiliation was intimately but obscurely connected to his imaginative narrative of exploring the shifting coastline of the Frisian Islands, his betwixt-and-between dedication to Britain and to Ireland eerily foreshadowed by his fictional narrative of patriotic adventure. In his thrilling tale of nautical adventure along the multiple estuaries of the Frisian coast, Childers adopts a marginal point of view and in so doing, suggests that coastwise navigation is at least partially a hermeneutic activity. Exploring the ever-changing intertidal zones of estuaries and sandy islands affords his two protagonists, Davies and Carruthers, privileged visual and cognitive access to the shore,

[24] The biographies by Boyle and McInerney both bear the almost inevitable title of *The Riddle of Erskine Childers*.

[25] Norman Donaldson, 'Introduction', in Erskine Childers, *The Riddle of the Sands: A Record of Secret Service*, ed. Norman Donaldson (Mineola, NY: Dover, 1976).

allowing them to perceive in the physical features of the seacoast and the human activities there plots and purposes that might otherwise remain hidden, naturalized by the quotidian terrestrial order of things. This reframing proved to be compelling, for *The Riddle of the Sands* was widely understood as a warning about the potential for German aggression at sea; in the longer term, it also suggests aesthetic innovation.

Childers develops the notion of coastal indeterminacy—of the shifting sands at the edge of the sea and their eponymous riddle—as a figure for an intellectual and physical freedom that transcends, or transgresses, the conventional boundaries of national identity in *The Riddle of the Sands*. And this in turn relates to the imperial experience as seaborne—John Darwin's recent histories of the British Empire provide excellent context for Childers's passion, as coastal navigation gleaned for him dangerous insights into the factitious nature of the nation-state. Perhaps this transformation from fervent nationalist and apologist for empire to passionate advocate for Irish Home Rule took place in part because Childers discovered in coastal navigation—Wicklow Harbour, the Thames Estuary, and the Frisian Islands—a critical vantage point from which to assess the workings of geopolitical forces made evident at the seacoast boundaries of nation-states. This critical perspective can be understood as an edge effect of coastal navigation, for it was by grappling with the conceptual uncertainties of seacoasts and their relationship to national politics that Childers contributed to world fiction and to world history. In *The Riddle of the Sands*, Childers explored the relationship between free individuals navigating in dangerous coastal waters and the integrity of the modern nation-state, not only as a geopolitical entity, but as an 'imagined community', to use Benedict Anderson's resonant phrase, subject to refiguration by those very individuals.[26] This reimagining, in the form of nautical adventure tale-cum-spy thriller, garnered Childers renown as a writer and political commentator as a relatively young man. His later, more active contribution to rethinking the contours of modern nation-states, in this case the United Kingdom, on the one hand, and the nascent independent Ireland, on the other, would eventually prove fatal.

Published during the build-up to the First World War, a time of mounting geopolitical tension with Kaiser Wilhelm's Germany that produced nationalistic literature demonizing the opponent in Britain and Germany, *The Riddle of the Sands* tells the story of two young Englishmen sailing a small sailboat—a converted lifeboat—called the *Dulcibella*. At a loss for what to do in London as the summer holiday drags on from

[26] Benedict Anderson, *Imagined Communities: Reflections on the Origin and Spread of Nationalism* (London: Verso, 2006).

August into September, Carruthers, a London civil servant and every bit the Edwardian gentleman, unexpectedly receives a letter from his old Oxford chum Davies inviting him to do a bit of yachting and duck-hunting in the East Frisian islands. Having declined other invitations to vacation in the country, and uninterested in the holiday haunts available to him in London, Carruthers complies with Davies's request to come along and bring, of all things, a prismatic compass and sundry other nautical gear with him, deciding on a whim that some fresh air and yachting might be just the thing. He only consents to go in the first place because he is at the end of his tether, desperate to get out of London, and imagines himself on the deck of an expensive yacht. Carruthers, the stiff, class-conscious, proper English gentleman, derives from Childers's own experiences as a clerk for the House of Commons.[27]

But if Carruthers, whom Trotter aptly describes as 'the sardonic, self-pitying, impressionable civil servant', resembles his creator in certain respects, the quiet, plain-spoken, enigmatic, yet unpretentious Davies, with his extraordinary seamanship skills and a passion for sailing, adventure, and ferreting out the truth behind appearances, more squarely resembles the author, as a brief look at his biography suggests.[28] Childers's first sailing yacht was a converted lifeboat named the *Vixen*, which he cruised extensively in shoal waters. This was the model for Davies's *Dulcibella*. Yet by choosing Carruthers, not Davies, to tell their tale and to develop as a complex narrative persona, Childers borrows a narrative trick from Herman Melville. Just as Melville's narrators are occasionally Vaudevillian figures of fun whose fears and prejudices generate tension and relief, so Carruthers plays the part of the prim English gentleman, a patriotic civil servant who begins as a callow prig and evolves into a more complex and sympathetic man of action and principle. It is a clever narrative gambit, for as Carruthers gets caught up in Davies's adventure, he becomes increasingly compelling as a narrator, his Britishness modulating from stiffness to pluckiness and his opinions from classist bigotry to unfeigned curiosity and engagement with something much larger than himself. Carruthers recounts his adventures with a kind of prissy contempt for Davies's 'yacht' modulating into growing interest, fascination, and eventually passionate dedication to unravelling the mystery upon which Davies has stumbled. For the two discover, in the sandy barrier islands at the estuaries of the Ems, Jade, Weser, and Elbe rivers, a carefully guarded secret of international significance.

[27] As David Trotter notes in his Introduction to the Oxford World's Classics edition of *The Riddle of the Sands: A Record of Secret Service* (Oxford: Oxford University Press, 1996), 1.

[28] Trotter, 'Introduction', 3.

By the standards of modern spy thrillers, *The Riddle of the Sands* is slow to get going, its descriptive, occasionally droll descriptions of the two characters' awkward interactions constantly alluding to the comedic brilliance of Jerome K. Jerome's estuarine Victorian boating classic *Three Men in a Boat*, written just fourteen years earlier. Childers gestures to Jerome's popular book in his amusing descriptions of the awkwardness between Davies and Carruthers on the latter's initial embarkation. Himself a veteran sailor of the Thames Estuary, Childers clearly took pleasure in characterizing Carruthers as a foppish prig who provides the butt of slapstick physical gags—the dripping deck that makes him uncomfortable in his bunk, the lack of space on Davies's little 'yacht' which requires the two men to move about like unwilling contortionists, and the endless mud, sullying Carruthers's visions of yachting as a leisure activity along with his clothes. While Davies's beloved Frisian coast initially resembles the Essex marshes, the educated banter of the two Oxford-educated gents is increasingly peppered with German phrases that complicate the Jerome-like humour by adding a dimension of alterity in the suggestion of linguistic indeterminacy. Why, we wonder, does Carruthers speak fluent German? Could he have a second government job as a spy? There is a mix of the estuarine and the coastal in these early scenes, heightened by landscape and seascape descriptions that emphasize the fungible boundaries of nation-states; these inevitably put the reader in mind of Conrad's opening descriptions in *Heart of Darkness*. Like the cruising yawl *Nellie* coming to rest in a Thames Estuary that creates in Marlow the impression of a primeval coastal wilderness from long ago, the *Dulcibella* in *The Riddle of the Sands* seems to float on the unsettled waters of an enigmatic shore pregnant with encrypted meaning.

Nothing prepares Carruthers for the vicissitudes of his yachting adventure on the muddy, low-lying coast of East Friesland. Arriving in an out-of-the way region with thoughts of his friends shooting in the country at an aristocratic estate and dressed for an elegant outing, Carruthers is confronted by his eccentric old schoolmate living aboard a tiny converted lifeboat, neither of them in any way conforming to Edwardian standards of yachting. Davies is not even dressed for the occasion: 'no cool white ducks or neat blue serge; and where was the snowy crowned yachting cap, that precious charm that so easily converts a landsman into a dashing mariner?'[29] Indeed, Davies has no interest in varnish or polished brass but is instead a rather down-at-heels if practical small-boat mariner. Just as he neglects the niceties of high-society yachting, so too does his frumpy little

[29] Childers, *The Riddle of the Sands*, 9.

boat, which is not an elegant, graceful swan designed by a Fife or Nicholson. As the self-pitying Carruthers notices upon surveying the odd little craft,

> What brass there was, on the tiller-head and elsewhere, was tarnished with sickly green. The decks had none of that creamy purity which Cowes expects, but were rough and grey, and showed tarry exhalations around the seams and rusty stains near the bows.[30]

With no standing head room and no Pimms, there was at least tinned tongue aboard. But the shock of discovering just how different Davies's notion of yachting is from his own nearly drives Carruthers back to London. More disquieting still is his growing sense that Davies harbours a secret and intends to hunt something else besides ducks. What Davies has stumbled upon before Carruthers's arrival on that low-lying coast, in addition to the shifting sands and sudden fogs endemic to the region, turns out to be a military plot of global significance. The Kaiser has been secretly plotting an invasion of England, amassing his invading fleet in the shifting sands and intricate coastal inlets and sluices of the East Frisian Islands, and, suspecting there is more to discover in the ever-shifting sands of that low-lying seacoast, the two men take it upon themselves to look into this plot and thwart it if they can. As Trotter notes, 'when Davies finally discloses that what he really has in mind is not a spot of duck-shooting but a spot of military reconnaissance, Carruthers finds it very hard to imagine his impetuous, disheveled companion as a master-spy'; yet the latter is hooked on the adventure nonetheless.[31]

Childers's nautical expertise is very much in evidence throughout the narrative, particularly in the vivid descriptions of Davies's feats of navigation in fog and 'thin waters'. Throughout the narrative, Childers develops the notion of coastal indeterminacy as a figure for the boundaries and frictions that separate and connect competing nation-states, those imagined communities that would eventually kill him, and the enigmas of unclear identities. 'Now what sort of coast is it?' Davies asks his shipmate at one point, answering his own question musingly, 'even on this small map you can see at once, all those wavy lines, shoals, and sand everywhere, blocking nine-tenths of the land altogether, and doing their best to block the other tenth where the great rivers run in'.[32] As the plot develops, a four-way relationship quickly develops between Davies, Carruthers, their adversary, the villain Dollmann, and Dollmann's daughter Clara, which foreshadows the themes of patriotism, treachery, passionate espousal of a cause, and

30 Ibid., 17. 31 Trotter, 'Introduction', 5.
32 Childers, *The Riddle of the Sands*, 58.

military invasion by sea that would become so fateful in the author's later years.

Dollmann owns a sailing vessel called the *Medusa*, and the reader learns, along with Carruthers, who listens as Davies tells of a narrow escape in rough weather and shallow water near the mouth of the Elbe, that all is not as it appears with this portentously named galliot and her elusive owner. The fact that Dollmann sails a North Sea galliot, a traditional shallow-draft sailing vessel, much larger than *Dulcibella*, used to transport cargo in the shallow waters of the North Sea's eastern coast, suggests that he is native to the region. His intimate knowledge of the local waters—a seacoast where local knowledge is particularly valuable due to the shifting sands and shallow channels—becomes a weapon when, under the guise of amicable nautical assistance, 'Herr' Dollmann attempts to mislead Davies to harbour through a shortcut and in so doing, nearly leads the Englishman and his little boat to perdition. In stormy weather on the Frisian coast, Dollmann, who appears to speak no English when Davies first encounters him (before Carruthers enters the story), shouts from the deck of the *Medusa* to a beleaguered Davies, aboard the tiny *Dulcibella*, 'Verstehen Sie? Short-cut through sands; follow me!' As Davies later notes to the astonished Carruthers, 'the last two sentences in downright English'.[33] Dollmann leads the way to a channel that amounts to a dead end amid the shoals, where Davies and his little vessel only survive by dint of luck and pluck, narrowly bumping over a sandbank to safety. Davies's misadventure in the sands transpires before the arrival of Carruthers: we learn of it when Davies finally divulges to his friend the true purpose of his invitation to come sailing. For Carruthers's fluent German, political interests, and connections make him particularly useful to his friend. In surviving the grounding, Davies injures his hand; when he later evades Carruthers's question about the injury with a vague brush-off, Carruthers and the reader begin to suspect that something is amiss.

Gradually, Carruthers gets caught up in the adventure, and the two young Englishmen spend the rest of their 'holiday', and the novel, energetically and with an increasing sense of urgency, ferreting out the reason for Dollmann's attempt to mislead and murder Davies. In this task, they undergo a series of sandy coastal adventures with some superb descriptions of coastal small-boat handling:

> When I last saw the *Medusa* she seemed to be charging it like a horse at a fence, and I took a rough bearing of her position by a hurried glance at the compass. At that very moment I thought she seemed to luff and show some

[33] Ibid., 55.

of her broadside; but a squall blotted her out and gave me hell with the tiller. After that she was lost in the white mist that hung over the line of breakers. I kept on my bearing as well as I could, but I was already out of the channel. By the look of the water, and as we neared the bank I saw it was all awash and without the vestige of an opening. I wasn't going to chuck her on to it without an effort; so, more by instinct that with any particular hope, I put the helm down, meaning to work her along the edge on the chance of spotting a way over. She was buried at once by the beam sea, and the jib flew to blazes; but the reefed stays'l stood, she recovered gamely, and I held on, though I knew it could only be for a few minutes, as the centre-plate was up, and she made frightful leeway towards the bank.[34]

Striking about the description is its technical specificity. Childers describes *Dulcibella* with pinpoint accuracy behaving as a small sailboat in shoal waters in a heavy onshore breeze, with nowhere to go but aground, will do. As this passage attests, Davies is a skilled boat-handler with an acute awareness of the challenges of sailing in unfamiliar shoal waters; so, too, was its author, whose detailed account of the seacoast and small-boat handling attest to Childers's minute attention to the particular challenges of small-boat handling on a shallow coast.

In the voice of Carruthers, the author is able to voice his love for the Frisian seacoast while also hurling his characters into an accelerating plotline of geopolitical intrigue. The Frisian coast vexes any simple notion of national boundaries: West Friesland belongs (and belonged) to the Netherlands, East Friesland to Germany, while Heligoland, the shore that stretches north to Schleswig-Holstein and Denmark, had been a battleground not long before Childers ventured there in the 1890s and remained a key strategic port held by the United Kingdom from 1814 to 1890, when Germany took possession.[35] The tension builds from the moment Carruthers arrives in Germany, the coastal landscape itself becoming a kind of antagonist. In a passage of resonant poetic prose, Carruthers describes the seemingly bleak landscape of the region in a narrative cartography. With the *Dulcibella* aground at low water, Carruthers finds the seacoast bleak, alluring, and vaguely threatening:

For miles in every direction lay a desert of sand. To the north it touched the horizon, and was only broken by the blue dot of Neuerk Island and its lighthouse. To the east it seemed also to stretch to infinity, but the smoke of

[34] Ibid., 49–50.

[35] Denmark ceded Heligoland to Great Britain in 1914. The war between Denmark and Germany over the northern portion of this coast is a major feature of the Danish author Carsten Jensen's 2008 novel *We, the Drowned*, trans. Charlotte Barslund, with Emma Ryder (New York: Houghton Mifflin Harcourt, 2010).

> a steamer showed where it was pierced by the stream of the Elbe. To the south it ran up to the pencil-line of the Hanover shore. Only to the west was its outline broken by any vestiges of the sea it had risen from. There it was astir with crawling white filaments, knotted confusedly at one point in the north-west, whence came a sibilant murmur as of the hissing of many snakes.[36]

The assonance and alliteration of this passage are palpable, poetically capturing the combination of captivation and bleakness that Carruthers perceives in the Frisian seacoast. While Carruthers learns the rudiments of sailing and coastal seamanship, Davies devotes himself to figuring out the coastal dynamics of tides, currents, and channels, as well as to divining the jealously guarded secret of the region that he has detected in the cagey behaviour of local officials and mariners. Their voyage proceeds as a deepening involvement in a kind of nautical masquerade, the two sailors feigning to hunt ducks while actually sleuthing out the eponymous riddle.

The narrative pace accelerates as the plot develops. From its slow start in London to its growing intrigue on the other side of the North Sea, the narrative modulates from sea story to spy thriller, with Davies and Carruthers feverishly playing the roles of an aquatic Watson and Holmes. Davies, with his nautical expertise and palpably bottled-up subjectivity, resembles a somewhat bumbling aquatic Holmes, while Carruthers, as the more staid sidekick whose background defines him, plays Watson. Together they eventually expose Dollmann as an English spy working for the Kaiser. He is not 'Herr' Dollmann at all, but an Englishman and 'a traitor in the German service'.[37] When Davies and Carruthers confront him with proof of their suspicions, Dollmann initially pretends to be a double agent working for the British government. The two young sleuths call his bluff, presenting evidence to the contrary as gathered by Carruthers in a brilliant clandestine mission in the preceding pages, and Dollmann takes his own life by slipping over the side of the yacht. His daughter, now aware of her father's treachery and in love with Davies, returns to Britain with her newfound love, a distinctly problematic union. For Clara Dollmann is the daughter of a traitor and would-be murderer, a desperate man in his element near the shifting sands of Friesland. There is something unsettling in this too-neat conclusion, and the reader is left wondering whether Carruthers, the consummate civil servant, will get all the credit for foiling the Kaiser's invasion plans while Davies sails off with his new love to parts unknown. The novel's suspense derives, like that of Buchan's *The Thirty-Nine Steps*, from the parallels between two plot trajectories, one literal and one conceptual: just as the protagonist

[36] Childers, *The Riddle of the Sands*, 79–80. [37] Ibid., 218.

(or protagonists) becomes obsessed with uncovering a hidden secret by decoding a series of cryptic clues, so too does he discover that he is (or they are) the object of a reciprocal curiosity. The physical game of cat-and-mouse parallels an intellectual game of geopolitical discovery and intrigue. Davies and Carruthers, like Richard Hannay in Buchan's novel, find themselves being pursued by the enemy, whose hidden plot they are in the act of discovering. Their inquiry into Dollmann's secret motives (and his identity) leads them to the gradual discovery of the Kaiser's plot to launch an invasion of Britain from the foggy, out-of-the-way coast of Friesland.

Perhaps the most extraordinary plot device in *The Riddle of the Sands*, in view of the author's subsequent biography and reputation, is the means by which Davies exposes Dollmann as an Englishman working for the Germans. He does so by remembering the author's portrait on the frontispiece of a small book in the library of the *Dulcibella*. This tiny library is stocked, as Carruthers observes, with three types of book: aids to coastal navigation ('pilots'), books 'on naval warfare', and books on 'cruising in small yachts'. Dollmann authored one of the latter, 'a guide for yachtsmen to a certain British estuary', as a younger man. 'Ass that I am not to have seen it before!' exclaims Davies, and points Carruthers to the book's frontispiece, where a younger Dollmann looks back at them.[38] Davies effects this discovery by returning to a shelf containing various classics of the genre, including Knight's *Falcon in the Baltic* and MacMullen's *Down Channel*, pointing out to Carruthers the portrait of the younger Dollmann on a book cover. This moment of discovery leads to the book's catastrophe, when the two younger men confront Dollmann with evidence of his treachery. When this occurs, towards the end of the novel, the reader experiences a momentary jolt of Dollmann's tragedy, for his exposure resonates with Aristotelian elements of tragedy—it is both *anagnorisis* and *peripeteia*, the instant of discovery and the sudden reversal of fortune, for the duplicitous mariner-villain. The reader cannot help but feel pity and fear on his behalf. So *The Riddle of the Sands* enters directly into dialogue with the small-boat narratives that inspired Childers himself. Sailor, author, and creature of the shifting sands, Dollmann becomes by the novel's end yet another alter ego for his author, but a much more troubling one than either Davies or Carruthers. For Dollmann's status as a traitor seems deeply connected to his passion for coastal sailing, while Davies's final voyage aboard Dollmann's vessel, with Dollmann's daughter aboard, suggests more is going on than a mere victory over a literary villain.

[38] Ibid., 138.

The embodiment of ambivalence towards national affiliation, Dollmann is an instance of literary projection on the part of his author. This extraordinary plot device induces a sense of historical foreshadowing in readers aware of Erskine Childers's subsequent biography, for the villainous Dollmann is at once an Englishman, an accomplished coastal mariner and equally accomplished nautical writer, and a creature of political intrigue whose national loyalties are very much in question. In still another eerie parallel with Childers's own last days, Dollmann keeps a gun hidden nearby. In the tense moments following their accusation of Dollmann, Carruthers warns him, 'no, I should let that pistol alone'.[39] The secret possession of a weapon in a time of deep political tension, combined with uncertainty about its owner's political loyalties, was precisely what led to Childers's own execution.

Whether or not the author intended them to do so, Carruthers, Davies, and Dollmann parallel the three phases of Childers's adult life. Hindsight lets us view the young Childers who penned *The Riddle of the Sands* as a man of divided roles, part Davies the pragmatic sailor, part Carruthers the man of politics, and part Dollmann the turncoat mariner with obscure motives. During the last two decades of his life, Childers would transform into a version of his own villain 'Herr' Dollmann, not by means of any overt villainy, but by working for the benefit of a foreign power, along a lightly policed coastline. The parallels between Dollmann and the author run even deeper. While Dollmann sails the *Medusa*, a ketch built along Frisian lines, his creator sailed a foreign craft as well, the *Asgard*, a gaff yawl designed and built by the Norwegian boat designer Colin Archer, who, in another twist of national identity stranger than fiction, was himself a man of two nations. The fictional *Medusa* and the historical (and historic) *Asgard* shared a similar rig (gaff yawl, gaff ketch), a nearly identical size, and other similarities (both, for example, were indigenous to the eastern North Sea). Perhaps the most celebrated boat designer in Norwegian history, Archer garnered fame for his innovative designs that incorporated traditional Norse elements (double-ended hulls of heavy displacement with a distinct tumblehome).[40] Yet Archer himself, the great Norwegian naval architect, was of Scots parentage. Childers, then, inhabited a nautical culture constituted by transcultural elements (sailboats, arms, charts) circulated on the boundaries of nation-states and empires. Like Parnell and Shackleton, Childers was British at the margins, sailing and thinking

[39] Ibid., 219.

[40] Archer's greatest success, the ship *Fram*, was designed for polar exploration and made famous by Fridtjof Nansen and Roald Amundsen in their expeditions to Arctic and Antarctic waters.

along the edges of an empire that was created and maintained as a patchwork of interlinked coastal sites.

Like Davies and Carruthers, Childers could not help poking about in the shallows policed by powerful national-political interests. British imperialism, as much an imaginary entity as a material one, functioned just as long as the territorial integrity of nation-states could be policed. It was John Stuart Mill who noted, in *England and Ireland*, that the root of the political antagonism between the two nations was a failure of imagination. 'The difficulty of governing Ireland', Mill argued, 'lies entirely in our own minds; it is an incapability of understanding'.[41] For expressing this sentiment, Mill was pilloried as a 'thoroughgoing apostle of Communism' and accused by one Lord Bessborough of being 'a Fenian'.[42] Like Mill before him, Childers would be reviled by those for whom patriotism and national identity stood as fixed, trans-historical categories constitutively exclusive of other affiliations. This, too, was a failure of imagination, for Childers's support of Irish independence can also be understood as an expression of patriotic sentiment, a desire, on the part of an Englishman, to rethink his country's colonial governance of a people eager to create their own 'imagined community'. I have suggested that Childers's capacity to reimagine the contours of the United Kingdom derived, in some part, from his expertise as a coastal mariner. For the coastal mariner's point of view is fundamentally liminal and beyond national or territorial affiliation, born of the margins, interstices, and gaps—of the ecotone—that delineates and complicates political boundaries, and borne up by a saltwater realm that owes no political allegiance. Coastal navigation affords intellectual edge effects that can glean powerful—and dangerous—insights into the factitious nature of sociocultural constructs such as the nation-state. Writers and mariners, who are sometimes one and the same, have long felt the allure of this perspective, as well as of the seacoast, that geocultural frontier where land and sea generate an ever-changing boundary and the imagination finds room to explore.

[41] John Stuart Mill, *England and Ireland* (London: Longmans, Green, Reader, and Dyer, 1868), quoted in Ranelagh, *A Short History of Ireland*, 129.

[42] Ranelagh, *A Short History of Ireland*, 130.

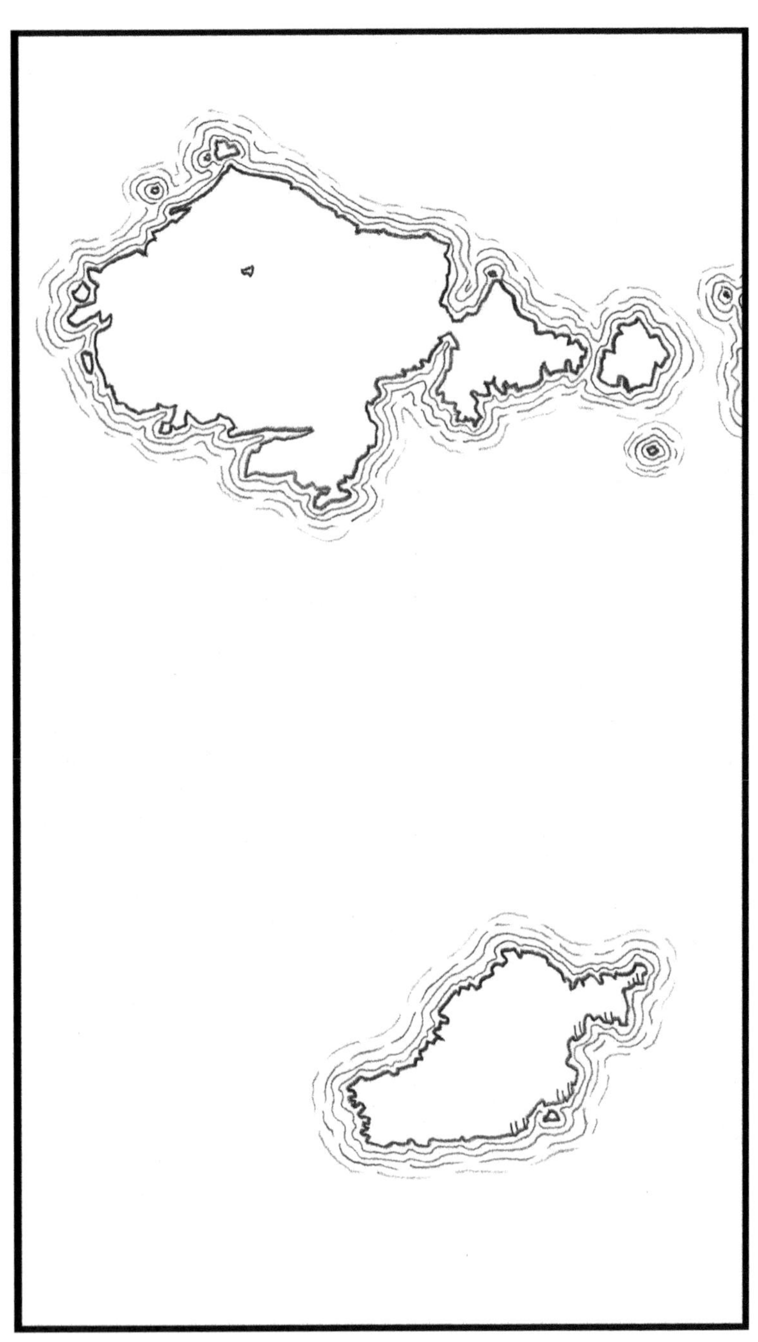

8

Ronald Lockley and the Archipelagic Imagination

Damian Walford Davies

Cardiff-born Ronald Mathias Lockley (1903–2000) suspected he was conceived on an island. Narrated at the beginning of *Myself When Young: The Making of a Naturalist* (1979)—a late-career amplification of earlier mappings of his multiple island identities—is a memory of his 'first deep-water voyage'.[1] The defining experience occurred in the company of his father, who at the time sported a 'black imperial beard'. An editor of train timetables for the *Red Rail Guide*, locked in a feckless cycle of debt and gambling that made his wife, Emily Margaret, despair, Harry Lockley was mostly absent from his son's childhood world. Lockley recalls being rowed out by his father 'over illimitable waters' and making landfall on an islet 'fifty paces in diameter'. He 'scrambled ashore from the prow of the skiff':

> Small green-yellow birds were darting and calling in the jungly foliage of purple loosestrife, willowherb and mimulus, under the towering boughs and shivering leaves of the poplars and weeping willows. Water-voles were plopping in and out of reedy banks . . .
>
> You could lose your way in the dense vegetation. Ronald did not go far. A magpie suddenly screamed, causing him to retreat, but all he could see was a wall of greenery shutting him in. He was lost. He called loudly in brief claustrophobic fear.
>
> 'Here, son,' the reassuring voice was just around the corner.
>
> 'Saw a big black and white bird. Made a terr'ble noise!'
>
> 'Lots of birds here. Must have been a magpie. D'you like the island? It's a favourite spot with your mother, too.'
>
> 'I 'member Mother said somethin'. Was I born'd here?'[2]

The island in question was 'in the middle of Cardiff's municipal lake'. 'Possibly I had been conceived there', Lockley remarks, noting that his

[1] R. M. Lockley, *Myself When Young: The Making of a Naturalist* (London: André Deutsch, 1979), 11.

[2] Lockley, *Myself When Young*, 12–13.

parents 'had also been there on the fine November Sunday' a few hours before he began '[his] struggles to be born'.[3]

Adam Nicolson has recently drawn attention to Lockley's 'half-boy, half-man style of adventuring'.[4] Cohabiting in this passage in a teasing discursive ecology typical of Lockley's writing are the naturalist's insistence on plain naming and recording, the imaginative writer's summoning of place, and an irony that does more than merely communicate the disjunction between a child's experience of tropical terrors and human-made municipal Welsh reality. Embedded here also, I suggest, is the frame of a Robinsonade—that classic adventure genre that was central, as Elizabeth DeLoughrey notes, 'to the indoctrination of young British boys into the emerging ideologies of masculine British nationalism and colonialism'.[5] Through that frame, the primal site of Lockley's originary island becomes a complex relational node, distinctively itself but also inevitably linked to an archipelago of fictive and actual islands and their natural, colonial, and postcolonial histories. Lockley's account emphasizes an invasion of the island's natural order, its non-human otherness, and its oppressive boundedness; at the same time, it is a narrative of return, a history of homing. The narrative knowingly configures the island in Roath Park as at once bourgeois recreational ground and exoticized, eroticized, illicit space, colonized by autochthonous and non-native flora. It is a site of both observed fact and fabling, sanctuary and terror.

1. LOCATING LOCKLEY

The reputation of Lockley as a pioneering ethologist, field biologist, 'new naturalist', ornithologist, conservationist, islophile, and paradigmatic island dweller is assured. His name is linked indissolubly with the treeless 'bare table of sandstone', 'wild Atlantic plateau', and 'remote little ornithological kingdom' of Skokholm island, off the coast of Pembrokeshire, whose stewardship the dissident twenty-four-year-old took in late 1927 as an 'experiment in a way of living'.[6] 'Our island lies beyond any point of land', Lockley wrote:

[3] Ibid., 14.

[4] R. M. Lockley, *Letters from Skokholm* (1947; Stanbridge: Little Toller Books, 2010), 18.

[5] See Elizabeth DeLoughrey, '"The Litany of Islands, The Rosary of Archipelagos": Caribbean and Pacific Archipelagraphy', *ARIEL: A Review of International English Literature*, 32 (January 2001), 22.

[6] Lockley, *Letters from Skokholm*, 41, 42, 103; John Buxton and R. M. Lockley, *Island of Skomer* (London: Staples Press, 1950), 10.

> There is no guiding cape or finger of land jutting towards it, as with the sister islands of Skomer and Ramsey. For this reason every bird that visits us is a true migrant.[7]

And every human, too, the logic runs. Here, Skokholm is an island (and condition) beyond cartographic deixis, seemingly beyond the interpellation of the mainland. (Mis-)named 'the loneliest man in the British Isles', Lockley lived on Skokholm with his wife and young daughter until 1940, restoring the farm buildings and hedge walls, living as a shepherd, fisherman, rabbit-catcher (and rabbit-exterminator), and bird-ringer.[8] It was here that he conducted ornithological research, erecting Heligoland traps and establishing the 260-acre island of red rock as a world-renowned bird observatory (the first in Britain). Skokholm—the Norse name signifies 'island in the sound'—had been uninhabited, in human terms, for twenty years before his arrival. In naturalist and conservationist circles, Lockley is linked in particular with the four creatures whose 'private lives' he laid bare through discipline-defining Welsh island and mainland fieldwork: the burrow-breeding Manx shearwater, the gannet, the Atlantic grey seal, and the rabbit. As is well known, Richard Adams generously recorded in *Watership Down* his debt to Lockley's classic study, *The Private Life of the Rabbit* (1964), which served Adams both as scrupulous scientific guide and creative prompt for the imaginative inhabitation of lapine psychology.[9]

Likewise, Lockley's importance as a prolific writer on natural history is generally acknowledged. However, he occupies fascinatingly ambiguous territory between the scientific professional and pioneering amateur. Never subject to institutionalized codes, his work is the product of an excentric sensibility. Alongside figures such as Frank Fraser Darling (with whom he collaborated), Lockley developed during the 1930s an ethology that, in Hayden Lorimer's words, 'willingly submitted to "unreason" and "uncommon" sorts of observation'—a science both 'radical and rational, variously regarded as serious minded and, in its anthropomorphism, quasi-scientific and dangerously maverick'.[10] In one of his most accomplished

[7] R. M. Lockley, *Dream Island Days: A Record of the Simple Life* (London: H. F. & G. Witherby, 1943), 124. This book is a revision and conflation of Lockley's *Dream Island* (1930) and *Island Days* (1934).

[8] R. M. Lockley, *Dear Islandman*, ed. Ann Mark (Gomer: Llandysul, 1996), 86.

[9] See Richard Adams, *Watership Down* (1972; Harmondsworth: Penguin, 1974), 8. Adams contributed the introduction to the American edition of Lockley's study, in which he refers to his 'deep debt' to 'this exceptional work of observation and natural history'; see *The Private Life of The Rabbit* (1964; Woodbridge: Boydell, 1985), 5–6.

[10] Hayden Lorimer, 'Forces of Nature, Forms of Life: Calibrating Ethology and Phenomenology', in Ben Anderson and Paul Harrison (eds), *Taking-Place: Non-Representational Theories and Geography* (Farnham: Ashgate, 2010), 57.

(and self-reflexive) works of ethology, *Letters from Skokholm* (1947), recently reissued by the Little Toller imprint as a 'classic' piece of nature writing, Lockley notes:

> The tendency is to write of birds as complete automatons. . . . Such writing is dead. . . . Surely we need to present our discoveries in a more living way, in the way of Jean Henri Fabre and Maurice Maeterlinck.[11]

If Lockley's tenure on Skokholm, which was always relativized and triangulated by the time he spent in various mainland dwellings and in inter-island transit, was an 'experiment in a way of living', then his remarkably diverse output can be regarded as a sustained experiment in ways of writing that 'living'.[12] Lockley has not been read whole. The layered iterations and radical hybridity of his island and related inland writing have not received the sustained critical attention they deserve, nor has his place in what John Brannigan has recently termed 'archipelagic modernism' been precisely calibrated.[13] Spanning sixty-six years, some sixty books, and a raft of scientific and popular articles, Lockley's work constitutes a complex ecology of literary genres, forms, and archipelagic 'scripts' that articulate a holistic encounter with—and performance of—Welsh island space as both a natural and culturally mediated phenomenon. There is an uncanniness to reading Lockley that derives from a practice of his that may at first seem to be repetition but which is in fact a commitment to reinscribing and inflecting material between editions and across generic boundaries so as to keep a particular episode, observation, or formulation open and negotiable. Collapsing the border between science and subjectivity, record and phenomenological response, the diversity and generic miscibility of his work actively resist a unitary discourse of the Atlantic edge.

Further, Lockley's writings of the 1930s and 1940s advocate a focus on geographical peripheries that reconstitutes them as centres. His observation and management of the Skokholm ecosystem naturalized a habit of relational thinking that involved a fundamentally archipelagic turn (whose literary reflexes I have already noted). In this chapter, I want to identify Lockley's importance as an innovative archipelagic thinker whose works—tidal in their insistent, layering returns to nodal places and former island-inland selves—anticipate very recent theoretical debates concerning archipelagic zones, 'aquapelagic assemblages' (defined by Philip Hayward

[11] See Lockley, *Letters from Skokholm*, 14.

[12] Ann Lockley refers to the family's 'itinerant existence between our various dwellings' (*Island Child: My Life on Skokholm with R. M. Lockley* (Llanrwst: Gwasg Carreg Gwalch, 2013), 71).

[13] See John Brannigan, *Archipelagic Modernism: Literature in the Irish and British Isles, 1870–1970* (Edinburgh: Edinburgh University Press, 2015), 1–20 and *passim*.

as 'the integrated space of islands and their adjacent waters and seafloors'), and island 'chorographies' (the delineation of spatial particularity) in the burgeoning transdisciplinary field of Island Studies.[14]

2. GRAPHIC SCRIPTS: TOWARDS LOCKLEY'S ARCHIPELAGRAPHY

A constellation of images from Lockley's texts, together with a literary portrait of Lockley that appears in a novel in which he is summoned in fictionalized form, offer a platform from which I will make a case for the following: his profound relevance to the contemporary discipline of nissology (defined by Grant McCall as 'the study of islands on their own terms' and by Christian Depraetere as 'a science of island thinking'), his major contribution to the island writing project, and his role in articulating a 'reterritorialization' of British and Welsh identities.[15] My chosen images typify some of the characteristic scripts and effects of Lockley's 'archipelagraphy'—a term I borrow from the work of DeLoughrey to identify the range of forms and 'different combinations of affect, materiality, performance, things' in which Lockley inscribes the Atlantic and global archipelagos and their maritime zones.[16] As Elaine Stratford and others have noted, to 'envision the archipelago' is to engage in a work of 'counter-mapping' that unsettles 'imperial binaries'.[17] Lockley intervenes in that project in seminal ways.

The first image, a wood engraving by C. F. Tunnicliffe, appears in *Letters from Skokholm* (see Figure 8.1).[18] It depicts two great black-backed

[14] See Philip Hayward, 'Aquapelagos and Aquapelagic Assemblages: Towards an Integrated Study of Island Societies and Marine Environments', *Shima: The International Journal of Research into Island Cultures*, 6 (2012), 6; Philip Hayward, 'The Constitution of Assemblages and the Aquapelagality of Haida Gwaii', *Shima: The International Journal of Research into Island Cultures*, 6 (2012), 1, 4.

[15] See Grant McCall, 'Nissology: A Proposal for Consideration', *Journal of the Pacific Society*, 17 (October 1994), 2; Christian Depraetere, 'The Challenge of Nissology: A Global Outlook on the World Archipelago, Part II: The Global and Scientific Vocation of Nissology', *Island Studies Journal*, 3 (2008), 24. I take the term 'reterritorialization' from Elaine Stratford et al., 'Envisioning the Archipelago', *Island Studies Journal*, 6 (2011), 124.

[16] See DeLoughrey, 'The Litany of Islands', 23. The concept of an 'archipelagraphy' is currently being developed into psychogeographical territory: see Pippa Marland, 'The "Good Step" and Dwelling in Tim Robinson's *Stones of Aran*: The Advent of Psycho-archipelagraphy', *Ecozon*, 6 (2015), 7–24. For the term 'Atlantic archipelago' (originally J. G. A. Pocock's), see Brannigan, *Archipelagic Modernism*, 6–7.

[17] Stratford et al., 'Envisioning the Archipelago', 114, 124.

[18] Lockley, *Letters from Skokholm*, 14.

Figure 8.1. Wood engraving of Skokholm by C. F. Tunnicliffe, *Letters from Skokholm* (1947).

gulls on a moss-grown stone wall on the elevated ground of the 'Knoll', looking north under a darkly scored sky over the renovated roof of the Skokholm farmhouse towards the neighbouring island of Skomer. A small flock of sheep is strung out in the middle distance, with the minutely drawn figure of a lone man on the cliff edge beyond. It is Lockley himself, here scaled down by distance, decentred to emphasize the suspension of human primacy and self-interest demanded by his intense ethological focus. At the same time, Lockley's writing, as we shall see, communicates a robust human personality and articulates startling recognitions and transformations of island selves.

My second image is the pictorial map of Skokholm (see Figure 8.2) spread over the pastedown and endsheet (both front and back) of *The Island* (1969)—at the time, only the latest in a textual archipelago of mutually illuminating Skokholm accounts by Lockley, each taking its full meaning from the range of intervening island texts, just as the islands of an archipelago (in Paul Sharrad's formulation) 'owe their identity not just to what they individually contain but to the sea between them'.[19] Drawn most probably by Tunnicliffe, the graphic map offers a bird's-eye view of the island's outline, with natural features ('Spy Rock', 'The Bog') and objects of the built environment ('House' and its accompanying 'Wheel House', 'Light House', and 'Tram Line') marked, and with an attempt to represent the hydrography of treacherous Jack Sound and 'the Wild Goose Race and its subsidiary tides'.[20] The shape of the island sears itself on the reader's consciousness, so often is it reproduced across Lockley's work—albeit in different cartographic representations that insist on defamiliarizing encounters with island forms. Further, the scale at which the island is represented—large enough for it to appear as a substantive body of land around which the island-rocks off Crab Bay and The Neck are ranged—asks the reader to confront a crucial nissological question posed by Godfrey Baldacchino (a question Lockley's work constantly negotiates):

> what exactly is an *island*?... geographers remind us of the *fractal* nature of islands: with larger magnification, what may have been a small island off a mainland itself becomes 'the mainland' for even smaller islands.[21]

Elements of Skokholm's contours recur fractally throughout Lockley's oeuvre in the form of graphic representations of Welsh, English, Irish, Scottish, Icelandic, German, and Danish islands of the Atlantic and North Sea archipelagos with whose human, natural, and literary histories he was intimately familiar. It was in relation to these that Skokholm's own significance was necessarily—archipelagically—to be understood. In *I Know an Island*, it is clear that Lockley savours the discovery of a copy of Liam

[19] Quoted in DeLoughrey, 'The Litany of Islands', 44.

[20] R. M. Lockley, *Inland Farm* (London: H. F. & G. Witherby, 1943), 12.

[21] Godfrey Baldacchino, 'Studying Islands: On Whose Terms? Some Epistemological and Methodological Challenges to the Pursuit of Island Studies', *Island Studies Journal*, 3 (2008), 47.

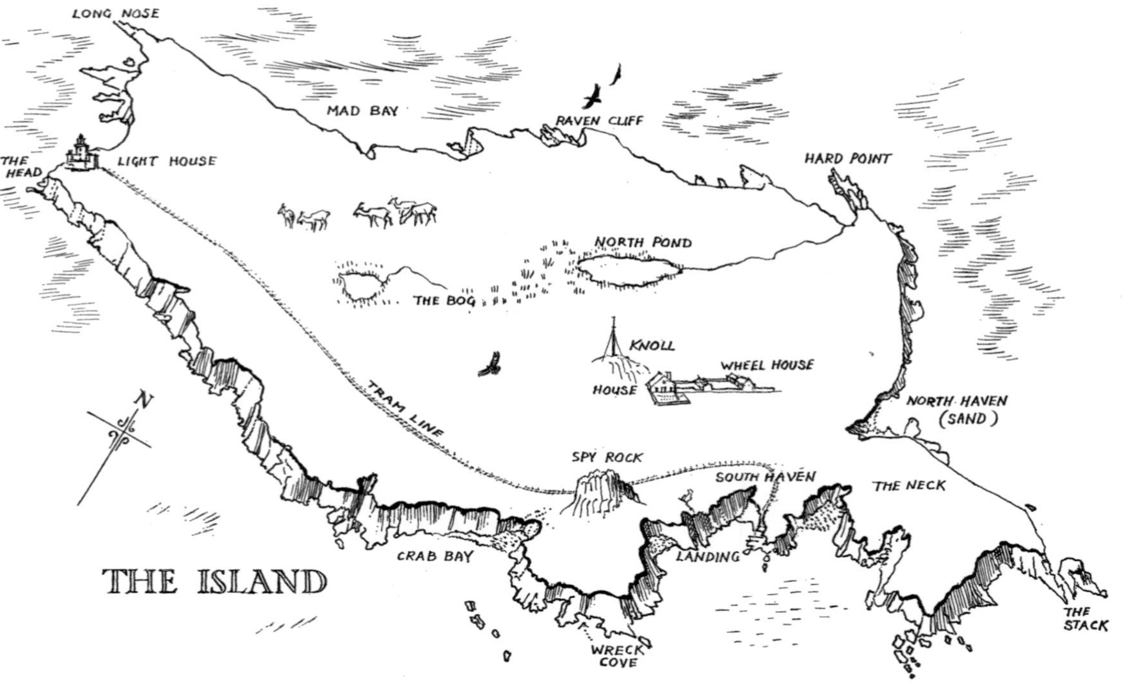

Figure 8.2. Pictorial map of Skokholm, *The Island* (1969).

O'Flaherty's island novel, *The Black Soul* (1924), in the house named 'Cristin' on Bardsey Island. And at the moment in *Letters to Skokholm* at which Lockley learns that his brother-in-law addressee, the poet and ornithologist John Buxton (who knew and loved Skokholm), has been captured in Norway and is being held as a prisoner of war, the letters become archipelagic enunciations that seek to bridge the connection between the ambiguous, relational freedom of Skokholm and Buxton's POW camp (Oflag VII-B, Eichstätt, Bavaria): 'You will in a sense be as enisled as we are, and your observations will be limited to the fauna of that entity of your camp and its perimeter'.[22]

My third image is taken from the one-reel short, *The Private Life of the Gannets*, filmed in 1934 on the island of Grassholm, north-west of Skokholm (see Figure 8.3). It was the first natural history documentary to win an Oscar (Lockley claimed that the idea was his and was hurt by the fact that he was billed as having only 'assisted' in the making of the film, while its producer and director, the distinguished zoologist and evolutionary

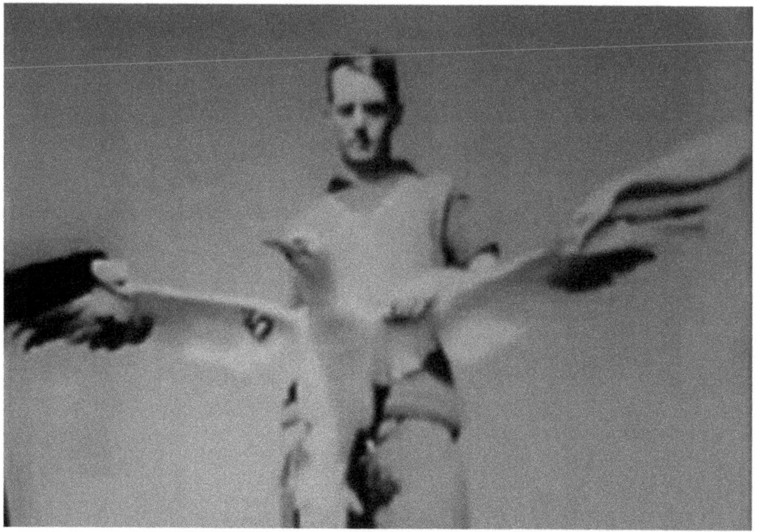

Figure 8.3. Frame from the one-reel short, *The Private Life of the Gannets* (1934).

[22] Lockley, *Letters from Skokholm*, 159; and see Adam Nicolson's remarks in his introduction, 19. For the story of the interned Buxton and his fellow conservationists and ornithologists John Barrett, Peter Conder, and George Waterston, see Derek Niemann, *Birds in a Cage... The Unlikely Beginnings of Modern Wildlife Conservation* (London: Short Books, 2012).

biologist Julian Huxley, 'should walk away with all the honours').[23] Two minutes into the reel (which begins with a voiceover that directs us westward to Grassholm from centrist English coordinates), Lockley is shown holding in front of him a gannet, great six-feet wings outspread, by its scapulars; the stylized commentary runs: 'What a bird it is!—designed as a perfect piece of living machinery'. It is an uncanny image: for a moment, what Lorimer terms the 'interspecies boundary' collapses and Lockley himself seems winged—a Grassholm denizen whom Huxley has come from London to study.[24]

Four maps are next. Together they exemplify a Lockleyan cartography that also constitutes an ontology. The map headed 'The Islands' in Lockley's *I Know an Island* (1938); the representation of 'The British Isles' (including Ireland, undivided) in *Islands Round Britain* (1945); the map identifying the breeding grounds of the grey seal in *The Seals and the Curragh* (1954); and the chart showing 'homing experiments with Manx shearwaters' in his groundbreaking 1942 study (call it a biography) of the bird all prompt a profound decentring (see Figures 8.4–8.7).[25] In the first three maps, the 'mainland' bodies of Britain, Ireland, continental Europe, and Iceland are unmarked. Statehood is erased (though Doris Lockley was to give Skokholm its own homemade flag, displaying 'three petrels rampant'—an act that both performed and ironized territorialization).[26] It is the islands, large and small, that are named in detailed edgework around the coasts. One reads *around* the landmasses that ordinarily prescribe our geographical, political, and cultural perspectives. Lockley's maps are the forerunners of Christian Depraetere's 2008 global 'biogeographical' map that shows 'Island patterns webbing the continents'—a reminder that 'islands are not just local hot spots, but the cornerstones of a global, pan-continental equilibrium'.[27] What is particularly striking in Lockley's archipelagraphy is the way the majority of the named entities cluster off the western seaboard, mapping a 'Celtic fringe' and a series of 'bits and pieces . . . [usually] considered as epiphenomena' (in the words of Depraetere) that now become a group of newly aligned, newly privileged, chorographies.[28] At the same time, these defamiliarizing maps create

[23] See Ann Lockley, *Island Child*, 58–9.

[24] Lorimer, 'Forces of Nature, Forms of Life', 66.

[25] R. M. Lockley, *I Know an Island* (London: George G. Harrap & Co., 1938), 13; *Islands Round Britain* (London: Collins, 1945), 15; *The Seals and the Curragh, Introducing the Natural History of the Grey Seal of the North Atlantic* (London: The Scientific Book Club, 1954), 145; *Shearwaters* (London: J. M. Dent, 1942), 185.

[26] See Lockley, *Dream Island Days*, 52, 168.

[27] See Depraetere, 'The Challenge of Nissology . . . Part II', 24–5, 26.

[28] Christian Depraetere, 'The Challenge of Nissology: A Global Outlook on the World Archipelago, Part I: Scene Setting the World Archipelago', *Island Studies Journal*, 3 (2008), 3.

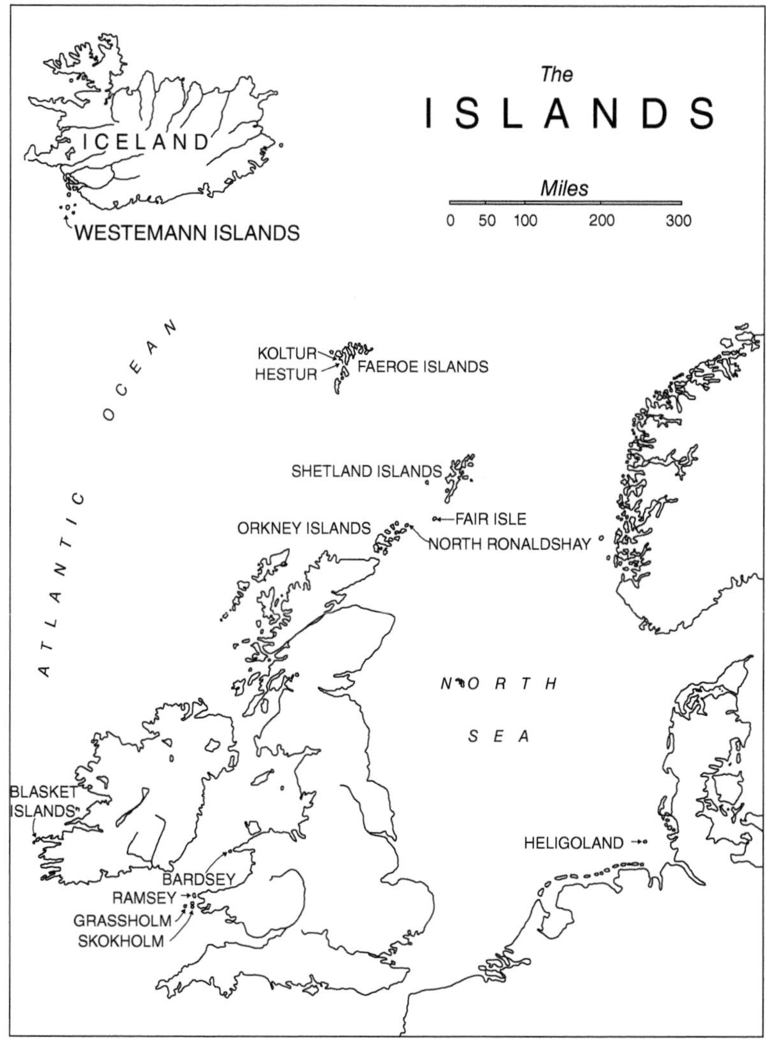

Figure 8.4. 'The Islands', *I Know an Island* (1938).

something of a *trompe l'oeil* effect, whereby the status of the 'mainlands' as likewise islanded (islands in a 'glocal' sea of islands) comes refreshingly into view.[29] In both cases, Lockley dramatically inflects what Depraetere

[29] Baldacchino, 'Studying Islands: On Whose Terms?', 50.

Figure 8.5. 'The British Isles', *Islands Round Britain* (1945).

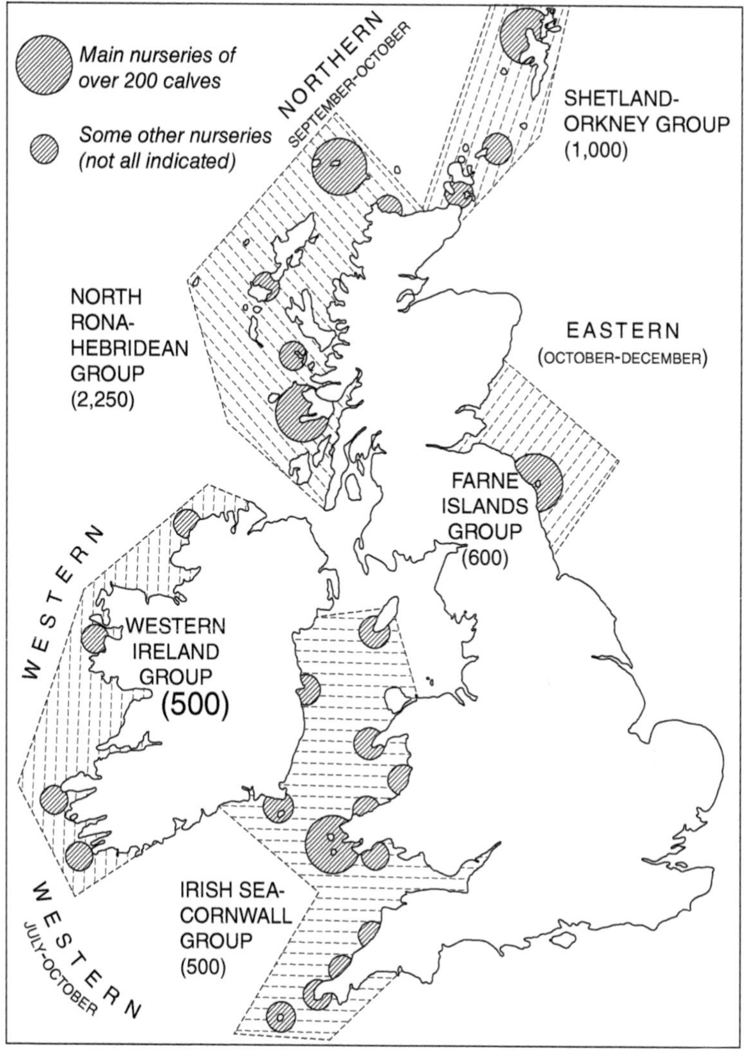

Figure 8.6. Map of grey seal breeding grounds, *The Seals and the Curragh* (1954).

calls a 'continental bias'.[30] In the map from the *Shearwaters* volume, which details the homing vectors of birds released by Lockley from as far afield as Venice and (through the offices of a friend) Boston, trans-European and transatlantic lines of return are shown converging dramatically on

[30] Depraetere, 'The Challenge of Nissology... Part I', 3.

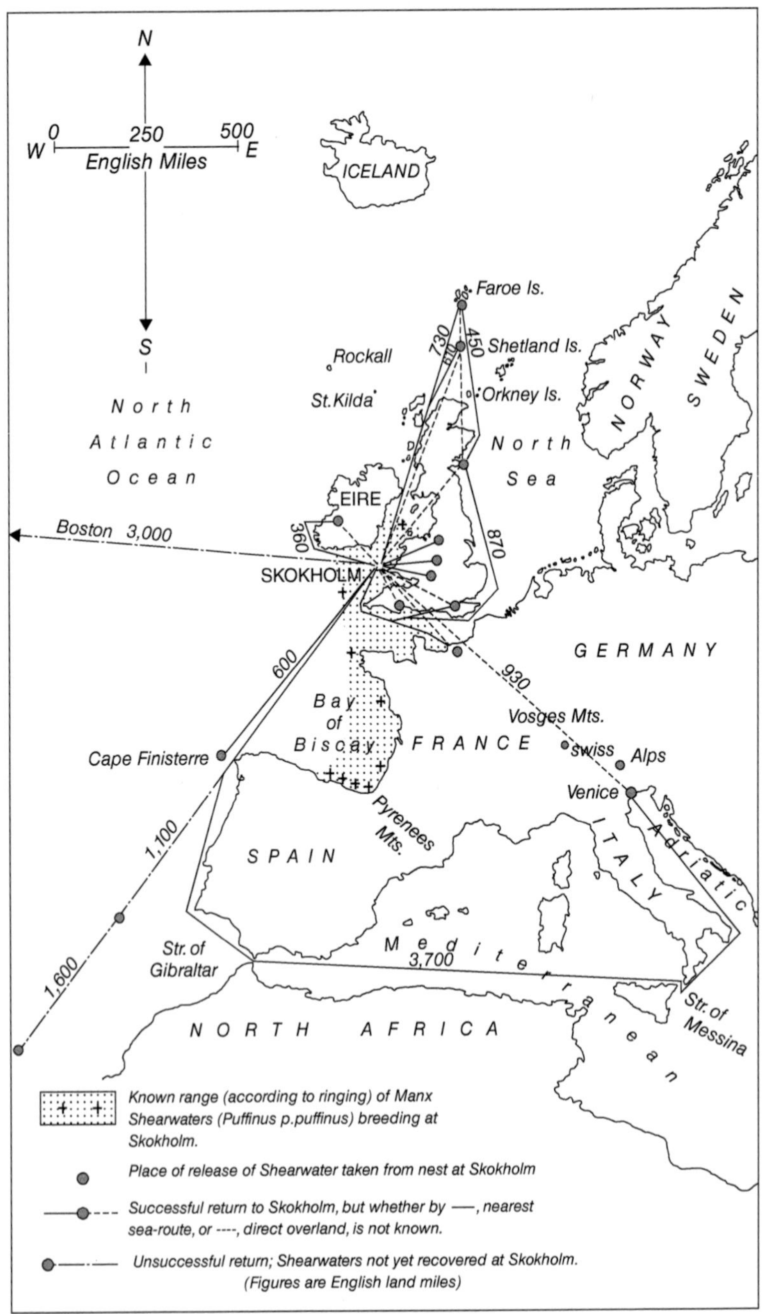

Figure 8.7. 'Homing Experiments with Manx Shearwaters', *Shearwaters* (1942).

Skokholm. The seal map charts a non-human 'aquaculture' of the 'Atlantic edge', locating the mammals' nursery grounds in the form of circles of different magnitudes within more extensive sea-zones that link Ireland, Wales, and western England on the one hand, and Scotland and eastern England on the other.[31] Thus, the island frame of the author's ethological project stimulates a refocusing of archipelagic relations that carries a geopolitical *frisson*. Taken together, these maps of what one might call peripheral centres contribute to the counter-mapping agendas of Lockley's wider archipelagraphy.

The penultimate set of images is likewise uncanny (see Figures 8.8–8.10). The images appear in the Skokholm text *Early Morning Island* (1939), subtitled *A Dish of Sprats*—a literary performance at once curious and characteristic in which Lockley ventriloquizes his eight-year-old daughter's imaginative response to Skokholm in a generically hybrid and often surreal sequence of encounters with the island environment and its

Figure 8.8. Ann Lockley and the *Alice Williams* figurehead, *Early Morning Island* (1939).

[31] See Lorimer, 'Forces of Nature, Forms of Life', 66.

Figure 8.9. Ann and Alice Williams, *Early Morning Island* (1939).

Figure 8.10. The Lockley family, *Early Morning Island* (1939).

articulate non-human inhabitants. (The influence of Lewis Carroll is everywhere felt, having first manifested itself in a letter to his wife in which Lockley views an unreal Skokholm from the mainland 'through the Looking Glass'.)[32] The book is illustrated by a portfolio of staged (and not a little eerie) photographs of nine-year-old Ann, alongside conventional images fit for the *Countryman* magazine that record island wildlife. In one photograph, Ann appears on the cliff at the entrance to South Haven, holding a nosegay, cheek-to-cheek with the female figurehead of the schooner, *Alice Williams*, whose welcome cargo of coal Lockley salvaged when the vessel was wrecked on the island cliffs in February 1928.[33] The figurehead, dressed 'in the fashion of the eighteen-fifties' with 'an old-fashioned tight bodice' and 'a rosary of jet and a black cross that matched her raven hair', was mended and placed by Lockley high above the harbour.[34] A companion photograph shows Ann lying asleep on an island bank of bluebells, with the figurehead in the distance, looking out to sea—a female form of equivocal symbolic significance that gathers to itself the personae of watcher, welcomer, siren-wrecker, and archipelagic hailer of shores beyond.[35] The book's final photograph captures a more kinetic act of hailing: Ann appears with her parents and the family friend and fellow Skokholm-dweller, George Henry Owen Harris (known as 'The Baron'), all in silhouette on high Spy Rock, looking out over the length of the island, their arms stretched high towards the setting sun.[36] It is another suggestively equivocal Skokholm script, encoding a gesture of human overlordship, the subordination of the human to the natural, an inter-island salutation (they are facing west, where, as Lockley frequently emphasizes, 'the nearest land... is South America'), and an act of desperate SOS signalling.[37]

My final example is taken from the close of Richard Adams's anti-vivisection parable, *The Plague Dogs* (1977). In the company of the celebrated conservationist Sir Peter Scott (pioneer at Slimbridge), Lockley is summoned in the novel's metafictional tailpiece as what one might call *deus ex insula*. Breaking the fictional spell in a transgressive piece of metafiction, Adams presents the two naturalists at sea between the Calf of Man and the coast of the Lake District in a 'converted lifeboat named

32 Lockley, *Dear Islandman*, 146.

33 R. M. Lockley, *Early Morning Island, or A Dish of Sprats* (London: George G. Harrap & Co., 1939), 39.

34 See Lockley, *Dream Island Days*, 35; and *Dear Islandman*, 159–62.

35 Lockley, *Early Morning Island*, 42.

36 Ibid., 77.

37 Lockley, *Letters from Skokholm*, 24; see also Lockley, *Dream Island Days*, 11; and *I Know an Island*, 57.

the *Orielton*' (the name of the neglected manor near Pembroke—'just the same size as [Skokholm], and ringed with a splendid ancient stone wall in place of the white Atlantic surf'—where Lockley, following conversations with Fraser Darling, G. P. Wells, Eric Linklater, Richard Church, Compton Mackenzie, and Julian Huxley, conducted his trailblazing study of rabbits between 1954 and 1962).[38] They have been 'putting in at several islands off the Welsh coast to visit old haunts of Lockley's', 'staying a night each at the bird observatories on Skokholm and Bardsey'.[39] Sitting 'at the helm, cutting beef for sandwiches off the bone and reflecting on the frame of things disjointed', Adams's Lockley conducts a debate with Peter Scott on anthropomorphism, 'ignorant sentimentality' (including Adams's own) 'about animals and birds', and the destruction visited by humans on other species. What follows is the novel's climax. Lockley spots the two exhausted canine protagonists, Rowf and Snitter, in the water. Close to death, fleeing from a hue and cry, they are rescued and brought to land. Throughout the exchange that follows on the beach, Lockley remains half on the shingle and half in the surf, holding the Orielton 'aground as the tide flowed'. It is he who finally calls for re-embarkation: 'I think it's time we were sailin' away. Are you fit, Peter?'[40] I suggest that Adams's bold *Verfremdungseffekt*, his choice of inter-island, tidal space as the novel's paradigmatic location of debate and 'salvage', and the novel's imaginative collapsing of the human–non-human boundary all testify to his close attention to the scripts of Lockley's archipelagraphy. In *The Plague Dogs*, Adams summons Lockley as both ethological and literary guru.[41]

3. ISLAND-MAKING

Lockley's islophilia (James Michener's term 'nesomania' also seems apt) began early.[42] It was, I suggest, the product of multiple cultural, psychological, psychosexual, and imaginative factors. Lockley's mother moved her young family from Cardiff to 'the nearby residential village' of

38 Richard Adams, *The Plague Dogs* (London: Allen Lane, 1977), 439; R. M. Lockley, *Orielton: The Human and Natural History of a Welsh Manor* (1977; Harmondsworth: Penguin, 1980), 45.

39 Adams, *The Plague Dogs*, 439.

40 Ibid., 458.

41 Lockley and Adams, accompanied by the photographer Peter Hirst-Smith, were to undertake an Antarctic trip together, an account of which was published as *Voyage Through the Antarctic* (London: Allen Lane, 1982). By that time, Lockley, having remarried twice, had been living in New Zealand for twelve years, where his conservationist and ethological work continued.

42 Quoted by DeLoughrey, 'The Litany of Islands', 23.

Whitchurch (fast becoming a suburb) to set up a boarding school. It is clear from the account offered in *Myself When Young* that in this 'complacently conventional bourgeois' and anglophone world, Lockley developed a deep interest in the natural history and wider ontologies of bounded spaces.[43] They were both refuges and testing grounds, ranging from the 'walled-in pleasance' of his mother's Whitchurch garden and its abutting fields to 'Moorhen Island', the 'small island hidden in a swamp' and 'bird-metropolis' near the industrial artery of the Glamorganshire Canal where young 'Ron' enterprisingly built a hut, botanized, observed birds, and developed an islocentric outlook.[44] In the context of his later career, this act of island-*creation* can be seen as part of what he calls the 'healthy sloughing of the soft shell of our suburban existence'—a response to what he seems to have recognized early as the normative behavioural codes of his class and culture in the interwar years.[45] Such carvings-out of bounded topographies can also be seen as a complex reaction to developing gender and sexual identities that were themselves perceived as frustratingly delimited. As 'the only permanent male' in an overwhelmingly female domestic space, Lockley describes himself as 'surrounded and hedged with femininity—four sisters, a mother, female servants and mistresses, and many girl pupils'.[46] Considered in the context of his avid consumption of *Robinson Crusoe*, *The Swiss Family Robinson*, and *The Coral Island*, and his discovery of the philosophical frame he subconsciously craved in Thoreau's *Walden* (which left him 'mentally stunned'), Lockley's early acts of seeking out, and seeking to know, enisled spaces were attempts both to enact and to escape models of British bourgeois, colonialist masculinity.[47] They also raise issues of the claims of stewardship vs ownership and solitariness vs connectedness that his writing would seek to work through. Further, the hybrid environments of his early island cartographies—hinterlands where the boundaries between the industrial and the rural, the domestic and the wild, were not fixed, and in which he encountered social and linguistic Welsh identities that differed markedly from his own—inform the archipelagic energies of his thinking and the inveterate acts of ventriloquization that layer his writing.[48]

Lockley's career is marked from the first by uncanny propagations of island space. They are not replications, since that term denies each new island form its particularity, at whatever scale. As I have suggested,

[43] Lockley, *Myself When Young*, 15. [44] Ibid., 30, 106–8, 148.
[45] Ibid., 178. [46] Ibid., 31. [47] Ibid., 237.
[48] See Lockley, *Myself When Young*, 17, 184–94.

Lockley's is an island-*making* imagination. As well as works such as Charles Waterton's *Wanderings in South America* (1825), the young Lockley read avidly in island geography, familiarizing himself with the names and shapes of the small islands of the Atlantic archipelago, tracing 'the outlines and main features' of the Pembrokeshire islands from 'scale maps in Cardiff Library' until he 'knew their topography by heart'.[49] At the farm in the Beggan Valley near St Mellons, north-east of Cardiff, which he took on as a nineteen-year-old with his sister Enid (having been persuaded of the impracticability of accomplishing a 'disappearing trick' and removing himself to the 'long-deserted' island of North Rona in the Outer Hebrides), he constructed around an 'old oak in the centre of the lower field' a 'broad moat in the soft alluvial soil':

> The excavated material, heaped around the tree, would quickly raise an island and deepen the 'sea' around it. This island would provide sanctuary for birds and wild plants.... One shore of the island would be lined with flag, reed and rush for the nesting of dabchick, mallard and moorhen; above this vegetation would be low bushes for the convenience of sedge- and reed-warblers, reed-bunting, whitethroats and blackcap. In short, I would re-create the Moorhen Island of tender memory, but with the advantage of owning the freehold.[50]

'The ten acres of the farm became an island for me', he notes, recognizing an aspect of islands that postcolonial and globally inflected modalities of twenty-first-century nissology tend to regard with suspicion—namely, their status as 'paradigms of hard-edgedness', 'absolute entities', 'territories', 'closed (read manageable) systems, amenable to study', and 'unit[s] of analysis'.[51] This was to be one of Skokholm's great attractions. And yet Lockley's proliferating island sites (which after his departure from Skokholm were to include two 'enisled' farms in Pembrokeshire) point to the need he felt to render all bounded sites archipelagic. Seeking to understand and enact the island condition (what he called the 'island complex') as both dwelling and archipelagic 'hopping', Lockley anticipates what has become an orthodoxy in Island Studies in an age of 'global information networks' and migration: the conception of shorelines as being, in the words of Pete Hay, 'alive with relational meaning', 'permeable' phenomena that 'invite transgression; inspire restlessness; demand to be breached'—'portal[s] to roads and sea-trails fanning out to other (is)lands'.[52] What

49 Ibid., 176. 50 Ibid., 239, 259.

51 See Pete Hay, 'A Phenomenology of Islands', *Island Studies Journal*, 1 (2006), 22; Godfrey Baldacchino, 'Islands, Island Studies, Island Studies Journal', *Island Studies Journal*, 1 (2006), 5, 9; Baldacchino, 'Studying Islands: On Whose Terms?', 39.

52 See Hay, 'A Phenomenology of Islands', 24, 23.

Lockley called 'the delicate truth' of bird migration was itself a living embodiment of archipelagic connectivity.[53]

4. LENSES ON THE ISLAND PROJECT

Lockley's decision to take the twenty-one-year lease on Skokholm in 1927 was in part motivated by a search for an 'island autonomy' that he explicitly contrasted with a 'herd excitement', pathological 'unrest', and an 'unnatural craving for money' that he associated specifically with the metropolis.[54] He would refer to a mode of dwelling 'away from the artificiality of man's conurbial life' (the coinage conjures 'connubial'; one senses a Freudian slip).[55] He was to trade human suburbs, towns, and cities for life among Skokholm's 'great metropolis of shearwater burrows' and its puffin 'townships' with their 40,000 'aldermanic' denizens.[56] Yet at the same time as they articulate a faith in the island project, certain of the literary and mythological lenses through which Lockley's early encounters with Skokholm are figured resonate with core anxieties. These include the fear that Welsh island space may erode social identity, agency, and the possibility of actualization in history; the opposite fear, that island space can never offer sanctuary and immunity from history's violence; the inevitability of a return to a world of 'unrest'; and the effect of island dwelling on human conceptions of 'home' and on instincts of 'homing'. In a letter of 18 February 1928 to his wife Doris ('Do') from the point of embarkation for Skokholm, he bemoans the uncooperative winds, remarking that 'if this goes on we'll never get to Tir Nan Og [*sic*]'.[57] The reference to *Tír na nÓg* sees him playing Oisín to his wife's Niamh, drawing into the narrative of their imminent translation to the island a fretfulness concerning homesickness, acts of forgetting, and the inevitability (and necessity) of shocking returns to 'history' (contemporary Ireland's included) and to social ties. We have already encountered Lockley the ethologist on the island of Grassholm, out in the sea beyond Skokholm; it was where he and Do spent their wedding night, among the stir, stench, and 'moulted white down' of the gannet colony.[58] What he would later term the 'reality of returning—an abrupt waking' to mainland modernity is also, inescapably, embodied in Grassholm's guano-encrusted

53 Lockley, *Letters from Skokholm*, 53.
54 Lockley, *I Know an Island*, 91, 230–1.
55 Lockley, *The Island* (London: André Deutsch, 1969), 21.
56 Lockley, *Dream Island Days*, 125; *Letters from Skokholm*, 153.
57 Lockley, *Dear Islandman*, 148; see also *Letters from Skokholm*, 13.
58 Lockley, *Dream Island Days*, 57.

rock and its surrounding sea-zones, given the fact that, as Lockley acknowledges, it figures in the second branch of the *Mabinogi* as *Gwales*, the island where the survivors of the war in Ireland feast in historical amnesia until the forbidden door onto the Bristol Channel is opened and traumatic historical consciousness forces a return to political and social 'centres'.[59] Lockley also deployed Keats at the start of his Skokholm tenure as a way of getting a purchase on vectors of removal and return. Finding 'the day birds in chorus [—] larks, curlew, lapwings, wheatears' as he 'cross[ed] the bog at sunrise', Lockley hears 'the clang of *Alice Williams*'s fog bell' (used to announce island mealtimes) and enters the house 'to open the new casement windows of the living room; these truly look out over the foam of perilous seas of fairy lands forlorn'.[60] This allusive, compacted Skokholm script focuses the competing trajectories of Keats's 'Ode to a Nightingale'—first a flight from 'The weariness, the fever, and the fret' into a relation with what Lorimer terms the 'pace and purpose' of the non-human, then an obligatory tolling back ('Forlorn! the very word is like a bell / To toll me back') to a febrile human world and to an acculturated 'sole self' removed from imaginative ethological and archipelagic connectivity.[61]

The Tempest provides another lens through which Lockley initially sought to understand his relation both to Skokholm and to various social groupings and ideological movements in the early 1930s. Following *Dream Island: A Record of the Simple Life* (1930)—his first work of what we would now call autobiographical creative non-fiction (the term 'record' belies its imaginative figurings)—Lockley offered in his first novel, *The Island Dwellers* (1932), a contemporary Welsh archipelagic revisioning of *The Tempest*. This fascinatingly unstable fiction of the first few Skokholm years is part eco-romance, part thriller, part autobiography, part natural history, complete with a map (with 'currents indicated') and an ethnographic preface emphasizing the Scandinavian, Flemish, and 'refugee' blood of the (anglophone) inhabitants of 'the extreme south-westerly peninsula of Wales'.[62] *The Island Dwellers* enshrines Lockley's developing brand of ethology by registering, at moments of both crisis and resolution in the narrative, 'mode[s] of being' that mark 'intensities of relation' with the natural world.[63] It also conducts a dialogue with Shakespeare's island play to reflect on rights of dwelling and possession, acts of colonization,

[59] Lockley, *Dear Islandman*, 247; and see Lockley's article on Grassholm in *The Countryman*, 11 (July 1935), 426.

[60] Lockley, *Dear Islandman*, 248.

[61] Lorimer, 'Forces of Nature, Forms of Life', 66; John Keats, *The Complete Poems*, ed. John Barnard, 2nd edn (Harmondsworth: Penguin, 1977), 348.

[62] R. M. Lockley, *The Island Dwellers* (London: Putnam, 1932), 1.

[63] Lorimer, 'Forces of Nature, Forms of Life', 66.

the relation of centres to peripheries, and the inauthenticity of faddy modern island 'movements' (whose beginnings can be traced to the 'loose theorizing... indulged in by idealists who sip their morning coffee in ultra-fashionable urban cafés', as Lockley was to put it in *Islands Round Britain*).[64] Anticipating the recent insight of Island Studies that aquapelagos are necessarily '*performed* entities', Lockley seeks a purchase on his own plural identities and accountability as a newly 'embedded' ethologist and as a (Anglo-)Welsh island dweller through multiple self-figurings enabled by the novel form.[65] Thus, aspects of his own identity and cultural trajectory are performed not only in the character of Prosper Bernard, the non-native 'guardian' of the 'Lower Island' and holder of its fragile lease, but also in the persona of artist Peter Williamson, the Londoner who offers him a loan; Prosper's wife Mary, whom mainland gossip configures as a witch since she seems never to have left the island, and whose buried body becomes the site of the novel's most passionate reflection on island embeddedness; the 'addled town folks' of the 'London Thoreauvian Society' who wish to purchase the island to practise 'the crazy beliefs of that poverty-stricken consumptive'; and also Prosper's wild, creaturely son Mark, a Caliban figure consistently located in the novel at the frontier between species.[66] In an archipelagic move that recalibrates the established dialectic between the mainland and Prosper's Lower Island, Lockley has Mark flee from the law to 'Green Island'—Grassholm—where he is found 'delirious in the recess in the cliff beneath the gannetry', having achieved ambiguous sanctuary in the realm of the great birds that 'made no attempt to molest him' as they 'gaz[ed] at him dispassionately with their cold, fishy eyes, in which the white iris accentuated the coldness of the stare'.[67] 'The Islant [*sic*] belongs to Prosper by right of everything in the world' is the local blacksmith's response to the question of possession posed early in the novel.[68] Lockley's inflection of Caliban's claim to his island, in defiance of Prospero, in *The Tempest*—'This island's mine by Sycorax my mother, / Which thou tak'st from me'—suggestively collapses competing human and non-human claims (and gender identities) in the light of Prosper Bernard's sensitive stewardship of the island's ecology and the imaginative 'version of dwelling' he and his family have chosen.[69] The novel focuses a debate about possession that continues throughout Lockley's writing;

[64] Lockley, *Islands Round Britain*, 25.

[65] Hayward, 'Aquapelagos and Aquapelagic Assemblages', 6; Lorimer, 'Forces of Nature, Forms of Life', 57.

[66] Lockley, *The Island Dwellers*, 34; Lorimer, 'Forces of Nature, Forms of Life', 66.

[67] Lockley, *The Island Dwellers*, 225, 213.

[68] Ibid., 17.

[69] William Shakespeare, *The Tempest*, ed. Stephen Orgel (Oxford: Oxford University Press, 1998), 119 (I. ii. 331–2); Lorimer, 'Forces of Nature, Forms of Life', 66.

it would manifest itself in other works in assertions of ownership ('The joy of possession is emphasized on an island; every bird that flies to our shores is instantly labelled ours'—'labelled', there, carrying the sense of 'ringed' and thus 'tracked'); in guarded articulations of non-human entitlements ('When I see our ravens I have a feeling, almost, that this island is not mine, but theirs'); and in explicit acknowledgements of prior rights of occupancy ('Birds are ever the true, the constant freeholders of Skokholm').[70]

5. 'NOT QUITE AT HOMENESS': LOCKLEY'S ARCHIPELAGIC UNCANNY

The terms of such a debate lead us to a core feature of Lockley's project. Elaine Stratford has identified a feature of the archipelagic imagination she calls a 'not quite at homeness'.[71] I see this condition energizing Lockley's work in the form of modes of 'being, knowing and doing' that are *creatively unsettling* in their commitment both to what Ian Maxwell terms the 'charismatic idiosyncrasy' of place and to the notion that place is a 'mutually constituted and co-constructed' category.[72] It is also present in Lockley's desire to hold subjective and objective knowledges in productive balance (and tension) and to experience a multifarious world's bracing *unhomeliness* in the very act of establishing on Skokholm not so much 'science-at-home' as 'science-*as*-home', as Hayden Lorimer smartly puts it.[73] Call this need the archipelagic uncanny—a way of preserving an agile, plural response to the world that recognizes 'disjuncture' and 'disruption' as well as 'connection and entanglement' as core features of island experience.[74]

A classic example is the chapter titled 'A Walk Around the Island' that appeared first as an article in *The Countryman* and then in *Island Days* (1934). In this ludic, masterfully controlled piece, the speaker leads the middle-class reader-tourist around Skokholm. Attention is drawn not only to the island's manifest beauties, but also to scenes of predation, with the result that we are interpellated into the ecology of an uncanny Skokholm that is at once pastoral-maritime *refugio*, erotic space, and killing ground:

[70] Lockley, *Dream Island Days*, 124; *Letters from Skokholm*, 43; *Shearwaters*, xi.

[71] Stratford et al., 'Envisioning the Archipelago', 117.

[72] Ian Maxwell, 'Seas as Places: Towards a Maritime Chorography', *Shima: The International Journal of Research into Island Cultures*, 6 (2012), 23; Stratford et al., 'Envisioning the Archipelago', 113.

[73] Lorimer, 'Forces of Nature, Forms of Life', 66.

[74] See Stratford et al., 'Envisioning the Archipelago', 114.

> The great black-backed gulls have adorned their nests here with the skulls and skins of their feathered victims, like a Bornean head-hunter his kraal... over there a black-back has just killed a rabbit.... When we pick up the fledgling it is quite dead. We shall leave it. No bird will touch the hateful meat, but before it is cold the bottle-flies will have found it, and for the rest there are the eager burying-beetles and the red and black ants.... A wilder, prettier spot for love-making could not be imagined.... As it is, [the shearwaters] suffer hideously: every one that does not find cover before light is massacred by the gulls; just here their wings and breastbones litter the cliff-edge, their skulls peep out from clumps of thrift.[75]

Welcome, neo-Thoreauvian stranger (Lockley says), to the terrible beauty of the Welsh archipelago. Lockley, I suggest, is fruitfully encountered through strategies of uncanny reading that recognize in his nature writing a nuanced modality of war writing. The series of themed micro-studies of the island's natural history in *Letters from Skokholm*—begun at a 'critical moment in history' in 1939, when Lockley expected to have to evacuate the island at any time—are to be read, I argue, as a complex ethological version of the wartime Mass Observation and 'Recording Britain' projects.[76] The book's affecting phenomenology of place, its minutely observed chorography of dependent relations, make it a moving war book—a summative 'performance' of the island and of an unsettled island self uncannily pressured by the obscenities of war, written (as we have seen) to a combatant and prisoner of the 'Nazi machine'.[77]

In his insightful discussion of the contributions of Lockley and Frank Fraser Darling to a mid-twentieth-century scientific project that 'work[ed] the shifting tideline between ethology and phenomenology', Lorimer emphasizes both Lockley's search for modes of 'attunement' with the natural world and his acknowledgement that

> the recalibration of relations necessary for greater levels of intimacy still requires an on-going acceptance that disjuncture occurs in the middle of connectivities, and that there remain untold forces of nature always occurring, and non-human lives always existing; unannounced; unadorned, wholly on their own account.[78]

What such principles necessitated was a self-conscious engagement with the challenges of writing particularity, relation(ality), and otherness. Maps, drawings (by Lockley's wife, Doris), photographs, and lists of fauna and flora, together with tabular data on dates of egg laying, hatching, incubation

75 Lockley, *Dream Island Days*, 115–16.

76 Lockley, *Letters from Skokholm*, 28.

77 Ibid., 159. The 'performed' nature of the project is noted by Adam Nicolson in his introduction, 18.

78 Lorimer, 'Forces of Nature, Forms of Life', 70.

periods, and fledging, coexist fluidly in the literary ecology of Lockley's works as ways of seeking knowledge of and attunements with the non-human, while simultaneously conceding (and celebrating) its very otherness. As already noted, an unwillingness to settle into a single literary script or genre, together with the constant reclamation of previously published material and diary entries in a creative cycle of imaginative salvage, result in an uncanny body of work that keeps the reader's own relation to the Atlantic archipelago and to Lockley himself open and creatively unstable—in a word, archipelagic. What may at first seem a *problem* of style and register can in fact be seen as a highly self-conscious juxtaposition and conflation of scientific and literary discourses and categories whose layeredness is an expression of Lockley's ecological and nissological principles.

The Atlantic (and global) aquapelago cannot by definition be written monologically, but only relationally and plurally. Hence, Lockley's commitment to the creative narrativization of scientific discovery sits alongside the presentation of tabular data; his constant recourse to dialogue alongside description and observation; his ventriloquizations of the non-human ('Crayfish said, rather wistfully, I thought: "Curious, in fact most odd, how the tides work here"') alongside his repeated attempts to render the 'scream of the Manx shearwater' ('a catcall and a cockcrow uttered simultaneously and cut off with a sharp knife before the finish'; 'Kŭck-kŭck-kŭck-ōōōō').[79] Kept punctiliously from the early 1940s during his post-Skokholm farming experiments on the inland Pembrokeshire farm of Cwmgloyne and on the peninsula called Dinas Island in the early 1940s, Lockley's farming diary becomes in *The Golden Year* (1948) the basis for a work that occupies threshold territory between nature notes ('In the deep wood the rare elecampane is in flower'), a reflection on post-war farming practices ('It is more and more clear to me that this western shore is not ideal for seed clover production'), fictional narrative, and a study of his relationship with his wife, from whom he was by that time divorced.[80]

Hybrid discourses, now accompanied by uncanny photomontage ('atrociously faked photographs', in the words of Lockley's daughter), also characterize the single-species 'study', *The Seals of the Curragh*, first drafted as a novel and inspired by his discovery, during wartime reconnaissance work for Naval Intelligence, of a seal-breeding site he called 'The Red Wilderness' on the north Pembrokeshire littoral.[81] Those acts of

[79] Lockley, *Early Morning Island*, 60–1; *Shearwaters*, 5; *Dream Island Days*, 119, 16.

[80] R. M. Lockley, *The Golden Year* (London: H. F. & G. Witherby, 1948), 113, 139. See also the first two books of Lockley's farming trilogy: *Inland Farm* (London: H. F. & G. Witherby, 1943) and *The Island Farmers* (H. F. & G. Witherby, 1946).

[81] Ann Lockley, *Island Child*, 274.

intense watching and surveillance—seal observation and wartime scouting—would be revisited and further transformed in *Seal Woman* (1974), in which the speaker is initiated into a new form of being and dwelling by a woman ambiguously located at the interspecies boundary. Hayden Lorimer refers to 'narratives of affiliation and mutuality that Fraser Darling and Lockley fashioned out of their seal colony encounters' and their connection 'with charismatic individuals and their on-going life histories'.[82] Attuning oneself to the behaviour of 'animal lives' required 'that conditioned aspects of human-ness fall away'; Lockley's and Fraser Darling's influential ventriloquization and narrativization of animal 'histories', Lorimer notes, 'speak volubly of their biographers' own transformations' on the Atlantic edge.[83] (In an article in *The Countryman* published on the eve of the family's enforced departure from Skokholm in the summer of 1940, Doris Lockley wrote: 'like a seal, I went ashore for the birth of my daughter'.)[84] Combining ethological research and folk myth (indigenous voices beyond the orthodoxies of science that 'spoke otherwise of animality'),[85] *Seal Woman* can be fruitfully encountered as a transgressive conservationist fantasy in which ethological research, war trauma, sexual desire, and Lockley's own 'ex-isle' identity are narrativized along an axis that links the metropolis, the Irish coast, secret seal holms, the submarine environments of the Atlantic archipelago, and total war. Preparing an island shelter for his seal-bride, the transformed narrator takes to

> herborizing in every sheltered nook of our green cradle in the Holm of Seals. I made a border of fig-marigolds, tapestry for our palliasse of sun-dried holcus blades. The mesembryanthemum can live without roots in that salt air.[86]

The discourse is an unabashed archipelagic conflation that draws together scientific observation, popular nature writing, and the poetic botany of a Shakespearean romance. In no way does a novel like *Seal Woman* 'interrupt' Lockley's writings on natural history, as Lorimer claims.[87] Rather, natural history enters into a testing ecology with fiction and fantasy.

82 Lorimer, 'Forces of Nature, Forms of Life', 65.

83 Ibid., 66.

84 Doris Lockley, 'The Woman's Side of Island Life', *The Countryman: A Quarterly Non-Party Review and Miscellany of Rural Life and Work for the English-speaking World*, 21 (July–August–September 1940), 269.

85 Lorimer, 'Forces of Nature, Forms of Life', 57.

86 Lockley, *Seal Woman* (1974; Sydney: Hicks Smith, 1976), 104.

87 Lorimer, 'Forces of Nature, Forms of Life', 64.

Further, Lockley's engagement in *Seal Woman*, and throughout his work, with the 'three-dimensionality' of aquapelagic space, with routes/roots and with the movements of waters, anticipates the recent formulation in cultural geography and Island Studies of two concepts that seek a dynamic purchase on the land–sea and natural–historical entanglements of the archi/aquapelago. The first is the notion of a 'maritory'—an understanding of the sea–land assemblage that goes beyond the 'surface model' of the aquapelago.[88] The second is the concept of 'tidalectics', developed from its initial postcolonial context in the work of Kamau Brathwaite into 'a dynamic model' of geography, history, cultural interaction, and ontology to signify (one's experience of) 'recursive' rhythms and routes that link (but never erase the difference between) sea and land.[89] A work like Lockley's second novel, *The Sea's a Thief* (1936), which deploys the novel form to write tides and tideraces, island sounds, death-by-water, and recursive sea-passages between the economic and ethnic territories of Pembrokeshire's northern Welshry and southern Englishry, is tidalectic *avant la lettre*.

Lockley's lasting legacy is, I suggest, a challengingly capacious archipelagraphy that asks us to consider modes of dwelling in these islands as imaginative acts. Characterized by an openness to disparate categories of experience, such acts call for complex ecologies of verbal and graphic expression. For Lockley, island ontologies were at once a distinctive experience of life at the Atlantic edge, a shared global condition, and a transferable tool of relational thinking. Phenomenological modalities of cultural geography will find in Lockley's writings richly various and flexible patterns of mapping space. As I have argued, central to his contribution is a principle of 'not quite at homeness'—a hybrid sensibility in which an acute attunement to idiosyncrasies of place and non-human forms of life is naturalized alongside a distrust of essentialism and a desire for connectivity that actively courts disjunction. Fiercely historicist, too, Lockley's work asks us to reach our own accommodation with that unsettled condition of unhomeliness in the context of global conflict, population displacement, environmental degradation, and whatever polities

[88] See Christian Fleury, 'The Island/Sea/Territory Relationship: Towards a Broader and Three-dimensional View of the Aquapelagic Assemblage', *Shima: The International Journal of Research into Island Culture*, 7 (2013), 1–13.

[89] See Elizabeth DeLoughrey, *Routes and Roots: Navigating Caribbean and Pacific Island Literatures* (Honolulu: University of Hawai'i Press, 2007), 2; Anna Reckin, 'Tidalectic Lectures: Kamau Brathwaite's Prose/Poetry as Sound-Space', *Anthurium: A Caribbean Studies Journal*, 1 (2003), 1–16.

we wish 'this unnameable constellation of islands', in Andrew McNeillie's phrase, to take.[90] Lockley's ethological project was also a deeply personal journey. Writing the non-human inescapably involved writing the self. His environmentalist credentials are predicated not on the elision of our humanness, but on the need to assert—and contest—it creatively and dissidently in new forms. The question the three-year-old Lockley asked his father on that artificial municipal island in Cardiff was a promising starting point: 'Was I born'd here?'

[90] Andrew McNeillie, 'Editorial', *Archipelago*, 1 (2007), vii.

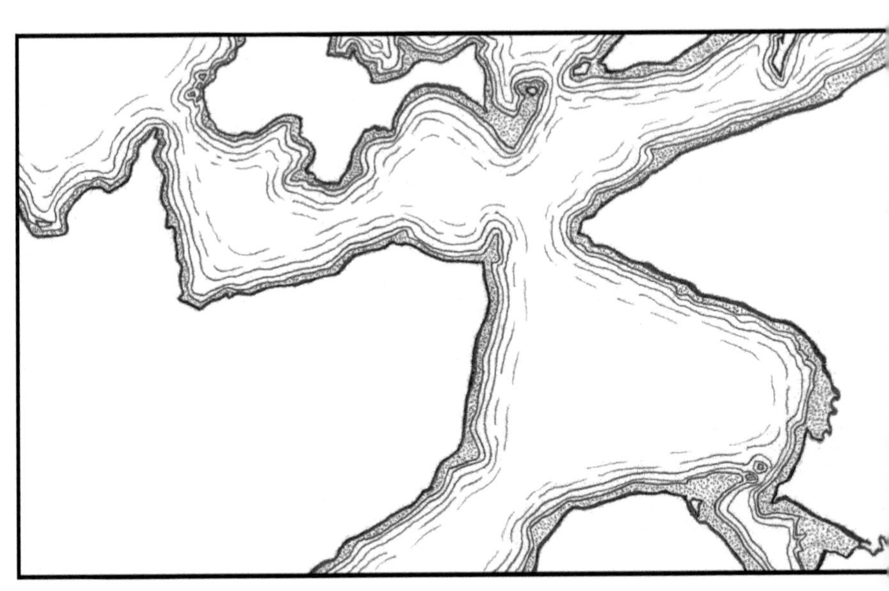

9

Maude Delap's Domestic Science

Island Spaces and Gendered Fieldwork in Irish Natural History

Nessa Cronin

Maude Jane Delap (1866–1953) is primarily remembered today for her contribution to Irish and British natural history through her work elaborating the complex life cycle of the jellyfish and for her contribution with her sister Constance to a maritime survey of Valentia Harbour, Co. Kerry in 1895–6. Her contribution to Valentia's maritime ecologies is embedded within the gendered geographies of late Victorian Britain and Ireland, and a critical examination of her work offers a more nuanced understanding of the wider networks of scientific and scholarly life in this period.[1] Other than brief acknowledgements by Robert Lloyd Praeger, an obituary in *The Irish Naturalists' Journal*, and biographical notes or short articles by Tim Collins, Mary Mulvihill, Anne Byrne, and Breda Joy, there has been very little written on Delap's life and work, and there has been no critical attention paid to her contribution to our understanding of Irish natural history and contemporary coastal heritages in Ireland and Britain today.[2] The study of Delap and her island home, as one chapter in the history of Atlantic coastal heritages, demands a careful assessment of the particular intellectual milieu in which Delap worked for most of her adult life, as well

[1] The term 'maritime ecologies' refers to the study of marine biology, zoology, botany, and folklore associated with the science and culture of maritime life in Ireland. I would like to thank the following for their comments and suggestions on earlier drafts of this chapter: Juliana Adelman, John Brannigan, Timothy Collins, Diarmid Finnegan, Tadhg Foley, Méabh Ní Fhuarth※áin, and Dorinda Outram. Thanks also to staff at the Valentia Island Heritage Centre; National Museum of Ireland, Dublin; National Marine Biological Library, Plymouth; and *The Kerry Magazine* and Kerry County Library. Finally, many thanks to Joanna Lee, who kindly gave me access to Delap family archival material.

[2] Robert Lloyd Praeger, *Natural History of Ireland: A Sketch of its Flora and Fauna* (1949; New York: Barnes and Noble Books, 1972), 285.

as a consideration of the broader cultural and social worlds of what I term 'the spaces of domestic science' in late Victorian Ireland. While much scholarly work on women naturalists and travellers in this period often focuses on women from elite backgrounds and metropolitan contexts, I argue that a critical rereading of late Victorian scientific culture can be elucidated through the lens of geography and gender in showing alternative pathways of, and to, scientific knowledge in Ireland in this period. In terms of a metropolitan, colonial geography with London at its core, a rethinking of the margins of the margin (an island off the west coast of Ireland) helps us to explain how an 'uneducated' Rector's daughter on an island off the coast of Kerry became an international expert in maritime ecologies, culminating in the offer of a professional position in Plymouth, membership of the Linnaean Society, and indeed the highest accolade a natural scientist can attain in having a new species named in honour of her contribution to the natural sciences. In more ways than one, then, Maude Delap (and her island home) challenges the received narrative of the Victorian scientist by her gender, travel, and value of local place as a scientific space. Delap's life and work therefore offer an alternative view of a world on the Atlantic edge, a marginal world that was also simultaneously at the heart of the imperial sciences and fieldwork cultures of Victorian Britain.

This chapter also seeks to open up wider questions relating to the European spaces and cultures of natural history. It argues that rethinking the *sites* of travel, discovery, and knowledge production challenges us to recalibrate the formation of natural science in a European and colonial context and that the spaces of such 'universal' discoveries often have local roots. In this, I am rehearsing Dorinda Outram's argument that earlier concepts of chorography and eighteenth-century natural history that foregrounded 'the embeddedness of the natural order in a particular land' were dispensed with upon the advent of enlightenment ideas of science 'as the paradigmatically "universal" endeavour'.[3] The particularities of place were therefore replaced with a universalizing narrative that naturalized European space and language, often being translated and transported to non-European contexts. In particular, the Linnaean system was seen as liberating natural history from 'superstitious theory' and also from national prejudice (particularly from the English perspective, removing it away from a continental, i.e. French, influence). If Thomas Kuhn could argue for a *temporal* reappraisal of the history of science to

[3] Dorinda Outram, 'The History of Natural History: Grand History or Local Lore?', in John Wilson Foster (ed.), *Nature in Ireland: A Scientific and Cultural History* (Dublin: Lilliput Press, 1997), 470.

foreground 'the historical integrity of that science in its own time', I would similarly claim the need to demonstrate the *spatiality* of science—that natural history needs to be put into its time *and* place.[4] Outram also maintains that the 'mythology of science outside social production' has to be regarded as being 'a luxury of lands with settled histories where the society that produces science is not itself in question'.[5] In offering a deeper exploration as to the gendered sets of fieldwork practices associated with late Victorian scientific culture, the chapter makes a wider argument as to the situated nature of knowledge formation, production, and circulation, and argues that as a cultural phenomenon (with values attached), there is nothing 'natural' about the study, writing, and practice of natural history, particularly in colonial contexts.

1. ISLAND SPACES

Maude Jane Delap was born in 1866 at Templecrone Rectory, Dungloe, County Donegal, the seventh of ten children born to the Reverend Alexander Delap (1830–1906) and Anna Jane Delap (née Goslett, 1831–1914). In 1874, the family moved from Donegal to Valentia Island, a small island off the Iveragh Peninsula, Co. Kerry, where her father was appointed rector of Valentia and Caherciveen.[6] Reverend Delap undertook the journey by boat to transport the family furniture, while Mrs Delap and the children travelled down by land. In the rectory at Reenellen, Knightstown, Valentia, Maude would maintain a laboratory in a room she later called 'The Department'. Between 1895 and 1896, she was actively involved with the Valentia Harbour Survey, a survey of the flora and fauna of Valentia by a team of eight naturalists and scientists, led by Professor Edward T. Browne of University College London.[7] Her contribution, along with that of her sister, Constance (better known as Connie, 1868–1935), is noted in the final publication of the survey in the *Proceedings of the Royal Irish Academy* (Vol. 5, 1898–1900). It appears that Reverend Delap was locally well known and liked, and in his 'Memories of a Loving Alien', Peter Delap records an incident with his

[4] Thomas Kuhn quoted in Nicholas Jardine and Emma Spary, 'The Natures of Cultural History', in Nicholas Jardine, J. A. Secord, and Emma Spary (eds), *Cultures of Natural History* (Cambridge: Cambridge University Press, 1996), 6.

[5] Outram, 'The History of Natural History', 470.

[6] Valentia Island is also referred to as 'Valencia Island' in this period.

[7] See E. T. Browne, I. Thompson, F. H. Gamble et al., 'The Fauna and Flora of Valencia Harbour on the West Coast of Ireland', *Proceedings of the Royal Irish Academy*, 21 (1899), 667–854.

grandfather. 'There is a sad stereotype of the Church of Ireland clergymen of yesterday as a lackey of the establishment', he writes. 'Not all were so, my cousin Rhoda once asked "Grandfather, what are the Catholics?" and got a sharp reply: "Never ask me that child, we are all God's children"'.[8] The Delap sisters were equally liked and respected, with Peter Delap recollecting that 'Wherever we went, she [Maude] was instantly recognized and greeted with delight'. He notes that his grand-aunt Maude 'was an old-school Victorian all-round naturalist' and that 'we learned so very much from her'.[9] In an interview with Joanna Lee, a grand-niece of Maude Delap, Lee recalls that it was noted in the family that 'Mary told you what should be done, Maude got it done, and Connie was the one who comforted you'.[10] After her father's death, Maude's mother and her sisters (also unmarried) led a largely self-sufficient life on the island by growing their fruit and vegetables (including grapes and peaches in their greenhouse) and selling gladioli and lilies for a supplementary income. Prayers were said before breakfast, alcohol was not consumed, and rabbit and fish were often served for dinner. Grand-nieces and nephews remember the sisters as wearing Edwardian-style clothes well into the twentieth century ('they dressed fifty years out of date'), which they felt was out of a sense both of social propriety and economic necessity.[11] Peter Delap notes that this was not out of 'prudishness', but a 'compulsion to preserve a low profile', as 'ostentation was intolerable in the face of poverty', which was evident throughout the island at the time.[12]

As with many self-taught female natural scientists, Maude had no formal education and was greatly influenced by her father's interest in marine biology, zoology, and botany. It is not clear from the existing archives what exactly her father's engagement was with Darwinism, but as Thomas Duddy has noted, 'What you get in Ireland in the nineteenth century is a spectrum of responses'.[13] Reverend Delap, primarily as a man of religion, in addition to being an avid amateur naturalist, may well have fallen into a category of natural scientists that could 'blend' science and religion by following the precepts of evolution, but explained godly design through the employment of a natural theology which showed that 'divine unity' lay beneath the diversity of animal and organic structures.[14] Following

[8] Peter Delap, 'Memories of a Loving Alien', unpublished memoir, n.d., 3. I am grateful to Joanna Lee for this source.

[9] Ibid., 1.

[10] Personal interview with Joanna Lee, Dublin, 25 November 2013.

[11] Ibid.

[12] Delap, 'Memories of a Loving Alien', 2.

[13] Thomas Duddy, 'The Irish Response to Darwinism', in Róisín Jones and Martin Steer (eds), *Darwin, Praeger and the Clare Island Surveys* (Dublin: Royal Irish Academy, 2009), 10–11.

[14] See Thomas Duddy (ed.), *The Irish Response to Darwinism*, 6 vols (Bristol: Thoemmes Continuum, 2003).

her father's example, Delap sent specimens and samples to the Natural History Museum in London and in 1894 started a correspondence with Dr Robert Francis Scharff, curator of the Dublin Natural History Museum, sending him regular observations, field notes, letters, preserved specimens, and sketch drawings—a practice she would retain with the Museum until 1949.[15] In 1906, she was offered a post in the Marine Biological Station at Plymouth, but turned it down, in her great-nephew John Barlee's account as her father reputedly stated that 'No daughter of mine will leave home, except as a married woman!'[16] The reality of leaving Valentia at this stage of her life, as she was then approaching forty, in addition to leaving her sisters, may well have been additional considerations as to why Delap did not take up the position.

During the interwar years, she was the official recorder of whale-strandings in south-west Ireland for a study conducted by Dr Francis Charles Fraser of the British Museum. Her scientific work was internationally acknowledged in 1928 when zoologists Oskar Carlgren and T. A. Stephenson named a sea anemone after her, *Edwardsia Delapiae*.[17] In this, Delap is unusual in having a species named after a woman and becomes embedded within a masculine tradition 'that used naming as a form of recognition of accomplishments'.[18] In 1936, her contribution to marine biology was acknowledged when she was made an Associate of the Linnaean Society in London.[19] There are over forty references to her contribution to the Valentia Survey, and there are eighty-one noted entries of donations of specimens to the National Museum of Ireland's natural history database under the name of 'Delap'.[20] Between 1901 and 1924, she published over fifteen articles in journals and magazines such as the *Irish Naturalist*, *Kerry Archaeological Magazine*, and *Fisheries Ireland* and

[15] On Scharff, see Juliana Adelman, 'Evolution on Display: Promoting Irish Natural History and Darwinism at the Dublin Science and Art Museum', *The British Journal for the History of Science*, 38 (2005), 411–36.

[16] John Barlee quoted in Anne Byrne, 'Untangling the Medusa', in Patricia Deevey and Mary Mulvihill (eds), *Stars, Shells and Bluebells: Women Scientists and Pioneers* (Dublin: WITS, 1997), 104.

[17] As noted in a report for the National Parks and Wildlife Service of Ireland, 'Survey of the Distribution of the Anemone *Edwardsia Delapiae* (Carlgren and Stephenson, 1928) in Valentia Harbour and Portmagee Channel SAC, Co. Kerry', *Report for the National Parks and Wildlife Service of Ireland*, by MERC Consultancy, available at https://www.npws.ie/sites/default/files/publications/pdf/MERC_2007_Survey_for_Edwardsia_Delapiae.pdf, accessed 13 January 2017.

[18] Mona Domosh, 'Towards a Feminist Historiography of Geography', *Transactions of the Institute of British Geographers*, 16 (1991), 101.

[19] Women had only been admitted as members to the Linnaean Society in 1905.

[20] Some of these are under A. J. Delap (Maude's father), but most are singularly attributed to M. J. Delap.

contributed notes and information to scholars in the areas of botany, zoology, marine science, folklore, and anthropology throughout her lifetime.[21]

In many ways, Delap's home, Valentia Island, is an exception to all the perceived 'rules' concerning island life in Ireland at this time. Due to its physical location, as an island off the west Kerry coast (measuring almost seven miles by two miles in size), one could be forgiven for thinking its remote location would hold a distinct disadvantage for the island and its inhabitants. It is, however, precisely the location of the island that led to its prosperity and to its exceptional status in nineteenth- and twentieth-century Ireland. Valentia may have been physically cut off from the Irish mainland, but it was intellectually, scientifically, and economically connected to the rest of the world in many different ways. Such connections to the cultural and scientific worlds of metropolitan Dublin, London, and New York can be attributed to the location of a telegraph station, weather station, and an observatory on the island, in addition to extensive fishing and mining industries established since the early 1800s. By the time of the Valentia Survey, the island was seen as an open laboratory, with science as its bridge to the world. Valentia was indeed then 'a different Irish island', and was markedly different to other islands along a western Irish coastline that would become familiar, if not over-determined, to tourists, artists, and scholars during the Irish Cultural Revival period (*c.*1890s–1920s).[22]

The flow of visitors for scientific and scholarly research purposes to the island over the years (engineers, scientists, marine biologists) finally culminated with a decision made by Browne to locate an extensive marine survey on Valentia in the mid-1890s. The decision to locate the study on the island was in part informed by the interest in natural science of Reverend Delap (who was already well known through his previous activities in the Belfast Field Club) and the availability of existing infrastructure. With the arrival of the survey team in 1895, through their father's interest in natural history and the hosting of survey visitors at Reenellen, Maude and Constance would become centrally involved with Browne's study and would continue to log information and collect specimens for him years after the initial 'official' fieldwork had been completed. In Irish, if not in European terms in this period, the only other comparable island to receive such multidisciplinary attention would be Lambay Island, Co. Dublin, with the survey of its flora and fauna in 1905–6.[23]

[21] She was also recorded as being a member of *Cumann Béaloideas na hÉireann* (The Folklore Association of Ireland) in 1948.

[22] Nellie O'Cleirigh, *Valentia: A Different Kind of Irish Island* (Dublin: Portobello Press, 1992).

[23] Both the Valentia and Lambay surveys in many ways laid the template for the more famous Clare Island Survey (County Mayo), led by Robert Lloyd Praeger and conducted by

Valentia can be seen, therefore, as an exemplary (if not exceptional) maritime site of national and imperial fieldwork that then was re-produced, displayed, and published in various urban contexts. What we find are sometimes competing sets of cultural geographies produced by different fieldwork practices and cultural epistemes. As Diarmid Finnegan stresses in his work on the connections between fieldwork and the natural sciences in the Scottish Highlands in the same period, 'a distinction between the locational geographies of mountain fieldwork and the geographies produced through that same fieldwork remains a useful heuristic'.[24] This distinction is indeed a critical one and is one that will be discussed more fully in the remainder of this chapter in terms of how Valentia both *enabled* and *produced* culturally encoded fieldwork practices within the context of its own local, national, and imperial geographies. In producing a whole set of public, imperial, and gendered maritime geographies, Valentia opens up one set of discussions of how other marginal, coastal, island spaces align themselves with, and possibly alter, metropolitan narratives of gender and modernity, the implications of which largely remain to be explored in Irish and international contexts. This leads us then necessarily to examine not just what is being studied in terms of local or national cultures of natural history, but to ask in what broader epistemological spaces are those cultures and knowledges implicitly embedded, particularly when considering the spaces of the gendered body, nation, and empire.

2. GENDERED GEOGRAPHIES

In a 1992 review of *Women in the Field: America's Pioneering Women Naturalists*, Barbara L. Peckarsky notes that the preface to the book refers to the 'attributes' these pioneer women naturalists had in common. Many of them seemed to share some (if not all) of the following personal characteristics: modesty; none liked typically 'women's things' like housework or clothes, although it is interestingly noted that 'most of them did enjoy cooking for their friends'; some had been 'favourite daughters of enlightened fathers'; and many had independent mothers as role models. Of the twenty-five women portrayed in the book, most never married or started their careers after their husbands died; six had supportive husbands;

a team of over 200 experts from the Royal Irish Academy and the Royal Society of London, 1909–11.

24 Diarmid A. Finnegan, 'Naturalising the Highlands: Geographies of Mountain Fieldwork in Late-Victorian Scotland', *Journal of Historical Geography*, 33 (2007), 814.

two were actively discouraged by husbands; two had children; some gave their material to men for subsequent publication; the majority were self-taught; and finally, most did not hold professional positions or status during their lifetimes.[25] To this list we can add another typology based on more recent work in literary history and feminist cultural geography to highlight other sociocultural factors, particularly questions of class and socio-economic status. Often, such women tended to be wealthy from privileged and well-connected backgrounds and therefore different constraints of domesticity and respectability did not always apply. They often had sufficient private funds to pay for travel, fieldwork, and laboratory materials, and indeed their subscriptions to field clubs and related societies often helped to keep such organizations financially afloat.[26] They primarily used private (often family) connections and operated within a highly interconnected, and in many cases international, intellectual milieu. They efficiently used personal connections and letters of introduction with individuals to engage with scientific and scholarly communities and learned societies. In addition to the above, they often held access to knowledge networks (infrastructure and technologies) of the period: journals, books, associations, institutions, and field clubs, in addition to access to postal and telegraphic services and transport networks.[27] They were often dependent on a previous connection from a father, brother, and/or husband, and often remained dependent on that link for future research and work, and indeed for their livelihoods. Such networks were more often than not highly gendered, and one can easily trace what feminist geographer Gillian Rose has called 'paternal lines of descent' in women scientists and their families across Britain and Ireland in this period.[28]

The strategies employed by such women also entailed the negotiation of a limited set of permitted practices within highly prescribed and gendered spaces. Such women engaged in the study of natural history by participating in learned practices such as the submitting of paintings for public display; the collecting of biological specimens, for private and public collections; giving provision in the field or in texts (to male scientists) of

[25] Barbara Peckarsky, 'Review of *Women in the Field: America's Pioneering Women Naturalists* by M. M. Bonata', *Journal of the New York Entomological Society*, 100 (1992), 640.

[26] I am indebted to Timothy Collins for this note with regard to the role of women's subscriptions to field clubs in Ireland in particular.

[27] The expansion of local railway lines that connect to national and international networks across Ireland and Britain in this period is of particular importance, both in terms of the transfer of specimens to museums and also in allowing for the efficient organization of surveys and field club outings in a relatively short period of time.

[28] Gillian Rose, 'Tradition and Paternity: Same Difference?', *Transactions of the Institute of British Geographers*, 20 (1995), 415.

specimens and Latin names for species encountered; and the citation of the expertise of male authorities to authenticate and validate their own work. They also engaged in a variety of activities that challenged masculinist ideals of fieldwork, such as walking, climbing, rowing, cycling, and extensive travelling; they observed and recorded by drawing, sketching, painting, logging, writing, and photographing; they displayed through exhibitions, lectures, and publication; and they contributed by translating, transcribing, and donating funds and specimens to scientific projects. Other outlets for the translation of privately accumulated knowledge into more open and public spaces include letter writing, the publication of journals and travel narratives, being the authors of 'popular science', and the writing of educational books on natural history and science for children.

Cheryl McEwan notes the 'separate spheres' argument that has dominated much critique of Victorian culture in terms of the construction of homosocial spheres in the realms of culture, science, and the family.[29] She focuses on the articulation of gendered notions of 'separate spheres' in the construction of science and scientific geography and argues that there is still a problematic contemporary legacy regarding the maintenance of such gendered spaces and categories of knowledge with regard to contemporary professionalization of geography and geographical teaching and praxis in the academy today.[30] She argues that 'women's struggle to be recognized as scientists has a long history' and notes that while popular science for middle-class women increased during the eighteenth century, so did 'the gap between professionalism and amateurism, high and popular science'. Women in this period often became the 'unpaid "invisible assistants" to scientific husbands or fathers in the home, because they were barred from universities'.[31] Individuals such as Ann Lee, Anna Blackburne, Sarah Abbot, and Mary Kingsley are often cited as examples of the limitations placed on women with an active interest in science and natural history in this period.[32] The public works of men were, therefore, 'often based on a certain extent on the "invisible", private, amateur work of women taking place in the domestic realm'.[33]

The concepts of 'the field' and 'fieldwork' (with the attendant spatial and epistemological assumptions) need to be critically unpacked and

[29] Cheryl McEwan, 'Gender, Science and Physical Geography in Nineteenth-Century Britain', *Area*, 30 (1998), 215–23.

[30] Ibid., 220–1. [31] Ibid., 216.

[32] See Gerry Kearns, 'The Imperial Subject: Geography and Travel in the Work of Mary Kingsley and Halford Mackinder', *Transactions of the Institute of British Geographers*, 22 (1997), 450–72.

[33] McEwan, 'Gender, Science and Physical Geography', 216.

evaluated to investigate the different registers of Delap's spaces in the study of natural history and the maritime ecologies of Valentia Island. In a special issue of *cultural geographies* dedicated to the concept of 'field cultures', guest editor Philip Crang notes how the concept of 'the field' developed within the history of natural science and within studies of scientific culture.[34] Crang foregrounds that field cultures represented local cultures, in that 'what was done in places imagined and performed as field sites was central not only to the formation of scientific cultures of knowledge such as natural history—but also to placed civic identities'.[35] Drawing on the work of H. Kuklick and R. E. Kohler, Crang comments that the field is therefore 'a privileged location for knowing nature and culture, and a setting for place-specific practices of knowing'.[36] In their analysis of natural history societies in late Victorian Scotland, Charles W. J. Withers and Diarmid A. Finnegan develop the connection between local, civic, and imperial knowledges. Through an examination of how fieldwork contributed to the development of scientific fields, they argue that working and being 'in the field' helped to promote civic identity through scientific conduct in this period.[37] While they do not examine this aspect of Victorian field culture in terms of gender, in their conclusion they acknowledge that 'there is, of course, more to consider'—'the gendered nature of fieldwork' being one such consideration they cite as meriting further critical study.[38]

Little critical attention has been paid to the actual empirical use of 'domestic' space in science, particularly in the context of the gendering of the natural sciences and the role that amateur women scientists, field-workers, and naturalists played in the constructions of modern European science.[39] As Outram notes, 'natural history fieldwork was squarely associated with a tradition which linked curiosity to movement'—a tradition that required the precondition of political, economic, and gendered freedom to be mobile in the first instance.[40] Women were admitted into some scholarly and learned societies, but it was still very much within the context of being the exception rather than the rule. What we have then are what Jeanne Kay Guelke and Karen Morin call 'competing sets of cultural

34 Philip Crang, 'Field Cultures', *cultural geographies*, 10 (2003), 251–2.

35 Ibid., 251.

36 Ibid., 252.

37 Charles W. J. Withers and Diarmid A. Finnegan, 'Natural History Societies, Fieldwork and Local Knowledge in Nineteenth-Century Scotland: Towards a Historical Geography of Civic Science', *cultural geographies*, 10 (2003), 334–53.

38 Ibid., 347.

39 Dorinda Outram, 'New Spaces in Natural History', in Jardine, Secord, and Spary (eds), *Cultures of Natural History*, 253.

40 Ibid., 255.

practices' within the context of Victorian natural history and science, and of women's opportunities and place within such practices.[41] In the Irish context, this was silently enabled by the possibility of the relatively free movement of people across boundaries and places, which in many ways was merged with the cultural rather than the political spheres in the post-Parnellite era of the 1890s. Less formal gatherings, such as regional field clubs and associated national unions, can offer a different and more regionally nuanced picture. The presence and activities of such field clubs also presumed an ability to walk and leisurely roam across the Irish countryside with relative ease. While some, like Praeger, may have regarded the Belfast Naturalists' Field Club as 'a second university in which I formed friendships which, despite the disparity of age, remained warm and intimate and through which I acquired a knowledge of field-lore, botanical, zoological and geological, which stood to me throughout my life', for many women in Britain and Ireland at this time, such field clubs served as *first* universities, in addition to being regarded as 'Field and Flirtation Societies' because they were mixed and often allowed women full membership.[42]

As Kirsten Aletta Greer and Jeanne Kay Guelke note in their study of bird-watching in Southern Ontario from 1791–1886, there were three key influences on birdwatching practices in Canada at this time. The first influence was the transfer of British natural history to its overseas colonies; second, the popularity of American naturalists was of note; and finally, the rise of Canada's own incipient nationalism played into narratives of place, nation, and belonging.[43] In many ways, a similar pattern can be seen to emerge in Ireland through the rise in field clubs, amateur associations, and the participation of men and women from different social backgrounds in nineteenth-century Ireland.[44] These two sets of distinct spaces

[41] Jeanne Kay Guelke and Karen M. Morin, 'Gender, Nature, Empire: Women Naturalists in Nineteenth Century British Travel Literature', *Transactions of the Institute of British Geographers*, 26 (2001), 311.

[42] Robert Lloyd Praeger, *Some Irish Naturalists: A Biographical Note-Book* (Dundalk: Dundalgan Press, 1949), 17, as cited in Timothy Collins, 'Praeger in the West: Naturalists and Antiquarians in Connemara and the Islands 1894–1914', *Journal of the Galway Archaeological and Historical Society*, 45 (1993), 124.

[43] Kirsten Aletta Greer and Jeanne Kay Guelke, '"Intrepid Naturalists and Polite Observers": Gender and Recreational Birdwatching in Southern Ontario, 1791–1886', *Journal of Sport History*, 30 (2003), 323–46.

[44] The Belfast Field Club was established in 1863, the Dublin Naturalists' Field Club in 1886, the Cork Naturalists' Field Club in 1892, the Limerick Naturalist Field Club in 1892, and the North Munster Archaeological Society (established in 1908) amalgamated with the Limerick Field Club to become the Thomand Archaeological Society and Field Club in 1929. The role and influence that Ulster-based learned groups and societies, and in particular the Belfast Field Club, had on subsequent national work in natural history and science cannot be overestimated and would be worthy of further study.

(public/private, masculine/feminine) were not mutually exclusive, and some overlap did occur, as with the blurring of the categories of the home study and domestic laboratory. McEwan argues that scientific production by women very often took place in a 'third space' between these two gendered spheres. While women were denied access to the laboratories of learned and scholarly institutions, 'many middle class women were actively encouraged to engage in scientific pursuits in the private, domestic laboratory'. This was primarily aimed at the class of 'leisured women', as it was thought that the menial and mechanical nature of the work was a suitable hobby for such individuals, while also allowing for more 'intelligent' women to be relieved of depression and boredom. The laboratory was therefore seen as 'an extension of the domestic sphere'. Fieldwork, which entailed the 'finding' of material and the 'creation' of data in the field (as opposed to in the study or laboratory), also involved 'the exercise of a particular kind of masculinity'.[45] In this formulation, the 'field' is feminized, something to be observed, conquered, and managed, with the 'work' being an heroic, manly occupation and operation. In this sense, Victorian fieldwork follows on from what Felix Driver has noted as being a masculine 'geography militant' in nineteenth-century imperial Britain.[46] Again, as McEwan notes,

> As the spaces of empire were gendered, so the field as a site for geographical research was constructed simultaneously as a feminized backdrop for the playing out of particular kinds of masculinity. The exclusion of women from the field, therefore, was naturalized by its construction as *public* space.[47]

She goes on to note that women of course did transgress these spaces during the nineteenth century, 'but rarely as professional scientists or geographers'.[48] It is, however, also important to consider how fieldwork offered women an alternative space and opportunity to engage with science at a time when advanced education and professional membership of learned societies was closed to them.[49] As Mona Domosh observes, 'Denied access to the academic training that would confer on them the appropriate status as "scientists", women like Mary Kingsley, Mary Graunt, Isabella Bird, and Marianne North found that fieldwork in the sense of exploration was as

[45] McEwan, 'Gender, Science and Physical Geography', 217.

[46] Felix Driver, *Geography Militant: Cultures of Exploration and Empire* (Oxford and Cambridge, MA: Wiley Blackwell, 2001).

[47] McEwan, 'Gender, Science and Physical Geography', 218.

[48] Ibid.

[49] There are many instances of women scientists having their papers read out by men to learned societies in this period, as they were unable to be present (as women) in such proceedings.

open to them as to anyone with adequate resources'.[50] In the following section, an exploration of what those 'adequate resources' might entail, in terms of other forms of social and intellectual capital, is offered in terms of the contents of the Delap Archive. The archive comprises many different materials and artefacts relating to Delap's life and work on the island spanning over eighty years, but a select number of items are chosen for discussion that highlight the different sets of cultural practices associated with the gendered geographies of Irish and British natural history in this period.

3. 'THE DEPARTMENT'—A ROOM OF ONE'S OWN

The Valentia Island Visitor Centre opened in 1986 as a volunteer-run heritage centre. It is housed in the former Knightstown National School (est. 1861), and there are three main display rooms, one of which contains the archive relating to the life and work of Maude Delap. The centre holds materials relating to Delap's work in particular, and items displayed include her field notebooks, bell jars, and the microscope from 'The Department'. Several items from this archive stand out as being of importance in terms of the social spaces of natural history in this period; such spaces are shaped and informed by cultures of reading, writing, and drawing and are deeply embedded within field cultures of observation, experimentation, and display. First, the *Illustrated Index of British Shells* (1859) by George Brettingham Sowerby was given by William Kinsey Dower to the Delap children in *c.*1873–6 (as noted by hand in the title page), and shows the role of natural history books and the scientific education for children in this period. As a standard text, Sowerby's volume indicates the increasing popularization of natural history (with children and young adults becoming an increasingly important market) and also shows that the Delap household was one in which such books would be welcome gifts. The book itself bears the signs of use and reuse, mostly in the same hand with many observational 'ticks' in pencil, often with various locations cited in the margins in Maude's hand.

The presence of shell, bone, and coral specimens in the Delap Archive illustrates the collecting and preserving practices that Delap experimented with, in addition to demonstrating the range of interests she had in Valentia's natural environment (see Figure 9.1). She also encouraged other islanders to collect specimens as well and wrote to the Dublin

[50] Domosh, 'Towards a Feminist Historiography', 96.

Figure 9.1. Window with specimens from the Delap Archive, Valentia Island Heritage Centre, Co. Kerry. Photograph, Nessa Cronin, 2013.

Natural History Museum on several occasions that they should pay for such specimens when and where possible to encourage further local fieldwork in the region. While there are many stories surrounding Delap's energy and fastidiousness, one incident in particular, 'Aunt Maude's Whale', as retold by John Barlee, gives an indication of the practicalities of fieldwork on Valentia at the time. It also illustrates how her garden functioned as an extension of the third space, where her private laboratory and public fieldwork melded into one.

Before the Second World War, the renowned whale expert Dr Fraser of the British Museum published several reports concerning whale-strandings across Britain and Ireland. Fraser recruited a body of watchers to send reports to him at intervals and as Barlee recalls, Maude 'was provided with books and notes on how to identify the different species and so became the official reporter for her corner of Ireland'.[51] Barlee notes that sometime in the 1920s, Maude became aware that 'a whale had been thrown up "on the rocks beyond the lighthouse", so she set out, accompanied by her handyman Mike, and an increasing crowd of hangers-on and small boys'. The whale was reported as being about sixteen feet

[51] John Barlee, 'Aunt Maude's Whale', unpublished manuscript, n.d., 1.

long, 'probably weighed a ton or two', and had already started to decompose. Maude decided that it was a specimen of True's Beaked Whale—a rare species discovered from an incomplete specimen in 1913 in North Carolina, which had been examined and described by Dr True of the New York Museum. Maude went home and sent a letter seeking instructions from the museum; writing was her preferred mode of communication, as Barlee informs us that 'the telephone had been invented by then but Aunt Maude never used one'. Within a few days, she received a letter with the instruction to cut off the head and flippers, send them on to the museum as soon as possible, and bury the skeleton in a safe place so that 'the skeleton could be recovered "in due course"'. Armed with 'an assortment of butchering implements', the whale was disarticulated and 'cut into manageable lumps', and then carried by cart to her garden, where she proceeded to take the flesh off the bones. In this it appears that Maude was assisted by a local man, Michael or 'Mike' (no surname given in the record), who also worked to help maintain the house and garden for the sisters. After photographing the head, she 'wrapped it and the flippers in newspaper and sacking and put them into a wooden case and dispatched them to the Museum'; usually this was done by train. The remainder of the whale was buried in the asparagus patch in the garden. A couple of years later, a letter came from the museum asking for the remaining bones to be sent up to Dublin—'Up came the asparagus and a large number of still very smelly bones were recovered and sent to the Museum'. Then yet another letter arrived, announcing that two bones were missing—the vestigial pelvic bones. So, 'up came the long-suffering asparagus' and Mike and Maude spent several days sieving through the earth searching for the lost bones, when a telegram arrived from the museum: 'Stop! New York Museum informs us that True's Beaked Whale does not possess vestigial pelvic bones'.[52]

The zoological register of the National Museum of Ireland states that the whale was stranded in April 1935, with the head and flippers being forwarded in May of that year. The skeleton was 'buried by Miss Delap and sent to the Museum in 1936'. This incident shows that Maude undertook the physical work of identifying and obtaining specimens, was in regular contact with both the Dublin and London Museums (via letters and telegrams), and was familiar with the practice of sending specimens to Dublin (via ferry-rail networks). What is also of note is that while the initial impetus in terms of observing whales in the area came from the British Museum, it was to the National Museum that Delap

[52] Ibid.

deposited her physical specimens, which would indicate her affiliation with the sense of an Irish natural history and a civic responsibility to have that logged and recorded, and displayed in what was then a newly re-formed national collection in Free State Ireland.

4. RETHINKING IRISH MARITIME HISTORIES

Delap never left her home on Valentia and was kept busy with her work at the local hospital and fisherman's tea rooms, in addition to documenting and occasionally publishing her findings and observations concerning the maritime life of the region. She remained unmarried, and references both from family interviews and published sources indicate that she had fallen in love with Browne during his time in Ireland in the 1890s but that the affection was not reciprocated (he married his assistant Miss M. Robinson in 1909). Notwithstanding this, Delap sent him violets on his birthday every year until his death in 1937.[53] She died on 23 July 1953 and was buried with her sisters in the Church of Ireland graveyard near Knightstown. Joanna Lee noted that Mrs Dore, the Delaps' housekeeper, looked after each of the three sisters as they became ill. She would sit outside their door at night in case she was needed and publicly keened the loss of each sister's passing. Peter Delap recollects, 'At the end, she would sit for hours outside Aunt Mary's bedroom door, and wrapped in her shawl, drawing on a little clay pipe and ever alert for a sound from within'.[54] A somewhat belated obituary notice in *The Irish Naturalists' Journal* in 1958 lists Delap's published papers, as well as noting her generosity and contribution to the study of Irish natural history during her lifetime. The notice additionally observed that:

> Until she was over seventy she was quite prepared to go out fishing in a small rowing boat, and gardened vigorously in spite of very arthritic hands. Although she long out-lived her sisters, and saw everything she had loved and respected sinking into disrepute, she remained cheerful, serene and intensely interested in world affairs.[55]

Delap left most of her 'Department' specimens and collections to John Barlee, but unfortunately, the preservatives had not been replaced, and much of what was left decayed into sludge. Some of her other specimens

53 Patricia M. Byrne, 'Delap, Maude Jane', in James McGuire and James Quinn (eds), *Dictionary of Irish Biography* (Cambridge: Cambridge University Press, 2009), 157–8.

54 Delap, 'Memories of a Loving Alien', 6.

55 N. F. McMillan and W. J. Rees, 'Maude Jane Delap (1866–1953)', *The Irish Naturalists' Journal*, 12 (1958), 222.

are catalogued and kept in the Natural History Museum in Dublin, with the head of True's Beaked Whale on permanent display on the first floor (see Figures 9.2a and 9.2b). Here her work remains on public display, along with other specimens collected from the region, and items registered from 'E.T. Browne' may well include specimens that were silently collected and presented to him by Constance and Maude Delap.

The legacy of Delap can be regarded in terms of rethinking the borders of the study of natural history, in foregrounding the contribution that 'marginal' and island spaces made to Victorian field cultures in this period. It also opens up questions as to the interconnections between local places that become sites of enquiry and transnational scientific cultures, in terms of rethinking the *spatiality of science* (domestic, local, imperial) in which practices of natural history are embedded. This is of particular importance when thinking of the contributions that amateur and professional naturalists and scholars equally made (often working alongside each other in the field, and one relying on the other for a different form of knowledge) to a nascent sense of an *Irish* natural history that was visually symbolized by, and housed within, the new Dublin Natural History Museum. Finally, in opening up an alternative narrative of the sociology of fieldwork and 'domestic science', it foregrounds the necessity to take into account the

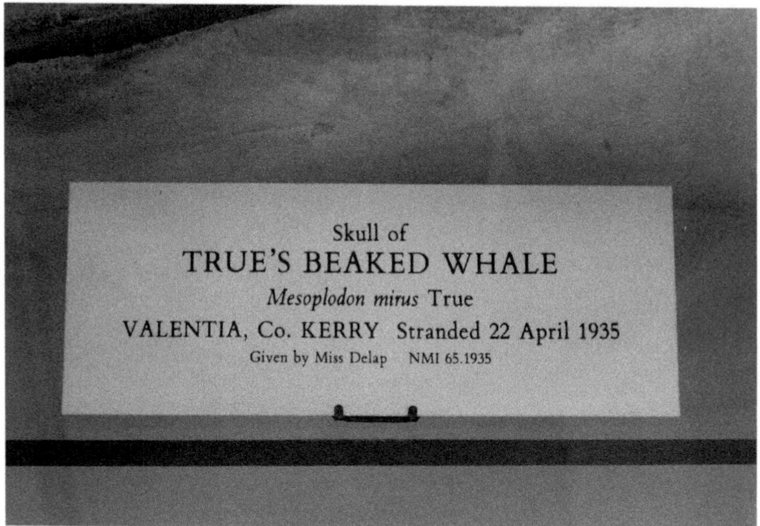

Figure 9.2a. Maude Delap's specimen of True's Beaked Whale on permanent display (detail). Natural History Museum, Dublin. Photograph, Nessa Cronin, 2014.

Figure 9.2b. Maude Delap's specimen of True's Beaked Whale (bottom right-hand corner) on permanent display. Natural History Museum, Dublin. Photograph, Nessa Cronin, 2014.

gendered geographies of the 'making' of natural history and various scientific practices in this period. The complex web of connections that linked Valentia to the scientific worlds of Dublin, London, and New York also served an intellectual social network that stretched across Maude Delap's life and career as an 'amateur' natural scientist. While Delap's maritime life and work is rooted in the island space of Valentia in this period, it also made a contribution beyond those shores and compels us to rethink the spaces of domestic science and fieldwork cultures in a broader Atlantic context.

10

Science at the Seaside

Pleasure Hunts in Victorian Devon

Kyriaki Hadjiafxendi and John Plunkett

In 1858, the versatile thinker and writer, George Henry Lewes, declared that the lovely sea anemone was 'now the ornament of countless drawing-rooms, studies, and back parlours, as well as the delight of unnumbered amateurs'.[1] The mid-Victorian period witnessed a popular fascination with marine biology and, more particularly, with the ecology of the seashore. Lewes's own volume, his *Sea-Side Studies at Ilfracombe, Tenby, the Scilly Isles, and Jersey* (1858), was part of this fashion, and based on a long coastal tour made by Lewes and his partner, Marian Evans Lewes (soon to become famous as George Eliot), from May to August 1856. Their decision to begin their excursion in Ilfracombe, North Devon was no accident. They were heading to a locale that was attracting increasing numbers of natural history enthusiasts, inspired by volumes such as Philip Henry Gosse's *A Naturalist's Rambles on the Devonshire Coast* (1853), Charles Kingsley's *Glaucus; or, The Wonders of the Shore* (1855), and George Tugwell's *A Manual of the Sea-Anemones Commonly Found on the English Coast* (1856). This chapter argues that the rich history of writing about the Devon coastline played an important role in the growth of Victorian popular science. While the popularity of Gosse, Kingsley, and marine biology more generally has been well documented, little critical attention has been given to why a small, relatively remote coastal zone inspired such attention. In explaining how the rock pools and beaches of Victorian Devon were especially suited for those enthused by natural history, our aim is to illustrate a neglected aspect of the history of popular science and British seaside tourism.

[1] George Henry Lewes, *Sea-Side Studies at Ilfracombe, Tenby, the Scilly Isles, and Jersey* (Edinburgh: William Blackwood and Sons, 1858), 114.

This chapter focuses on two entwined spaces: the first of these is the physical and imaginative place of the Devon coast and the role it played in the making of scientific knowledge. Recent scholarship in the history of science has demonstrated that scientific knowledge is not abstract or universal, but is spatially conditioned and produced. Simon Naylor has pointed out that 'It is not always the case that science only exerts its influence onto place; places also affect science and how it is received'.[2] Spatial approaches have been particularly productive in analysing nineteenth-century popular science because it was conducted at so many different venues and locales. Aileen Fyfe and Bernard Lightman pose the key questions: 'where might people encounter and interact with the sciences, and what sorts of experiences might they have there?'[3] A number of recent studies have examined the scientific culture of provincial towns, cities, and regions within Britain.[4] While providing confirmation of just how pervasive the provision of popular science was, such scholarship has produced a much more heterogeneous national picture than was hitherto the case.

The scientific importance that North Devon acquired because of its rich coastal ecology contrasted with its peripheral geographical position. The Victorians were fascinated by the liminal world of the seashore and the meanings they attached to this space form the second focus of our chapter. Seaside science concentrated on the biodiversity discoverable in the littoral zone between sea and land, part of whose appeal was that it was constantly being renewed and remade by the tide. Contemporary writer Linda Cracknell has described the intertidal zone as a space that 'enlivens imaginations; secreting the extraordinary in the ordinary rhythm of ebb and flow; swash and backwash. This is where transformation is possible, where nothing stays the same, where there are junctions of opportunity to gain wisdom.'[5] Gosse and Kingsley would have approved of such sentiments; indeed, they acquired popularity as pioneers in the study of the secret life of the seashore and the exploration of its imaginative appeal. Gosse dedicated

2 Simon Naylor, *Regionalizing Science: Placing Knowledges in Victorian England* (London: Pickering and Chatto, 2010), 3. See also David N. Livingstone, *Putting Science in Its Place: Geographies of Scientific Knowledge* (Chicago: University of Chicago Press, 2003); and David N. Livingstone and Charles W. J. Withers (eds), *Geographies of Nineteenth-Century Science* (Chicago: University of Chicago Press, 2011).

3 Aileen Fyfe and Bernard Lightman, 'Science in the Marketplace: An Introduction', in Aileen Fyfe and Bernard Lightman (eds), *Science in the Marketplace: Nineteenth-Century Sites and Experiences* (Chicago: University of Chicago Press, 2007), 4.

4 See Juliana Adelman, *Communities of Science in Nineteenth-Century Ireland* (London: Pickering and Chatto, 2009); and Diarmid A. Finnegan, *Natural History Societies and Civic Culture in Victorian Scotland* (London: Pickering and Chatto, 2009).

5 Linda Cracknell and Owain Jones, 'A Conversational Essay on Tides', available at https://tidalcultures.wordpress.com/a-conversational-essay-on-tides-by-linda-cracknell-and-owain-jones, accessed 9 January 2017.

a whole volume to *The Romance of Natural History* (1860), while in *Glaucus*, Kingsley claimed that zoophytes and microscopic animalcules found on every shore fuelled the curiosity of the public more than the large dinosaur sculptures at the new Sydenham Crystal Palace.[6] This widespread interest was accentuated by Gosse's popularization of the aquarium; its role in reproducing, domesticating, and making mobile the space of the seashore is described in the latter part of this chapter.

1. THE NORTH DEVON COAST AND THE ROMANCE OF NATURAL HISTORY

So why did seaside science come to the fore in the specific cultural moment of the 1850s? What was behind this fascination with the Devon coastline? The answers to these questions lie in a combination of geography, improvements in transportation, a revolution in popular publishing, and changing patterns of leisure and tourism. Domestic tourism had started to blossom during the Napoleonic Wars; one area to benefit was Devon and its coastal resorts, particularly Torquay, thanks largely to its picturesque views and the widespread belief in the health-giving effects of sea air. Transport links, however, remained poor, particularly when it came to reaching North Devon. In 1817, it took Frances Burney over twenty-five hours to travel the 110 miles from Bath to Ilfracombe.[7] It was not until the advent of widespread rail travel in the second half of the nineteenth century that domestic tourism would really take off; the attraction of North Devon in the 1850s was that it had come much more within reach for genteel visitors but still retained a fashionable remoteness.

The GWR train line to Bristol was completed in June 1841, but North Devon had to wait for its rail connection until the Exeter to Barnstaple Line opened on 12 July 1853. Less than three years later, when Marian Evans Lewes and George Henry Lewes arrived in Ilfracombe on 9 May 1856, they were able to travel on this new line via Bristol and Exeter; however, they still had to cover the final eleven miles by coach. In 1851, Ilfracombe only had a population of 3,677; but it was growing quickly.[8] When Charlotte Chanter described the appearance of the local coastline in the summer of 1855, she noted the increase in bathing machines and the

[6] Charles Kingsley, *Glaucus; or, The Wonders of the Shore* (1855: Cambridge: Macmillan and Co., 1859), 33.

[7] John F. Travis, *The Rise of the Devon Seaside Resorts 1750–1950* (Exeter: Exeter University Press, 1993), 71.

[8] Ibid., 77.

popularity of natural history exploration. The 'mushroom-like' appearance of the bathing machines turns them into 'novelty' specimens like the anemones natural historians sought to collect:

> [the shore has] thirty five of those novel brown mushrooms, who have for the last two years have infested the sea coast, all seated together so close that you could not have passed between them: besides sundry other specimens in groups of half-a-dozen, some perched upon the rocks, some sketching, some making holes in muslin, others again diving into 'rock pools' after unfortunate anemones.[9]

Chanter was the sister of Charles Kingsley and the wife of the Reverend John Mills Chanter of Holy Trinity Church, Ilfracombe. Her own guidebook was often mentioned alongside those of Gosse and Kingsley. Her *Ferny Combes: A Ramble after Ferns in the Glens and Valleys of Devonshire* (1856) helped to make visiting Devon for its ferns an activity to rival the search for anemones. (Articles on this subject appeared around this time in *Good Words*, *Leisure Hour*, and *Once a Week*.)[10]

The development of tourism, particularly as undertaken by the genteel and educated, went hand-in-hand with the growth of popular science. The pursuit of scientific discovery, in all its forms, seeped into many aspects of Victorian cultural and civic life. As a leisure pursuit, popular science combined pleasure, curiosity, and spectacle with an enlightenment desire to better understand the surrounding world. Its success was aided by a widespread belief in rational recreation; that is, in the idea that leisure time should be used for improvement as well as for amusement. Aileen Fyfe has argued that, from the 1850s, 'there is more evidence of the sciences in tourist literature. A growing enthusiasm for the out-of-doors helped inspire popular interest in natural history, especially but not only at the seaside'.[11] Freed from the urban environment, rock pooling, fossil hunting, searching after local flora and fauna—all provided a hands-on method of finding out more about the natural world. At the beginning of *Glaucus*, Kingsley addresses a putative urban tourist, urging him not to join the 'ignoble army of idlers', but to earnestly examine the shore to find wonders

[9] Charlotte Chanter, *Ferny Combes: A Ramble after Ferns in the Glens and Valleys of Devonshire* (London: Lovell Reeve, 1856), 25–6.

[10] 'A Summer's Study of Ferns', *Good Words*, 1 (December 1860): 423–4; 'Summer in Devonshire', *Once a Week*, 7 (26 July 1862), 121–4; 'A Trip to North Devon', *Leisure Hour* (10 May 1862), 297–8.

[11] Aileen Fyfe, 'Natural History and the Victorian Tourist: From Landscapes to Rock-Pools', in Livingstone and Withers (eds), *Geographies of Nineteenth-Century Science*, 380.

'around you at every step, stranger than ever opium-eater dreamed'.[12] He leads his reader-tourist away from the artificiality of cultured spaces down to the Torbay shoreline, a space of amazement and strangeness:

> Follow us, then, reader in imagination, out of the gay watering place, with its London shops and London equipages, along the broad road beneath the sunny limestone cliff tufted with golden furze; past the huge oaks and green slopes of Tor Abbey. . . . And once there, before we look at anything else, come down straight to the sea marge; for yonder lies, just left by the retiring tide, a mass of life such as you will seldom see again.[13]

As a physical, educational, and imaginative activity, science at the seaside offered multiple pleasures, while simultaneously satisfying the belief in rational recreation.

The rise of outdoor natural history pursuits, and even the social freedoms of the seashore, do not fully explain why Devon became the dominant place in the fashion for popular science. Its appeal for marine biology resided in the unique position of its coast, especially in North Devon, vis-à-vis the Atlantic Ocean, Irish Sea, and English Channel. Gosse, like Kingsley, initially moved to Torquay, arriving on 29 January 1852 to rest and recuperate following a period of nervous dyspepsia and ill health in London, likely due to overwork. With his wife and two-year-old son, Edmund, he subsequently moved to Ilfracombe in April 1852.[14] Yet his initial choice of Torquay was not just for his wellbeing, but had a scientific rationale. The littoral zoologist worked best at spring tides and the times of low water in Devon made marine biology a socially and scientifically viable activity:

> In many parts of the English coast the lowest water occurs at about six o'clock in the morning or evening, a time inconvenient in many ways, and particularly to an invalid. In Devonshire, on the days of the new and full moon, the lowest tide is near the middle of the day.[15]

Gosse was keenly attuned to the tidal movements that made the Devon seashore an abundant source of marine life. It was a distinct if small 'bio-region'—to use Robert L. Thayer Jr's term—an area that is 'literally and etymologically a "life-place"—a unique region defined by natural (rather

[12] Kingsley, *Glaucus*, 14. [13] Ibid., 62–3.

[14] Philip Gosse's life in Devon is excellently described in Ann Thwaite, *Glimpses of the Wonderful: The Life of Philip Henry Gosse* (London: Faber and Faber, 2002), 170–203.

[15] Edmund Gosse, *The Life of Philip Henry Gosse F.R.S.* (London: Routledge, Kegan Paul, Trench, Trubner and Co., 1890), 236.

than political) boundaries with a geographic, climatic, hydrological, and ecological character capable of supporting unique human and nonhuman living communities.'[16] As Gosse outlined in *A Naturalist's Rambles on the Devonshire Coast*, the shape of the Bristol Channel and the adjacent coasts offers 'peculiar facilities for the study of those marine animals whose proper sphere of existence is the wide ocean'.[17] The prevailing westerly winds moving the surface waters of the Atlantic propelled large numbers of sea creatures along the shores of Portugal, Spain, and France; subsequently, a number of them passed through the English Channel. Another large portion was turned northward by the projecting point of Cornwall into the funnel of the Irish Sea; this marine life had to either head out into the North Sea or were forced into the narrowing confines of the Bristol Channel.

Of the three locations—the shores of the English Channel, the Irish Sea, and the Bristol Channel—it is the latter, being closed, that is most likely to retain the biodiversity of the specimens carried by the waves, linking the Devonshire coast with global tidal movements. The tides in the Bristol Channel are routinely claimed to be the second highest tides in the world. The prevailing winds pushing sea life towards the Cornish shore, combined with the current that followed the bending shore around to North Devon, ensured that the southern side of the channel would be particularly rich in marine life; 'thus the rocky coves and inlets of North Devon might be expected to be more than usually rich in those rare and accidental stragglers, which the waves bring in from their roamings in the boundless sea'.[18] North Devon might have been looked down upon as a rural periphery relative to the economic and cultural dominance of Victorian London and the industrial cities of northern England, yet its coast was a privileged littoral space; a natural edge that was both boundary and receptacle for the tidal flow of Atlantic marine ecology and that fuelled a fascination, to quote Owain Jones, 'for tides and the odd world of the intertidal zone which switches from land to sea, from one space to other space'.[19]

Charles Kingsley's promotion of seaside science similarly sought to make the rich coastal ecology of Devon integral to its cultural identity. Kingsley, who was born in Holne, Devon, had spent much of his childhood in Clovelly on the North Devon coast; he first travelled to Torquay in South Devon in the winter and spring of 1854 for health reasons, needing a respite from the ill effects of the damp Rectory at Eversley,

[16] Robert L. Thayer Jr, *LifePlace: Bioregional Thought and Practice* (Berkeley: University of California Press, 2003), 3.

[17] Philip Henry Gosse, *A Naturalist's Rambles on the Devonshire Coast* (London: John van Voorst, 1853), 363.

[18] Ibid., 364.

[19] Cracknell and Jones, 'A Conversational Essay on Tides'.

Hampshire, his home as parish Rector. Inspired by a new-found friendship with Gosse and his belief in the healing powers of nature, Kingsley spent many happy hours fossicking on the seashore, declaring a passion for natural history: 'how I am happier now in classifying a new polype, or solving a geognostic problem of strata, or any other bit of hard Baconian induction, than in writing all the novels in the world'.[20] He regularly sent Gosse samples after the latter had moved back to London, and, like his friend, Kingsley's passion for natural history stemmed from his conviction that it showed a convergence of science and theology. Kingsley's work at Torquay led to an article on 'The Wonders of the Shore' for the *North British Review* in 1854, which was subsequently expanded into *Glaucus*.

Kingsley, like Gosse, celebrated the Torquay area for its 'delicious Italian climate', while the distinct geological 'variety of its rocks, aspects, and sea-floors' gave it 'an abundance and variety of animal and vegetable life, unequalled, perhaps, in any other part of Great Britain.'[21] He went further than Gosse, though, in promoting a tradition of seaside science for Devon. Thanks to the pioneering work of Amelia Griffiths, Colonel George Montagu, and William Turton, Kingsley claimed that the area could lay claim to be the 'original home of marine zoology and botany in England'.[22] Kingsley's *Westward Ho!* (1855) similarly mythologizes the history of the West Country. Beginning in Bideford, North Devon, with the early life of the novel's hero, Amyas Leigh, it retells the story of his involvement in Elizabethan maritime struggles against the Spanish. The lesson is clear; the victories achieved by the men of Devon paved the way for the dominance of British imperialism founded on maritime supremacy. Famously, *Westward Ho!* helped to popularize the North Devon coast to such an extent that a village was founded after its name to cater for the influx of tourists.

In keeping with the way their work stemmed from the study of a particular bioregion, much of the influence of Gosse and Kingsley was due to the fact that they promoted a new type of living natural history, one that was spatially orientated and not dominated by the naturalist's study or the taxidermied sample. Such an approach to the tidal life of Devon was concerned with the necessity of understanding specimens in relationship to their dynamic coastal environment, which metamorphosed on a daily basis thanks to its tidal rhythms, secreting 'the extraordinary in the ordinary rhythm of ebb and flow; swash and backwash.'[23] Prior to his

[20] Charles Kingsley, *Novels, Poems and Letters of Charles Kingsley: Letters and Memoirs*, ed. Fanny Kingsley, 2 vols (New York and London: Co-operative Publication Society, 1899), i. 328.

[21] Kingsley, *Glaucus*, 61–2.

[22] Ibid., 61.

[23] Cracknell and Jones, 'A Conversational Essay on Tides'.

arrival in Devon, Gosse had travelled and published extensively, including *The Ocean* (SPCK, 1845), *Popular British Ornithology* (1849), *Natural History: Reptiles* (SPCK, 1850), and *A Naturalist's Sojourn in Jamaica* (1851). In the preface to his Jamaica volume, he criticized the established type of natural history that he would depart from in his seashore volumes:

> Natural History is far too much a science of dead things; a *necrology*. It is mainly conversant with dry skins, furred or feathered, blackened, shrivelled, and hay-stuffed; with objects, some admirably beautiful, some hideously ugly, impaled on pins, and arranged in rows in cork drawers.... These distorted things are described; their scales, plates, feathers counted; their forms copied, all shrivelled and stiffened as they are;... their limbs, members, and organs measured, and the results recorded in thousandths of an inch; two names are given to every one; the whole is enveloped in a mystic cloud of Graeco-Latino-English phraseology (often barbaric enough); and this is Natural History![24]

For Gosse, his natural history practice was definitely not a necrology. Rather, it was an evaluative discourse of tidal landscapes under a process of change, one that 'investigates and records the condition of living things, of things in a state of nature'; it would research their affections, stratagems, wants, habit, and actions through 'their connection with the inanimate world around them'.[25] This approach, which necessarily relied on understanding animal or marine life in the dynamic context of the ecosystems they inhabited, gave them a characterization: their physicality was animated on the page and they were brought to life through Gosse's skills of observation and precise description, both verbally and visually.

Gosse's experiences were detailed in *A Naturalist's Rambles on the Devonshire Coast* (1853) and *Sea-Side Pleasures* (1853), anonymously published for the SPCK and written with his wife, Emily. These books emphasized that the seashore was a liminal space, a site of emotional epiphany and scientific wonder in which one could find, as Nicholas Allen, Nick Groom, and Jos Smith have noted, 'forms within forms, scales within scales, and worlds within worlds'.[26] Gosse, like Kingsley, proclaimed the strange and beautiful miniature creatures that were by his readers' feet on the seashore if they only knew where to look. His style of writing was not a systematic study of zoology, but rather a lively and immediate record of his exploration of the North Devon coast. The reader

24 Philip Henry Gosse, *A Naturalist's Sojourn in Jamaica* (London: Longman, Brown, Green, and Longmans, 1851), v.

25 Ibid., vii.

26 Nicholas Allen, Nick Groom, and Jos Smith, 'Introduction', this volume, 1.

was his companion, evoking the romance of natural history in multiple emotive registers through the kinaesthetic of his expeditions:

> I ask you to listen with me to the carol of the lark, and the hum of the wild bee; I ask you to stand with me at the edge of the precipice and mark the glories of the setting sun; to watch with me the mantling tide as it rolls inward, and roars among the hollow caves; I ask you to share with me the delightful emotions which the contemplation of unbounded beauty and beneficence ever calls up in the cultivated mind.[27]

Gosse's commitment to taking his audience with him extended beyond the pages of his books. On his second stay at Ilfracombe in 1855, he even ran his own regular shore class, which involved spending an hour or two on the shore every day when tide permitted; if the weather was inclement, he would run an indoor class on observing and identifying the specimens they had collected. (Gosse would repeat the exercise in Torquay in 1857.)[28]

Gosse's work was richly illustrated with his own beautiful and intricate drawings (his father had been a miniature painter and passed on much of his technique); his illustrations were an important extension of his aim to make visible and accessible to his readers the strange seashore world—with all the gorgeousness of its translucent colours. As the vivid detail of Figure 10.1 suggests, the ability to look anew into these rock pool worlds was being fostered by the availability and cheapness of good-quality microscopes, the production of which had been revolutionized in the 1840s due to improvements in glassmaking.[29] The refinement of dredging, a technique Gosse employed on occasion, also produced a host of new marine varieties to study.[30] The teeming world of life in a drop of water, whether of the River Thames or the seashore, was a frequent trope of popular science; Gosse himself published *Evenings at the Microscope* (1859), in which looking through the device became an act of revelation and a journey into an exotic land. The microscope reaffirmed and made visible more of God's glory but was equally 'like the work of some mighty genie of Oriental fable'.[31]

[27] Gosse, *A Naturalist's Rambles on the Devonshire Coast*, vi.

[28] Thwaite, *Glimpses of the Wonderful*, 231.

[29] See Isobel Armstrong, *Glassworlds: Glass Culture and the Material Imagination 1830–1880* (Oxford: Oxford University Press, 2008), 52–3, 317–28.

[30] See David Elliston Allen, *The Naturalist in Britain: A Social History* (Princeton: Princeton University Press, 1976), 115–17.

[31] Philip Henry Gosse, *Evenings at the Microscope; Or, Researches among the Minuter Organs and Forms of Animal Life* (London: SPCK, 1859), v.

Figure 10.1. Philip Henry Gosse, 'Caryophyllia Smithii', in *A Naturalist's Rambles on the Devonshire Coast* (London: John van Voorst, 1853).

Gosse and Kingsley both show the overdetermined meanings invested in the scientific survey of the seashore. Kingsley, an Anglican clergyman, and Gosse, a man of equally deep religious conviction and a member of the Plymouth Brethren, were part of an influential corpus of popular science books, which looked 'back to the natural theology tradition and in their writings offered new audiences a vivid glimpse of the design they perceived in nature.'[32] For Kingsley, the pursuit of natural history was a means of self-improvement that was invested with a muscular Gothic heroism. Far from being a dilettante activity, fossicking among rock pools after zoophytes was a rugged, moral pursuit of God's truth and beauty:

[32] Bernard Lightman, *Victorian Popularizers of Science: Designing Nature for New Audiences* (Chicago: University of Chicago Press, 2007), ix.

> Let no one think that this same Natural History is a pursuit fitted only for effeminate or pedantic men. I should say, rather, that the qualifications required for a perfect naturalist are as many and as lofty as were required, by old chivalrous writers, for the perfect knight-errant of the Middle Ages; for (to sketch an ideal, of which I am happy to say our race now affords many a fair realization) our perfect naturalist should be strong in body; able to haul a dredge, climb a rock, turn a boulder...
>
> For his moral character, he must, like a knight of old, be first of all gentle and courteous, ready and able to ingratiate himself with the poor, the ignorant, and the savage; not only because foreign travel will be often otherwise impossible, but because he knows how much invaluable local information can be only obtained from fishermen, miners, hunters, and tillers of the soil. Next, he should be brave and enterprising, and withal patient and undaunted... He must be of a reverent turn of mind also... wondering at the commonest, but not surprised by the most strange; free from the idols of size and sensuous loveliness; able to see grandeur in the minutest objects, beauty in the most ungainly; estimating each thing not carnally, as the vulgar do, by its size or its pleasantness to the senses, but spiritually, by the amount of Divine thought revealed to him therein...[33]

Rather than pursuing an abstract mode of knowledge in controlled, sterile conditions, Kingsley's naturalist-knight has to fully embed himself in a locality—its people and its topology—to understand its natural history. This figure is an embodiment of Kingsley's radical politics, all attentive to the neglected grandeur of the commonplace and minutiae of the world. Francis O'Gorman has argued that '*Glaucus* deploys the language of nature as exotic artefact recurrently, fashioning coastal natural history as an encounter with landscapes to wonder at and strange forms to marvel over.'[34] O'Gorman rightly notes that Kingsley's exoticism is a kind of discourse that colonizes nature; however, it also makes the seashore a space for questing, exploration and discovery. It is in this vein of defining masculinity through a raw physicality that rock pooling—and science at the seaside more generally—was proposed as a means of rejuvenating the male body, providing Gosse, Kingsley, or any other prospective natural historian with a vigour which city life would sap from them.

Kingsley's naturalist-knight may have celebrated the masculine prowess of seaside science, but there is no doubt that, as an activity, much of its popularity stemmed from its take-up by women. Collecting marine specimens was an improving and genteel activity in which women were

[33] Kingsley, *Glaucus*, 44–6.

[34] Francis O'Gorman, '"More Interesting than all the books, save one": Charles Kingsley's Construction of Natural History', in Juliet John and Alice Jenkins (eds), *Rethinking Victorian Culture* (Basingstoke: Macmillan, 2000), 156 (147–61).

encouraged to participate. When Reverend George Tugwell poked fun at the craze for marine biology in a September 1856 article for *Fraser's Magazine*, he pictured it as a feminine phenomenon, mocking women's pretension to be scientific: 'our lady friend carries home a jar of marine pickles, invests in a Gosse and a Kingsley, and before morning is on the high-road to a state of confirmed "thalassian" (*v.* Gosse) monomania'.[35] The symptoms included a predilection for zoological nomenclature; a dressing table covered in pudding basins and confectioners' jars, all holding marine samplings; and expensive dresses ruined by seaweed and saltwater. Tugwell, a keen naturalist, was a curate at Ilfracombe during this time and was about to publish *A Manual of the Sea-Anemones Commonly Found on the English Coast*; three months prior to the article being published, he had met with George Henry Lewes and George Eliot during their visit, even accompanying them on some of their outings along the Ilfracombe shore and giving them three anemones from his collection.[36]

Eliot, who recorded her recollections of her trip to Ilfracombe in her journal, was fully immersed in the scientific expeditions undertaken with Lewes. In a letter, she enthusiastically describes the clutter created by their fieldwork:

> You would laugh to see our room decked with yellow pie-dishes, a *footpan*, glass jars and phials, all full of zoophytes or molluscs or annelids—and still more to see the eager interest with which we rush to our 'preserves' in the morning to see if there has been any mortality among them in the night.[37]

Lewes's work, which was initially published as papers in *Blackwood's Edinburgh Magazine* before appearing in *Sea-Side Studies*, records the same sense of excitement, obsession, even disorientation, at the phantasmagoric world of polypes and molluscs when seen through the microscope:

> The typical forms *took possession of me*. They were ever present in my waking thoughts; they filled my dreams with fantastic images; they came in troops as I lay awake during meditative morning hours; they teased me as I turned restlessly from side to side at night; they made all things converge towards them.[38]

35 [George Tugwell], 'Science by the Sea Side', *Fraser's Magazine*, 54 (September 1856), 254 (253–60).

36 See Kathryn Hughes, *George Eliot: The Last Victorian* (London: Cooper Square Press, 2001), 173.

37 George Eliot, *The George Eliot Letters*, ed. Gordon S. Haight, 9 vols (New Haven and London: Yale University Press, 1954–78), ii. 252.

38 Lewes, *Sea-Side Studies*, 34.

COMMON OBJECTS AT THE SEA-SIDE—GENERALLY FOUND UPON THE ROCKS AT LOW WATER.

Figure 10.2. [John Leech], 'Common Objects at the Seaside—Generally Found upon the Rocks at Low Water', *Punch*, 35 (21 August 1858), 76.

The visit to Ilfracombe was an enabling point in both their careers. In addition to helping Lewes research and write up *Sea-Side Studies*, George Eliot commenced writing fiction immediately after the trip. The incorporation of natural history and scientific tropes in her novels is renowned, as is her commitment to a realism founded on detailed observation of the seemingly unimportant minutiae of the material world. There is also a telling coda to their stay; another female tourist, the twenty-six year old Eliza Brightwen, arrived in Ilfracombe for a day trip to gather ferns on the very same day they departed: she would go on to become a renowned writer-naturalist in the 1890s.[39]

While George Eliot's success story undermines Tugwell's gentle satire of women's engagement with natural history, he was not the only one to mock the feminine preoccupation with the seashore. A caricature from *Punch* similarly shows a group of female marine enthusiasts, all with bums in air (see Figure 10.2). Entitled 'Common Objects at the Seaside—Generally

[39] Eliza Brightwen, *Eliza Brightwen, Naturalist & Philanthropist; An Autobiography*, ed. W. H. Chesson, introd. Edmund Gosse (New York: American Tract Society, 1909), 55. Other notable publications by women in the field include Anne Pratt, *Chapters on the Common Things of the Sea-Side* (London: SPCK, 1850); and Margaret Gatty, *Parables from Nature* (London: Bell and Daldy, 1855–71) and *British Sea-Weeds* (London: Bell and Daldy, 1863).

Found upon the Rocks at Low Water', the title alludes to the extremely successful set of popular science handbooks that were beginning to be published by Rev. J. G. Wood: *Common Objects of the Sea Shore* (1857), *The Common Objects of the Country* (1858), and *Common Objects of the Microscope* (1861). All but one of the collectors in the engraving are female; their rather unsuitable crinolines (another of *Punch*'s favourite targets) imbue them with the appearance of the anemones they are trying so fervently to collect. As Jonathan Smith notes, 'Their search for "common objects at the seaside" converts *them* into objects of an implicitly male gaze.'[40]

The impact of the works of Gosse, Kingsley, Chanter, and Lewes, among numerous others, owed much to the revolution in printing and publishing that produced cheaper books and periodicals for an ever-larger readership. In recent years, numerous scholars have demonstrated the importance of Victorian print media in shaping public perceptions of scientific debates.[41] Sales figures for popular science books were high and formed a notable part of popular publishing. Wood's *Common Objects of the Sea Shore* sold 15,000 copies in its first year and 14,000 in its second. *Glaucus* went into four editions in the first four years after its publication, while Gosse's *A Naturalist's Rambles on the Devonshire Coast* enjoyed a print run of 1,500 copies and earned him the handsome sum of £70.[42] Gosse continued to educate the public on the ever-changing world of the seashore, publishing works full of practical advice on marine collection. *A Year at the Shore* (1865) was a collection of articles initially published in *Good Words*; despite its temporal focus, it was based on the littoral life of Devon, as was *Land and Sea* (1865), another volume published for the SPCK.

The locatedness of Gosse's natural history writing sits paradoxically alongside the geographical distribution achieved due to advances in book circulation and distribution. Thanks to all of the various publications on marine biology, the North Devon coast had certainly found its metier. In the decades after their books' publication, Gosse and Kingsley's books continue to be invariably mentioned in articles promoting the Devon

[40] Jonathan Smith, *Charles Darwin and Victorian Visual Culture* (Cambridge: Cambridge University Press, 2006), 72.

[41] See Lightman, *Victorian Popularizers of Nature*; James A. Secord, *Victorian Sensation: The Extraordinary Publication, Reception, and Secret Authorship of* Vestiges of the Natural History of Creation (Chicago: University of Chicago Press, 2000); Geoffrey Cantor, Gowan Dawson, Graeme Gooday, Richard Noakes, Sally Shuttleworth, and Jonathan R. Topham (eds), *Science in the Nineteenth-Century Periodical: Reading the Magazine of Nature* (Cambridge: Cambridge University Press, 2004); and Aileen Fyfe, *Science and Salvation: Evangelical Popular Science Publishing in Victorian Britain* (Chicago: University of Chicago Press, 2004).

[42] Lightman, *Victorian Popularizers of Science*, 75; Fyfe, 'Natural History and the Victorian Tourist', 388, 398; Edmund Gosse, *The Life of Philip Henry Gosse F. R. S.*, 245.

coastline as ideal for those interested in naturalist expeditions. In *London Society* of 1867, Ilfracombe was portrayed as still obsessed with natural history:

> I must here remark that it is not very much use in coming to Ilfracombe unless you have some little taste for natural history. Socially it is everything here. You are hardly fit to live unless you know everything about anemones. Nearly every house, I suppose, has got its aquarium. You are at any moment liable to remarks about zoophytes like the madrepore and polype.... Let me strongly advise my friends to bring down with them a set of natural history books if they would fully enjoy this marvellous coast and what is still more important, 'be in the fashion'.[43]

The particular appeal of Ilfracombe (and the and the role that guidebooks played in shaping its reputation and encouraging natural history tourism) was similarly described in the *North Devon Journal* in 1871:

> Like pebble-hunting at Hastings, Ilfracombe has also its speciality of amusement—natural history; everyone hunts for anemones, sea shells, and sea weeds, and everyone has got an aquarium. If you wish to stand well with Ilfracombe society you must, if not already in love with its marvellous beauties, go in for natural history. Bring your books by Gosse,—'Sea and Land', 'A Year at the Sea Shore', your Catlow and Woodward; your 'Common objects' and 'Common Shells', and, above all, Kingsley's 'Glaucus', and you will find work and use for all.[44]

In addition to these specialist works, general guidebooks for tourists were part of the increase in printed matter for sale, and could also advertise the pleasures of natural history. Fyfe has noted that the first John Murray handbooks produced were those for *London* and *Devon* in 1851.[45] Tellingly, in her examination of the revisions made for the 1856 edition of Murray's *Devon* handbook, Fyfe points out how Gosse's reputation was exploited to promote Ilfracombe as a resort; it was noted, 'It is a favourite haunt of those wonderful and beautiful forms of life so recently brought to our notice by men such as Gosse'.[46] These lines were still present in the eighth edition of 1872, but disappeared by the eleventh edition of 1895; their removal testifies to the much more commercial character of late Victorian seaside culture, which replaced the earlier romance of natural history.

[43] 'Ilfracombe', *London Society: An Illustrated Magazine of Light and Amusing Literature for Hours of Relaxation*, 12 (July 1867), 28.
[44] 'At Ilfracombe', *North Devon Journal*, 2 November 1871, 6.
[45] Fyfe, 'Natural History and the Victorian Tourist of science', 390.
[46] Quoted in Ibid., 390.

2. THE AQUARIUM: 'OH! I DO LIKE TO BE BESIDE THE SEASIDE'

Railways and steamships were able to take many more tourists to the coast; thanks to Gosse, though, those enamoured of their experience were able to recreate their own seashore space through the latest fashionable accoutrement for the home: the marine aquarium. The coast would no longer be a peripheral or remote space, but was now mobile and reproducible, part of the domestic interior. The impetus to reproduce the beauty of nature within the Victorian home was already evident in the Wardian case, which had become popular in the 1840s and 1850s as a decorative artefact. It allowed exotic ferns and other plants to thrive within an unhealthy urban atmosphere by enclosing them within the controlled temperature of an airtight glass container. The marine vivarium satisfied a similar drive to observe, domesticate, and conserve nature.

Gosse cannot take credit for inventing the aquarium, but rather for developing and popularizing it. The question of who can claim primacy is complicated by a number of contemporaneous developments; however, the rock pools of North and South Devon figure significantly in its development. Rebecca Stott has argued that Anna Thynne, wife of Reverend Lord John Thynne, Sub-Dean of Westminster Abbey, should receive more recognition.[47] An enthusiast for geology and marine biology, while in Torquay in 1846 Thynne collected some madrepores and sponges from the seashore; she wanted to study them further and transported them to Ashburnham House, which was part of Westminster Abbey. At her London home, she kept them in glass cases and discovered that, by transferring some of the water from one receptacle to another in front of an open window, the water could be aerated and the madrepores kept alive. Later, in 1847, she had sea plants brought from Torquay to aid the tanks and was able to maintain her specimens for another two years.

Although Thynne did not publish her work until much later, her discovery was another example of the important contribution of women to Victorian popular science. It was Gosse and another scientist, Robert Warington, who were working at the same time on the problem of how to keep sea organisms alive for long periods in tanks and jars, who succeeded in popularizing the aquarium.[48] Gosse's key contribution was to refine

[47] See Rebecca Stott, *Theatres of Glass: The Woman Who Brought the Sea to the City* (London: Short Books, 2003).

[48] See Natascha Adamowsky, *The Mysterious Science of the Sea, 1775–1943* (2015; Abingdon: Routledge, 2016), on the relative claims of each.

and commercialize the seawater model such that it became the latest decorative craze of the 1850s.[49] Natascha Adamowsky has pointed out that, prior to 1852, 'aquariums were mostly cylindrical glass containers with a few fish or invertebrates inside. After this date, they came to be viewed as the living space for a marine community and an idealised miniature landscape'.[50] Gosse's perfected version of the aquarium emerges directly out of his work on the littoral zone of North Devon, as well as from his commitment to a natural history based on investigating and collecting living specimens. His description of how he had managed to sustain a living seawater collection was published at the end of *A Naturalist's Rambles on the Devonshire Coast.*

In a triumph of his overall approach to natural history, Gosse discovered that marine life could only survive as part of an ecosystem. On their own in a tank, starfish and anemones were doomed due to the diminution in oxygen levels; however, when paired with living vegetation, the oxygen produced counterbalanced what was used by the marine life therein. In 1850, when Gosse was first engaged in the study of microscopic Rotifera, he noticed that by allowing aquatic weeds to grow in the glass vases in which he kept the Rotifera, they were able to survive and multiply. Gosse renewed his experiments while at Torquay and Ilfracombe. Motivated by his desire to sustain the many specimens he collected, he devised an extremely effective formula for artificial seawater that could be used for refreshing the tank if it was located a long way from the coast. For Gosse, the vivarium offered an embodiment of his belief that the most 'interesting parts, by far, of published natural history, are those minute, but most graphic particulars, which have been gathered by an attentive watching of individual animals'.[51]

In 1852, he advised on the building of around a dozen freshwater and marine aquaria for public exhibition at the Zoological Gardens at Regent's Park: he stocked them with around 200 specimens of marine animals and plants he had brought up from Ilfracombe two months previously.[52] The attraction opened on 22 May 1853, immediately after the release of *A Naturalist's Rambles on the Devonshire Coast*. The *Illustrated London News* declared that visitors would no longer have to journey to the sea to discover the exquisite biodiversity of the English coast:

[49] On the development of the aquarium, see 'Aquarium History', available at http://parlouraquariums.org.uk/HomePages/historyHome.html, accessed 2 February 2017.

[50] Adamowsky, *The Mysterious Science of the Sea, 1775–1943*, 115.

[51] Philip Gosse, *The Aquarium: An Unveiling of the Wonders of the Deep Sea* (London: John van Voorst, 1854), v.

[52] Edmund Gosse, *The Life of Philip Henry Gosse F. R. S.*, 244.

> But, in this new undertaking of the Zoological Society, we have not only an illustration of the colour and form of these animals, which no pencil can approach, but a means of observing their habits and economy which far surpasses any opportunity which has been within the reach even of the authors to whom we have referred; and the student may now, without the expense of a journey to the sea, without the use of the dredge, or any other exertion than that of a visit to Regent's Park, find himself, in a museum of living nature, where he will find, from time to time, all the rarest as well as the most common of the inhabitants of the British seas . . .[53]

This living-picture exhibition of the seashore did not entail the difficulties and physical travails of rock pool rambling; the specimens were guaranteed to be present, and there was little travel required, and the large plate-glass tanks offered a more transparent viewpoint than most tidal pools. As Figure 10.3 demonstrates, whereas anemones when seen at low tide were a closed mass, in their underwater condition at the aquarium, observers could see them unfurled in all their beauty. Crowds thronged to this new attraction. On Whit Monday of 1853, 22,000 people visited the exhibition, exceeding the numbers seen at the Zoological Gardens during the height of the Great Exhibition of 1851.[54] Next to open in Britain was the Derby Museum in Liverpool in 1857. Never to be outdone, P. T. Barnum

Figure 10.3. 'The Aquatic Vivarium at the Zoological Gardens, Regent's Park', *Illustrated London News*, (28 May 1853), 420.

[53] 'The Aquatic Vivarium at the Zoological Gardens, Regent's Park', *Illustrated London News*, 28 May 1853, 420.
[54] Ibid.

created the first American aquarium in 1856 in New York as part of his Barnum's American Museum. Other large public aquaria subsequently opened at the Crystal Palace (1871), Brighton (1872), and in a number of European cities.

The excitement caused by Gosse's perfection of the marine aquarium made them the latest craze. Gosse himself did much to inspire the fashion as *A Naturalist's Rambles on the Devonshire Coast* led to *The Aquarium: The Unveiling of the Wonders of the Deep Sea* (1854), in which he elaborated in more detail its theory and practice. Tellingly, until the volume went to press, it was entitled 'The Mimic Sea'; the title testifies to the impetus not only to artificially reproduce the littoral world, but also to deconstruct the boundary between land and sea. Whereas coastal landscapes are always changing thanks to tidal ebb and flow, within the vivarium's controlled environment a mimic miniature seashore could be brought into the home for conservation and the edification of all. Henry Butler made a similar point in *The Family Aquarium; Or, Aqua-Vivarium* (1858), proclaiming its scientific and artistic virtues as a replica, its provision of observational epiphanies in the same vein as the microscope and telescope:

> That extraordinary combination of science and art may be called the crowning glory of the spirit of discovery characteristic of the nineteenth century. It opens to our inquisitive gaze the hidden chambers of the deep.... It presents us with a miniature facsimile of the fascinating reality in its exquisite colours, and replete with its inexplicable revelations. It exhibits, in other words, LIFE BELOW THE BILLOWS in all its surprising shapes, and amid all its amazing phenomena.[55]

A number of other books and journal articles provided instruction on how to install one's own home aquarium. Gosse's book illustrated a design for a fountain aquarium (see Figure 10.4); there were various other designs in Edwin Lankester's *The Aquavivarium* (1856), while Shirley Hibberd's 1857 edition of his *Rustic Adornments for Homes of Taste, and Recreations for Town Folk* pictured one with a cast-iron decorated base.

Aquaria came in all varieties for all classes; the 'coast' was now everywhere. The *Literary Gazette* was just one journal to poke fun at their ubiquity but, in so doing, makes clear that it was its very accessibility that led to its appeal:

> It was almost as if we went to bed one night innocent of anything but... having seen some glass tanks at the Zoological Gardens, and rose to find

[55] Henry D. Butler, *The Family Aquarium; Or, Aqua-Vivarium* (New York: Dick and Fitzgerald, 1857), 11.

Figure 10.4. Philip Henry Gosse, 'Fountain Aquarium', in *The Aquarium: An Unveiling of the Wonders of the Deep Sea* (London: John van Voorst, 1854), 254.

> every naturalist's shop, half the fishing tackle houses, and all the filtered water and ginger-pop establishments, displaying elegant assortments of living, swimming fishes, gracefully meandering amid groves of water plants, every little nondescript shop up a by-court feasting the eyes of admiring urchins with dim-looking bottles, in which 'tittlebats' and minnows and 'water-efts' sprawled and wrangled, while more than half the centre drawing-room windows in the more fashionable parts of the town appeared furnished with an ornamental chest of plate glass, with a shingly, rocky, weedy bottom, and numerous silvery fishes, and other marine animals of strange shapes . . . [56]

Aquaria were like many other popular exhibitions of the period, such as panoramas, lantern slides, and stereoscopes, in offering an experience of a country, landscape, or region where the viewer did not have to leave the comfort of their own home or city. Everyone could be beside the seaside. Unsurprisingly, part of the success of the domestic

[56] 'Book Review', *Literary Gazette*, 21 August 1858, 236.

aquarium was its appeal to women, and *Punch* could not resist picturing 'The Bursting of Old Mrs Twaddle's Aqua-Vivarium', in which a genteel drawing room was turned into a seascape with Mrs Twaddle endeavouring to pick up her favourite eel with her coal tongs.[57] Kingsley wrote approvingly that 'if Mr. Gosse's presages be correct, a few years more will see every clever lady with her "aquarium," and live sea-anemones and algae will suppliant "crochet" and Berlin wool'.[58] The refined feminine accomplishments—polite but artificial—should be supplanted by the healthier concern with natural history.

At least one visitor to Ilfracombe set up an aquarium as a living souvenir of time spent in North Devon; the Anglo-Irish novelist, Anna Maria Hall (who usually published under Mrs S. C. Hall), visited Ilfracombe and Torquay in the autumn of 1855. She was accompanied by her husband, Samuel Carter Hall, editor of the *Art Journal* and a prominent journalist: the couple are another example of the area's ability to attract well-known literary figures. Writing in the *Art Journal* in 1856, Anna Maria Hall describes her trials and tribulations in maintaining her seawater vivarium. While in Ilfracombe, they stayed with the daughter of a Mr Heale, who had become as 'familiar with *"Madrepores"* and *"Sabellas"* and *"Actinae"* of all kinds, as the generality of pretty village maidens are with primroses and buttercups'.[59] She found that even the small children of Torquay and Ilfracombe had been caught up in the new fashion and 'come to the seaside visitor with a bunch of "zoophytes," as they used to do with a young bird or a bouquet'.[60] One small boy reportedly brought her a worm in triumph, describing it as a sea serpent.

Anna Maria and Samuel Carter Hall also spent their time in Devon gathering ferns as much as actinae, filling their lodgings with all kinds of marine specimens. She even met Gosse when he was leading his seashore seminar and subsequently relied on both his books and personal advice when putting together her aquarium. Anna Maria Hall's touching account reveals the decorative, contemplative, and theological meanings that were got out of her many hours watching life inside the tank:

> During the past winter, those 'blossoms of the sea' have afforded me a great deal of enjoyment. Every bit of weed and rock—every zoophyte—has its little history. I have beguiled some lonely midnight moments by placing my

[57] 'Terrific Accident. Bursting of Old Mrs Twaddle's Aqua-Vivarium', *Punch* (19 December 1857), 250.

[58] [Charles Kingsley], 'A Popular History of British Zoophytes or Corallines', *North British Review*, 22 (November 1854), 1.

[59] Mrs S. C. Hall, 'A New Pleasure', *Art Journal*, 17 (May 1856), (145–7).

[60] Ibid., 147.

> candle, so as to reproduce different effects of light and shade on my mimic ocean; and those dim links between vegetable and animal life have carried me back, without an effort, to the delicious scenes from whence they came.
>
> How patiently have we watched the receding tide, to enable us to explore the mysteries of some tide pool, difficult of access, but richly repaying our exertions by the abundance and variety of its inhabitants! . . .
>
> It is impossible to admire these beautiful creatures, and the simple labours by which they exist, without thinking of HIM who, insignificant as they may appear, works for them and in them. Surely, if HE cares for them—which cannot, except by the contentment they exhibit, acknowledge HIS bounty—how much more will HE care for us.[61]

The many hours Anna Maria Hall spent studying and arranging the specimens—observing the dignified life and simple labour of the creatures—is a counterpoint to the oft-satirized feminine fascination with the secret life of the intertidal zone. As Adamowsky notes, the aquarium offered 'a theatre of exotic forms that were perpetually changing, a continuum of the strangest metamorphoses and paradoxical symbioses'.[62] Hall's 'mimic ocean', taken from Ilfracombe and Torquay, was more than just a commemoration of a pleasant holiday and an evocation of the blessed hierarchy of nature; it ebbed and flowed in her body through her emotions like a tide.

To sum up, seaside science emerged at a unique moment; it was a convergence of the popularity of natural history, particularly among the genteel, with the rise of coastal Devon as a tourist resort for those self-same visitors. Gosse's achievements were not endlessly reproducible across different locales; his volume, *Tenby: A Sea-Side Holiday* (1856), which attempted to repeat the success of his Devon work, sold very well but did not have the same influence. Indeed, so popular was the seaside science inspired by Gosse and others that, on coming to Tenby, he found that amateur naturalists had got there before him and removed a great volume of species; he bemoaned the fact that probably only one in six anemones they captured actually made it into an aquarium: 'if the visitors were gainers to the same extent that the rocks are losers, there would be less cause for regret'.[63] It was the same for Devon; Gosse was soon to protest that the coastline of all the fashionable watering places on the south and west coast was being stripped:

> Since the opening of sea-science to the million, such has been the invasion of the shore by crinoline and collecting jars, that you may search all the likely and promising rocks within reach of Torquay, which a few years ago were

[61] Ibid. [62] Adamowsky, *The Mysterious Science of the Sea*, 1775–1943.

[63] Edmund Gosse, *The Life of Philip Henry Gosse F. R. S.*, 264.

> like gardens with full-blossomed anemones and antheas, and come home with an empty jar and aching heart, all being now swept as clean as the palm of your hand![64]

It was not solely overenthusiastic amateurs that were to blame for pleasure hunting, though; the popularity of natural history had a commercial element (of which the growth in scientific publishing was but one element), with a cadre of professional collectors and small tradesmen emerging, who would collect as many as ten dozen anemones in a single tide.

Tugwell was equally splenetic towards those who were infected by the new-found desire to be thought 'scientific', those who were more concerned with fashion than nature; he declaimed against them as 'swarming on our coasts like blow-flies in summer time—infesting our *soirees* and *conversaziones* in the London season'.[65] The geographical remoteness of the North Devon coast, which led to its initial popularity among a certain cultural set, had lost its cachet now that it had become more touristy. The ventures of Gosse, Tugwell, Kingsley, and others became the victim of their own success; promoting hands-on engagement with the life of the seashore may have recreated innumerable miniature seascapes through domestic aquaria, but it was unsustainable to the marine ecosystems from which the specimens came. Gosse's and Kingsley's natural theology encouraged wonder towards the subjective life of non-human entities; they stressed the value, beauty and sentience of ordinary seashore life. At the same time, however, their ecological appreciation was often riven with contradictions that stemmed from a hierarchical view of nature and the drive to popularize natural history. Thus, the pleasure hunts of marine biology were founded on the particular ecology of the Devon coast; yet the fashion for seaside science also produced the aquarium—where you could take the shore back home with you and recreate it according to your taste. This reduction of nature to a decorative artefact undermined the locatedness that made the seashore a space of social freedom and scientific curiosity. Coastal landscapes are always changing thanks to tidal ebb and flow. But, as Victorian natural historians came to realize, they were also subject to human cultivation and the growth of the tourist industry with serious ecological consequences.

64 Philip Henry Gosse, *Land and Sea* (London: James Nisbet, 1865), 251.
65 [Tugwell], 'Science by the Sea Side', 255.

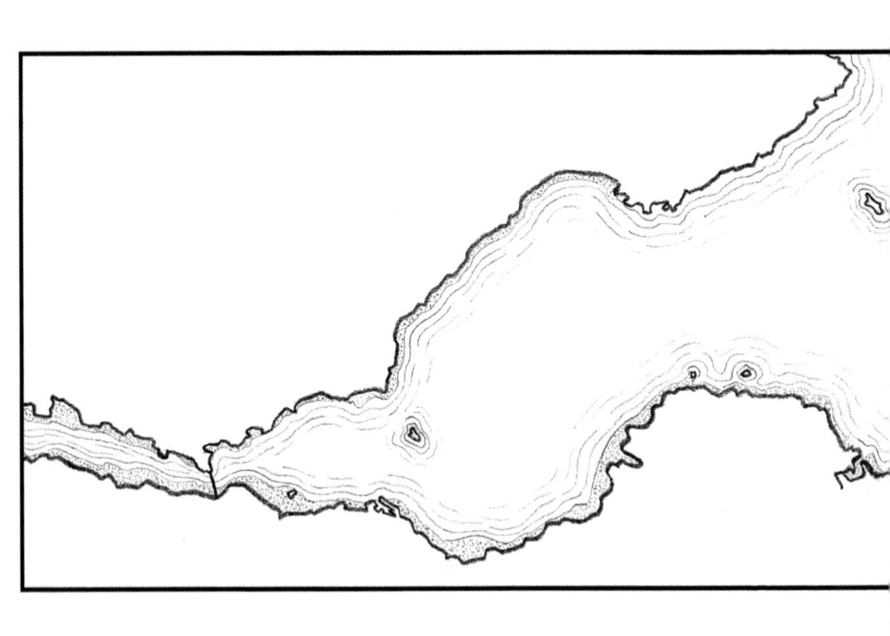

11

Seeing Through Water

The Paintings of Zarh Pritchard

Margaret Cohen

Water molecules, 800 times denser than air, present an opaque atmosphere where human vision struggles for orientation. Coastal environments, where the presence of water saturates the land, are one arena where water's optical challenges abound. Marine fog and mist are hazardous to travel, whether on roads or by boat; however, their depictions have inspired visual artists across history. The Romantics, notably, attended to these conditions, which defied the Enlightenment criterion of clarity. When the critic John Ruskin defended J. M. W. Turner in his first book, *Modern Painters*, published when he was twenty-four, he extolled Turner's interest in fog and haze. Many contemporaries in the 1840s charged that Turner's late paintings were marred by their lack of definition. Thus, an 1842 review of 'Snow Storm—Steam Boat off a Harbour's Mouth making Signals in Shallow Water and going by the Lead. The Author was in this Storm on the Night the Ariel left Harwich' objected that 'Where the steam-boat is—where the harbour begins, or where it ends—which are the signals, and which the author in the *Ariel*... are matters past our finding out'.[1] Ruskin, in contrast, understood Turner as inspired by the specific, murky meteorological conditions of the coast. In his view, 'Snow Storm' was 'one of the very grandest statements of sea-motion, mist, and light that has ever been put on canvas, even by Turner'.[2]

[1] *Athenaeum* (14 May 1842), cited from David Blayney Brown, Amy Concannon, and Sam Smiles (eds), *J. M. W. Turner: Painting Set Free* (Los Angeles: J. Paul Getty Museum, 2014), 158.

[2] John Ruskin, *Modern Painters* (Boston: Adamant Media Corporation, 2005 [reprint of 1906 edition published by George Allen, London]), i. 404. Contemporary art historian T. J. Clark offers a related account of the opaque atmosphere of steam in the nineteenth century at the juncture of denotation and artistic effect when he discusses its use as a signature of artistic modernism, in conjunction with technological modernization. Even as the haze around steam accompanied a challenge to mimetic art, through its optical condition, working as 'a figure of emptying and evanescence... It was always also an

Turner's exquisite depictions of the visual specificity of aquatic murk belong to a lineage where the marine environment would be a privileged subject to examine the artistic effects yielded by seeing through water, continuing through the sea and riverscapes of influential Western artists such as Claude Monet and James Whistler to the recent images of Japanese photographer Hiroshi Sugimoto. One aspect of this environment neglected for its aesthetic effect has been the underwater realm, which was in the nineteenth and first part of the twentieth centuries difficult to access and yet more difficult to characterize, due to the strange properties of its optics. In an atmosphere entirely composed of dense water molecules, light waves behave in a different way. A pervasive haze, for example, softens our view of the environment. Depth of field is radically diminished and difficult to gauge, and colours and forms appear differently as well.

Such optical conditions were still unknown at the time of Turner. However, during the latter half of the nineteenth century, science and technology had started to penetrate the obscurity beneath the water's surface in the most technologically advanced nations, notably the United Kingdom and the United States, as well as Germany and France.[3] Helmet diving took off in the 1830s, with innovations yielding the modern closed helmet diving suit, and the technology of the time was used for work in coastal waters, notably for marine engineering and salvage. In keeping with this practical orientation, writing about the conditions beneath the surface was at first purely technical and professional. It is indicative of the lag between technical development and the realization of diving technology's non-specialist appeal that one of the first non-professional portrayals of optics beneath the surface is in an 1888 essay by Robert Louis Stevenson. From a family of marine engineers and initially destined for such a career, Stevenson writes about persuading a professional diver to let him use equipment off-limits to amateurs to descend into the depths in 'The Education of an Engineer' (1888). There, Stevenson discovers a hazy world of 'twilight'. His first impressions of undersea optics from shallow depths are of a 'low green heaven mottled with

image of power. Steam could be harnessed; steam could be compressed': T. J. Clark, 'Modernism, Postmodernism and Steam', *October*, 100 (2002), 156, 157.

3 As Helen Rozwadowski has detailed, the factors catalyzing this penetration were complex. They involved developments in biology, geology, engineering, communications, warfare, and the culture of the spectacle. Once human perception, action, and curiosity were immersed in the depths, the underwater imagination blossomed as well. On the opening of the underwater frontier, see Helen Rozwadowski, *Fathoming the Ocean: The Discovery and Exploration of the Deep Sea* (Cambridge, MA: Harvard University Press, 2008); see also Robert Marx, *The History of Underwater Exploration* (New York: Dover, 1990). Bernd Brunner offers a concise history of the modern aquarium, important in bringing the depths to general audiences on land, in *The Ocean at Home: An Illustrated History of the Aquarium* (New York: Princeton Architectural Press, 2005).

vanishing bells of white; looking around ... nothing but a green gloaming, somewhat opaque but very restful and delicious'. In resurfacing, Stevenson's language reaches Shakespearean heights, as emerging in the 'trough of a swell', he passes from the green to 'a glory of rosy, almost of sanguine light—the multitudinous seas incarnadined'.[4] The reference to *Macbeth* does not make much sense in the context of Stevenson's observations of perception during his dive. However, perhaps Stevenson was reading Ruskin on marine atmosphere in art, as Stevenson's language does directly echo Ruskin's praise for the late Turner's rendering of marine atmosphere. The phrase, specifically, concludes Ruskin's discussion of 'The Slave Ship (Slavers Throwing Overboard the Dead and Dying)' (1840), immediately following Turner's defence of 'Snow Storm' in *Modern Painters*. There, Ruskin observes, the guilt of the ship 'mixes its flaming flood with the sunlight, and, cast far along the desolate heave of the sepulchral waves, incarnadines the multitudinous sea'.[5]

Stevenson was ahead of his time, for it was not until the first decades of the twentieth century that a wider community started to learn what it looked like under the waves. By this time, naturalists and adventurers were starting to use diving suits to observe the underwater environment, diving from small boats off coasts, notably in warm waters in this era before gear enabling insulation against cold water. They wrote about what they saw, and one artist, Walter Howlison 'Zarh' Pritchard, depicted it based on direct observation. Nancy Dustin Wall Moure observes that the underwater realm had interested a few painters in the latter half of the century, such as Edward Moran, the older brother of the famous American landscape painter Thomas Moran, who imagined the valley of the sea off the coast of Great Britain in 1862. She continues,

> The American Frederick Stuart Church ... completed imaginative underwater views featuring mermaids. Winslow Homer ... created a few split focus paintings that show scenes both above and below the water such as *The Mink Pond* (1891).[6]

Additionally, from a scientific perspective, a stunning set of early images of coral reefs were made by the Austrian Baron Ransonnet-Villez from his observations in a diving bell, published in his *Sketches of the Inhabitants, Animal Life and Vegetation in the Lowlands and High Mountains of Ceylon, as well as of the Submarine Scenery near the Coast* (1867).

[4] Robert Louis Stevenson, 'The Education of an Engineer', *Scribners* (November 1888), 638, 639.

[5] Ruskin, *Modern Painters*, 405.

[6] Nancy Dustin Wall Moure, *The World of Zarh Pritchard* (Carmel, CA: William Karges Fine Art, 1999), 12.

However, Pritchard was the first artist to draft paintings based on observation *en pleine mer*, and to study this subject throughout his career.

As a result, the specific optics of underwater coasts, as this chapter will discuss, inspired his imaginative creations, which were at the intersection of art and naturalist documentation. Moure observes that 'the closest "marine" painter from whom Pritchard could have taken inspiration was probably... Turner', and in particular 'his grandly magnificent atmospheric views'.[7] However, Turner observed from the surface—in contrast to Pritchard's perspective—and Pritchard's favourite depth for observing was around thirty feet. To prepare a water-resistant picture surface, Pritchard told a reporter, he followed the advice of Wera Hiko, a chief of Tongolo New Zealand, using a skin soaked in boiled-down flax.[8] To the prepared leather, Pritchard applied oils squeezed directly out of tubes onto a palette and used a brush soaked in linseed oil. Pritchard also reported sketching underwater with pastel crayons. He gives a vivid description of the need to work swiftly: 'A tiny mistake because a fish has come too near and the whole sketch is spoiled'.[9] How many of Pritchard's paintings were in fact done underwater is unclear—many were probably at least finished on land, if not drafted entirely from preliminary underwater sketches.

Pritchard was born in Madras in 1866 to Anglo-Irish parents. He was educated in Scotland, where, a century before modern wet and drysuits, he started diving in the frigid Firth of Forth, opening his eyes under water and observing. Little has been confirmed about his early life, but by his own account these dives inspired him to render what he saw. He studied art and design in Edinburgh, and then began his career in the London theatrical scene in the 1890s, where he designed 'costumes, stage accessories, and interior decorations for stage personalities, all on undersea themes'.[10] After he suffered from pneumonia, doctors advised that he go to a warm, dry climate, and he eventually moved to California and then the South Pacific for his health. Bishop in California would become the home he would return to from his forays across the globe to dive in new locations and meet scientists, gallery owners, museum representatives, and patrons.

While Pritchard's works have been forgotten today, they were appreciated in their time for their alluring, mysterious atmosphere, as well as for

7 Ibid, 9–10.

8 M. B. Levick, 'Paintings Under the Sea', *New York Times* (5 August 1923), 10.

9 Pritchard, quoted in Malcolm Vaughan, 'Painting Beauty under the Sea', *Los Angeles Times* (8 July 1928), 113.

10 Elizabeth Shor, 'Zarh H. Pritchard, A Biography', copyright 2010, available at http://scilib.ucsd.edu/sio/hist/Shor-Pritchard.pdf; I thank Elizabeth Shor for generously sharing with me her detailed research on Pritchard. Two published accounts of Pritchard's life are Moure, *The World of Zarh Pritchard*, and the chapter on Pritchard in Thomas Burgess, *Take Me Under the Sea: The Dream Merchants of the Deep* (Salem: Ocean Archives, 1994).

offering a window onto a hitherto unknown area of the planet before the advent of underwater colour photography. They were purchased by royalty and the wealthy in Europe, the United States, and Japan, including theatrical celebrities like Sarah Bernhardt and Ellen Terry, as well as by, among others, the Musée du Luxembourg in Paris, the Boston Fine Arts Museum, and the Brooklyn Museum. Pritchard's paintings were at the same time admired by scientists of the marine environment, such as the oceanographer Prince Albert I of Monaco and the ichthyologist David Starr Jordan, who became the first president of Stanford University. In the 1910s and 1920s, Pritchard's works were acquired by institutions with missions of scientific investigation and popularization, such as the Scripps Institution of Oceanography in La Jolla, the American Museum of Natural History in New York, and the Cleveland Natural History Museum. Albert I purchased eleven paintings by Pritchard for the Musée Océanographique in Monaco shown at a 1921 exhibition at the prestigious Galerie Georges Petit in Paris, where Pritchard later had another exhibition in 1925.

Throughout Pritchard's underwater imagery, he returned to two favourite settings: the west coast of Scotland, and the waters off Tahiti, where he had first used a diving helmet in 1902. The paintings of Scottish waters feature magnificent kelp forests and basalt formations, rendered with an extraordinarily nuanced range of blues and greens at about thirty feet, his preferred depth for depiction. In some of them, faint orange bream lead our eye down into the depths, gliding mysteriously, as is illustrated by 'Bream in 25 Feet of Water Off the West Coast of Scotland' (1910) in the collection of the Brooklyn Museum (see Figure 11.1). The paintings in the clearer, warm waters of Tahiti, similarly at Pritchard's preferred depth of thirty feet, are in a more varied palette of yellows, purples, and oranges, also inspired by the physical conditions of the undersea. In *Beneath Tropic Seas* (1928), the American naturalist, adventurer, and inventor of the bathysphere, William Beebe, wrote, 'One artist, Zarh Pritchard, has brought to canvas, evanescence of hue, tenuousness of tint... probably because he paints under water'.[11] Beebe took one of Pritchard's underwater scenes as the frontispiece for this book.

In the remainder of this chapter, I analyse the qualities of seeing through water that fascinated Pritchard, using three paintings done by Pritchard off the coast of Tahiti in the 1910s. I use these paintings because I have been able to see them first-hand, an observation critical in understanding the

[11] William Beebe, *Beneath Tropic Seas: A Record of Diving among the Coral Reefs of Haiti* (New York and London: G. P. Putnam's Sons, 1928), 38. Beebe perhaps accorded a painter pride of place in his study because the first underwater photographers were preoccupied with 'realistic' questions, such as how to minimize the differences between underwater optics and optics on land; furthermore, when Beebe wrote in 1928, colour film was not fast enough for the low light conditions underwater.

Figure 11.1. Zarh Pritchard, 'Bream in 25 Feet of Water Off the West Coast of Scotland' (1910), courtesy of the Brooklyn Museum. Pastel image.

subtlety of Pritchard's rendering of colour and atmosphere. This focus may seem removed from the Atlantic; however, the fact that Pritchard's scope ranged from the waters off of western Scotland to Tahiti make an important point about maritime and marine topics. Their study often takes us beyond both national borders, and even aquatically defined regions, in keeping with the supra-national nature of ocean environments and biology, as well as its social practice. The ocean, is, after all, a realm of our planet that exceeds the control of the nation-state, and where humans contend with natural forces, from the weather to fish, which are themselves indifferent to national boundaries. Many arenas of ocean activity have, moreover, long been hospitable to international cultures and peripatetic people, from the inception of global ocean travel in the early modern period. Beginning in this era, too, news from the ocean came around the world, and those who followed it were unfettered by a national point of view. Such ocean internationalism certainly characterizes Pritchard's far-flung career. For him, the waters off Scotland and the water off of Tahiti were differing but related opportunities to limn the beauty of aqueous opticality.

In praising Pritchard's painting in *Beneath Tropic Seas*, Beebe singled out 'the pastel film of [what he called Pritchard's] *aquatic perspective*', which 'No aquarium tank c[ould] ever show', along with 'the mystery and beauty of this undersea world of color', not perceptible from the surface, even in a 'glass-bottomed boat'.[12] A lush example of Pritchard's 'aquatic perspective' is the painting titled 'Parrot Fish and Poisson d'or amongst the Coral in the Lagoon of Papara TAHITI' (*c.*1910), donated to the Scripps Institution of Oceanography in 1917, and still on display there today (see Figure 11.2).[13] As the title indicates, the image draws our gaze to a delicately patterned fish, which floats right of centre and slightly below the picture's midpoint, a traditional focal point in landscape painting. The left side of the image is bounded in the foreground by a reef, which delimits our field of view, almost like a wing flat in the theatre, and which also helps draw our eye towards the centre of the scene. From the fish, which is a species of Pacific wrasse, the yellowtail coris, our eyes move up along the reef towards three dimmer yellow butterfly fish, at the top of the painting. The butterfly fish form a group—a visual echo of the coris in the centre—poised at a similar downward slope. Undulating purplish,

[12] Ibid.

[13] I thank Peter Brueggeman for his erudition and generosity in helping me to understand the details of Pritchard's paintings and how they correspond to optics at depth, when he showed them to me before his recent retirement as curator of the Scripps Institution of Oceanography's Special Collections and Archive; I also thank him for photographs of the paintings used in this chapter. According to Brueggeman (email communication, 22 February 2012),

> Ellen Scripps gave the paintings to SIO. The gift year/date is uncertain. The gift is noted in an art object file here in Scripps Archives by a handwritten reference to SIO director [Malcolm] Vaughan's papers as saying he mentioned the paintings in the Aquarium in 1924. . . . Paperwork on the paintings in the art object file here in Scripps Archives says it was gifted in 1910 with no attribution.

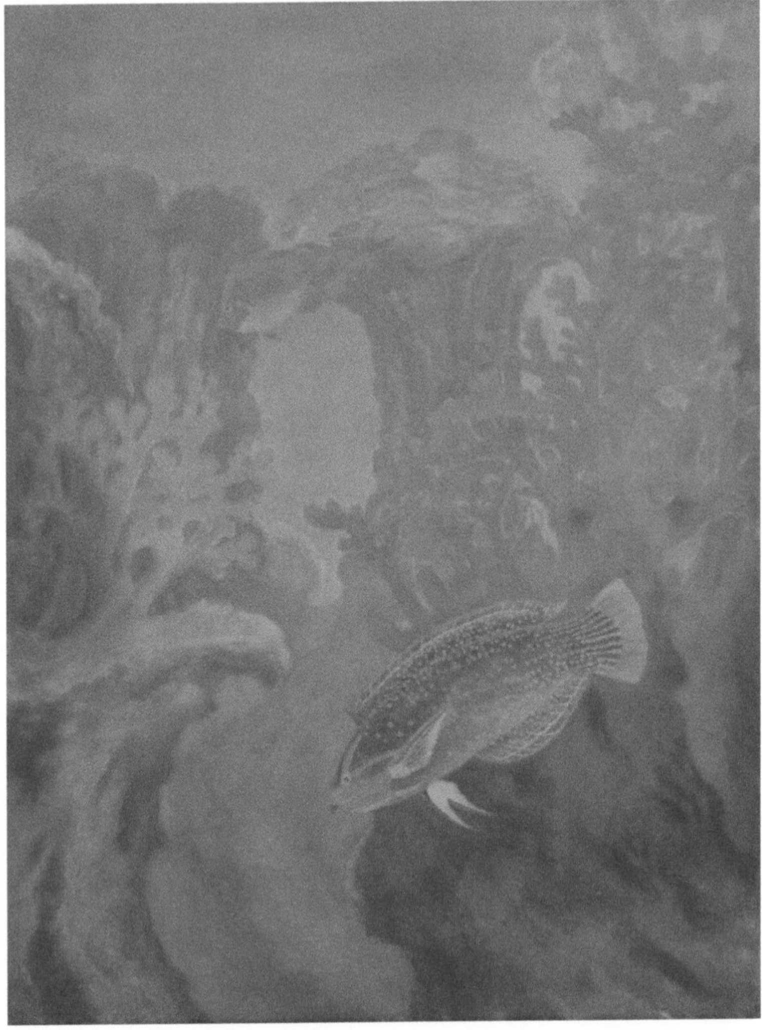

Figure 11.2. Zarh Pritchard, 'Parrot Fish and Poisson d'or amongst the Coral in the Lagoon of Papara TAHITI' (1910). Oil on animal skin. Courtesy of the Scripps Institution of Oceanography, UC San Diego.

blueish, and yellowish stalks of living coral divide the foreground and the background, organized along the diagonal axis of the swimming fish. The coral fronds blur into more massive solid coral heads, sedimentations of once-living organisms.

To today's viewers used to contemporary underwater photography and unfamiliar with first-hand visual perception, Pritchard's picture appears faded and washed out. Our expectation, however, that an underwater scene would be clear and bright is the result of a long history of photographic technique working to compensate for what happens to light when seen through the medium of water, one that is 800 times denser than air. When we see through water, unaided by artificial lighting or corrective lenses, we perceive a pervasive haze and pastel colouring. These conditions occur because water molecules slow down light, absorb it and scatter it. The refractive index of light—which is to say, the ratio of the speed of light in a substance to the speed of light in a vacuum—in water is about 1.3, in comparison to the refractive index of light in air, which is close to 1. Further disrupting and refracting light underwater are 'minute particles suspended in water', and also, at shallow depths, the way sunlight is refracted or diffused by the texture of the ocean's surface. As Thomas Burgess observes of Pritchard's work, 'No attempt was ever made to sharpen or refine images that were naturally softened' in the aqueous atmosphere.[14] Burgess also emphasizes Pritchard's own counter-intuitive observation that underwater, 'not one object looks wet or glitters', in contrast to the optics of wet surfaces viewed through the atmosphere of air.[15]

Considering Pritchard's paintings with the eye of a marine scientist, J. Malcolm Shick notes that Pritchard was 'among the first to recognize the altered submarine spectrum', characterized by distinctive colour loss at different depths.[16] For Shick, Pritchard's observations are based on physical reality:

> as one goes deeper, not only is there less light to be seen, but long red wavelengths disappear first, followed by the progressively shorter orange, yellow and green. Blue light is left to penetrate deepest.

Although the exact depth of colour loss depends on a number of local conditions (how turbid the water is, the strength of the light above the water, and the turbulence of the surface), Pritchard's palette in the painting of the coris indicates typical coloration at thirty feet in the clear waters of Tahiti. In Pritchard's words, 'The coloring beneath the ocean is all in the lowest tones, merging from deep indigo and purple into the higher, delicate tints of pale greens, grays, and yellows'.[17]

To say that colour is muted is not to say that it is uniform, as Beebe remarked. In the chapter praising Pritchard in *Beneath Tropic Seas*, 'No-Man's-Land Five Fathoms Down', Beebe expresses the colour subtleties of

[14] Burgess, *Take Me Under the Sea*, 137.

[15] 'A Conversation with Zahr H. Pritchard, Recorded by the Editor', *Asia*, 234 (March 1924), 219.

[16] J. Malcolm Shick, 'Otherworldly', in *Underwater*, catalogue for a Towner Touring exhibition curated by Angela Kingston (2010), 34.

[17] Cited in Vaughan, 'Painting Beauty under the Sea', 113.

this new underwater frontier with a vocabulary of enchantment, marking the limits of standard denotative description. To cite Beebe, 'We need a whole new vocabulary, new adjectives, adequately to describe the designs and colors of under sea', which he also calls the 'exquisite magic, of ineffable, colorful mystery' that is 'the theme of this watery world'.[18] The comparison of Pritchard's coris to the coris as it looks in today's photography emphasizes Pritchard's interest in muted underwater colouring, where, in Beebe's words, 'the harshest, most gaudy parrotfish' appear like a Chinese print or an 'age-mellowed-tapestry' in this 'fairyworld'. Pritchard's age-mellowed vision of a gaudy fish is only possible, that is to say, when observing optics at depth. While Pritchard may very well have gathered information about the physical details of the coris from specimens on land, their patterns would have shown brightly when first caught, as they would when seen behind the glass of an aquarium, before the colour faded when the fish died.

Doubt has been cast upon whether Pritchard did in fact paint his pictures underwater, or indeed based them on observation under the sea at all, or whether this claim was a publicity stunt. Pritchard's knowledge of the haze underwater, however, as well as the specific coloration of differing water depths, is one indication confirming the authenticity of his observation. Another is his handling of the kind of perspective through which to express seeing through such a thick aquatic haze. Pritchard's paintings really do devise a kind of 'aquatic perspective', to cite Beebe, if we take perspective, in the specifically pictorial sense, as the geometry of composition. Pritchard immerses us in his watery world through altering the conventions of linear perspective, a basic paradigm of rendering three-dimensional space in two dimensions since the Renaissance. Pritchard's turn away from linear perspective is in the spirit of the visual practices of his time. In *Suspension of Perception*, Jonathan Crary describes the later nineteenth century as an era in transatlantic modernity when the image's stability as a coherent window onto a scene started to decompose, along with the integrity of the observing subject.[19] Pritchard's art emerges from this network of visual practices, though he brings a unique twist on such destabilization through his familiarity with underwater optics.

[18] Beebe, *Beneath Tropic Seas*, 7.

[19] See Jonathan Crary, *Suspensions of Perception: Attention, Spectacle, and Modern Culture* (Cambridge, MA: MIT Press, 1999). Crary finds this decomposition across a range of practices and media, from the paintings of the Impressionists and Post-Impressionists to fashion plates, stereoscopic views, and early cinema. One particularly intriguing point of contact for Pritchard is Crary's analysis of how Georges Seurat flattened out illusionistic theatrical space (the chapter '1888: Illuminations of Disenchantment'). Although we lack most details of Pritchard's career before 1902, we do know he worked as a set designer and interior decorator in the 1890s.

In jettisoning linear perspective, Pritchard is doing justice to an environment utterly unsuitable to the famous pictorial convention's founding assumptions.[20] These foundations, according to Panofsky, include a 'ground plane [which] . . . clearly permits us to read not only the sizes, but also the distances of the individual bodies arrayed on it'.[21] Geometric forms are placed on this ground plane, and they recede proportionally. In such an oft-cited example as Raphael's *School of Athens* in the Vatican (1509–11), diminishing architectural elements, like pillars, tiles, and stairs, aid our ability to measure depth. The culmination of recession in linear perspective is the single vanishing point on the horizon. Orthogonal lines meet at this vanishing point, often endowed with narrative intensity, as in the Raphael fresco, where the lines lead our eyes back to the spot where Plato and Aristotle converse.

Multiple aspects of the founding conventions of linear perspective are, however, entirely at odds with underwater optics. Linear perspective relies on a substantial depth of field to create the impression of an enveloping environment. The poor visibility underwater, however, radically diminishes the ability to perceive distance. The furthest the eye can see in the clearest of water, distilled water, is only 250 feet. Martin Edge gives some striking figures on this reduced visibility in his practical guide, *The Underwater Photographer*. 'Such is the density of water', writes Edge, 'that people compare a picture taken in 0.5 m of water with a picture on land taken 800 m away'.[22] Because visibility is so radically diminished, objects do not come at us from a distant horizon; rather, they loom suddenly into view. 'How can life be organized in a world without horizons?' asked Philippe Diolé, a writer diving with the French Navy team that pioneered SCUBA in the 1940s, striving to convey a sense of our visual disorientation beneath the water's surface.[23] The same question might be transposed to the problem of rendering this environment in two dimensions as well.

There are theatrical elements to the compressed depth in the painting of the coris, such as the coral reefs that work like wing flats to focus attention on the centre of the scene.

[20] In the words of S. M. Luria and Jo Ann S. Kinney in a *Science* article concerned, among other things, with the reason that divers make errors underwater, 'an underwater object is usually viewed by light that is insufficient and drastically changed in wavelength, and the optical image has been modified in size and position' (S. M. Luria and Jo Ann S. Kinney, 'Underwater Vision', *Science*, 167 (1970), 1454).

[21] Erwin Panofsky, *Perspective as Symbolic Form*, trans. Christopher S. Wood (Cambridge, MA: MIT Press, 1999), 57.

[22] Martin Edge, *The Underwater Photographer*, 3rd edn (Oxford: Elsevier, 2008), 8.

[23] Philippe Diolé, *The Undersea Adventure*, trans. Alan Ross (London: Sidgwick & Jackson, 1953), 23.

Linear perspective's mathematical system of proportional recession is also ill-suited to capturing underwater optics because we are not only near-sighted underwater, but prone to confusion. The denser medium of water magnifies objects. Stereoscopic vision, in addition, does not work well. This is particularly true close up, when the brain experiences a conflict between the tactile knowledge of distance and underwater magnification. But it is also true in distances beyond our reach, because, as Helen Ross explains, stereoscopic perception depends on 'the disparity in the images received by the two eyes [which] is a fairly powerful cue to the relative distance of objects, and contributes a great deal to the sensation of dimensionality'. In mist, as underwater, 'the low contrast of the images makes the disparity difficult to detect, and stereoscopic acuity is much poorer than would be predicted on the grounds of retinal image alone'.[24] In describing the feeling of being at depth, Pritchard observes that 'Rocks and cliffs in the dim light assume an appearance of inconceivable size'.[25] Pritchard also notes how hard it is to orient oneself: even touching bottom underwater was 'as if one were temporarily resting . . . on a rapidly dissolving fragment of some far planet'.[26]

Another important aspect of the phenomenology of vision beneath the ocean's surface challenging linear perspective involves the very possibility of a straight line, essential to the orthogonals of the vanishing point. As Ross observes, 'Refraction from the face-mask [makes] . . . straight lines appear curved'. Pritchard was using a helmet rather than the later face mask, but the helmet, too, uses the glass essential for creating a layer of air where human vision can operate effectively, and whose opening also limits the field of view. Of the limits of this field apropos of the effect of the face mask, Ross writes that 'points on the left of the face-mask are displaced to the left, and those on the right to the right'. It is particularly difficult to adapt to 'two opposing distortions'.[27]

Such opposing distortions are even more of a challenge to the abstracted monocular vision of linear perspective than to stereoscopic vision on land. Nor, of course, do optics underwater ever achieve anything like linear perspective's immobility. Underwater, everything is truly an environment *mobilis in mobile*, to cite Verne's famous phrase from *Vingt mille lieues sous les mers*. Natural phenomena are washed by surge and sway, and the observer too is in motion. Pritchard's interest in depicting such undulations is the focus of

[24] Helen Ross, 'Mist, Murk, and Visual Perception', *New Scientist*, 66 (1975), 659.

[25] Vaughan, 'Painting Beauty under the Sea', 113.

[26] Pritchard, interview in *Asia*, 219.

[27] Helen Ross, *Behaviour and Perception in Strange Environments* (London: George Allen & Unwin, 1974), 57.

a picture painted around 1910, also donated to the Scripps Institution of Oceanography by Ellen Scripps, which portrays a school of damselfish in the lagoon of Maara, Tahiti.[28] In this image, the tentacles of the sea anemones have been swept to the right, highlighting the force of the surge, a factor in fish behaviour. In contrast, the damselfish, facing to the left, swim into the surge. The realism of these details is one more indication that Pritchard did in fact paint his pictures based on observation at depth, for such behaviour would be hard to guess on land, where the fish might just as well be presumed to be swept along by the current, as would a human swimmer.

In an environment so at odds with linear perspective, Pritchard comes up with alternative techniques of composition to express conditions of underwater optics. The basis of his composition of underwater scenes is a type of perspective developed during the Renaissance to show hazy objects on the remote horizon. 'Aerial perspective' was the term coined by Leonardo da Vinci when he considered the haziness of buildings and mountains in the distance. The cues to orientation at a remote distance, according to da Vinci, are variations in colour: da Vinci advised that buildings be depicted as 'blue, almost of the same hue as the atmosphere': 'the appearance presented by a group of buildings on the far side of the wall . . . as seen above the top of the wall look to be the same size', but 'if in painting you wish to make one seem farther away than another you must make the atmosphere somewhat heavy'.[29]

Characterizing perception underwater, Helen Ross observes that 'Aerial perspective is a much more important cue under water than on land—partly because the loss of contrast is more noticeable, and partly because other distance cues are reduced or absent'.[30] Pritchard intuits Ross's observation in his renditions of the underwater environment, which take the techniques of aerial perspective and apply them to the 'middle distance', a phrase from Pritchard's observation about the unique quality of the underwater experience of distance. Pritchard declares, 'Nowhere does substance appear beyond the middle distance. Material forms insensibly vanish into the veils of surrounding color.'[31]

We can see Pritchard transposing aerial perspective into the middle distance in the picture of the coris, if we look, for example, at how he conveys the sense that the butterfly fish are in the background of the painting. Although these fish cannot be more than 100 or 200 feet away,

[28] See page 5 of Shor's biography for a copy of this painting.
[29] *The Notebooks of Leonardo da Vinci*, ed. and trans. Edward MacCurdy (New York: George Braziller, 1955), 295.
[30] Ross, *Behaviour and Perception in Strange Environments*, 50.
[31] Pritchard, interview in *Asia*, 219.

Figure 11.3. Zarh Pritchard, untitled ['Moorish Idols'], *c.*1910. Oil on animal skin. Courtesy of the Scripps Institution of Oceanography, UC San Diego.

most likely significantly less, they take on the chartreuse colour of their atmosphere. Also adhering to conventions of aerial perspective, the colour of this portion of the pictures is dimmer than the foreground. In yet a third aspect of aerial perspective, the forms of the butterfly fish get progressively blurrier, conveying the sense that they recede.

Pritchard moves aerial perspective even closer to the foreground of the scene in a third painting at the Scripps Institution of Oceanography, also donated by Ellen Scripps and painted around 1910 (see Figure 11.3). This picture shows a pair of Moorish idols, similarly at about thirty feet deep in the waters off Tahiti. While the Moorish idols are at the front of the scene, Pritchard shows us the tail end of the long dorsal fin of the fish on the left as it disappears into the haze and takes on the colour of the background. The fish in Pritchard's paintings are often a self-conscious element, reminding the viewer that a perceiving human is necessary to convey the world beneath the surface of the sea. In the image of the Moorish idols, the fish draws attention to Pritchard's perspectival techniques, reminding us of his efforts to adapt long-standing Western perspectival conventions to aquatic visuality. While he uses aerial perspective to capture the pervasive underwater haze, the subject that recedes into this haze is a variety of fish that is striped. Depicting how the stripes recede proportionally, Pritchard uses the Moorish idol's bands of black and white, like the tiled floor that is a prominent way to establish spatial orientation in the paradigm of linear perspective.

The aesthetic effect of Pritchard's distinctive 'aquatic perspective', to use Beebe's phrase, is one of ineffably pleasing disorientation. Distances have an enigmatic quality, and the imprecise, softened edges of underwater forms shrouded in a haze make the scene somewhat illegible. Pritchard also uses other techniques based on seeing through water to enhance the viewer's subtle disorientation. In the picture of the Moorish idols, as in the picture of the coris, it is difficult to gauge the scale of the scene. This is partly due to the distortions previously mentioned, coupled with the low light. Yet another reason why we cannot fix size is the fractal nature of the reef formations in the images. Both the coral heads and living branches exist in a range of scales.[32] There is no human figure or recognizable architecture in the landscape to serve as a yardstick, as in the Raphael 'School of Athens'.

Yet another source of disorientation in Pritchard's underwater scenes is his treatment of the opposition between horizontal and vertical axes, foundational to linear perspective and to our orientation on land as well. But in water, the perceiver finds that this opposition starts to erode. Floating in this dense medium where gravity is attenuated, it is easy to become confused about the anchoring axes of horizontal and vertical, along with the difference between foreground and background. Areas of Pritchard's painting express this confusion. In the picture of the coris, for example, the reef bordering the painting on the left would seem to be a vertical form at the forefront of the picture plane. The blue swathe behind the coris also appears as a vertical coral reef in the picture's foreground. But the swathe between these two reefs, composed of vague forms, can signify either depth or distance. Does, for example, the blue at the very bottom of the picture lead the eye towards the back of the scene, or down to depths outside the picture's frame?[33]

Pritchard recounts that he was an avid reader of Verne's *Vingt mille lieues sous les mers* as a child. Once we grasp Pritchard's attention to the specific conditions of underwater optics, we can understand his disappointment with the novel when he started to dive. Shick notes a number of Verne's scientific mistakes in sequences such as the promenade through the submarine forest of Crespo, where Verne's narrator, Professor Aronnax, dons a diving suit and accompanies Captain Nemo. Beguiled by

[32] I thank Gert van Tonder for this insight, gained in conversation at the Stanford Humanities Center, 2012.

[33] Thus, da Vinci comments that to make buildings appear remote, they should be given a bluish cast.

the beauty of the scene, Aronnax writes, for example, about the light thirty feet beneath the surface of the ocean, just the coastal depths at which Pritchard painted his wrasse. In this environment, according to Aronnax,

> The sun's rays struck the surface of the waves at an oblique angle, and the light was decomposed by the refraction as if passing through a prism. It fell on the flowers, rocks, plantlets, shells and polyps, and shaded their edges with all the colours of the solar spectrum. It was a marvel, a feast for the eyes.[34]

Pritchard's paintings, in contrast, respect that, at thirty feet below the surface, light is not perceived as through a prism and red has dropped off the scale.

The problems with rendering optics at the depths of *Vingt mille lieues sous les mers* extend to the novel's whimsical original illustrations. Compare Pritchard's painting of the damselfish in Tahiti swimming into the surge with Alphonse de Neuville and Edouard Riou's image of Aronnax's stroll through Crespo (see Figure 11.4).[35] There is expansive depth of field in the Verne illustration, in comparison to Pritchard's middle distance. In the novel's image, the jellyfish recede proportionally, extending like balloons into the horizon, in contrast to the dimming of the coral reefs as they recede in Pritchard's painting. Verne's illustrators have made the jellyfish look shiny, with light glinting off their balloons, and the divers have shadows, as if seen through air. While Pritchard's damselfish and sea anemones move reacting to the surge, the jellyfish hang with their tentacles straight down in the original illustrations of Verne.

My point in comparing the underwater environments imagined at the time of Verne and those depicted by Pritchard is not to rank one over the other. It is, rather, to underscore the different sources of physically inspired enchantment for each, shaped by the access to technologies of underwater visualization at the time. Shick observes that Verne 'probably gained his own underwater visions in the Paris aquarium', or at least in the shallows easily accessible to amateur naturalists of his era—when, it might be added, Verne and his illustrators were not simply projecting onto underwater conditions the optics of air.[36] Experiencing the transparency of the underwater world in Verne's novel, observers nonetheless retain their terrestrial reference points intact.

For Verne and his illustrators, the crystalline, glistening underwater vistas are based on fusing glimpses of underwater life offered by the aquarium with terrestrial conditions of visuality. They evince a blend of secular enchantment and optimism that is one powerful mood of Verne's

[34] Jules Verne, *Twenty Thousand Leagues Under the Sea*, trans. and ed. William Butcher (New York: Oxford University Press, 1998), 109. See Shick's comments on this passage, 'Otherworldly', 34.

[35] See Shor, 'Biography', 5.

[36] Shick, 'Otherworldly', 34.

Figure 11.4. Walk through the underwater forest of Crespo, *Vingt mille lieues sous les mers* (Paris: J. Hetzel, 1870), plate by Alphonse de Neuville and Edouard Riou, engraved by Hildibrand.

science fiction. Pritchard is an artist as well, and he too creates a mood and tone with his underwater portrayal. For Pritchard, the reality of optics at depth, so distorting when compared to optics on land, creates a dreamy, emotional tone. Contemporaries noted this effect when praising his pictures. Jiro Harada, His Imperial Japanese Majesty's Commission to the Pan Pacific International Exhibition, in a letter to Pritchard written from San Francisco in 1915, thus described Louvre curator Jean Guiffrey's reaction to the artist's work as 'a remark in French which you told me meant "words cannot express"'. In Harada's assessment, mixing Guiffrey's observations with his own, Guiffrey was 'deeply moved by your paintings, their uniqueness and charm and delight in the mysterious harmony of colors revealing something more than the eye can see'. 'Wonderful', Harada reports Guiffrey commenting about 'the submarine picture of shoals of fishes apparently worshipping the image of Buddha'.[37]

[37] Jiro Harada, letter to Zarh Pritchard (San Francisco, 17 July 1915) in the catalogue for an exhibition of the work of Pritchard held at the Grace Nicholson Gallery in Pasadena, 1925.

Pritchard himself suggested that the experience of underwater perception was one akin to an ecstatic state. In his comments in *Asia*, he expressed such heightened awareness with a vocabulary of magic and enchantment. 'When one leaves the resounding, splashing surface . . . to enter the depths below', he stated, 'one is astounded by the sensation that some sudden magic spell has swept away every drop of the water, replacing it with a soft, all-enveloping atmosphere.' 'At one moment going over a deep strait in Tahiti in my diving suit', he tells his interviewer, 'I was an atom suspended in the center of a limitless, horizontal-banded sphere of translucent color.'[38] This experience, he says, recalled to him lines from Cardinal Newman's *Dream of Gerontius* describing 'the experience of the spirit immediately after death'. The Newman line is: 'As though I were a sphere, and capable/To be accosted thus'.[39] This feeling of being suspended produces what Pritchard describes as 'an indescribable feeling of happiness', inspired by the physical conditions of water rather than intimations of a transcendent spiritual life.

Due to his attentiveness to the reality of underwater optics, Pritchard created lush, muted environments, whose strange organic forms and decorative flatness resonate with *art nouveau*, an artistic movement that shaped his practice in theatre and design during the 1890s. The disorientation, at the same time, diverges from some of the prettier *art nouveau* scenes and intensifies with details of Pritchard's depiction that come from the inspiration of the artist rather than the observation of the ichthyologist. Note the eye of the coris, with a white pupil and blue iris, spanning the distinction between human and fish.[40] Note, too, the lips, more like human lips than those of a fish, in being so 'distinctly offset from the head coloration'.[41] The lips of Pritchard's coris resemble specifically the lips of a made-up young woman, with their bow form brought out by the red, almost as if the fish were wearing lipstick. The striking red is itself a fantasy element amid Pritchard's otherwise realistic portrayal of underwater colour, for he was aware that at the depth of thirty feet, reds had faded out. Such blurring of species extends the haze of underwater optics to

[38] Pritchard, interview in *Asia*, 218–19.

[39] John Henry Newman, *The Dream of Gerontius*, ed. Maurice Francis Egan (New York: Longmans, Green, and Co., 1910), 35.

[40] In his chapter on Pritchard in *Take Me Under the Sea*, Burgess declares, 'He descended to a land engulfed in monotones; yet once there, he transposed the bright prismatics of the surface world and he often fearlessly redesigned shapes and forms to suit his fancy' (159). This transposition is not consistent, nor is it purely whimsical. The alternative sexualities of marine life fascinated the surrealists, notably the scientific, surrealist filmmaker Jean Painlevé.

[41] Philip Hastings, email to Elizabeth Shor (12 January 2012); I thank Philip Hastings for his help in understanding the painting, and also Elizabeth Shor for putting us in touch, and sharing his comments with me.

epistemology, as Pritchard's imagined environment intimates a world where divisions among Enlightenment categories break down.

In the case of the sensitive wrasse, the divisions are those between animal and human, as well as nature and artifice. Another fundamental identity distinction, between male and female, may also be at issue, depending on what Pritchard knew of the coris's life cycle. As ichthyologist Philip Hastings observes, corises 'are hermaphroditic, spawning first as females and changing sex to male, signaled by a significant change in color'.[42] Despite the feminine red lips, the specimen in Pritchard's picture has the coloring of 'a large male'. Whether the hermaphroditism of the coris was known to ichthyologists in 1910, let alone Pritchard, is not clear, but naturalists were fascinated by the hermaphroditism of marine organisms from the time of Darwin. Even if we interpret the image based on its visual information alone, the coris has a phallic appendage with his raised front dorsal fin, along with the feminine red bowed lips. Again, we can only wonder if Pritchard knew that corises raise their front dorsal fins in displays of mating and aggression.

When William Beebe put into words the pleasures of the phenomenology of underwater perception in *Beneath Tropic Seas*, he emphasized the effect of achieving an altered psychological state, which was a kind of relaxation. In one passage, Beebe describes, for example, how he became riveted on

> a great font of a sponge. It was not especially striking in size nor of perfect symmetry nor of unusual brilliance—a greyish violet as I remember, but it was *satisfying*, a characteristic indefinite but very real if only we will relax before things about us and let unimportantness fade away.[43]

In this passage, underwater optics are the portal to an experience that sounds like a drug trip; they enable a kind of profane illumination, to use the phrase of Walter Benjamin: 'a materialistic, anthropological inspiration, to which hashish, opium, or whatever else can give an introductory lesson'.[44] When Ruskin defended Turner against his critics for the hazy contours of his late works, he qualified them as magnificent expressions of the sublime: an aesthetic that characterizes the pleasure we take in portrayals of awe-inspiring power. However, Pritchard's alluring, yet slightly disturbing underwater imagery, coupled with Beebe's lyrical descriptions, suggests that along with the sublime, the profane illumination is also an expressive concept for the pleasures of seeing through water.

[42] Ibid. [43] Beebe, *Beneath Tropic Seas*, 42.

[44] Walter Benjamin, 'Surrealism—The Last Snapshot of the European Intelligentsia', in Walter Benjamin, *Reflections*, ed. Peter Demetz (New York: Harcourt Brace Jovanovich, 1975), 179. Benjamin published this essay a year after Beebe's *Beneath Tropic Seas*.

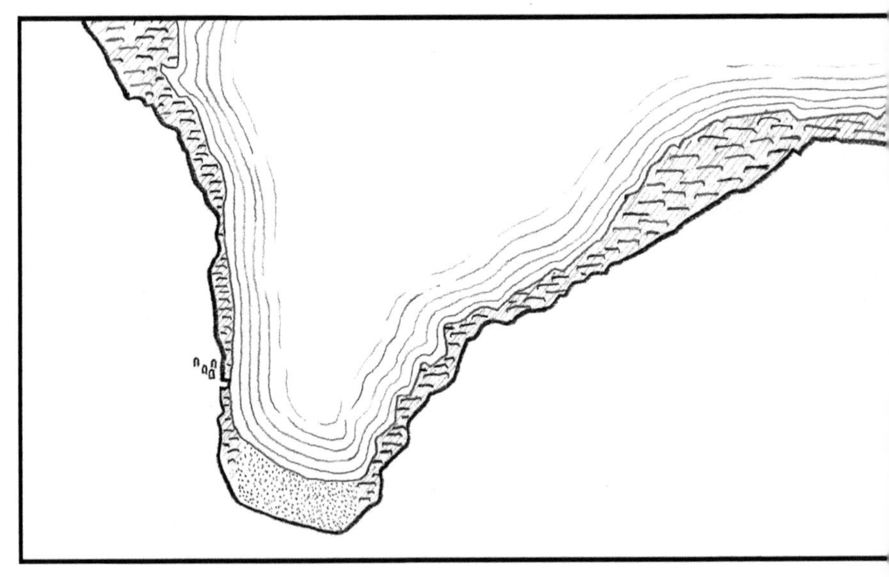

12

In the Labyrinth

Annotating Aran

Andrew McNeillie

The *Irish Times* of Saturday, 10 March 2001 carried an almost full-page, illustrated review by Tim Robinson, entitled 'Faithful to the Last unto Aran'. The book in question was *An Aran Keening* by Andrew McNeillie, which the Lilliput Press, original publisher of Robinson's *Stones of Aran*, had just that week launched at the Irish Writers' Centre in Dublin.

The review paid the book many a fine compliment and at one point remarked: 'Reading between the lines of one of his [McNeillie's] guarded reports of gossip, I realise that he knows only the beginning of a story of which I know only the end'. That was to prompt me as I read his Aran books to consider carefully the contexts of his observations and 'reports', wherever these were not overtly or overly pursued, wherever I knew the 'beginnings' or even the 'ends' of things he either didn't know or chose to omit.

Total knowledge or 'the complete description of a place' is an impossibility, even were it desirable. (Robinson calls it an 'unfulfillable ideal'. I call it the end of the world, as fatal as a return to Eden, where there is really nothing to do, unless bite into the apple and start the story again.) Places—local habitations—are inexhaustible. There is no way through or out of their labyrinth that may be called definitive or complete. Of course, this is something of which Robinson is sharply aware. His art is a high-wire balancing act between the poles of less and more.

I had preceded the Robinsonian 'watch' on Aran by four years, through all but a year from November 1968. *Stones of Aran: Pilgrimage* had come out in 1986 and its sequel, *Labyrinth*, in 1995. These were major works in a new form of topography and antiquarianism of extraordinary artistry, all but peerless in the tradition, a species of Proustian chorography, I like to call it. (For me, only Thoreau and Synge spring to mind as being as artful—differently artful—in the genre.) My effort was in an altogether lesser league, but the publication of Tim Robinson's books cast a great shadow over my enterprise, which for many years could not find a publisher. I had been unable to read them in those years simply out of fear, anxiety as to influence, territorial resentment, and so on.

1. QUANTUM JUMP

It was at an event some years later—a 'Roundstone Conversation' in Cambridge—that I began to speculate on the Robinson *oeuvre*, by then expanded to include the volumes on Connemara with regard to future scholarship. (The third volume in the Connemara trilogy was just out or about to be.) I wondered what might be involved in creating an annotated edition of his work, as surely one day it will be attempted, a necessary undertaking, using the extensive archive of notebooks and other documents now housed in state-of-the-art conditions in the James Hardiman Library at the National University of Ireland, Galway.

I suggested to the participants at the 'Conversation' that there was important work to be done one day, annotating Tim Robinson. No sooner had it been said than we learned the man had himself already explored the idea, providing footnotes to the passage 'Sworn to the Tower' that opens *Stones of Aran: Part II: Labyrinth* (down to the end of the entire section). There is not space enough to reproduce text and all fourteen footnotes in their entirety here. So I will attempt to provide the more substantive of them, aided by a note Tim sent me about his approach:

> Here's the annotated bit of *Labyrinth* . . . I wrote it long ago in response to a request for something on how I write. Not knowing the answer to that, I decided to take a piece of text and see where the various images etc. in it came from. There's no implication that the reader is supposed to pick up on all these echoes from a lifetime of miscellaneous reading. They install a tone, rather than impart information.

This is itself revealing information. It prompts us to consider the artful management of that tone and the reading and thinking that underwrite it. *Stones of Aran* is nothing if not formally exquisite. It is also immensely literary. The author's 'miscellaneous reading' is remarkable in its range and for the intensity with which at times it surfaces. His first three notes don't take us beyond the three elements of his title. 'Stones of Aran' is annotated:

> The book engages with an unfulfillable ideal, the complete description of a place. The title asserts that the rough terrain and rural culture of Aran are as important, or can be made so by close attention, as the glories of Venice. However, Ruskin's title is *The Stones of Venice*; that is, all of them that

> matter, whereas mine hints that there are innumerable other stones of Aran equally worth describing which I have not been able to work into this book.

The note to 'Part II: Labyrinth' reads:

> The first part of the book, *Pilgrimage*, is in the form of a walk around the coast of the biggest of the three Aran Islands, Árainn itself, and the second, *Labyrinth*, deals with its interior. Several years elapsed between the completion of the first and the final and major reworking of the second part, and the first chapter of *Labyrinth*, 'Sworn to the Tower', describes and enacts the process of getting started again.

And of 'Sworn to the Tower' itself we learn:

> The title is from Goethe's *Faust*, Part II, the song of Faust's watchman Lynceus, the lynx-eyed Argonaut: 'Zum Sehen geboren, / Zum Schauen bestellt, / Dem Turme geschworen / Gefällt mir die Welt.' ('Born to see, / Set to watch, / Sworn to the tower, / I love the world.') This does not mean that I am writing only for those likely to recognise such quotes, which indeed I have only picked up half-understood and at random; the phrase itself has enough resonances—of dedication to a high cause, of fate and the quest—to do its work here. But these three words have long been important to me, and emerged from my memory to energise this beginning. Artistry in the sort of writing I care for consists in tuning and amplifying the resonances of each phrase by adjustment of its context. One could imagine writing a whole book just to give three words their adequate setting.

The passage about 'finding an entrance to the labyrinth' being preceded by 'another labyrinth' created by the fact that the author no longer lives on Aran provides a key revelation. 'My sight-lines and thought-lines to it are', he writes,

> interrupted by the thick boggy hills and dazzling waters of Connemara. I am too far for touch, too near for Proustian telescopy.

The note to this reads:

> Through 'automatic memory'—memory not consciously conserved but spontaneously evoked by a taste or other sensation, the narrator of Proust's *A la Recherche*... recaptured tracts of his distant past with the vivacity of immediate experience; references to this idea are frequent in my book. Venice is the common ground of Proust and Ruskin, whose intensity of vision he admired. In 'A Fool and his Gold' (*Labyrinth*, p. 211), when I wonder if all the stones of Aran are worth one uneven paving stone in San Marco, I am thinking of the uneven pavingstone Proust's narrator felt underfoot in a Paris courtyard, that reminded him of one in San Marco and so restored to him a lost chapter of his life; thus even in that moment of

> dejection it is no small matter I am pitting Aran against, but a crucial nexus of European culture.

Robinson's one-sided contretemps with Synge on the matter of the Irish name for the maidenhair fern prompts the following:

> I haven't read Bloom's *The Anxiety of Influence*, but I know well what he means! However in a labyrinth progress can only be by trial and error, and my anxiety before the precedent of Synge's elegant slim work stimulates a forward movement: having misguidedly introduced the maidenhair fern, I take it as my guide into the substance of my book in the next section, 'Maidenhair'.

This is a significant revelation, not simply as to the matter of literary precursors, but as to method. We are relayed forward, ever deeper into the maze, by the slenderest means, as we might be by the encodings of a novel. Only in this case, the means are tangibly apparent and it is the method we construe. As to which, perhaps the most illuminating note provided is that to the author's 'preferred literary transition, a slinking behind my own back':

> Although at this point it appears I have not yet begun, a lot of information about the starting-point has already been covertly conveyed. A favorite mode of modern or perhaps postmodern writing is self-referential—the discussion or explication of what the writer is doing or trying to do. Of course behind this screen of apparent frankness one can be doing something else entirely. In an earlier draft instead of 'a slinking behind my own back' I had written 'a quantum slink'. What we all vaguely know from science about quantum jumps is that they are sudden, unpredictable miracle-like transitions with no intermediate stages; slinking on the other hand is a smooth operation usually with duplicitous forethought. So the quantum slink might have been an arresting oxymoron for the literary trickery I am owning up to here, but finally I decided it was a little too obtrusive and jokey in tone. However, 'quantum jumps' hung around in my mind and eventually found their place in the next sentence, indicating what tricky material I have undertaken to treat.

As I read *Stones of Aran*, I find myself caught in a kind of inner running commentary, expanding on the text, most of all at the heart of my own island labyrinth, the village of Cillmhuirbhigh.

2. SHADOW OF AN ISLANDMAN

Some years ago, I opened my email one day to find a message from a man I did not know from Adam. It suggested I click on an attached link. I clicked as instructed. No, it was not a scam from someone in Nigeria. It was a revelation from Michael Muldoon on Aran.

To my wonder, I was taken to '35 results with search query "tom hernon"' in the George Pickow Image Collection, James Hardiman Library. Among the images was one captioned: 'Photograph of a young man rowing a currach, Aran Islands. The young man is either Tom or Sonny Hernon' (see Figure 12.1). The author of the identification—was it the late George Pickow himself?—I do not know. I was startled to see the image and believed I knew at once that the young man at the 'sticks' rowing a currach was Tom Hernon, not his brother Sonny.

The condition of the negatives from which the Pickow collection may be reproduced is not the best. What we see of Tom Hernon is more a shadow of an islandman, light years from a sharp, digital, many-pixelated image. But I believe that I would know him anywhere, even in the shadows, as far away as 1952. Under the pseudonym Gregory Feaney, he featured centrally in *An Aran Keening*. He was in many respects its hero and my foil. There were many more photographs in the collection, some identifying their human subjects, others unannotated. But seeing Tom and his

Figure 12.1. Photograph of a young man rowing a currach, Aran Islands. March 1952. The young man is either Tom or Sonny Hernon. Courtesy of the James Hardiman Library, National University of Ireland, Galway.

mother among them gave me pause and made my hand shake briefly. One or two of the other images featured people I knew personally or by sight. Others among them defeat even the older generation of islanders now and pass unidentified, if not unrecorded, into oblivion.

The Pickows embarked for Aran in the early spring of 1952, and as the photographs generally suggest, were well received by the islanders. Eighteen years on from Robert Flaherty's classic *Man of Aran* film, and in the long wake of J. M. Synge, the islanders were already acutely aware of their attraction for the outside world. The full power of that attraction had still to be visited upon them in 1968, but it was by then well established.

For my part, it was one thing, and heartening, to see, or to believe one was seeing, in several images in the collection, the brothers Tom and Sonny Hernon. It was quite another to see shots of their mother, Annie, at her spinning wheel, and at a simple, improvised loom weaving a *crios* (the islands' traditional highly coloured belt of woven wool) (see Figures 12.2 and 12.3). I felt that I had sat more than once in the chair against which

Figure 12.2. Photograph of a woman operating a spinning wheel, Aran Islands. March 1952. The woman is Annie Hernon. Courtesy of the James Hardiman Library, National University of Ireland, Galway.

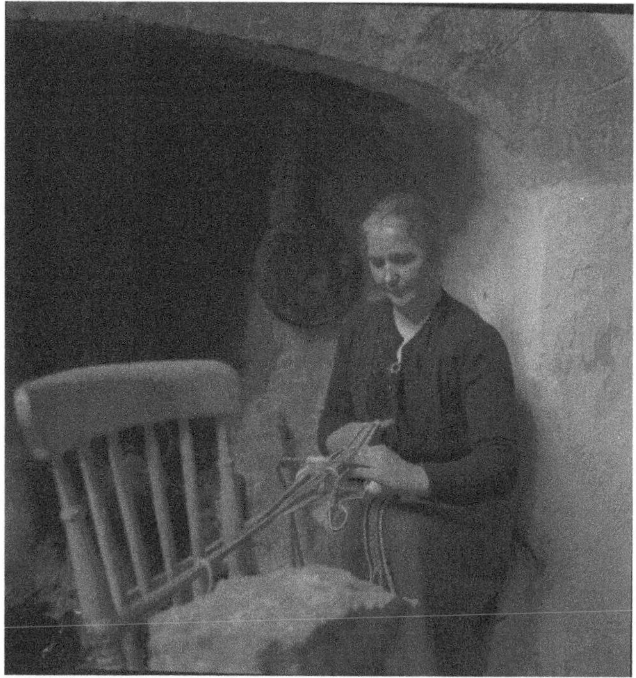

Figure 12.3. Photograph of a woman weaving a crios, Aran Islands. March 1952. The woman is Annie Hernon. Courtesy of the James Hardiman Library, National University of Ireland, Galway.

the 'loom' in the picture is braced. Or else it had been one of the same design. I knew that spinning wheel, just as I knew the drift nets in the shoreline photographs, but only when they were redundant, stowed away in the great stone outhouse, or 'store' as they called it, at the back of the Hernon home. (I remember how I used to look longingly at the old nets piled up there among the beams, coveting them in one of my innumerable fishing fantasies. I also remember Tom telling me that some of the bigger timbers holding up the roof had been washed ashore from ships sunk in the war.)

I rented my house from Annie Hernon. I ate her soda bread every day and bought my milk from her each morning. I sat in her kitchen, with Tom and his sister Margaret, and sometimes Sonny would come over from 'the big house', where now he lived married to Bridget. Annie would speak now and then of her late husband Pat Phaddy. He it was who once heard a voice speak from under a stone he was lifting. He was building a wall, just beyond the village. The voice scared the life out of him, and he abandoned his work, there and then. You could still see where the wall halted, in mid-course, in the middle of nowhere, enclosing nothing. I never found it. Tim Robinson got to the story too. He tells us that the voice had said 'Listen! Listen!' But I did not hear what it said because Annie Hernon had no chance to tell me. Her son Tom, embarrassed at the story, interrupted her to dismiss it all as 'just imagination', while his mother, flustered by him, protested it was not. Among Pickow's images is one of Pat Phaddy standing by the hearth in full song. I have been told that he would no doubt be singing his favourite, 'Sagart na Cúile Báine'—'The Faire Haired Priest', or by another interpretation, 'A Priest from Cúil Bhán' (in Co. Mayo).

Where the house with the big hearth stood, in which several of the pictures were taken, I was at a loss to say. As far as I knew, it was not to be found in Cill Mhuirbhigh sixteen years later when I arrived there. I have since been told that the hearth was a film set, in what they called 'The Man of Aran cottages'—Flaherty's purpose-built 'studios', just a little inshore, west of Cill Mhuirbhigh quay. By 1968, the property was in an extremely dilapidated condition, boarded up and infested by a huge colony of rats. The images in the Pickow Collection of Annie and her husband, and of the *ceilidh*, in which Sonny Hernon dances with Bridget Johnson of 'the big house', were to a degree performances, enactments, staged for Pickow and Ritchie. They were not quite true to everyday life, some seven years after the Second World War. They were self-conscious Aran in performance, in a purpose-built studio.

3. MOOCHING ABOUT

On the afternoon of 1 May 2012, I embarked for Aran. I have been going back once or twice a year for some years now. But this time, I boarded the ferry in the company of Tim Robinson. It was momentous for me. He wasn't sure whether it was his first time back to the big island in ten years—or was it eight? What was clear is that it was an occasion of the greatest moment for him. 'Faithful to the Last unto Aran'—that phrase of Ruskinian resonance he had used in his review of my book—came back to me as we crossed from Ros an Mhíl, two veterans of the slower and more arduous sailings from Galway in the old days, aboard the legendary, and none-too-stable, *Naomh Eanna*. Tim seemed beyond reach, as if dreaming awake. Who might guess what quantum jumps were going on in his head between past and present? We fairly flew across, with an easterly wind astern and scarcely a pitch or a roll. The modern boats offer none of the old thrills and spills, unless the weather is very bad indeed.

My friend Michael Muldoon had the sorest throat and was running a temperature. But there he was, up from his bed to greet us at the newly expanded harbour, with its extensive car park and elaborate traffic system, and he took us to our lodgings, at the 'Dormer', defending the modernization as he drove, as if to forestall any disapproval. 'Don't mention the buses!' one of the jarveys would call out after Tim, just a little later, as we set out on our first walk together. 'Don't . . . ' they called, amid much laughter. Respect and affection on Aran for Tim Robinson are palpable. But a writer is a writer and the general suspicion of such beings in such a place is that, whatever else they may be, they are also a species of trouble. If they are worth their salt, that is.

I had come with some 'trouble' of my own. I had had prints made for the occasion of about thirty of the photographs from Pickow's lens. I wanted to give one set to an elderly but vigorously active islander I knew. I saw him shortly after we arrived, on the corner below 'The American Bar', and gave the pictures to him at once. He was with two other men. My friend, to whom I have given old photos before, was delighted by them, fascinated to look into them and puzzle to identify the people they portrayed from so long ago. I was keen to show him the picture of Tom Hernon rowing a currach. But on seeing it, he exchanged looks with his fellows. They seemed to think it was not Tom. They were doubting Toms. Were they remembering or seeing, or forgetting what they never saw into?

Their doubt surprised and baffled me and haunted the rest of my stay. But with Tim Robinson for company, I had much to distract me from Tom Hernon and his shadow. We walked for hours that first evening and then headed back to our lodgings. It is a long enough road on to Cill Rónáin from Fearann an Choirce (Oatquarter—at the east–west divide of the island). It is the more so if you set out by Bothar na gCreag (Rocks Road), the straight, unmettled, undulating back road to Gort na gCapall (Field of the Horse), high above the Atlantic. 'The best road in the world', as Tim agrees. But it is a fair step round from start to finish, no matter the sights and conversation, the placelore and botanizing, or Tim's whistling Debussy's 'The Girl with the Flaxen Hair' now and then, and we were ready for our supper by the time we got back.

With the great labour and triumph of his island studies, his account of the Burren, and now the Connemara trilogy behind him, Tim spoke of his wish to move away from facts and to write more philosophically—as he has done before in *My Time in Space* and elsewhere. I had heard him speak in Cambridge of a work in hand: 'Where are the Nows of Yesteryear?'—with apologies to Villon and the depths of snow. But now he spoke of a new enquiry into the nature of 'gravity' and its potential as metaphor.

He was not sure where it was going, but he used his glass to explain that *its* centre of gravity was not in its base, where I might take it to be, but just above it. The centre of gravity of a high jumper performing a Fosbury flop, he was at pains to tell me, is just *below* the bar.[1]

Glasses, bars. . . . I looked across to where the men sat on their stools or leant talking to each other, their points (and pints) of gravity beginning to drift from true in pursuing the truth or falsehood of the proposition that *in Guinness veritas*. So perhaps what we think we know is not where we take it to be? And where we are is not quite where we think we are, especially under the magnetic influence of Guinness on an empty stomach. An image I am convinced is of Tom Hernon might not be of him at all. Tim also speculated on an idea for an 'installation'. This was to be centred round a single thalecress plant and had already caught the interest of Dublin's Hugh Lane Gallery. Thalecress (*Arabdiopsis thaliana*) is what botanists call a model organism (it is the first plant to have its entire genome sequenced). One of its names is 'Mouse-ear cress'. In experimental terms, it is to botany what the mouse is to biology.

I listened carefully and watched the men at the bar. I was mindful that Tim had in his pocket a little book about Schopenhauer. He had picked it up in Edinburgh when he was a young man a long time ago. It was for him what the poet Geoffrey Hill calls 'a comfort book'. I wondered if Schopenhauer figured at all in Tim's current speculations. But at the back of my mind I was brooding on facts and shadows. Might I be mistaken about Tom Hernon? Nothing could persuade me that I didn't know my man. I knew his face so well. Could the university library be misinformed as to those thirty-five results under the 'search term': 'Tom Hernon'? Could I not trust my mind's eye, my imagining memory? Oh, where were the nows of yesteryear and what of my centre of gravity? I felt that I had failed both Tom Hernon and myself. And things worsened the next day.

At the end of the third day, Tim and I said our goodbyes. He was heading for home. The weather had turned. Great white combers came up Galway Bay, testily. It would be a choppy crossing into the teeth of the wind. By nightfall, the rain lashed in and, later, at about eleven o'clock, from my rain-blurred window I saw the lifeboat go out. I do not know what drama it attended. But Tim would be safely home by then, I knew.

Well before the evening was over, just as Tim had gone, I was tracked down by Pádraig Ó Tuathail. He suggested a pint of Guinness, to be

[1] Some of this work has since been published. For 'Where are the Nows of Yesteryear?' and other work of its kind, see *Connemara and Elsewhere* (Prism: Royal Irish Academy, 2014) edited by Jane Conroy with contributions by John Elder, Nicolas Fève, and Tim Robinson. For 'The Centre of Gravity', see *Archipelago*, 10 (2015), 60–5.

followed by supper in Chill Éinne, prepared by his wife Mary O'Hara, the famous soprano and harpist. She is a dab hand, as I was to discover, at a hedgerow salad, one worthy to be set before even the botanizing Tim Robinson, had he only been there to join us.

In the bar, we met a man I will not name, but he was a native of Cill Mhuirbhigh and the eldest son of a family I knew well in my time. I showed him my photograph of Tom Hernon in a currach, thinking that though not quite of Tom's generation, still he would know him at once. But he had left his glasses at home. I offered mine but they did not help. He could only dimly make the figure out. It was little better than a blur, a shadowy impression to him, but glasses or no glasses, shadow or not, he expressed doubt. He was not seeing, but remembering, remembering something at least, something I had never heard before.

'Tom was never in a currach,' he said, flatly. 'He was born with his legs back to front.'

The expression took me aback. What could it mean? A form of hip *dysplasia*, perhaps, a not entirely uncommon condition in newborn infants? But 'back to front'? I could not help myself. A whole sequence of cartoon images of Tom ran through my mind, their legs on back to front.

'He wouldn't have been any good in a currach.'

'But he was a fine bareback horseman,' I said, remembering vividly Tom mastering the yet unbroken Grey Fella, 'surely. . . .'

'Just for the camera,' said Padraig, 'I think. . . . They were doing things for the camera. . . .'

I suppose we might say that they were engaged in 'quantum slinks', doing things behind their own backs, to engage the world as if they were pioneering postmodernists.

4. FOOTNOTE

I found myself on my last full day drawn to the case of Alfred Tizzard. He is buried in the graveyard that stands on a little promontory above Cill Mhuirbhigh Bay.

It is a classic *cimetière marin* where the dead lie within the perpetual sound of the sea, as it booms and hisses and rips and, on calm days, nestles, in a horseshoe bay of the whitest sand you ever saw. 'The old recumbent gravestones here are hard to read except in certain lights', Tim Robinson tells us, and goes on,

> now and then, in necrological mood, I used to kick through the tousled grass and little sandpits to see what death-notices were being posted by the circling

> sun. Old limestone and new marble agree that Hernon is the predominant name in the cemetery's mortal catchment area, principally the village itself. There are also many small, blank boulders marking the graves of those too young, too numerous or too humble to have been granted even one parting line by the hard art of writing. A stray occupies a discreet corner: A. Tizzard, a Royal Air Force gunner, fished up in the nets in 1941.

I remember vividly the morning, early in 1969, that I first came upon Alfred's grave. How surprising and moving it was to find, like a sudden shadow or shade cast under the wall, in the far south-west corner—a corner of a foreign field that *never* will be Rupert Brooke's forever England, although the headstone bears the RAF's emblem with its eagle and famous motto: 'Per Adua Ad Astra'—'Through Adversity to the Stars'. A strange presence in what had been a neutral Ireland. Then beneath the official device: '540427 FLIGHT SERGEANT/A. TIZZARD/AIR GUNNER ROYAL AIR FORCE/21ST APRIL 1941 AGE 26'. And at the foot of the stone: 'IN LOVING MEMORY / MUM AND DAD / SISTER AND BROTHERS / THY WILL BE DONE'.

Thy Will be done. . . . It was a day of clear blue, that last day I had to myself, after Tim had gone. The wind veered little, no more than a degree or two about north-east. Such a wind soon settles the sea along the leeward southern side of the island and opens the view right down the coast of Ireland. To the north-east itself it clears the far-away Twelve Pins of Connemara into a skyline worthy of the painter Paul Henry's impressionism.

It was May, but it scorched by midday like high summer. I took the best road in the world and went down to the Atlantic's edge at Port Bhéal an Dúin (Port of the Fort's Mouth), below Gort na gCapall (Field of the Horse), birthplace of the O'Flaherty brothers, Tom and Liam. (It moved me to see a 'For Sale' sign up in front of their family home. Surely, I thought, it should be acquired for the Irish nation?) I loitered thereabouts a while before setting off for Cill Mhuirbhigh, as if in the old days, heading for home.

My comfort book this trip was nothing as challenging as Schopenhauer. It was a battered old first edition of Tom O'Flaherty's *Aranmen All*, a work published in 1934, a classic of the Aran canon unduly neglected. Its opening chapter, 'Mackerel Nets', set at Cill Mhuirbhigh Bay, came to feel peculiarly potent in conjunction with Alfred Tizzard. It was highly affecting too in that I have waited for the dawn there myself a good few black inkwash mornings, though not in such company, attending the tide.

> The waves thundered on the sandy shore of Port Murvey. Eighty men, the crews of twenty-eight currachs, sat under the walls waiting for daybreak.

Thirty-four years later, there was only one currach in use at Cill Mhuirbhigh, and two men to row it, out and back to a half-decker moored in the bay, or to tend to a lobster storage cage. But the power of the sea out beyond and the tide-rip from North Sound is the same as ever it was, the same as when Alfred's body was suddenly brought up short in the meshes of what in April or May would probably have been a trammel net. O'Flaherty tells dramatically of the hazards and the precision needed to read and time the notorious 'Big Breaker'. Life and death could hang literally on knife-edge decisions to cut losses or not.

I went up into the crescent field at the back of the bay to the little fringe of dune above the shore, to lie down among the marram and close my eyes. I lay there remembering. Such a haul in my sound-warp net of memories to bring aboard. It was hearing the drone of the Aer Arann plane, on a sightseeing tour circling overhead, combing round above the cliff fort and raking off down the island, that really prompted me to think of Alfred. What a terrible reminder the sound of an aircraft would be to him.

'I swear they do that to torment me,' I heard him say. 'Curse the day Aer Arann was invented.'

Up until then, I had thought of him as happy there in a resting place I covet myself, an airy tomb, a sweet place of silver sand and porous limestone. You could lie there day and night, listening to the sea in its various tempi and to the waders, and in spring the cuckoo, the lark, and once the corncrake, but not now, and the trit-trot still of hoofbeats, in and out of hearing. But Tim Robinson had filled my head with another version of the afterlife, that of the Irish-language novelist Máirtín Ó Cadhain's *Cré na Cille*—'Graveyard Clay'—in which the dead go at it with all the spite and malice of the living on a bad day, arguing among themselves and maintaining a caustic running commentary on those above, yet to join them. Tim was at that date collaborating on an English version of *Cré na Cille*, a deeply challenging work to translate, not least for its play with Irish dialects.

5. COASTAL COMMAND

When at last I reached home—if home is where you live—I kept glimpsing Alfred's shadow in the back country of my mind. I began to research him and had one or two strange meetings with him, moments of Pathé newsreel. I heard him speak:

> Three fishermen hauled me up in their nets.
> I spilled inboard with the catch.

Little left to keep my corpse together,
All slime and slither to the touch.
It was Spring . . . That much I remember.
I heard them talking over their oars.
I heard them faintly.
I could not make out a word . . .

I heard ropes hissing as they were hauled inboard. As Alfred's shade would have done, I heard voices speaking in Irish. *Seo, breathnaigh, na páipéir atá air. An bhfuil tú in ann déanamh amach cén t-ainm atá air? AL-FRED TIZZ-ARD.* Here, look at the papers that are on him. Can you make out his name? AL-FRED TIZZ-ARD. I saw battleships sailing close to the island and aeroplanes as they roared overhead. I dwelt on the terror and horror of war. I tried to imagine Alfred's life and the inevitable solitude and fear even within comradeship that he would feel. I could not imagine him, as Yeats imagines his Irish airman, proclaiming 'The years to come seemed waste of breath, / A waste of breath the years behind / In balance with this life, this death'.

I pursued the Ministry of Defence to know what record they had of Flight Sergeant Alfred Tizzard. They took months to come up with anything. The people involved seem overwhelmed with enquiries in our age of lost identity and heritage.

The Atlantic front was speedier. I soon began to receive communiqués from Aran. I now learnt that the nets that caught Alfred belonged to Brian Peter Stephen Hernon, a man I had known, a neighbour. It seems that two brothers, Tom and Bartley Feeney Hernon, were also present. I knew them too. What is more, I had once rowed in a currach with Tom Feeney, out to the Callagh in the far west, to inspect lobster pots, and with us was Mikey MacDonough (leading character in the story to which Tim Robinson knew the end and I only the beginning), now, in spirit only, a neighbour of Alfred, lost at sea, as a memorial stone records. They were all my neighbours once, as they are all Alfred's neighbours now, resting on their oars above Cill Mhuirbhigh Bay. Do not forget them, quite, such memorials say. But what's in a name is more than a name can say through time. There's many a thing more lasting than a person, the written word chief among them. And so I write this, as footnotes to their names, as a stay against total oblivion.

Brian Hernon had taken it on himself to give Alfred a Christian burial. He consulted no one, certainly not the priest. The grave was originally marked by a wooden cross made by Coley Gill, a shipwright at Cill Rónáin. This was altogether a great act of independence and reverence for life. Later, someone came out from England with the 'official' RAF headstone; he was brought to the graveyard by Dara the postman by pony and trap. Not every fallen airman or seaman found at sea was so treated. Nor was there any want of them. Some islanders in those days would not take a body from the sea, for fear the sea would exact its price and one day claim them in return.

By the strangest of coincidences, the shipwright Coley Gill had a sister who served with Alfred's sister, as a nurse in the British Army. This meant that when Alfred's parents, Cecil and Emily, came out to visit their son's grave, they had a connection with one of the strong island families. It would have made a major difference to their experience. At what point and in what season they made the journey, I do not know. But the voyage out to the islands would have been from Galway aboard the *Dun Aengus*, as in 1952 it was for George and Jean Pickow. We might think of the Tizzards crossing Ireland by train from Dublin, to Dublin from Holyhead or Liverpool. The long journey all the way from Littlehampton on the banks of the River Arun in West Sussex must have been one of intense reflection and feeling, surreal in its last leg down Galway Bay, tiring physically and emotionally. Imagine the Tizzards gazing out from the train, hour upon hour. Imagine what they had been through, learning of Alfred's death, as one can only learn such things, suddenly, irrevocably, with a sickening shock.

They had experienced the war directly too. Littlehampton lay on the flight-path to and from Portsmouth and Southampton. In the spring of 1941, German planes bombed Littlehampton nearly every night, their Heinkels thundering overheard. A local historian has recorded incidents, telling how one day a German airman fell to earth, and as he plummeted, one of his flying-boots fell off and flew away. His pocket watch dropped too, invisibly, to be found still ticking, like a bomb, in someone's garden. It is odd perhaps to think of anyone in Goering's ultra-modern Luftwaffe depending on a pocket watch.

The Tizzards would have felt the hours of travel weigh on them, steadily and slowly. It was a slower world and a slower Ireland then, and the West a far wilder edge of Europe than today (so it was even in 1968). How many nights had they spent on their way? How long did they stay on the island and in what weather? They had come in their grief thinking to make arrangements for the return of their son's remains. But it seems the island worked its magic on them, as it can nowhere more overwhelmingly than at Cill Mhuirbhigh. They chose instead Aran's shore over that of Arun. A vowel of difference and a world.

Alfred Tizzard's last hours on earth were of course in the air and possibly on water. What records of his last sortie survive in the MoD's archive do not even list him by name. But we know he was aboard a Catalina seaplane, AH532 of 210 Squadron, that took off from Oban at nearly a quarter-to-six on the evening of Saturday, 19 April 1941. His pilot was Flight Lieutenant Henry Francis Dempster Breese, aged twenty-two—a doomed youth, son of a doomed father. Air Vice-Marshall Charles Dempster Breese, of Knightsbridge, had been a casualty the month before, killed in a prang on 5 March 1941, in transit somewhere in the North of Scotland. Otherwise, of Alfred's comrades, only Warrant Officer Clifford Bond and Sergeant Alexander Vaughan McRae are listed in the record.

A full complement aboard a Catalina would number ten, all trained 'air gunners', in addition to whatever other duties they had. The Catalinas could stay in the air for twenty-four hours, and in the Atlantic Theatre, it was the aircraft that went farthest and first to meet homebound convoys, to scour the seas for U-boats, and to respond to attacks from enemy aircraft, especially the dreaded Focke-Wulf Condor. The perils—the seeming interminable monotony, the cold and inevitable exhaustion—were extreme. Theirs was coastal work with a difference. 'It was presently noticed', an official account of this period relates,

> that the fatigue from which they suffered on returning from long sorties was severe. The time it took them to concentrate their thoughts and reply to questions during their interrogation was considerable and there were many complaints of air sickness.

All this would have been Alfred Tizzard's routine lot, right up to the fatal moment, the exact nature of which we cannot know.

From Oban, AH532 flew to Loch Erne in the North of Ireland, alighting at ten-to-eight, and, at a quarter-past-nine that night, it took off again down the Donegal Corridor, to escort a convoy. *Coastal Command*, an HMSO publication of 1943, enables us to imagine something more of Alfred's experience:

> A quarter of an hour after the captain and his companions have come on board, the rigger prepares to let go the moorings. One of the fitters then starts first one, then the other engine.... This fills the boat with fumes, which will disperse when she is in the air. The engines are warmed up one after the other, so that the flying boat turns in circles first one way, then the other, like a mayfly in the eddy of a stream. The Catalina then taxies slowly to the flare-path... after the rigger has reported that all hatches are closed, the klaxon sounds. The Catalina moves slowly at first, then with swiftly-gathered speed. The take-off has begun.

But this time, alighting and debriefing would not follow. The next night, 21 April, at half-past eight, a Sunderland Short set out to search for survivors. About an hour later, a message from Stranraer gave a bearing. Then in another hour, the Sunderland's rear gunner sighted flares to starboard. Parachute flares were dropped at once and the aircraft combed the area methodically, to no avail. A last weak signal, presumed to be from the Catalina's crew, was received at twenty-past-one.

Around an hour later, the Sunderland headed for Eagle Island, Co. Mayo, to dead reckon her position. At just gone a quarter-to-five in the morning, she was at Slyne Head (an archipelago about nine miles south-west of Clifden, Co. Galway). They searched doggedly as before but found nothing. At last, they turned for home, one has to think, with heavy hearts and bleak thoughts, as ballast to their fatigue. Then all at once—at ten to nine—they came under attack from a Focke-Wulf Condor. Their number might have been up, just as in an instant Alfred's had been. But the plane broke off, as suddenly as it had engaged them, at about 1000 yards, without hitting.

So the Sunderland was waterborne at Lough Erne at 10.15 on the Tuesday morning, and back by the afternoon on the Firth of Lorn, known in wartime as the 'Oban Road'. The crew would eventually go to their billets in one or other of the town's main seafront hotels, perhaps 'The Great Western' or 'The Esplanade', 'The Alexandra' or 'The Marine'.

At some point, we cannot know how much later, Brian Hernon and his fellows pushed their currach off from the strand at Cillmhuirbhigh and rowed out to retrieve their nets, to see what luck had brought them.

13

Fugitive Allegiances

The Good Ship *Archipelago* and the Atlantic Edge

Jos Smith

The written and visual works published over the last decade in the literary journal *Archipelago* (2007–present) have produced a distinctive and enduring landscape vision of Britain and Ireland clustered around the Atlantic edge. It is a vision of a craggy, sea-swept, but inhabited periphery that has found a surprising purchase in the cultural imagination of the twenty-first century. However, unlike many other more amenable of what Joanne Parker has called the 'countless vying maps' of these isles, this vision exists at an argumentative tilt to the more conventional orientation.[1] It privileges and celebrates the northern and western margins of what the journal has come to refer to as the 'unnameable archipelago', its channels and seas, its firths and bays, its peninsulas, and of course, its many islands.[2] It celebrates, too, the languages, cultures, and place names of these locales and micro-regions, exploring their uncertain relations to the inland world and, in particular, to a partially devolved Britain. Julian Bell's striking, monochrome illustration, which has appeared on every front cover so far, shows the British and Irish archipelago as glimpsed all at once looking down through diving gannets from somewhere in the north-west out beyond St Kilda. Most of the south east is occluded behind the head of a gannet in the foreground or is disappearing under shadow near a dark and slightly curved horizon. In fact, we see more of Normandy's Cotentin peninsula poking up towards the West Country (a reminder of those old connections between the fishing communities of northern France and Cornwall) than we see of Kent, Sussex, Hampshire, or any of the 'Home Counties'. 'I would like [a] somewhat tilting, distorted map', the journal's editor suggested to the artist, 'pushed to the lower right hand frame of the picture, with

[1] Joanne Parker, *Britannia Obscura: Mapping Britain's Hidden Landscapes* (London: Jonathan Cape, 2014), xi.

[2] Andrew McNeillie, 'Editorial', *Archipelago*, 1 (2007), vii.

south-east England chopped off by the frame.'[3] At first glimpse, it does take a moment to 'discover' Britain and Ireland upside down in the image. But as you do so, there is a mental reorientation that reveals the wider agenda of resisting an Anglocentric and metropolitan view of the Isles.

There are layers of significance to this reorientation. The argument between centre and periphery—in which the periphery is summoned up in all its linguistic variety and ecological richness—is important in its own right. Many of the journal's launch events over the years have taken place in that most central of English locations in Oxford, in the Bodleian Library no less, and have involved invocations of landscapes and seascapes as remote and coastal as the litany of the shipping forecast. There is a quality of 'speaking back' to the centre about this, and a sense in which the journal is attempting to inculcate a corrective literary culture. However, looking a little more closely reveals a sense in which the periphery is reconfigured as an *archipelagic* space, in the way in which this has been explored in recent work in Island Studies, exchanging its sense of being on an edge relative to the south-eastern centre for one more consciously '*between* and *among* islands', a space in which allegiances are all the stronger for being plural and mobile.[4] Multiple places come into dialogue with one another in this vision and the connecting seas and channels themselves become spaces of creative activity. If the 'unnameable archipelago' presents a challenge to the more conventional representations of Britain and Ireland, then it is with this image of constellated richness, an image of small places fiercely alive and renegotiating their identities in relation to the old and unwieldy 'sovereigntyscape'.[5]

Archipelago's editor, Andrew McNeillie, is a poet and author himself who was, at the time of the first edition, emerging from a career as a literature publisher and commissioning editor in Oxford. He started the Clutag Press in 2000, where he had been hand-setting and printing poetry by new and established poets. *Archipelago* would go on to be the primary output for Clutag, though other publications have included original works by Geoffrey Hill, Tom Paulin, and Anne Stevenson among others. *Archipelago* 1 was launched in 2007 at an event in Cambridge organized by Robert Macfarlane in memory of the late Roger Deakin. In the opening editorial, McNeillie made the following, memorable claim:

[3] Letter from Andrew McNeillie to Robert Macfarlane, 12 March 2006 (RobMacletter.doc) in Clutag Press archive (uncatalogued), Bodleian Library, Oxford.

[4] Stratford, Baldacchino, McMahon, Farbotko, and Harwood, 'Envisioning the Archipelago', 124.

[5] Tom Nairn, *After Britain: New Labour and the Return of Scotland* (London: Granta, 2000), 125.

> Extraordinary will be its preoccupations with landscape, with documentary and remembrance, with wilderness and wet, with natural and cultural histories, with language and languages, with the littoral and the vestigial, the geological, and topographical, with climates, in terms of both meteorology, ecology and environment; and all these things as metaphor, liminal and subliminal, at the margins, in the unnameable constellation of islands on the Eastern Atlantic coast, known variously in other millennia as Britain, Great Britain, Britain and Ireland etc.[6]

For Alan Riach, such 'Extraordinary... preoccupations' have led the journal to offer something of a 'corrective' to Modernism's 'forensic detachment', one that, for the artist of this new millennium, 'bears the weight of conscious connection with his or her society, family, language and national history'.[7] As such, we have marginal twentieth-century figures such as Ian Niall, Seton Gordon, Ivor Gurney, and Jack Clemo (not to mention the less marginal presiding shadow of Hugh MacDiarmid), revisited and reconsidered. They are reconsidered not *in spite* of their 'regionalism', but because, through their vivid and felt connections to place, the journal suggests, we discover our understanding of these islands enlarged, their landscapes and their literatures enriched by being so carefully located. Behind this celebration of geographical and linguistic diversity, Riach goes on, is an insistence on 'the understanding that imperial authority is always being resisted by people in places unconquered by metropolitan centralism, unimagined by its arbiters of canonicity'.[8] The recovery of such figures from the century just gone has helped to determine coordinates for what might even be called an early twenty-first-century literary movement now, one intimately invested in the diverse cultural geographies of the archipelago.

In this sense, the journal has helped to nurture a contemporary literature that is also 'archipelagic' in the recent particular sense that John Kerrigan has proposed for literary criticism. Kerrigan's groundbreaking work on the seventeenth century, *Archipelagic English* (2008) (in which Andrew McNeillie is thanked as an early reader), describes its critical approach as 'archipelagic', after the historian J. G. A. Pocock, who voiced concerns about the suspicious English bias to British history writing as early as the 1970s.[9] There have now been key publications in archipelagic criticism for the

[6] McNeillie, 'Editorial', vii.

[7] Alan Riach, 'Archipelago', in *PN Review*, 37 (September/October 2010), 48.

[8] Ibid.

[9] J. G. A. Pocock, *The Discovery of Islands: Essays in British History* (Cambridge: Cambridge University Press, 2005).

eighteenth century and, more recently, for twentieth-century modernism.[10] Kerrigan describes the methodology as an attempt to 'strip away modern Anglocentric and Victorian imperial paradigms' and to 'recover the long, braided histories played out across the British-Irish archipelago between three kingdoms, four countries, divided regions, variable ethnicities and religiously determined allegiances'.[11] The term 'archipelagic', he claims, designates a 'geopolitical unit or zone'; it does so 'neutrally (avoiding the assumptions loaded into "the British Isles"); and it implies a devolved, interconnected account of what went on around the islands'.[12] McNeillie's editorial work has helped to direct this historical and literary critical method into a forward-looking attempt to shape this contemporary literary movement for the twenty-first century.

While the journal is in English and has always published English translations, it has reached out to a range of the different languages of the archipelago. In the very first issue, there was an essay by Mark Williams on contemporary Scottish Gaelic language poetry, for example. The following few lines are translated from Fearghas MacFhionnlaigh's long Scottish nationalist poem 'The Midge' and suggest a characteristic form of cultural resilience:

> Tha mi beag, agus is toil leam na rudan beaga:
> an sìol adhlaict' a sgoltas an cabhsair;
> an t-sileag uisg' a chaitheas a' chlach;
> a' ghainmhein mhìn a thiodhlaiceas am biorramaid;
> a' chiad eun a chuireas fàilt' air a' ghréin;
> an dùthaich bheag, an cànan beag;
> facal na fìrinn as truime na 'n Domhan.
> (I am small, and I like the small things:
> the buried seed that splits the sidewalk;
> the water-drop that devours the stone;
> the grain of sand that inters the pyramid;
> the first bird that welcomes the sun;
> the little country, the little language;
> the word of truth that is heavier than the world.)[13]

[10] Philip Schwyzer and Simon Mealor (eds), *Archipelagic Identities: Literature and Identity in the Atlantic Archipelago, 1550–1800* (Aldershot: Ashgate, 2004); and John Brannigan, *Archipelagic Modernism: Literature in the Irish and British Isles, 1890–1970* (Edinburgh: Edinburgh University Press, 2015).

[11] John Kerrigan, *Archipelagic English: Literature, History and Politics, 1603–1707* (Oxford: Oxford University Press, 2008), 2.

[12] Ibid., vii.

[13] In Mark Williams, 'The Old Song', *Archipelago*, 1 (2007), 81.

'The little language' is poised on the wild edges here, ready to swell over these images of city and empire. There is Irish Gaelic poetry of the Blaskets from Rody Gorman too, and a close attention to the distinctive linguistic contours of place throughout. There is one poem in particular that stands out, though, capturing as it does the journal's attitude to language and the cultural diversity of the archipelago. This is a rare instance of the St Kildan dialect given in Scottish Gaelic, with a stanza and loan words borrowed from a particularly monastic version of English by the contemporary poet Peter Mackay. The way this poem has been translated over two pages, its complicated plaiting of the two languages and the one dialect, suggests some carefully made editorial decisions. English loan words appear in the Gaelic version and the same words are in Gaelic in the English translation. St Kildan words are glossed in the Scottish version, Scottish words in the English version.[14] It is a fine example of those 'long braided histories' that John Kerrigan describes, and testament to the richness they produce.

The journal has inflected this 'archipelagic' perspective in its own distinctive way, then, and its preoccupations with place have extended into an ecology of the isles that is important in its own right as well. In a review of the first edition, one of its most regular contributors, Robert Macfarlane, glosses his own understanding of the adjective 'archipelagic' and proposes it as a description of a broader tendency in contemporary British and Irish art and literature concerned with landscape:

> It can be hard to know what to call this new body of work. 'Landscape art' is blandly tepid. 'Nature writing' is sapless and text-specific. 'Pastoral' summons swains and greenswards. 'Environmental' has become gummed by politics. Perhaps the adjective 'archipelagic' might serve, catching as it does at imaginings that are chthonic, marine, elemental and felt.[15]

Archipelago's treatment of the geology, birdlife, wildflowers, and the imaginative significance of the sea itself has also celebrated the richness of this slightly different meaning to the 'archipelagic'. Elemental nature on the coastal edges of the archipelago has become allied with the 'little languages' described by Fearghas MacFhionnlaigh above. Both are part of this 'littoral and vestigial' vision of the Atlantic edge. However, far from being an idealized version of 'the wild'—a hotly disputed term recently—the ecologies of the archipelago are often revealed to be vulnerable, depleted, and polluted. Tim Dee captured this sense when, in *Archipelago*

[14] Peter Mackay, 'Escodus à Hiort', *Archipelago*, 4 (2009), 26–7.

[15] Robert Macfarlane, 'Go Wild in the Country', *The Guardian* (14 July 2007), 13.

5, he suggested that what we mean by 'nature' when we talk about 'nature writing' today may have changed:

> Country diaries survive in some newspapers but DDT, species losses, and Ted Hughes' gore-poetics saw off the nice in the 1970s, while nature itself—under the human heel—has been pushed, bloodied, shrunken and ruined to the front of the stage ever since. There, even enfeebled, it has called for new descriptions, fresh thoughts.[16]

Writing of Tory Island, Robert Macfarlane himself, in an uneasy and curious coupling of adjectives, suggests of the littered coastline that 'the abject and the sublime are never far apart here'.[17] *Archipelago* has brought together its celebration of a rich diversity of cultures and languages with this fascination for the 'chthonic' and 'elemental'. 'Littoral and vestigial' as both may seem at times, the imaginative power of the journal has been to mark their resilience and actively stimulate new work at the intersection of these two senses of 'archipelagic'. It has drawn attention to the intrinsic link between a richly plural constellation of cultures and the diverse ecosystems and topographies from which they have emerged and to which they are indebted.

1. AN ARAN KEENING

McNeillie has extended a metaphor through a number of artworks and editorials for *Archipelago*, in which the journal itself has figured as a boat setting out to sea with its net spread wide for new writing. Ishmael has been occasionally alluded to,[18] but the metaphor of the 'good ship archipelago' eventually settled on a more ordinary fishing vessel venturing out from coast to coast, gathering in news from place to place.[19] It is a more modest metaphor, but with a nod to the almost prophetic grandiosity of W. S. Graham's 'The Nightfishing' too, suggesting that fine line between ordinary experience and extraordinary perception.[20] For example, in one such instance of this extended metaphor, the 'good ship archipelago' is described as once or twice a year making landfall 'to

[16] Tim Dee, 'Nature Writing', *Archipelago*, 5 (2011), 22.

[17] Robert Macfarlane, 'Tory Island', *Archipelago*, 3 (2009), 40.

[18] Andrew McNeillie, 'Editorial', *Archipelago*, 3 (2009), n.p.

[19] Andrew McNeillie, 'Unchartered Waters', www.clutagpress.com (19 November 2011), accessed 15 January 2015.

[20] A watercolour by McNeillie published on the journal's blog shows the 'good ship' at sea at night and written in the sky is 'THE NIGHTFISHING'. 'Hope and Anchor', www.clutagpress.com (3 October 2014), accessed 15 January 2015.

publish . . . and be damned in the arc-light glare of the dawn fish-market'.[21] In this, the coast itself takes on a particular meaning too, as the edge of our conventional world, criss-crossed in search of fresh experiences and refreshing perspectives. Such experiences and perspectives are delivered like a prescription to an ailing, inland society, its 'post-Thatcherian mismanagement culture' for whom 'growth' is a 'religion', 'quantity the be-all, and nothing for quality (of life), unless approved by the Committee for Homogeny and signed off by some hubristic Walter Mitty'.[22] There are precedents for such a critical, sea-borne position on inland life. Jonathan Raban has described a nineteenth-century prose genre of the 'sailing-alone book': John MacGregor, R. T. McMullan, and E. E. Middleton all went to sea in the 1860s 'to teach the land a lesson' in journeys that treated the sea as 'that biblical wilderness in which the true prophet must temporarily dwell'.[23] Raban himself, more forgivingly, sails around the coast of Britain as a way of exploring the question of England in 1982. The difference in *Archipelago* is marked, though, as McNeillie is never alone in his 'good ship'. The whole process is founded on a sociable advocacy of plural views on the Isles that would have been abhorrent to the disgruntled Tory politics of these Victorian men.

The metaphor of this 'good ship' as a fishing vessel is particularly apt when we consider that the vast majority of the literary or artistic contributions either involve travel between islands or tracing a form of coastal geography. Locating on a map of Britain and Ireland whatever poems and essays from these ten editions it is possible to locate reveals the majority to be north-westerly, all but a handful to be marine or coastal, and almost all of those that are not north-westerly to be nonetheless coastal.[24] Such an overarching attempt to understand a place through a view from its edge or, to borrow Tim Robinson's phrase, through a 'view from the horizon' suggests a certain fugitive allegiance, an allegiance pledged to the ongoing lived experience, to the instability of place as it is being redreamed at the edges, celebrating complexity, divergence, difference, and local distinctiveness, all in contradistinction to the unified idea of a nation-state, certainly in contradistinction to that 'Committee for Homogeny'.[25]

21 Andrew McNeillie, 'Memories are Made of Fish', www.clutagpress.com (28 March 2012), accessed 15 January 2015.

22 Andrew McNeillie, 'Editorial', *Archipelago*, 5 (2011), n.p.

23 Jonathan Raban, *The Oxford Book of the Sea* (Oxford: Oxford University Press, 1992), 25–6.

24 Of course, it is not possible to place all contributions on a map, but it is also worth noting that the majority of those contributions that are not mappable concern themselves with subjects that may yet be considered marginal in some sense: geology, fishing, Gaelic language, birds, sea life, and the like.

25 Tim Robinson, *The View from the Horizon* (London: Coracle Press, 1999).

In such fugitive allegiances there is a sense of being in between islands that seems appropriate enough for an editor whose own lineage draws on a Scottish family line, a Welsh childhood, a very formative year on the Aran Islands, and a career spent in Oxfordshire. But in this there is also a broad and very modern understanding of *place* itself that emerges here. 'Places', writes the philosopher Edward Casey, 'are matters of experience . . . [w]e make trial of them in culturally specific ways'; being in or from a place is a part of 'an ongoing cultural process with an experimental edge'.[26] This 'edge' that Casey describes here finds a topographical counterpart in the maze of north-west Atlantic coastlines as they appear in the journal. It is an edge being brought into focus and *worked* by the 'good ship archipelago', crossing back and forth, bringing images and languages, place names and stories, from here to there and back again. Doreen Massey captures the slant of recent work in geography on the subject of place when she describes it more dynamically as an 'event', as 'a constellation of processes rather than a thing'.[27] The image of a boat among the islands of an archipelago, gathering in and giving out news, endlessly renewing the relationships between places, seems apt for this dynamic understanding of place.

The sense of space and the rhythm of this trawling and island hopping are underpinned by McNeillie's own 'sea-pastoral adventure' when, in 1968, he spent a period of time living alone on the Aran Islands in the mouth of Galway Bay. Inspired by J. M. Synge's account of Aran as a young man, McNeillie had visited, fallen for the place, and returned later to stay for nearly a year with a trunk of books, tinned food, fishing tackle, and as much as he had been able to save in wages. The time had a profound effect on him just before he settled down to marriage and working life inland, but it would be thirty years before he published his travel memoir *An Aran Keening* (2001). The book draws on his journals of the time but is firmly grounded in the voice of the older man looking back ('Almost every plank of my vessel has been replaced since I first crossed Galway Bay').[28] Reviews of the book note the surprising decision of a young writer to set out for the periphery in the year of the general strikes, occupations, and protests that had brought Paris to its knees in 1968.[29] However, there is an erroneous assumption in this that the periphery is an

[26] Edward Casey, *Getting Back into Place: Toward a Renewed Understanding of the Place-World* (Bloomington: Indiana University Press, 1993), 31.

[27] Doreen Massey, *For Space* (London: Sage, 2005), 140–1.

[28] Andrew McNeillie, *An Aran Keening* (Dublin: Lilliput Press, 2001), x.

[29] Shawn Gillen, '*An Aran Keening*: Review', *New Hibernia Review*, 6 (2002), 156; and Aidan Higgins, 'Reviewed Books', *Books Ireland*, 240 (May 2001), 135.

apolitical space. Certainly, it is remote, arrived at by two long boat trips, with no electricity, no telephone but for one in the post office, and before television came and 'changed everything' (as one islander tells him when he returns in 2000).[30] But the decision to live somewhere remote should not be equated with the decision to somehow abandon the world. In fact, Clarrie Wallis has described the way, for a generation of young artists disillusioned with the city as a cultural centre, and venturing out to work in remote locations, 1968 represented 'a turning point away from technological optimism to preoccupations with ecology, conservation and a crisis of the 1970s as the British were uneasily forced to face their post-industrial and post-colonial future'.[31] McNeillie's own rural Welsh background, the literary coordinates of his youth ('Owen, Kavanagh, MacDiarmid, Thomas, Thomas, and Thomas'), and the presiding influence of his father, Ian Niall, have all weighted his own cultural allegiances to the west and the north anyway.[32]

Less an escape *from* Europe, or Wales, or London, or Britain behind him, the book represents rather an escape *into* a little-known world with a distinctive quality of experience, one that might serve as an educative comparison to later life in Britain. On the one hand, the Aran of 1968 is the 'elemental' archipelago that Macfarlane describes, a place in which McNeillie was able to 'learn about time as space', in which the moving constellations, the rhythm of the tides, weather, and the repetitive '*crex crex*' of the corncrake offer coordinates that supersede the clock and the British city's working day.[33] On the other hand, it is also a world vulnerable and susceptible to the pressures of modernity, and he has a keen eye for this. When he returns to write the postscript in 2000, the corncrake—such a forceful nocturnal presence in his journals—has become locally extinct to the islands and the local community itself is also described with an unsentimental sharpness of vision:

> though a community there was, skeletal yet interwoven, stressed with resistances and rivalries, and bound together by affections and loyalties, tragedy and comedy, common necessity no longer held it as intimately together as once it had. It was a symptom of the modern age, the incipient self-help era. And this was striking to observe because the past remained such an immediate neighbour. So intimate was it that some still wore its clothes next to their skin, and occupied its houses, and tuned their mindsets to its fading wavelengths.[34]

30 McNeillie, *An Aran Keening*, 217.

31 Clarrie Wallis, 'Making Tracks', in Clarrie Wallis (ed.), *Richard Long: Heaven and Earth* (London: Tate Publishing, 2009), 38.

32 McNeillie, *An Aran Keening*, 176. 33 Ibid., 47. 34 Ibid., 66.

McNeillie is, of course, to some degree insulated against much of the hardship involved in staving off the perils of poverty or hunger that attend any idleness for those who take their living from the sea or the land in such a remote place. He is, in his own words, 'the archetypal uninvited stranger' who will return to time's 'linear tyranny', such as it is in the city.[35] He is under no illusions about becoming part of the community, though he does, of course, make friends. Like Synge before him, he was there to glimpse and connect with a singular way of life 'right at the edge of the western world, in a northern sea, like living in the corner of a scene by Bruegel'.[36]

There is a moment that vividly recalls the Europe that he is supposed to have left behind him at one of the book's most westerly and peripheral locations, when he is fishing on the limestone pavements under the southern cliffs:

> I was still using my handline then and catching only pollack, when the mackerel came in a shoal a hundred yards wide and as deep as a three-storey house, deeper than the eye can see in even such clear water, a squad of helmeted militia, inch-perfect in their drill, like Red Square on May Day, or a Nuremberg rally, or riot police on high alert in the Paris streets of '68. Naïvely I raised my arm to throw a line—like a revolutionary with a Molotov cocktail on its sling—thinking I couldn't miss. But in the instant my arm went up, the thoroughbred shysters turned themselves inside out, turned on their tails and sped, like a startled flock of birds, thousands of them, in their phoney tiger stripes and metallic blue-green armour.[37]

In a moment of hallucinatory loneliness, the sudden swell of post-war Europe erupts, and disappears as quickly, leaving him standing and holding something he connects to a Molotov cocktail. The 'riot police', seen through the skin of water as if through a glass between worlds, disappear off into the dark again. '[P]honey' even lends the passage the air of Holden Caulfield's awkward and disgruntled relationship with the social world. The image offers a way of thinking about the spatial orientation of McNeillie's Aran to Europe, and to Britain, and to Ireland: a world, not separate, but brushing up against Europe, on its edge and affording a critical distance, from which the author is looking in, rebellious, resolved, and alone.

The counter image to this one is of the older McNeillie in later life 'delaying too long before the fishmonger's slab and fancying I can taste the salt-and-iodine, the mineral sea, and even hear it surge beneath the cloud

[35] Ibid., 91, 47. [36] Ibid., 193. [37] Ibid., 187–8.

of harrying herring gulls at the dead centre of England'.[38] In both images there is a sense of elsewhere brought to bear on the meaning of the given location, a plaiting together of disparate experiences. This sense of *elsewhere* and *between* that folds together centre and periphery comes across in McNeillie's poetry as well. In the playful and knotted short poem 'Belonging', a sense of place emerges that is spatially complex. The poem offers a disruption of the meaning of the word 'belonging' as we might recognize it as meaning 'rooted in' or 'possessed by', inflecting it with something paradoxically more fluid and mobile:

> Who put the longing into it?
> The longing to leave so that
> We might belong in longing
> To return again, and again?
>
> Who put the being into it?
> The being that is never the same
> So that when we come back to it
> All we have is a name?[39]

The sense of place and of belonging comes through the repeated process of departure and return as much as through location itself. To answer the rhetorical questions, nobody put either 'longing' or 'being' in the word 'belonging'—the *OED* directs us to entirely different roots for the word—and so the questions suggest a projection of a modern experience, the shifting emotions of a mobile life, carrying a collection of disparate worlds within and struggling to hold them in relation to one another.

In an early review of the journal, Fiona Stafford distinguishes between 'the isolation and individualism' of a literary *island* and a very different logic, distinctive to an archipelago, 'of clustering and analogy'.[40] The fugitive allegiance of 'the good ship archipelago', then, is something that began in McNeillie's own experience, an emotional tension that prompts the editor to re-imagine the Isles from the point of view of a boat crossing seas, collecting in news from the periphery, and building an alternative vision with which to answer back to the centre. In fact, the whole spatial organization of centre/periphery begins to come undone. McNeillie might have travelled out in 1968 from the centre to the periphery, but by the time he launched *Archipelago* as a journal, it was with this plural sense of clustered places, a sense of moving *among* a changing network of cultural centres.

[38] Ibid., xi.

[39] Andrew McNeillie, 'Belonging', *Now, Then* (Manchester: Carcanet Press, 2002), 65.

[40] Fiona Stafford, 'Review of *Archipelago* 1', *Times Literary Supplement* (2 November 2007), 24–5.

2. THE GOOD SHIP

The first issue of *Archipelago* begins with a short prose poem by Seamus Heaney describing a trip by boat back to the mainland, haunted by exchanges with a man who is himself 'a mystery to the islanders'.[41] It goes on to a coastal poem by Derek Mahon which characteristically contemplates the clash of modernity and our animal origins at the water's edge. The coordinates begin to come clear as this is followed by an essay that begins aboard another boat travelling out, not quite from the centre to the periphery, but from the south to a sea that is itself oddly central, the Irish Sea. Robert Macfarlane's essay describes a night spent on the island of Ynys Enlli off the Llŷn Peninsula, where he travels in search of what he describes as 'a tradition of archipelagic writing' that 'goes as far back as the Celtic *peregrini* of the sixth to tenth centuries AD'.[42] These '*peregrini*' were monks, solitaries, anchorites, and pilgrims who travelled 'in their thousands to the bays, forests, promontories, mountain-tops and islands of the Atlantic littoral'.[43] For Macfarlane, this is part of a wider project to pursue the contentious idea of 'wildness' across modern Britain and Ireland. The purpose of this trip in particular, though, is less an attempt to discover a modern and vestigial version of wildness itself on the island (though that is there too) than an attempt to trace something of the monks' own distinctive apprehension of life in this remote coastal world. Just as his earlier book, *Mountains of the Mind*, was a work less concerned with mountains than with the fascination that mountains inspire, it is by visiting the places in which these monks lived and wrote that Macfarlane endeavours to glimpse and connect with what fascinated *them* about the western islands and coastlines.

The story of these monks and their pilgrimage out to 'the brinks of Europe and beyond' suggests a movement between worlds, like McNeillie's, not just as an *escape from* the European world of their day, but as an *escape into* something worldly on its own peripheral terms. The monks' journey is initially described as an effort to 'act out a movement from history to eternity', but it does not remain 'eternity' for long as poetic sketches and Gaelic marginalia begin to locate their experience somewhere *between* history and eternity, a place of carefully differentiated animal noises, living weather, and a sense of wonder.[44]

41 Seamus Heaney, 'Our Mystery', *Archipelago*, 1 (2007), 1.

42 Macfarlane, 'Go Wild in the Country', 13.

43 Robert Macfarlane, 'Island', *Archipelago*, 1 (2007), 7.

44 Ibid., 8.

> Their poems speak eloquently of a passionate and precise relationship with nature, and of the blend of receptivity and detachment which characterized their interactions with it. Some of the poems read like jotted lists, or field notes: 'Swarms of bees, beetles, soft music of the world, a gentle humming; brent geese, barnacle geese, shortly before All Hallows, music of the dark wild torrent.' Others record single charmed instants: a blackbird calling from a gorse branch near Belfast Loch, foxes at play in a glade. Marban, a ninth-century hermit who lived in a hut in a fir-grove near Drum Rolach, wrote of the 'wind's voice against a branchy wood on a day of grey cloud'. A nameless monk, responsible for dry-stone walling on the island of North Rona in the ninth century, stopped his work to write a poem that spoke of the delight he felt at standing on a 'clear headland', looking over the 'smooth strand' to the 'calm sea', and hearing the calls of 'the wondrous birds'. A tenth-century copyist, working in an island monastery, paused long enough to scribble a note in Gaelic beside his Latin text. 'Pleasant to me is the glittering of the sun today upon these margins'.[45]

Monks who were apparently turning their backs on the world become transfixed here by different types of geese and carefully observed weather conditions, and are moved to express poetic figures such as the 'wind's voice'. The compulsion to write about these things arises to make a record and turn perception itself into something creative, interactive. 'Receptivity and detachment' is a frame of mind aspired to by ascetics of many religions for its blend of worldliness and transcendence, but it is also a fitting description of the mentality of many authors and artists associated with the journal and it may well be this that draws out the connection Macfarlane makes between the *peregrini* and 'archipelagic writing'. In the long poem that opens *Archipelago* 4, 'Instructions to a Saintly Poet', Douglas Dunn plays on this same writerly monasticism. To be detached is one thing, to forfeit the conventional social allegiances and sail a little closer to the edge of the known world with all the exposure and vulnerability that this might risk is another; but here 'receptivity' also suggests a willingness to take on new coordinates and to positively encourage a reorientation by them. It suggests an attempt to broaden the horizon and enlarge the familiar world; or rather to intensify the level of detail, complicating it with little-known local histories: to enlarge it by revealing its complexity.

One of the most important vehicles for the forms of minute local history that *Archipelago* has helped to bring aboard and conserve is the place name. Robin Robertson's long poem 'Leaving St Kilda' in *Archipelago* 4 is an extreme case in point and one of the most memorable. It invokes a long itinerary of place names spread over ten pages and is

[45] Ibid., 12.

interspersed with Norman Ackroyd's monochrome etchings of many of the places called to mind. The poem describes a journey towards the mainland from that outermost of the Hebridean islands, but it becomes at times a long list, naming cliffs and islands, sounds, and outlying rocks as it goes. The cartographer and author Tim Robinson has described place names as being like 'so many isolated lines from a lost epic of everyday life'.[46] They do certainly have this quality here; the Romantic fascination with the poem fragment is even called to mind at times. Robertson's poem seems to celebrate the way the place names gesture and allude to worlds loaded with memory in which story and history blend together: names such as 'The Well of Many Virtues', 'The Plain of Spells', 'The Stack of Doom', 'Point of the Strangers', and 'Skerry of the Son of the King of Norway'.[47] It is a poem which collects its intangible, linguistic geography into the public consciousness, but in doing so, it leaves it hanging precariously somewhere between celebration and elegy. The inclusion of Ackroyd's etchings on every other page also provides a visual topographical reference for the litany and generates a sense of immersion among the places named (see Figures 13.1 and 13.2).

The visual aesthetic that has helped to shape *Archipelago*'s distinctive version of the Atlantic edge is indebted to, more than anything, etchings such as these by Ackroyd that have appeared in every edition. Ackroyd has described finding his calling as an artist when a fisherman offered to take him out around the 450 ft red sandstone sea stack, the Old Man of Hoy, off the coast of the Orkney Islands.[48] Since then, he has spent a lifetime making engravings of the craggy outliers and islands of the north-west, sketching in fishing boats, then transferring to copperplate back home in London. Now, on an easel in his Bermondsey studio, there sits a map of Britain and Ireland with a cluster of pins in an arc around the north-west coast, one in every location at which he has worked. In understanding Ackroyd's art, it cannot be stressed enough just how important the role of the boat has been (and the fishermen who have taken him out) in providing him with those perspectives on the rocky edge. It is an art that exemplifies the sense of being '*between* and *among* islands' that comes across psychologically in so much of the writing of *Archipelago*.[49] Again and again, the view is from a point that is hazardous, exposed, engulfed, encompassed, and immersed, taking stock of the land from among its

[46] Tim Robinson, 'The Seanchaí and the Database', *Irish Pages*, 2 (2003), 51.
[47] Robin Robertson, 'Leaving St Kilda', *Archipelago*, 4 (2009), 19–21.
[48] *What Do Artists Do All Day. Part 1, Norman Ackroyd*, dir. Matthew Hill, BBC 4 (19 March 2013).
[49] Stratford, Baldacchino, et al., 'Envisioning the Archipelago', 124.

Figure 13.1. 'Conochair and the Gap', Norman Ackroyd (1989).

Figure 13.2. 'Stac Lee and Stac Armin', Norman Ackroyd (1989).

towering broken edges. Ackroyd's aesthetic is one of the 'chthonic' and 'elemental' archipelago that Macfarlane describes and this is something that is reflected in the technique itself as well. McNeillie describes how his etching process—an unpredictable technique for which trial-and-error is an important part—is 'as fickle and spectacular in its effects as the weather itself' and how it is unusually subject to 'immediate hazard and serendipity'.[50]

The elemental nature of Ackroyd's coastal etchings, the soft washes that suggest low cloud and curtains of rain—a product of his use of aquatint—might lend the works an almost abstract quality of dark forms receding and protruding on the picture plane, but he rarely shows a desire to abstract entirely. The titles of the etchings are always careful to locate the images as precisely as possible, and he, like Macfarlane, reminds us that these have been 'densely populated' places, places in which a culture has been delicately and patiently cultivated in connection to the topography and wildlife. In the foreword to a book of his Irish etchings, he reminds his reader:

> Many of the islands supported self-contained communities most of which are now abandoned. They have left moving reminders in the ruins of their villages and field systems. Nearly every island of any size has associations with early Christian saints, and their churches and oratories... High Island off Connemara boasts an extraordinarily sophisticated eighth century watermill system indicating that the monastery, on this almost inaccessible rock, must have supported a population of about fifty monks. On Inishkea, off Co. Mayo, a midden on Bailey Mor indicates a factory for boiling molluscs to extract the blue-purple pigment much used in scriptoria.[51]

Ackroyd's elemental archipelago, then, is one with cultural and historical depth, and this comes across too in his love of the place names. At an event celebrating ten years of Clutag Press in Oxford in 2011, in the Bodleian Library, he stood to offer from memory a litany of all the names of those places in which he has worked on the north-west coasts, one for every pin in that map in his studio. He asked the audience to imagine a compass extending an arm from his childhood home in the 'ancient kingdom of Elmet' and reaching out some 300-odd miles along the outer edge, evoking a peripheral geography from Muckle Flugga and Out Stack due north right round to the Great Famine graveyard at Skibbereen in the South of Ireland, pointing out the mix of languages (Gaelic, Scots, English, Norse) that make up this wide arc, and calling

50 Andrew McNeillie, 'Where Art Meets Sea', *Archipelago*, 4 (2009), 32.

51 Norman Ackroyd, *Irish Etchings 1987–2008* (Thirsk: Zillah Bell Gallery, 2009), 7.

them to mind as if bringing them to bear on that most central and landlocked of southern English counties.[52]

It is in Ackroyd's images that the metaphor of the 'good ship archipelago' has been sustained visually throughout, and the metaphor has come very close to reality as well. In one essay by McNeillie himself, a very literal boat plays host to a collaboration between Norman Ackroyd and the poet Douglas Dunn (a Welshman writing about a collaboration between an Englishman and Scotsman). The poet and artist travelled by boat together along various coasts to create *A Line in the Water*, a book of poetry and etchings published in 2009 by the Royal Academy of Arts.

> ... we boot our way toward
> Undersea dreamscapes, surreal, eel-fathomed
> Depths in the super-dark, the silent, dumbed,
> Unpainted and unwritten floors
> Of the visionary deep, the great outdoors,
> Geology, botany, sky, sea, birds, fish,
> So commonplace to here it's just outlandish.[53]

Together they have cut themselves loose of the security of the shore. The word 'outlandish' carries the pun that doing so permits them a certain imaginative license, brushing up against the wildness of the dream world and the surreal; a bubbling away of the unconscious that might, in time, be instructive to the landlocked, conscious mind.

From time to time, Dunn addresses Ackroyd directly and his 'wide night-view's nocturnal aquatint':

> For you are lovers of the East and North,
> The West, and waters, and your art's no-place,
> Invention's home, that better place to be.[54]

The 'no-place' of art here is Ackroyd's distinctive, boat-bound perspective, outside looking in, '*between* and *among* islands', a momentary embodiment of what Heaney has called the 'free creative imagination' in all its temporary and struggled-for suspension of allegiances, in all its tension with the 'constraints of religious, political, and domestic obligation'.[55] This is 'Invention's home', a paradoxically stable image for a boat balanced on the swelling waves. The boat becomes 'place' and 'no-place' at the same time, defined and undefined, at the edge on which place itself is being reappraised and renegotiated.

[52] This event was filmed and a DVD distributed with *Archipelago*, 8.

[53] In McNeillie, 'Where Art Meets Sea', 40–1.

[54] In Ibid., 42.

[55] Seamus Heaney, *Sweeney's Flight* (London: Faber and Faber, 1992), 87.

This is 'the good ship archipelago' itself, suspended in the connective interstices, home to creative collaborations, and producing a vision of the land in which the identities of, and the relationships between, nations, locations, regions, and micro-regions are open-ended questions calling for dynamic and inclusive responses. The achievement of *Archipelago* has been to offer a view of Britain, Northern Ireland, and Ireland that responds to political and cultural instabilities and the uncertainty they have produced by grounding a cultural vision of the archipelago at a local and human scale. It has refused the simplifications and abstractions of the 'Committee for Homogeny' and opted always for something more difficult and more complex, revealing in every locale the presence of a network of cultural and ecological relations and nurturing these relations as a resource. In the end, there is something recuperative about this vision. It has helped to conserve, but also to nurture, a cultural vitality on the margins at a time when this is much needed.

14

Afterword

Beyond the Blue Horizon

John R. Gillis

The point of greatest interest is the place where land and water meet.

Ralph Waldo Emerson[1]

As *Coastal Works* so amply illustrates, we have never been so conscious of shores as we are today. Artists and writers were the first to colonize coasts in the nineteenth century, drawing in their wake the urban elites of Europe and America, followed by the middle and, ultimately, the working classes. Edges are where you will find artists, and, because islands are all edges, they fetch up there in great numbers. On Monhegan Island, off the coast of Maine, America's most famous artist colony, painters jostle to set up their easels on the headlands made famous by three generations of Wyeths, Rockwell Kent, George Bellows, Edward Hopper, and so many others.

Islands have what Adam Nicolson has called 'edge potency', stimulating the imagination, opening up far horizons.[2] The harder the edge, the more dramatic the separation of land and water, the more appealing it is, one of the reasons why, until recently, the soft contours of coastal wetlands have had relatively little appeal to artists. But edges are as much the product of art and literature as they are their subjects. We like to think of edges as a product of nature, when, in fact, nature abhors sharp edges and lines of any kind.

Sharply defined coast lines originated in the minds of eighteenth-century cartographers and have become ever more deeply etched over time, ignoring the non-linear, fractal nature of the places where land meets

[1] Kenneth White, *On the Atlantic Edge: A Geopoetics Project* (Dingwall: Sandstone Press, 2006), 25.

[2] Adam Nicolson, *Seamanship: A Voyage along the Wild Coasts of the British Isles* (New York: HarperCollins, 2004), 45–66.

water. In reality, shores are what ecologists call an *ecotone*, boundary places where two ecosystems meet and interface, more like a seam than an edge, a connection rather than a separation. As Rachel Carson famously put it, 'always the edge of the sea remains an elusive and indefinable boundary'.[3] The ecotonal shore has been one of humanity's most generative habitats, spiritually as well as materially.

The first human colonization of the shore goes back almost 200,000 years, when *Homo sapiens* from the interior of Africa came down to the sea and then, using coastal routes, spread rapidly around the globe. Later, in the 'Age of Discovery', Europeans came by ship, using the shores for trade, fishing, and hunting. Until the era of the Industrial Revolution, shores were the most productive places on earth. It is only recently that people came there not to produce, but to consume. Recently, a large part of this consumption has become scopic, an abrupt change from earlier periods when the sea was a place of work, of a fully embodied rather than a purely visual experience. The shore was prime human habitat, a place known by embodied experience, but, until the modern era, rarely depicted in art or literature. Indeed, the first European seascapes of the early modern period focused more on ships than the sea itself, more on the near shore and harbours than on broader expanses.

Like landscape, seascape was a place before it was representation of place. Seascapes came late to Western art. They were the progeny of early modern landscape and history painting. The first examples of seascapes were, in fact, landscapes painted from the decks of Dutch ships, the artists facing landward rather than seaward. Until the nineteenth century, the genre did not focus on the water itself, but on harbours and ships at anchor, on naval battles and coastal happenings. The sea itself was mere backdrop to alongshore maritime activity. For millennia, the sea had represented chaos and danger, ugly and unfit for artistic representation. The first seascapes represented an effort to bring order and reduce fear by framing water by land, thus rendering it intelligible and less threatening. Water itself was only rarely depicted.[4]

It was not until the nineteenth century that the Western world turned to face the sea. This was the moment when seaside resorts developed and the aquarium, first popularized in the 1850s, brought the sea into the

[3] Rachel Carson, *The Edge of the Sea* (Boston: Houghton Mifflin, 1998); John R. Gillis, *The Human Shore: Seacoasts in History* (Chicago: University of Chicago Press, 2012); and Mark Monmonier, *Coastlines: How Mapmakers Form the World and Chart Environmental Change* (Chicago: University of Chicago Press, 2008).

[4] John Wilmerding, *A History of American Marine Painting* (Boston: Little, Brown, 1968), chs 1–3; Steven C. Boursa, *The Aesthetics of Landscape* (London: Belhaven Press, 1991), 4.

home. Seascapes that became so popular in the Victorian era focused mainly on the occupants of the foreshore, on fisher folk and the beaches, where women and children were the favourite subjects. What has been called 'pure seascape', focused on water itself, did not arrive until the 1890s. It was then that artists began to flock to cliffs and headlands, rendering paintings reflecting the awesome powers of the sea itself. This was the great accomplishment of the American painter Winslow Homer, whose work turned away from beach scenes, to face down the raging seas a few yards away from his studio at Prouts Point, Maine.[5] For twentieth-century painters like John Marin, 'the sea is so damned insistent that houses and land won't appear in my pictures'.[6]

The history of seascape reflected and, in turn, was affected by the changing perception of the relationship of sea and land. Once the shore became a fixed edge, a coast line, its ecotonal nature was obscured. Even as more and more people moved closer to the sea, few had any working relationship with it apart from the visual. Coasts became in the twentieth century places to see or be seen. Most visitors to the shore have no working, embodied experience of the sea.[7] Working waterfronts now make up a tiny fraction of littorals that are now far more devoted to recreation. In earlier periods, the shore was a place to be avoided except when work demanded. Coastal peoples built their houses well back from the shore, with windows facing inland. Those who made their living from the sea did not spend much time gazing at it. They knew it primarily through senses of hearing, smell, and touch, feeling it as much as seeing it. Today, people come down to the shore not to do, but to look. What the new pure seascape gained in edginess, it lost in its ability to do justice to the ecotonal qualities of coasts themselves and the nature of coastal life in general. The coast had ceased to be a place and the sea had become a view, a change reflected in art, but also a power force in coastal construction and management.

Painters taught the general public how to look at the sea. When Paul Theroux circumambulated the British Isles in the 1980s, he found the people there standing at the seaside and staring at the ocean. 'I believed that these people were fantasizing that they were over there on the waiting horizon, at sea. I seldom saw anyone with his back toward the sea', even in the worst of weathers. 'The British seem to me a people forever standing on

[5] David Tatham, 'Winslow Homer and the Sea', *Winslow Homer in the 1890s: Prout's Neck Observed* (New York: Hudson Hills Press, 1990), 81.

[6] Carl Little, *Maine Artists* (privately printed: Rockport, 1994), n.p.

[7] Gillis, *The Human Shore*, 128–57.

a crumbling coast and scanning the horizon.' What had once been the privilege of the leisured classes was now regarded as the right of everyman and everywoman. 'It was the poor person's way of going abroad', he wrote.[8]

'The sea is to be gazed at and even celebrated, but as an actual place of production and transportation it is largely hidden', writes Philip Steinberg.[9] People go to the beach 'to *watch*, not do'.[10] There life follows art. Now we all view the sea through artists' eyes, through the perspective of outsider, of someone *on* the coast, but not *of* the coast, someone who lives *by* the sea, but does not know how to live *with* it. Coasts which were once seen as broad zones where history was made are now a kind of non-place where we turn our backs not just to land, but to the past itself. Both maritime art and maritime history encourage us to overlook the coast, to turn it into the edge of something else rather than the special place it actually is.

A lot of work gets done on coasts today, but, unlike the past, little of it is manual; most is mental and imaginative.[11] Working waterfronts are now hemmed in by great stretches of shore where doing nothing appears to be the principal occupation. Fishers, clammers, reapers of seaweed, and mariners have been replaced by swimmers, surfers, sunbathers, and water-gazers. But it would be wrong to say that nothing is being accomplished on the beaches of contemporary Europe and America, for their idleness is an illusion. An immense amount of cultural work is going on there all the time, and not just by writers and artists. Beachgoers fashion themselves and their gender, race, and national identities at the edge of the sea. Learning to look for crucial cultural work that goes on there will reveal massive productivity not recorded in the measures of Gross National Product, but no less vital to the reproduction of modern society.

Modernity has torn down innumerable physical boundaries and closed many frontiers, but, at the same time, it has created a whole new set of prospects from which to view the world, real and imagined. Since the mid-nineteenth century, our favourite horizon has been the shore. Herman Melville was one of the first to notice the very modern phenomenon of water-gazing. He discovered it on Manhattan's waterfront: 'Here come the crowds, pacing straight for the water, and seeming bound for a dive.

[8] Paul Theroux, *Kingdom by the Sea: A Journey Around Great Britain* (Boston: Houghton Mifflin, 1983), 188.

[9] Philip E. Steinberg, *The Social Construction of the Ocean* (Cambridge: Cambridge University Press, 2001), 171.

[10] John R. Stilgoe, *Alongshore* (New Haven and London: Yale University Press, 1994), 407.

[11] Mike Brown and Barbara Humberton (eds), *Seascapes: Shaped by the Sea* (Farnham: Ashgate, 2015).

Strange! Nothing will content them but the extremist limit of land.'[12] A half-century later, the urban masses would find themselves a subway ride away on the beaches of Coney Island and other resorts, doing exactly the same thing. Today, we travel ever further for the unobstructed view.

People now fly halfway around the world just to sit on the beach. The highest-priced real estate is always that with a water view.[13] Water-gazing is something landlubbers do. The unobstructed horizons they seek are of no interest to mariners, who pay attention to what is in the water, not what is on the horizon. The landlubber's vision is pulled outward, but the mariner's focus is on what is hidden below the surface, and, if sailing, the winds above. As Paul Theroux discovered when he took up residence on Cape Cod, mariners and landlubbers have very different ways of seeing. The former 'does not distinguish between land and water, and keeps going, actually or mentally seeing shoals and eddies and sunken ships and rocks', while the latter sees only lines, one at the shore—the coastline—the other on the horizon where sky and water seem to intersect.[14] Neither is real, but this does not mean they are not consequential.

There is something about a shore, and especially an empty shore, that triggers the imagination. It is not the shore itself, or even the waters along the shore, that produce this effect. Rather, it is the mental construct of the horizon that draws us outward into a time and space of the *beyond*, where we escape reality, if only for a moment.[15] Deserts, plains, and arctic wastes are also known for their edge effects. 'The edge of any landscape . . . quickens an observer's expectations', writes Barry Lopez, but there is no horizon like that of water.[16] The blue horizon is one that can never be reached, always retreating as we approach it. Its beyond is ultimately unattainable, making it the safest repository for the dreams and nightmares we deposit there.

All cultures have their temporal and spatial edges. Without them, they would be at a loss to locate themselves. Some places draw their edges tight around them. The Maine artist, Eric Hopkins, whose paintings leave no doubt about the line that separates land and water, is convinced that

[12] Herman Melville, *Moby Dick* (New York: Barnes & Noble, 1993), 1–2.

[13] Wallace J. Nichols, *Blue Mind: The Surprising Science That Shows How Being Near, In, On, or Under Water Can Make you Happier, Healthier, More Connected, and Better at What You Do* (New York: Little, Brown, 2014); and Orvar Lofgren and Billy Elin, *The Secret World of Doing Nothing* (Berkeley: University of California Press, 2010).

[14] Paul Theroux, 'The True Size of Cape Cod', *Fresh-Air Fiend: Travel Writings, 1985–2000* (Boston: Houghton Mifflin, 2001), 148.

[15] Vincent Crapanzano, *Imaginative Horizons: An Essay in Literary-Philosophical Anthropology* (Chicago: University of Chicago Press, 2004), 14–15.

[16] Barry Lopez, *Arctic Dreams: Imagination and Desire in Northern Landscapes* (New York: Scribner's, 1986).

'islands are finite. You know where the edge of the world is. . . . You know where you stand'.[17] This is a particularly Western view, however, for Pacific islanders view their world as encompassing both land and sea. It is Western cartography that has taught them to see blue horizons.

The horizon itself is a feature of Western modernity. In earlier centuries, European and American societies organized their centres and left their edges ragged. But boundaries have become more clearly delineated over the last two centuries as Western territorial nation-states have become more insistent on surveying and fortifying their borders. They have exported these notions, drawing lines and dictating borders all over the globe. Many of these defy ecological and sociological reality, but they satisfy those who wish to set their edges. Put another way, horizons are not given but made, produced by a set of cultural practices originating on the shores of Europe and North America, but now found everywhere where sea and land meet.

Staring at the horizon, modernity's favourite form of daydreaming, is of relatively recent origins.[18] In the ancient world, the horizon was a very concrete thing, a boundary of stones separating one territory from another. Today, horizons are mental rather than physical. They mark the limit of our sensory perception, the point where imagination takes over. In a world that leaves so little room for imagination, we have to go ever further out to find space for it.

In earlier periods, Western peoples projected their imagining vertically, to the heavens and below into nether regions. In a cosmos organized vertically, high and low mattered more than near and far. Our medieval ancestors occupied a finite world of great depth but little breadth, but the 'Age of Discovery' changed all that, creating a world that, as Yi-Fu Tuan describes it, was 'broad in surface, low in ceiling'.[19] Since then, both time and space have become more linear and infinite. The old cosmos burst its bounds at the point that Biblical certainties were challenged by scientific notions of natural time and deep space that not only shattered old horizons, but created new imaginary ones.

Science has disenchanted all those realms, including the heavens, which once harboured human fantasy. When the world was fully explored, hopes and fears could no longer be projected in the same old places. The shore, which had sheltered mythical creatures like the mermaid, was rapidly demythologized. What had been a demonic place up to the eighteenth

[17] Eric Hopkins, personal communication.

[18] Lofgren and Elin, *The Secret World of Doing Nothing*; and Orvar Lofgren, *On Holiday: A History of Vacationing* (Berkeley: University of California Press, 1999).

[19] Gillis, *The Human Shore*, 154.

century now became a paradisiacal beach in the course of the nineteenth century. In the United States, the closing of the frontier, officially declared by the government in 1890, coincided with the emergence of new kinds of horizons, ones not for crossing, but for contemplating. In his study of what he calls the imaginative horizon, Vincent Crapanzano describes 'a beyond that is, by its very nature, unreachable in fact and in representation'.[20]

The triumph of modern notions of linear time and infinite space have made it more difficult to comprehend the nature of the shore itself. Conceptualizing it as an edge has obscured the reality of its *betweenness*, its ecotonal nature. Thinking of it as a border rather than a permeable *boundary*, we have entered into massive projects of sea-walling that have utterly changed the life that exists there. Sea-walling has been destructive of shores, conducive to beach erosion and the extinction of species that rely on the ebb and flow of the tides for their existence.

Of late, however, there has been a noticeable consciousness of the need to reconnect with water, and not just through the traditional marine occupation of fishing. More and more people are looking for the embodied experience that new water sports—surfing, diving, small-boat sailing, and kayaking—are providing. This is a potent sign of our need to reconnect with the sea, not just scopically, but in an embodied manner. Recently, Wallace J. Nichols has argued that we are all possessed of a 'blue mind', bequeathed to us by our long association with water, fresh and salt.[21] While one might be sceptical of his notion that our relationship to the sea is hardwired by human evolution, there is no doubt about our cultural connection to water, something that has been rediscovered by artists and writers in the present moment.

In the absence of land frontiers, the sea has become our new wilderness, a notion Thoreau championed as early as the mid-nineteenth century but that is now gaining new strength in the extreme sport movement which is so oriented to the sea. A sense of adventure and freedom, once associated with the land, has found new life there. A new generation tests itself by engaging with wind and wave, recovering skills that have been moribund in earlier generations. The worldwide popularity of surfing and the parallel renaissance of kayaking are only two of the many examples of the current embodied re-engagement with the sea.[22]

[20] Crapanzo, *Imaginative Horizons*, 14–15.

[21] Nichols, *Blue Mind*.

[22] Jon Anderson and Kimberley Peters (eds), *Water Worlds: Human Geographies of the Ocean* (Farnham: Ashgate, 2014).

Rather than seeing the shore as the edge of something else, it seems time to see it for itself, as one of those invaluable in-between places where two ecosystems meet and enrich one another, contributing so mightily to the physical and mental health of our planet. We will continue to focus on our imaginary blue horizons, but we need to pay attention to the green ecotonal nature of the shore itself.

Bibliography

Ackroyd, Norman, *Irish Etchings 1987–2008* (Thirsk: Zillah Bell Gallery, 2009).

Acts and Statutes made in a Parliament begun at Dublin, the Twelfth Day of November, Anno Dom. 1715 (Dublin, 1719).

Adamowsky, Natascha, *The Mysterious Science of the Sea 1775–1943* (Abingdon: Routledge, 2016).

Adams, Richard, *The Plague Dogs* (London: Allen Lane, 1977).

Adams, Richard, *Watership Down* (Harmondsworth: Penguin, 1974).

Adams, Richard and R. M. Lockley, *Voyage Through the Antarctic* (London: Allen Lane, 1982).

Adelman, Juliana, *Communities of Science in Nineteenth-Century Ireland* (London: Pickering and Chatto, 2009).

Adelman, Juliana, 'Evolution on Display: Promoting Irish Natural History and Darwinism at the Dublin Science and Art Museum', *The British Journal for the History of Science*, 38 (2005), 411–36.

Air Ministry, *Coastal Command: The Air Ministry Account of the Part Played by Coastal Command in the Battle of the Seas 1939–1942* (London: HMSO, 1943).

Alexander, Neal and James Moran (eds), *Regional Modernisms* (Edinburgh: Edinburgh University Press, 2013).

Allen, David Elliston, *The Naturalist in Britain* (Princeton: Princeton University Press, 1976).

Anderson, Benedict, *Imagined Communities: Reflections on the Origin and Spread of Nationalism* (London: Verso, 2006).

Anderson, Jon and Kimberley Peters (eds), *Water Worlds: Human Geographies of the Ocean* (Farnham: Ashgate, 2014).

[Anonymous], 'The Bublers Mirrour', in Paul Langford (ed.), *Walpole and the Robinocracy: The English Satirical Print* (Cambridge: Chadwyck-Healey, 1986), 38–9.

[Anonymous] [George Tugwell], 'Science by the Sea Side', *Fraser's Magazine*, 54 (September 1856), 254.

[Anonymous], *Thoughts of a Project for Draining the Irish Channel* (Dublin, 1722).

Armitage, David and Michael J. Braddick (eds), *The British Atlantic World, 1500–1800*, 2nd edn (New York: Palgrave, 2009).

Armstrong, Isobel, *Glassworlds: Glass Culture and the Material Imagination 1830–1880* (Oxford: Oxford University Press, 2008).

Arnold, Matthew, *The Complete Poems*, ed. K. Allott and M. Allott, 2nd rev. edn (London: Longman, 1979).

Auden, W. H. (ed.), *The Oxford Book of Light Verse* (London: Clarendon Press, 1938).

Auden, W. H. and Louis MacNeice, *Letters from Iceland* (1937; London: Faber and Faber, 1967).

Baldacchino, Godfrey, 'Islands, Island Studies, Island Studies Journal', *Island Studies Journal*, 1 (2006), 3–18.

Baldacchino, Godfrey, 'Studying Islands: On Whose Terms? Some Epistemological and Methodological Challenges to the Pursuit of Island Studies', *Island Studies Journal*, 3 (2008), 37–56.

Baldacchino, Godfrey and Eric Clark, 'Editorial', *cultural geographies*, 20 (2013), 129–34.

Barlee, John, 'Aunt Maude's Whale', unpublished manuscript, n.d.

Barlow, Edward, *An Exact Survey of the Tide* (London, 1722).

Barry, Kevin, *The City of Bohane* (London: Vintage, 2011).

Beebe, William, *Beneath Tropic Seas: A Record of Diving among the Coral Reefs of Haiti* (New York and London: G. P. Putnam's Sons, 1928).

Walter Benjamin, *Reflections*, ed. Peter Demetz (New York: Harcourt Brace Jovanovich, 1975).

Blake, William, *The Marriage of Heaven and Hell* (Oxford: Oxford University Press, 1985).

Bloom, Harold, *The Anxiety of Influence: A Theory of Poetry* (Oxford: Oxford University Press, 1973).

Boate, Gerard, *A Natural History of Ireland, in Three Parts* (Dublin, 1726).

Bolster, W. Jeffrey, *The Mortal Sea* (Cambridge: Belknap Press, 2013).

Boursa, Steven C., *The Aesthetics of Landscape* (London: Belhaven Press, 1991).

Boyd, David, *Norman Nicholson: A Critical Biography* (Seascale: Seascale Press, 2014).

Boyle, Andrew, *The Riddle of Erskine Childers* (London: Hutchinson, 1977).

Brannigan, John, *Archipelagic Modernism: Literature in the Irish and British Isles, 1890–1970* (Edinburgh: Edinburgh University Press, 2015).

Brayton, Dan, *Shakespeare's Ocean: An Ecocritical Exploration* (Charlottesville: University of Virginia Press, 2012).

Brearton, Fran and Edna Longley (eds), *Incorrigibly Plural: Louis MacNeice and his Legacy* (Manchester: Carcanet, 2012).

Brett, David, *A Book Around the Irish Sea: History Without Nations* (Dublin: Wordwell, 2009).

Brightwen, Eliza, *Eliza Brightwen, Naturalist & Philanthropist; An Autobiography*, ed. W. H. Chesson, introd. Edmund Gosse (New York: American Tract Society, 1909).

Brown, David Blayney, Amy Concannon, and Sam Smiles (eds), *J. M. W. Turner: Painting Set Free* (Los Angeles: J. Paul Getty Museum, 2014).

Brown, Mike and Barbara Humberton (eds), *Seascapes: Shaped by the Sea* (Farnham: Ashgate, 2015).

Brown, Terence, *The Literature of Ireland: Culture and Criticism* (Cambridge: Cambridge University Press, 2010).

Brown, Terence, '"What am I doing here?" Travel and MacNeice', in Brearton and Longley (eds), *Incorrigibly Plural*, 72–84.

Browne, E. T., I. Thompson, F. H. Gamble et al., 'The Fauna and Flora of Valencia Harbour on the West Coast of Ireland', *Proceedings of the Royal Irish Academy*, 21 (1899), 667–854.

Brunner, Bernd, *The Ocean at Home: An Illustrated History of the Aquarium* (New York: Princeton Architectural Press, 2005).

Burgess, Thomas, *Take Me Under the Sea: The Dream Merchants of the Deep* (Salem: Ocean Archives, 1994).

Burke, Edmund, 'Speech on Stamp Act Disturbances', in Paul Langford (ed.), *The Writings and Speeches of Edmund Burke: Volume II* (Oxford: Clarendon Press, 1981), 43–5.

Burke, Mary, '*Tinkers*': *Synge and the Cultural History of the Irish Traveller* (Oxford: Oxford University Press, 2009).

Burns, Robert, *The Poems and Songs of Robert Burns*, ed. James Kinsley, 3 vols (Oxford: Oxford University Press, 1968).

Burns, Robert, *The Works of Robert Burns*, ed. James Currie, 4 vols (Liverpool: J. McCreery, 1800).

Butler, Henry D., *The Family Aquarium; or, Aqua-Vivarium* (New York: Duck and Fitzgerald, 1857).

Buxton, John and R. M. Lockley, *Island of Skomer* (London: Staples Press, 1950).

Byrne, Anne, 'Untangling the Medusa', in Patricia Deevey and Mary Mulvihill (eds), *Stars, Shells and Bluebells: Women Scientists and Pioneers* (Dublin: WITS, 1997), 98–109.

Byrne, Patricia M., 'Delap, Maude Jane', in James McGuire and James Quinn (eds), *Dictionary of Irish Biography* (Cambridge: Cambridge University Press, 2009), 157–8.

Cannadine, David (ed.), *Empire, the Sea and Global History* (London: Palgrave, 2007).

Canny, Nicholas and Philip Morgan (eds), *The Oxford Handbook of the Atlantic World, 1450–1850* (Oxford: Oxford University Press, 2011).

Cantor, Geoffrey, Gowan Dawson, Graeme Gooday, Richard Noakes, Sally Shuttleworth, and Jon Topham (eds), *Science in the Nineteenth-Century Periodical: Reading the Magazine of Nature* (Cambridge: Cambridge University Press, 2004).

Carson, Ciaran, *Belfast Confetti* (Dublin: Gallery Press, 1989).

Carson, Ciaran, *The Star Factory* (London: Granta, 1997).

Carson, Rachel, *The Edge of the Sea* (Boston: Houghton Mifflin, 1998).

Carswell, John, *The South Sea Bubble* (Stanford: Stanford University Press, 1960).

Casey, Edward, *Getting Back into Place: Toward a Renewed Understanding of the Place-World* (Bloomington: Indiana University Press, 1993).

Chamberlayne, John, *Magnæ Britanniæ Notitia: or, The Present State of Great Britain; with Divers Remarks upon the Antient State Thereof* (London, 1726).

Chanter, Charlotte, *Ferny Combes: A Ramble After Ferns in the Glens and Valleys of Devonshire* (London: Lovell Reeve, 1856).

Chartered Institute of Logistics and Transport Report, *Vision 20:35 Cymru Wales*, in *Global Construction Review* (24 November 2014).

Childers, Erskine, *The Framework of Home Rule* (London: E. Arnold, 1911).

Childers, Erskine, *The Riddle of the Sands: A Record of Secret Service*, ed. Norman Donaldson (Mineola, NY: Dover, 1976).

Childers, Erskine, The *Riddle of the Sands: A Record of Secret Service*, ed. David Trotter (Oxford: Oxford University Press, 1996).

Clark, Heather, 'Leaving Barra, Leaving Inishmore: Islands in the Irish Protestant Imagination', *Canadian Journal of Irish Studies*, 35 (Fall 2009), 30–5.

Clark, T. J., 'Modernism, Postmodernism and Steam', *October*, 100 (2002), 154–74.

Cohen, Margaret, *The Novel and the Sea* (Princeton: Princeton University Press, 2009).

A Collection of Miscellany Letters, selected out of Mist's Weekly Journal, 4 vols (London, 1722–7).

Collins, Timothy, 'Praeger in the West: Naturalists and Antiquarians in Connemara and the Islands 1894–1914', *Journal of the Galway Archaeological and Historical Society*, 45 (1993), 124–54.

Colson, Nathaniel, *The Mariners New Kalendar* (London, 1701).

Conroy, Jane (ed.), *Connemara and Elsewhere* (Prism: Royal Irish Academy, 2014).

'A Conversation with Zahr H. Pritchard, Recorded by the Editor', *Asia*, 234 (March 1924), 217–20.

Cooper, David, 'Envisioning "the Cubist Fells": Ways of Seeing in the Poetry of Norman Nicholson', in Neal Alexander and David Cooper (eds), *Poetry & Geography: Space & Place in Post-War Poetry* (Liverpool: Liverpool University Press, 2013), 148–60.

Cooper, David, '"Matter Matters": Topographical and Theological Space in the Poetry of Norman Nicholson', *Yearbook of English Studies*, 39 (2009), 169–85.

Cooper, David, 'The Poetics of Place and Space: Wordsworth, Norman Nicholson and the Lake District', *Literature Compass*, 5 (2008), 807–21.

Cooper, David, '"The Post-Industrial Picturesque"?: Placing and Promoting Marginalized Millom', in John K. Walton and Jason Wood (eds), *The Making of a Cultural Landscape: The Lake District as a Tourist Destination, 1750–2010* (Aldershot: Ashgate, 2013), 241–62.

Corry, Geoffrey, 'The Dublin Bar: The Obstacle to the Improvement of the Port of Dublin', *Dublin Historical Record*, 23 (1970), 137–52.

Courcy Ireland, John de, *Ireland and the Irish in Maritime History* (Glendale Press: Dun Laoghaire, 1986).

Crang, Philip, 'Field Cultures', *cultural geographies*, 10 (2003), 251–2.

Crapanzano, Vincent, *Imaginative Horizons: An Essay in Literary-Philosophical Anthropology* (Chicago: University of Chicago Press, 2004).

Crary, Jonathan, *Suspensions of Perception: Attention, Spectacle, and Modern Culture* (Cambridge, MA: MIT Press, 1999).

Cromek, R. H., *Reliques of Robert Burns, Quarterly Review*, 1 (1809), 19–36.

Cunliffe, Barry, *Facing the Ocean: The Atlantic and Its Peoples, 8000 BC-AD 1500* (Oxford: Oxford University Press, 2001).

Cunningham, Valentine, *British Writers of the Thirties* (Oxford: Oxford University Press, 1988).

Cunningham, Valentine, 'MacNeice and Thirties (Classical) Pastoralism', in Brearton and Longley (eds), *Incorrigibly Plural*, 85–100.

Daly, Mary, *Dublin, The Deposed Capital: A Social and Economic History (1860–1914)* (Cork: Cork University Press, 1985).

Darwin, John, *The Empire Project: The Rise and Fall of the British World-System (1830–1970)* rev. edn (Cambridge: Cambridge University Press, 2011).

Darwin, John, *Unfinished Empire: The Global Expansion of Britain* (New York: Penguin, 2012).

Davenant, Charles, *A Postscript to a Discourse of Credit, and the Means and Methods of Restoring it* (London, 1701).

da Vinci, Leonardo, The *Notebooks of Leonardo da Vinci*, ed. and trans. Edward MacCurdy (New York: George Braziller, 1955).

Davis, Herbert (ed.), *The Prose Writings of Jonathan Swift*, 16 vols (Oxford: Basil Blackwell, 1939–74).

Dee, Tim, 'Nature Writing', *Archipelago*, 5 (2011), 21–30.

Deevey, Patricia and Mary Mulvihill (eds), *Stars, Shells and Bluebells: Women Scientists and Pioneers* (Dublin: WITS, 1997).

Defoe, Daniel, *A Tour Thro' the Whole Island of Great Britain, divided into Circuits or Journies*, 3 vols (London, 1724).

Delap, Maude J. and Constance Delap, 'Notes on the Plankton of Valencia Harbour, 1899–1901', *Annual Report on the Fisheries of Ireland, Scientific Investigations, 1902–1903*, Part II, Appendix I (1905), 3–19.

Delap, Peter, 'Memories of a Loving Alien', unpublished memoir, n.d.

DeLoughrey, Elizabeth, *Routes and Roots: Navigating Caribbean and Pacific Island Literatures* (Honolulu: University of Hawai'i Press, 2007).

DeLoughrey, Elizabeth, '"The Litany of Islands, The Rosary of Archipelagos": Caribbean and Pacific Archipelagraphy', *ARIEL: A Review of International English Literature*, 32 (January 2001), 21–51.

Democratic Unionist Party, *DUP Westminster Manifesto 2015* (Belfast: Democratic Unionist Party, 2015).

Depraetere, Christian, 'The Challenge of Nissology: A Global Outlook on the World Archipelago, Part I: Scene Setting the World Archipelago', *Island Studies Journal*, 3 (2008), 3–16.

Depraetere, Christian, 'The Challenge of Nissology: A Global Outlook on the World Archipelago, Part II: The Global and Scientific Vocation of Nissology', *Island Studies Journal*, 3 (2008), 17–36.

Dillon, Wentworth, fourth Earl of Roscommon, *Poems* (London, 1717).

Diolé, Philippe, *The Undersea Adventure*, trans. Alan Ross (London: Sidgwick & Jackson, 1953).

Dobbs, Arthur, *An Essay on the Trade and Improvement of Ireland* (Dublin, 1729–31).

Domosh, Mona, 'Towards a Feminist Historiography of Geography', *Transactions of the Institute of British Geographers*, 16 (1991), 95–104.

Driver, Felix, *Geography Militant: Cultures of Exploration and Empire* (Oxford and Cambridge, MA: Wiley Blackwell, 2001).

Duddy, Thomas (ed.), *The Irish Response to Darwinism*, 6 vols (Bristol: Thoemmes Continuum, 2003).

Duddy, Thomas, 'The Irish Response to Darwinism', in Róisín Jones and Martin Steer (eds), *Darwin, Praeger and the Clare Island Surveys* (Dublin: Royal Irish Academy, 2009), 10–11.

Duff, David and Catherine Jones (eds), *Scotland, Ireland and the Romantic Aesthetic* (Lewisburg: Bucknell University Press, 2007).

Dunn, Douglas, *New Selected Poems: 1964–2000* (London: Faber and Faber, 2003).

Durkheim, Émile, *Elementary Forms of the Religious Life* (New York: Free Press, 1965).

Dutton, Matthew, *The Office and Authority of a Justice of Peace for Ireland…* (Dublin, 1718).

Edge, Martin, *The Underwater Photographer*, 3rd edn (Oxford: Elsevier, 2008).

Eliot, George, *The George Eliot Letters*, ed. Gordon Haight, 7 vols (New Haven and London: Yale University Press, 1954).

Elliot, Marianne, *Wolfe Tone: Prophet of Irish Independence* (London: Yale University Press, 1989).

Escobar, Arturo, 'Culture Sits in Places: Reflections on Globalism and Subaltern Strategies of Localization', *Political Geography*, 20 (2001), 139–74.

Esty, Jed, *A Shrinking Island: Modernism and National Culture in England* (Princeton: Princeton University Press, 2004).

Evans, David, *A History of Nature Conservation in Britain* (London: Routledge, 1992).

Evans, Malcolm D., 'Maritime Boundary Delimitation', in Rothwell et al. (eds), *The Oxford Handbook of the Law of the Sea*, 254–79.

Finnegan, Diarmuid A., *Natural History Societies and Civic Culture in Victorian Scotland* (London: Pickering and Chatto, 2009).

Finnegan, Diarmuid A., 'Naturalising the Highlands: Geographies of Mountain Fieldwork in Late-Victorian Scotland', *Journal of Historical Geography*, 33 (2007), 791–815.

Fisk, Roger, *Scotland in Music* (Cambridge: Cambridge University Press, 1985).

Fitzgerald, Robert P., 'Science and Politics in Swift's Voyage to Laputa', *Journal of English and Germanic Philology*, 87 (1988), 213–29.

Flaherty, Robert, *Man of Aran* (London: Gaumont Picture Corporation Ltd, 1934).

Fleury, Christian, 'The Island/Sea/Territory Relationship: Towards a Broader and Three-dimensional View of the Aquapelagic Assemblage', *Shima: The International Journal of Research into Island Culture*, 7 (2013), 1–13.

Flood, Donal T., 'Dublin Bay in the 18th Century', *Dublin Historical Record*, 31 (1978), 129–41.

Foster, John Wilson (ed.), *Nature in Ireland: A Scientific and Cultural History* (Dublin: Lilliput Press, 1997).

Fyfe, Aileen, 'Natural History and the Victorian Tourist: From Landscapes to Rock-Pools', in David N. Livingstone and Charles Withers (eds), *Geographies of Nineteenth-Century Science* (Chicago: University of Chicago Press, 2011), 371–98.

Fyfe, Aileen, *Science and Salvation: Evangelical Popular Science Publishing in Victorian Britain* (Chicago: University of Chicago Press, 2004).

Games, Alison, 'Atlantic History: Definitions, Challenges, and Opportunities', *American Historical Review*, 111 (2006), 741–57.

Gardiner, Michael, *The Return of England in English Literature* (Basingstoke: Palgrave, 2012).

Gardner, Philip, *Norman Nicholson* (New York: Twayne, 1973).

Garrigan-Mattar, Sinead, *Science, Primitivism, and the Irish Revival* (Oxford: Oxford University Press, 2004).

Gatty, Margaret, *British Sea-Weeds* (London: Bell and Daldy, 1863).

Gatty, Margaret, *Parables from Nature* (London: Bell and Daldy, 1855–71).

Gillen, Shawn, '*An Aran Keening*: Review', *New Hibernia Review*, 6 (2002), 156.

Gilligan, H. A., *A History of the Port of Dublin* (Dublin: Gill and MacMillan, 1988).

Gillis, Alan, '"Any Dark Saying": Louis MacNeice in the Nineteen Fifties', *Irish University Review*, 42 (2012), 105–23.

Gillis, John R., *Islands of the Mind: How the Human Imagination Created the Atlantic World* (New York: Palgrave MacMillan, 2004).

Gillis, John R., *The Human Shore: Seacoasts in History* (Chicago: University of Chicago Press, 2012).

Goodby, John, 'Space, Narrative and Surveillance', in Elmer Kennedy-Andrews (ed.), *Ciaran Carson: Critical Essays* (Dublin: Four Courts, 2009), 66–85.

Gordon, Seton, *Islands of the West* (London: Cassell, 1933).

Gosse, Edmund, *The Life of Philip Henry Gosse F.R.S.* (London: Routledge, Kegan Paul, Trench, Trubner and Co., 1890).

Gosse, Philip Henry, *A Naturalist's Rambles on the Devonshire Coast* (London: John van Voorst, 1853).

Gosse, Philip Henry, *A Naturalist's Sojourn in Jamaica* (London: Longman, Brown, Green and Longman, 1851).

Gosse, Philip Henry, *Evenings at the Microscope; or, Researches Among the Minuter Organs and Forms of Animal Life* (London: SPCK, 1859).

Gosse, Philip Henry, *Land and Sea* (London: James Nisbet, 1865).

Gosse, Philip Henry, *The Aquarium: An Unveiling of the Wonders of the Deep Sea* (London: John van Voorst, 1854).

Greene, Jack P. and Philip D. Morgan (eds), *Atlantic History: A Critical Reappraisal* (New York: Palgrave, 2009).

Greer, Kirsten Aletta and Jeanne Kay Guelke, '"Intrepid Naturalists and Polite Observers": Gender and Recreational Birdwatching in Southern Ontario, 1791–1886', *Journal of Sport History*, 30 (2003), 323–46.

Groom, Nick, 'Gothic and Celtic Revivals: Antiquity and the Archipelago', in Robert DeMaria Jr, Heesok Chang, and Samantha Zacher (eds), *A Companion to British Literature*, 4 vols (Oxford: Wiley-Blackwell, 2014), iii. 361–79.

Guelke, Jeanne Kay and Karen M. Morin, 'Gender, Nature, Empire: Women Naturalists in Nineteenth Century British Travel Literature', *Transactions of the Institute of British Geographers*, 26 (2001), 306–26.

Hall, Mrs S. C., 'A New Pleasure', *Art Journal*, 17 (May 1856).

Hammond, Reginald J. W., *Guide to the Lake District, with an Outline Guide for Walkers, and a Special Section for Motorists* (London and Melbourne: Ward, Lock, and Co., 1950).

Harris, Alexandra, *Romantic Moderns* (London: Thames and Hudson, 2012).

Harris, Alexandra, 'The Secrets of England's Past Lie Buried in the Land', *New Statesman* (4 April 2011), 40–1.

Hay, Pete, 'A Phenomenology of Islands', *Island Studies Journal*, 1 (2006), 19–42.
Hayward, Philip, 'Aquapelagos and Aquapelagic Assemblages: Towards an Integrated Study of Island Societies and Marine Environments', *Shima: The International Journal of Research into Island Cultures*, 6 (2012), 1–11.
Hayward, Philip, 'The Constitution of Assemblages and the Aquapelagality of Haida Gwaii', *Shima: The International Journal of Research into Island Cultures*, 6 (2012), 1–14.
Heaney, Seamus, 'Our Mystery', *Archipelago*, 1 (2007), 1.
Heaney, Seamus, *Sweeney's Flight* (London: Faber and Faber, 1992).
Heise, Ursula, *Sense of Place and Sense of Planet* (Oxford: Oxford University Press, 2008).
Hewitt, Rachel, *Map of a Nation: A Biography of the Ordnance Survey* (London: Granta, 2010).
Higgins, Aidan, 'Reviewed Books', *Books Ireland*, 240 (May 2001), 135.
Howell, James, *Londinopolis; An Historicall Discourse or Perlustration of the City of London, the Imperial Chamber, and Chief Emporium of Great Britain* (London, 1657).
Hughes, Kathryn, *George Eliot: The Last Victorian* (London: Cooper Square Press, 2001).
Hume, James Deacon, *The Laws of the Customs* (London: Eyre & Strahan, 1826).
'Ilfracombe', *London Society: An Illustrated Magazine of Light and Amusing Literature for Hours of Relaxation*, 12/67 (July 1867), 25–31.
Illich, Ivan, *H_2O and the Waters of Forgetfulness: Reflections on the Historicity of 'Stuff'* (Dallas: Dallas Institute of Humanities and Culture, 1985).
International Hydrographic Organization, *Limits of Oceans and Seas* (Monte Carlo: International Hydrographic Organization, 1953).
Irving, Gordon, *The Solway Smugglers* (Dumfries: Robert Dinwiddie and Co., 1971).
Jackson, Kenneth Hurlstone (ed.), *A Celtic Miscellany*, rev. edn (Harmondsworth: Penguin, 1971).
Jardine, Nicholas, J. A. Secord, and Emma Spary (eds), *Cultures of Natural History* (Cambridge: Cambridge University Press, 1996).
Jardine, Nicholas and Emma Spary, 'The Natures of Cultural History', in Jardine, Secord, and Spary (eds), *Cultures of Natural History*, 3–13.
Jefferys, Nathaniel, *A Descriptive and Historical Account of the Isle of Man* (Newcastle upon Tyne, Preston & Heaton, n.d. [*c*.1810]).
Jensen, Carsten, *We, the Drowned*, trans. Charlotte Barslund, with Emma Ryder (New York: Houghton Mifflin Harcourt, 2010).
John, Juliet and Alice Jenkins (eds), *Rethinking Victorian Culture* (Basingstoke: Macmillan, 2000).
Johnson, Samuel, *A Dictionary of the English Language* (London, 1755–6).
Jones, Róisín and Martin Steer (eds), *Darwin, Praeger and the Clare Island Surveys* (Dublin: Royal Irish Academy, 2009).
Joyce, James, *A Portrait of the Artist as a Young Man*, ed. John Paul Riquelme (New York: Norton, 2007).

Justice, Alexander, *A General Treatise of the Dominion of the Sea: and A Compleat Body of the Sea-Laws...* (London, 1709).

Kavanagh, Patrick, 'Inniskeen Road: July Evening', in David Pierce (ed.), *Irish Writing in the Twentieth Century: A Reader* (Cork: Cork University Press, 2000), 456.

Kearney, Hugh, *The British Isles: A History of Four Nations*, 2nd edn (Cambridge: Cambridge University Press, 2006).

Kearns, Gerry, 'The Imperial Subject: Geography and Travel in the Work of Mary Kingsley and Halford Mackinder', *Transactions of the Institute of British Geographers*, 22 (1997), 450–72.

Keats, John, *The Complete Poems*, ed. John Barnard, 2nd edn (Harmondsworth: Penguin, 1977).

Kelly, James, 'Jonathan Swift and the Irish Economy in the 1720s', *Eighteenth-Century Ireland: Iris an dá chultúr*, 6 (1991), 7–36.

Kerrigan, John, *Archipelagic English: Literature, History, and Politics, 1603–1707* (Oxford: Oxford University Press, 2008).

Kerrigan, John, 'The Ticking Fear', *London Review of Books*, 30 (7 February 2008), 15–18.

Kingshill, Sophia and Jennifer Westwood, *The Fabled Coast: Legends & Traditions from around the Shores of Britain & Ireland* (London: Random House, 2012).

[Kingsley, Charles,] 'A Popular History of British Zoophytes or Corallines', *North British Review*, 22 (November 1854).

Kingsley, Charles, *Glaucus; or, The Wonders of the Shore* (1855; Cambridge: Macmillan and Co., 1859).

Kingsley, Charles, *Novels, Poems and Letters of Charles Kingsley: Letters and Memoirs*, ed. Fanny Kingsley, 2 vols (New York and London: Co-operative Publication Society, 1899).

Lehner, Stefanie, *Subaltern Ethics in Contemporary Scottish and Irish Literature: Tracing Counter-Histories* (London: Palgrave, 2011).

Lewes, George Henry, *Sea-Side Studies at Ilfracombe, Tenby, the Scilly Isles, and Jersey* (Edinburgh: William Blackwood and Sons, 1858).

Lightman, Bernard, *Victorian Popularizers of Nature* (Chicago: University of Chicago Press, 2007).

Lightman, Bernard and Aileen Fyfe, 'Science in the Marketplace: An Introduction', in Bernard Lightman and Aileen Fyfe (eds), *Science in the Marketplace: Nineteenth-Century Sites and Experiences* (Chicago: University of Chicago Press, 2007), 1–21.

Livingstone, David N., *Putting Science in its Place: Geographies of Scientific Knowledge* (Chicago: University of Chicago Press, 2003).

Livingstone, David N. and Charles Withers (eds), *Geographies of Nineteenth-Century Science* (Chicago: University of Chicago Press, 2011).

Lockley, Ann, *Island Child: My Life on Skokholm with R. M. Lockley* (Llanrwst: Gwasg Carreg Gwalch, 2013).

Lockley, Doris, 'The Woman's Side of Island Life', *The Countryman: A Quarterly Non-Party Review and Miscellany of Rural Life and Work for the English-speaking World*, 21 (July–August–September 1940), 265–74.

Lockley, R. M. ['Grassholm'], *The Countryman*, 11 (July 1935), 425–40.
Lockley, R. M., *Dear Islandman*, ed. Ann Mark (Gomer: Llandysul, 1996).
Lockley, R. M., *Dream Island Days: A Record of the Simple Life* (London: H. F. & G. Witherby, 1943).
Lockley, R. M., *Early Morning Island, or A Dish of Sprats* (London: George G. Harrap & Co., 1939).
Lockley, R. M., *The Golden Year* (London: H. F. & G. Witherby, 1948).
Lockley, R. M., *I Know an Island* (London: George G. Harrap & Co., 1938).
Lockley, R. M., *Inland Farm* (London: H. F. & G. Witherby, 1943).
Lockley, R. M., *The Island* (London: André Deutsch, 1969).
Lockley, R. M., *The Island Dwellers* (London: Putnam, 1932).
Lockley, R. M., *The Island Farmers* (London: H. F. & G. Witherby, 1946).
Lockley, R. M., *Islands Round Britain* (London: Collins, 1945).
Lockley, R. M., *Letters from Skokholm* (Stanbridge: Little Toller Books, 2010).
Lockley, R. M., *Myself When Young: The Making of a Naturalist* (London: André Deutsch, 1979).
Lockley, R. M., *Orielton: The Human and Natural History of a Welsh Manor* (Harmondsworth: Penguin, 1980).
Lockley, R. M., *The Private Life of The Rabbit* (Woodbridge: Boydell, 1985).
Lockley, R. M., *The Sea's a Thief* (London: Longman's, Green and Co., 1936).
Lockley, R. M., *Seal Woman* (Sydney: Hicks Smith, 1976).
Lockley, R. M., *The Seals and the Curragh, Introducing the Natural History of the Grey Seal of the North Atlantic* (London: The Scientific Book Club, 1954).
Lockley, R. M., *Shearwaters* (London: J. M. Dent, 1942).
Lofgren, Orvar and Billy Elin, *The Secret World of Doing Nothing* (Berkeley: University of California Press, 2010).
Lopez, Barry, *Arctic Dreams: Imagination and Desire in Northern Landscapes* (New York: Scribner's, 1986).
Lorimer, Hayden, 'Forces of Nature, Forms of Life: Calibrating Ethology and Phenomenology', in Ben Anderson and Paul Harrison (eds), *Taking-Place: Non-Representational Theories and Geography* (Farnham: Ashgate, 2010), 55–78.
Luria, S. M. and Jo Ann S. Kinney, 'Underwater Vision', *Science*, 167 (1970), 1454.
McCall, Grant, 'Nissology: A Proposal for Consideration', *Journal of the Pacific Society*, 17 (October 1994), 1–14.
McCaughan, Michael and John Appleby (eds), *The Irish Sea: Aspects of Maritime History* (Belfast: Institute of Irish Studies, 1989).
McDonald, Peter, *Louis MacNeice: The Poet in his Contexts* (Oxford: Clarendon Press, 1991).
McEwan, Cheryl, 'Gender, Science and Physical Geography in Nineteenth-Century Britain', *Area*, 30 (1998), 215–23.
Macfarlane, Robert, 'Island', *Archipelago*, 1 (2007), 5–23.
Macfarlane, Robert, *The Old Ways: A Journey on Foot* (London: Penguin, 2013).
Macfarlane, Robert, 'Tory Island', *Archipelago*, 3 (2009), 32–43.
McInerney, Michael, *The Riddle of Erskine Childers* (Dublin: E. & T. O'Brien, 1971).

Mackay, Peter, 'Escodus à Hiort', *Archipelago*, 4 (2009), 26–7.
Macky, John, *A Journey Through England. In Familiar Letters from a Gentlemam [sic] Here, to his Friend Abroad*, 2 vols, 2nd edn (London, 1724).
McMillan, N. F. and W. J. Rees, 'Maude Jane Delap (1866–1953)', *The Irish Naturalists' Journal*, 12 (1958), 221–2.
MacNeice, Louis, *The Agamemnon of Aeschylus* (London: Faber, 1936).
MacNeice, Louis, *The Collected Poems of Louis MacNeice*, ed. E. R. Dodds (New York: Oxford University Press, 1967).
MacNeice, Louis, *I Crossed the Minch*, introd. Tom Herron (1938; Edinburgh: Polygon, 2007).
MacNeice, Louis, *Letters of Louis MacNeice*, ed. Jonathan Allison (London: Faber, 2010).
McNeillie, Andrew, *An Aran Keening* (Dublin: Lilliput Press, 2001).
McNeillie, Andrew, 'Editorial', *Archipelago*, 1 (2007), vii–viii.
McNeillie, Andrew, 'Editorial', *Archipelago*, 3 (2009), n.p.
McNeillie, Andrew, 'Editorial', *Archipelago*, 5 (2011), n.p.
McNeillie, Andrew, *Now, Then* (Manchester: Carcanet Press, 2002).
McNeillie, Andrew, 'Where Art Meets Sea', *Archipelago*, 4 (2009), 31–43.
MacRobert, A. E., *To See Oursels*... (Dumfries and Galloway: Libraries, Information and Archives, 2001).
Magennis, Caroline, 'Re-writing Protestant History in the Novels of Glenn Patterson', *Irish Studies Review*, 23 (2015), 348–60.
Mandelbrot, Benoît, 'How Long Is the Coast of Britain? Statistical Self-Similarity and Fractional Dimension', *Science*, 156 (5 May 1967), 636–8.
Marland, Pippa, 'The "Good Step" and Dwelling in Tim Robinson's *Stones of Aran*: The Advent of Psycho-archipelagraphy', *Ecozon*, 6 (2015), 7–24.
Marx, Robert, *The History of Underwater Exploration* (New York: Dover, 1990).
Massey, Doreen, *For Space* (London: Sage, 2005).
Massey, Doreen, *Space, Place and Gender* (Cambridge: Cambridge University Press, 1994).
Matless, David, *Landscape and Englishness* (London: Reaktion, 1998).
Maxwell, Ian, 'Seas as Places: Towards a Maritime Chorography', *Shima: The International Journal of Research into Island Cultures*, 6 (2012), 22–4.
Melville, Herman, *Moby Dick* (New York: Barnes & Noble, 1993).
Miège, Guy, *The Present State of Great Britain and Ireland, in Three Parts*, 5th edn (London, 1723).
Mill, John Stuart, *England and Ireland* (London: Longmans, Green, Reader, and Dyer, 1868).
Mills, A. D., *A Dictionary of British Place Names* (Oxford: Oxford University Press, 1991).
Monmonier, Mark, *Coastlines: How Mapmakers Form the World and Chart Environmental Change* (Chicago: University of Chicago Press, 2008).
Moore, Alfred Stewart, *Linen* (New York: Macmillan, 1922).
Moore, Desmond F., 'The Port of Dublin', *Dublin Historical Record*, 16 (1961), 131–43.

Morton, Timothy, *The Ecological Thought* (Cambridge, MA: Harvard University Press, 2010).

Moure, Nancy Dustin Wall, *The World of Zarh Pritchard* (Carmel, CA: William Karges Fine Art, 1999).

Myers, Bill, *Millom Remembered* (Stroud: Tempus, 2004).

Nairn, Tom, *After Britain: New Labour and the Return of Scotland* (London: Granta, 2000).

National Parks and Wildlife Service of Ireland, 'Survey of the Distribution of the Anemone *Edwardsia Delapiae* (Carlgren and Stephenson, 1928) in Valentia Harbour and Portmagee Channel SAC, Co. Kerry', *Report for the National Parks and Wildlife Service of Ireland*, by MERC Consultancy.

Naylor, Simon, *Regionalizing Science: Placing Knowledges in Victorian England* (London: Pickering and Chatto, 2010).

Newman, John Henry, *The Dream of Gerontius*, ed. Maurice Francis Egan (New York: Longmans, Green, and Co., 1910).

Nichols, Wallace J., *Blue Mind: The Surprising Science That Shows How Being Near, In, On, or Under Water Can Make you Happier, Healthier, More Connected, and Better at What You Do* (New York: Little, Brown, 2014).

Nicholson, Norman, *Collected Poems*, ed. Neil Curry (London: Faber and Faber, 2008).

Nicholson, Norman, *Greater Lakeland* (London: Robert Hale, 1977).

Nicholson, Norman, *Wednesday Early Closing* (London: Faber and Faber, 1975).

Nicolson, Adam, *Seamanship: A Voyage along the Wild Coasts of the British Isles* (New York: HarperCollins, 2004).

Niemann, Derek, *Birds in a Cage... The Unlikely Beginnings of Modern Wildlife Conservation* (London: Short Books, 2012).

Nixon, Philip and Hugh Dias, *Exploring Solway History* (Derby: Breedon, 2007).

Norquay, Glenda and Gerry Smith (eds), *Across the Margins: Cultural Identity and Change in the Atlantic Archipelago* (Manchester: Manchester University Press, 2002).

'North Sea Drainage Project to Increase Area of Europe', *Modern Mechanics* (September 1930), 169.

O'Brien, Edward Conor Marshall, *Across Three Oceans* (London: E. Arnold, 1926).

Ó Cadhain, Máirtín, *Cré na Cille* (Baile Átha Cliath: Sairseal Agus Dill, 1949/65).

O'Cleirigh, Nellie, *Hardship and High Living: Irish Women's Lives, 1808–1923* (Dublin: Portobello Press, 2003).

O'Cleirigh, Nellie, *Valentia: A Different Kind of Irish Island* (Dublin: Portobello Press, 1992).

O'Flaherty, Tom, *Aranmen All* (Dublin: At the Sign of the Three Candles, 1934).

O'Gorman, Francis, '"More Interesting than all the books, save one": Charles Kingsley's Construction of Natural History', in Juliet John and Alice Jenkins (eds), *Rethinking Victorian Culture* (Basingstoke: Macmillan, 2000), 144–61.

Outram, Dorinda, 'New Spaces in Natural History', in Jardine, Secord, and Spary (eds), *Cultures of Natural History*, 249–65.

Outram, Dorinda, 'The History of Natural History: Grand History or Local Lore?', in John Wilson Foster (ed.), *Nature in Ireland: A Scientific and Cultural History* (Dublin: Lilliput Press, 1997), 461–71.

Panofsky, Erwin, *Perspective as Symbolic Form*, trans. Christopher S. Wood (Cambridge, MA: MIT Press, 1999).

Paor, Liam de, *On the Easter Proclamation and other Declarations* (Dublin: Four Courts, 1997).

Parker, Joanne, *Britannia Obscura: Mapping Britain's Hidden Landscapes* (London: Jonathan Cape, 2014).

Patten, C. J., *The Story of the Birds* (Sheffield: Pawson and Brailsford, 1928).

Patterson, Glenn, *The Mill for Grinding Old People Young* (London: Faber, 2012).

Pearce, Cathryn J., *Cornish Wrecking, 1700–1860: Reality and Popular Myth* (Woodbridge: Boydell Press, 2010).

Pearse, Patrick, 'On the Strand of Howth', *Plays, Stories, Poems* (Dublin: Talbot Press, 1966).

Pearson, Nels, *Irish Cosmopolitanism: Location and Dislocation in James Joyce, Elizabeth Bowen, and Samuel Beckett* (Gainesville: University of Florida Press, 2014).

Peckarsky, Barbara, 'Review of *Women in the Field: America's Pioneering Women Naturalists* by M. M. Bonata', *Journal of the New York Entomological Society*, 100 (1992), 638–40.

Perry, John, *An Account of the Stopping of Daggenham Breach* (London, 1721).

Perry, John, *An Answer to Objections against the Making of a Bason, with Reasons for the bettering of the Harbour of Dublin* (Dublin, 1721).

Perry, John, *The State of Russia, under the Present Czar* (London, 1716).

Petty, Sir William, *A Geographical Description of the Kingdom of Ireland, Newly Corrected & Improv'd by Actual Observations* (London, 1728).

Philbrick, Thomas, *James Fenimore Cooper and the Development of American Sea Fiction* (Cambridge, MA: Harvard University Press, 1961).

Pocock, J. G. A., *The Discovery of Islands: Essays in British History* (Cambridge: Cambridge University Press, 2005).

Pope, Alexander, *The Memoirs of the Extraordinary Life, Works, and Discoveries of Martinus Scriblerus*, ed. Charles Kerby-Miller (New York and Oxford: Oxford University Press, 1988).

Praeger, Robert Lloyd, *Natural History of Ireland: A Sketch of its Flora and Fauna* (1949; New York: Barnes and Noble Books, 1972).

Praeger, Robert Lloyd, *Some Irish Naturalists: A Biographical Note-Book* (Dundalk: Dundalgan Press, 1949).

Pratt, Anne, *Chapters on the Common Things of the Sea-Side* (London: SPCK, 1850).

Pritchard, Zarh H., 'A Conversation with Zarh H. Pritchard, Recorded by the Editor', *Asia*, 234 (March 1924), 219.

Proust, Marcel, *À la recherche du temps perdu*, 7 vols (Paris: Grasset and Gallimard, 1913–27).

Raban, Jonathan, *Coasting: A Private Voyage* (New York: Simon and Schuster, 1987).

Raban, Jonathan, *The Oxford Book of the Sea* (Oxford: Oxford University Press, 1992).

Ranelagh, John O'Beirne, *A Short History of Ireland*, 2nd edn (Cambridge: Cambridge University Press, 1994).

Reckin, Anna, 'Tidalectic Lectures: Kamau Brathwaite's Prose/Poetry as Sound-Space', *Anthurium: A Caribbean Studies Journal*, 1 (2003), 1–16.

Riach, Alan, 'Archipelago', in *PN Review*, 37 (September/October 2010), 48.

Roberts, Callum, *The Unnatural History of the Sea* (Washington, DC: Island Press, 2007).

Robertson, Robin, 'Leaving St Kilda', *Archipelago*, 4 (2009), 17–25.

Robinson, Tim, 'The Centre of Gravity', *Archipelago*, 10 (2015).

Robinson, Tim, *Connemara: A Little Gaelic Kingdom* (London: Penguin, 2012).

Robinson, Tim, *My Time in Space* (Dublin: Lilliput Press, 2001).

Robinson, Tim, 'The Seanchaí and the Database', *Irish Pages*, 2 (2003), 43–53.

Robinson, Tim, *Stones of Aran: Labyrinth* (Dublin: Lilliput Press, 1995).

Robinson, Tim, *Stones of Aran: Pilgrimage* (Dublin: Lilliput Press, 1986).

Robinson, Tim, *The View from the Horizon* (London: Coracle Press, 1999).

Rogers, Pat, 'Gulliver and the Engineers', *Modern Language Review*, 70 (1975), 260–70.

Rose, Gillian, 'Tradition and Paternity: Same Difference?', *Transactions of the Institute of British Geographers*, 20 (1995), 414–16.

Ross, Helen, *Behaviour and Perception in Strange Environments* (London: George Allen & Unwin, 1974).

Ross, Helen, 'Mist, Murk, and Visual Perception', *New Scientist*, 66 (1975), 659.

Rothwell, Donald R., Alex G. Oude Elferink, Karen N. Scott, and Tim Stephens (eds), *The Oxford Handbook of the Law of the Sea* (Oxford: Oxford University Press, 2015).

Rozwadowski, Helen, *Fathoming the Ocean: The Discovery and Exploration of the Deep Sea* (Cambridge, MA: Harvard University Press, 2008).

Ruskin, John, *The Library Edition of the Works of John Ruskin*, ed. E. T. Cook and A. Wedderburn, 39 vols (London: Allen, 1903–12).

Ruskin, John, *Modern Painters* (Boston: Adamant Media Corporation, 2005 [reprint of 1906 edition published by George Allen, London]).

Ruskin, John, *Praeterita*, ed. Francis O'Gorman (Oxford: Oxford University Press, 2012).

Ruskin, John, *Praeterita*, ed. Timothy Hilton (London and New York: Everyman, 2005).

Ruskin, John, *The Stones of Venice*, 3 vols (London: Smith Elder, 1851–3).

Saunders, James, *The Compleat Fisherman* (London, 1724).

Scammell, William (ed.), *Between Comets: For Norman Nicholson at 70* (Durham: Taxvs, 1984).

Schwyzer, Philip and Simon Mealor (eds), *Archipelagic Identities: Literature and Identity in the Atlantic Archipelago, 1550–1800* (Aldershot: Ashgate, 2004).

Scott, Walter, *Redgauntlet*, ed. G. A. M. Wood and David Hewitt (Edinburgh: Edinburgh University Press, 1997).

Scott, Walter, 'Review of R. H. Cromek, *Reliques of Robert Burns*', *Quarterly Review*, i (1809), 19–36.

Secord, Jim, *Victorian Sensation: The Extraordinary Publication, Reception, and Secret Authorship of* Vestiges of the Natural History of Creation (Chicago: University of Chicago Press, 2000).

Shakespeare, William, *The Tempest*, ed. Stephen Orgel (Oxford: Oxford University Press, 1998).

Singer, Christoph, *Sea Change: The Shore from Shakespeare to Banville* (Amsterdam: Brill Academic Publishers, 2014).

Slauter, Eric, 'History, Literature, and the Atlantic World', *William and Mary Quarterly*, 55 (2008), 135–61.

Smith, Jonathan, *Charles Darwin and Victorian Visual Culture* (Cambridge: Cambridge University Press, 2006).

Southward, Alan, Gerald Boalch, and Linda Maddock, 'Climatic Change and the Herring and Pilchard Fisheries of Devon and Cornwall', in David J. Starkey (ed.), *Devon's Coastline and Coastal Waters: Aspects of Man's Relationship with the Sea* (Exeter: Exeter University Press, 1988), 33–57.

Stafford, Fiona, 'Inhabited Solitudes: Wordsworth in Scotland, 1803', in David Duff and Catherine Jones (eds), *Scotland, Ireland and the Romantic Aesthetic* (Lewisburg: Bucknell University Press, 2007), 93–113.

Stafford, Fiona, *Local Attachments: The Province of Poetry* (Oxford: Oxford University Press, 2010).

Stafford, Fiona, 'Review of *Archipelago* 1', *Times Literary Supplement* (2 November 2007), 24–5.

Steinberg, Philip E., *The Social Construction of the Ocean* (Cambridge: Cambridge University Press, 2001).

Stevenson, Robert Louis, 'The Education of an Engineer', *Scribners* (November 1888), 634–41.

Stilgoe, John R., *Alongshore* (New Haven and London: Yale University Press, 1994).

Stott, Rebecca, *Theatres of Glass: The Woman Who Brought the Sea to the City* (London: Short Books, 2003).

Stratford, Elaine, Godfrey Baldacchino, Elizabeth MacMahon, Carol Farbotko, and Andrew Harwood, 'Envisioning the Archipelago', *Island Studies Journal*, 6 (2011), 113–30.

Swift, Jonathan, *The Bubble: A Poem* (London, 1721).

Swift, Jonathan, *The Correspondence of Jonathan Swift*, ed. Harold Williams, 5 vols (Oxford: Clarendon Press, 1963–5).

Swift, Jonathan, *Gulliver's Travels* [*Travels into Several Remote Nations of the World*], in *The Writings of Jonathan Swift*, ed. Robert A. Greenberg and William B. Piper (New York and London: W. W. Norton, 1973), i–xiv, 1–260.

Swift, Jonathan, *Miscellanies*, 4th edn (London, 1722).

Swift, Jonathan, *Miscellanies, The Second Volume* (London, 1727).

Tatham, David, *Winslow Homer in the 1890s: Prout's Neck Observed* (New York: Hudson Hills Press, 1990).

Thacker, Jeremy, *The Longitudes Examin'd. Beginning with a Short Epistle to the Longitudinarians, and Ending with the Description of a Smart, Pretty Machine of my own, which I am (almost) sure will do for the Longitude, and procure me the Twenty Thousand Pounds* (London, 1714).

Thayer Robert L., Jr, *LifePlace: Bioregional Thought and Practice* (Berkeley: University of California Press, 2003).

Theroux, Paul, *Fresh-Air Fiend: Travel Writings, 1985–2000* (Boston: Houghton Mifflin, 2001).

Theroux, Paul, *Kingdom by the Sea: A Journey Around Great Britain* (Boston: Houghton Mifflin, 1983).

Thomson, A. Landsborough, *Bird Migration* (London: Witherby, 1936).

Thomson, George, *Studies in Ancient Greek Society: The Prehistoric Aegean* (London: Lawrence and Wishart, 1949).

Thomson, George, *Island Home: The Blasket Heritage* (Dingle: Brandon, 1988).

Thwaite, Ann, *Glimpses of the Wonderful: The Life of Philip Henry Gosse* (London: Faber and Faber, 2002).

Travis, John, *The Rise of the Devon Seaside Resorts 1750–1950* (Exeter: Exeter University Press, 1993).

Verne, Jules, *Twenty Thousand Leagues Under the Sea*, trans. and ed. William Butcher (New York: Oxford University Press, 1998).

Viles, Heather and Tom Spencer, *Coastal Problems* (London: Edward Arnold, 1995).

Waldron, George, 'A Description of the Isle of Man: with some Useful and Entertaining Reflections on the Laws, Customs, and Manners of its Inhabitants', *Compleat Works, in Verse and Prose, of George Waldron, Gent. late of Queen's College, Oxon* (London, 1731), 91–191.

Walford Davies, Damian, *Cartographies of Culture: New Geographies of Welsh Writing in English* (Cardiff: University of Wales Press, 2012).

Wallis, Clarrie, 'Making Tracks', in Clarrie Wallis (ed.), *Richard Long: Heaven and Earth* (London: Tate Publishing, 2009), 33–61.

Ward, Edward, *The London-Spy Compleat* (London, 1700).

Welsh, Frank, *The Four Nations: A History of the United Kingdom* (New Haven and London: Yale University Press, 2003).

White, Kenneth, *On the Atlantic Edge: A Geopoetics Project* (Dingwall: Sandstone Press, 2006).

Williams, Mark, 'The Old Song', *Archipelago*, 1 (2007), 79–96.

Williams, Raymond, *Marxism and Literature* (Oxford: Oxford University Press, 1977).

Wills, Clair, *That Neutral Island: A Cultural History of Ireland During the Second World War* (London: Faber, 2007).

Wilmerding, John, *A History of American Marine Painting* (Boston: Little, Brown, 1968).

Withers, Charles W. J. and Diarmid A. Finnegan, 'Natural History Societies, Fieldwork and Local Knowledge in Nineteenth-Century Scotland: Towards a Historical Geography of Civic Science', *cultural geographies*, 10 (2003), 334–53.

Wordsworth, William, *William Wordsworth: Twenty-First Century Authors*, ed. Stephen Gill (Oxford: Oxford University Press, 2010).

Index

Page numbers in italics indicate illustrations.